CRUSH

CRUSH

The Triumph of California Wine

JOHN BRISCOE

UNIVERSITY OF NEVADA PRESS | Reno & Las Vegas

University of Nevada Press | Reno, Nevada 89557 USA, www.unpress.nevada.edu
Copyright © 2018 by University of Nevada Press. All rights reserved.
Cover photograph Radius Images / Alamy Stock Photo
Cover design by TG Design

LIBRARY OF CONGRESS CATALOGING-IN-PUBLICATION DATA
Names: Briscoe, John, author.
Title: Crush : the triumph of California wine / by John Briscoe.
Description: Reno : University of Nevada Press, 2017. | Includes bibliographical references and index.
Identifiers: ISBN 978-1-943859-49-8 (cloth : alk. paper) | ISBN 978-0-87417-715-2 (e-book) | LCCN 2017036463 (print) | LCCN 2017037617 (e-book)
Subjects: LCSH: Wine and wine making—California—History. | Wineries—California—History. | Vineyards—California—History. | Viticulture—California—History.
Classification: LCC TP557.5.C2 B75 2017 (print) | LCC TP557.5.C2 (e-book) | DDC 663/.209794—dc23
LC record available at https://lccn.loc.gov/2017036463

The paper used in this book meets the requirements of American National Standard for Information Sciences—Permanence of Paper for Printed Library Materials, ANSI/NISO Z39.48-1992 (R2002).

FIRST PRINTING

Manufactured in the United States of America

For Carol
and for Kevin Starr

—∞∞∞—

I was interested in California wine. Indeed, I am
interested in all wines, and have been all my life, from
the raisin wine that a schoolfellow kept secreted in
his play-box up to my last discovery, those notable
Valtellines, that once shone upon the board of Caesar.

The stirring sunlight, and the growing
vines, and the vats and bottles in the cavern,
made a pleasant music for the mind.

—ROBERT LOUIS STEVENSON,
The Silverado Squatters

Contents

Preface

Love of good living is one of the peculiarities
of the nation, possibly, but in California the
national weakness is a ruling passion.

—NOAH BROOKS, "Restaurant Life in San Francisco,"
Overland Monthly

CALIFORNIANS TALK WINE more than they do weather; but,
unlike weather, they actually do something about wine. They
swirl it, peer at and through it, inhale it, sip it, and guzzle it. They
also make it—in both small and prodigious quantities, and in
qualities ranging from nearly swill to rather swell.

And they write about it. Californians, native or adopted, have
been writing about wine for as long as they've been making it.
Father (now Saint) Junípero Serra, the Spanish founder of the
California mission system, bemoaned in his letters the short
supply of wine.[1] The putative father of California wine, Agoston
Haraszthy, wrote scientific treatises on it in the mid-nineteenth
century, both for the California legislature and for readers in general; he was followed by more historical—or, at least, anecdotal—
writers like Frona Eunice Wait. Writing about California wine
then proliferated in the twentieth century. Some discussed just
one variety—Zinfandel, for example; others described a particular growing region, like Napa Valley. Still others addressed only a
particular terroir—the particular blend of soil, climate, and sunlight that make any grape its own—within a region. Some are serious, scholarly works; some, though no less serious, are intended
for the nonacademic reader; and some, notwithstanding the very
self-serious nature of wine and winemaking in California, are
light, effervescent—even gossipy.

So why another book about California wine—or, more precisely, why this particular addition to the prolific and proliferating
literature on the subject? For one, the history of wine and winemaking in California is entwined with the tumultuous boom-
and-bust history of this state—even, dare I say, with the history of
the world. Yet the many excellent books on wine and its history

in California do not sufficiently reference or illuminate the larger history in which took place, for example, the fiasco of 1915—namely the Panama-Pacific International Exposition. Indeed, this leads to the second point: the 1915 debacle was just one of several crushing setbacks to the wine industry, and yet most histories recognize just the disaster brought on by Prohibition. And third, while several of the books have a richness, even a surfeit of details, none teases out the most pertinent strands of California's wine history—notable for five high points and four devastating low ones. One history of winemaking in California (assiduously researched, maddeningly unfootnoted) doesn't even mention a significant pinnacle of California winemaking, a blind tasting in Paris in 1976—even though the event occurred a mere seven years before that book's publication.

A fourth reason is particularly impressive. San Francisco's culinary tradition—and, by extension, California's—began in the Gold Rush of 1849, from which it catapulted to ambrosial heights. No city on earth, that we know of, had attained such greatness in any endeavor—be that food, wine, art, or military conquest—in such short order.

The wine tradition of California began as early as 1769. But it would take more than two hundred years before any authority would rank California wines as having achieved world-class status—and even then the winners would likely not have been selected had they been identified as Californian.

In the end, there are many stories of wine and California. This particular one suggested itself—with an insistent, almost audible ahem—as being worthy of writing. ▪

J. Gundlach & Co. California Vintage advertisement, from *Langley's San Francisco Directory for the Year Commencing May 1889.* Courtesy of the San Francisco History Center, San Francisco Public Library.

Notes

1. Serra, *Writings of Junípero Serra,* 1:263, 281.

Introduction

Providence has given us the most extended wine
country in the world, as if to complete our means of
industry, wealth, and human happiness; and who so
insensate as to place obstacles in its development?

—MATTHEW KELLER, "California Wines"

WHEN OUR FOREBEARS first made wine, how they did it, and
how their first vintage tasted, we'll never know. We do know
there were wine jars in the tomb of Scorpion I of Egypt, dating
from 3150 BCE. Scorpion's wines came not from Egypt, scholars
believe, but from the Jordan River valley.[1] Archaeologists digging
in Tel Kabri, a Canaanite site in what is today northern Israel,
recently disinterred one of "civilization's oldest and largest wine
cellars," which appeared to have housed the equivalent of three
thousand bottles of red and white wines. The cellar, thought to
be but one of many, was found in the ruins of a Canaanite palace dating from 1700 BCE—before the appearance of the bibli-
cal Hebrews.[2]

We also know that the kings and soldiers of the Trojan War
drank wine. In the Iliad and Odyssey Homer refers scores of
times to a "wine-dark sea"—notwithstanding that no vintage has
the color of the Aegean. When Achilles insults Agamemnon he
calls him a "wine sack"—or, in more modern translations, a "stag-
gering drunk."[3] Hecuba, mother of Troy's great warrior-prince
Hector, offers her son "some honeyed, mellow wine. When a
man's exhausted, wine will build his strength."[4] In fact, the fuss
that led to the Trojan War in the first place started years before at
the wedding feast of Peleus and Thetis, where the wine had, by all
accounts, flowed freely.[5]

Wine figures throughout the Old Testament. After the Flood,
Noah apparently planted a vineyard, made wine, got drunk, fell
asleep naked, and raged livid at his son for finding him so.[6] Eleven
generations later, Lot, his wife having been turned into a pillar
of salt, took up residence with his two daughters in a cave. On

successive nights the girls served him enough wine to make him oblivious, for reasons we'll leave unstated.[7]

Alexander the Great liked wine so much he had his own wine-pourer, a young man named Iollas. Indeed, wine may have been Alexander's undoing. Some historians state he died of alcoholism; others suspect that Iollas poisoned Alexander's wine at the behest of Iollas's father, Antipater, who had fallen out of favor with Alexander (and whose name sounds suspiciously seditious, like "anti-father").

A few centuries after Alexander, wine served as the dramatic tension for the New Testament story of the wedding feast at Cana. When the wine ran out, Jesus changed water into wine—and good wine at that. Of course, wine was poured at the Last Supper as well.[8]

In the common era, winemaking was, interestingly, imported to France twice. First came the Phoenicians, who settled Marseilles in 600 BCE. As André L. Simon notes in his book *The Noble Grapes and the Great Wines of France,* the Phoenicians "had no need to bring cuttings of their own Eastern vines: they had only to prune, train, and tend the [wild] native vines in order to get better grapes and to make wine." Five hundred years later, when Julius Caesar came to, saw, and conquered Gaul, he bid the lands nearest essential waterways be stripped of their trees so as to prevent unexpected assault by hidden, resentful natives. Caesar then encouraged pliant residents to plant vineyards in the river valleys of the Loire, Marne, Rhône, Saône, and Seine. But he didn't do this just to produce wine; by this means he also sought to more deeply root the locals to their soil—as well as to him. When Crassus extended Roman dominion to the Atlantic a few years afterward, he found a flourishing viticulture already rooted in the area we know as Bordeaux.[9]

The Romans in turn most likely introduced wine to England.[10] And though the English today cherish their red Bordeaux—their "Claret" (a word, which rhymes with carrot, not found in French today)—they've never quite gotten the hang of making it. And so they import it, from France in particular.

In 1066 William the Bastard, Duke of Normandy, made preparations to set off for England—during a visit of Halley's comet, no less—to wage a battle that would profoundly turn history and remake the English language. He packed axes and adzes, lances, spears, and Norman wine, what we now consider French wine. We know this because the great historical authority on the subject,

The thirty-seventh tableau of the Bayeux Tapestry depicts a cask of wine being loaded for William the Conqueror's Norman invasion of England in 1066. Courtesy of Granger–Historical Picture Archive.

the Bayeux Tapestry, depicts all facets of the expedition and triumph, including the Battle of Hastings itself. The tapestry's thirty-seventh tableau—the entire magnificent piece is nearly seventy-five yards long—shows a cask of wine being loaded for the expedition. After defeating King Harold at Hastings on October 14, 1066, William the Conqueror became King William I of England. In addition to French wines, William brought French and Latin, which commingled with the Anglo-Saxon Old English. Its offspring, Middle English, was the English of Chaucer.

More than four hundred years later the king and queen of Spain, Ferdinand II of Aragon and Isabella I of Castile, dispatched a Genovese sailor on what many thought was the errand of a fool, or at least an errand funded by fools. Christopher Columbus, in ships that included casks of wine, sailed west on the third of August, 1492, seeking a new sea route to what we consider the East Indies. Instead, he made landfall two months later in the West Indies—probably on the island of San Salvador in today's Bahamas—making him the "discoverer" of the New World. The native peoples of this New World had no wine that we know of, notwithstanding that the Vikings, who had themselves "discovered" the New World five centuries earlier, had named it "Vinland."

And so, wine found its way to the New World: first to its east; then, in the fullness of time, to its west.

To tell the story of wine in California, it's best to begin with the history of one of its first cities, San Francisco. Some would say San Francisco was founded in the same year the United States declared its independence, 1776. In that year, two sites were founded for St. Francis of Assisi: a Roman Catholic mission still known as Mission Dolores, and a military garrison (in Spanish, presidio) near the tip of the Golden Gate. Others would claim San Francisco wasn't much to speak of until 1835, when, as "Yerba Buena," it was founded as a village or pueblo under Mexican law—its center a good three or four miles from either the mission or presidio, in the heart of what is known today as Chinatown. (As of 1821, "Alta California" was considered part of Mexico, having exerted its independence from Spain in its own war for independence.) The pueblo didn't get its formal name until 1847, when Yerba Buena was officially renamed San Francisco; by then the region was considered American territory. In 1847, San Francisco was a somnolent, remote agglomeration of sand and sand fleas, hills, fog, marshes, and mud, boasting roughly five hundred people and about as many dogs.[11]

Regardless of when San Francisco was founded, one cannot say it was a "city" in any sense of the word until 1849. In that year, the population of San Francisco swelled from fewer than five hundred to twenty-five or thirty or fifty thousand—no one knows for sure. To quote J. S. Holliday's book title, the world rushed in: along every overland route where a trail was blazed (or wasn't), or by sea around Cape Horn or via the jungle of Panama or across the Pacific—through the Golden Gate to San Francisco. Eighteen forty-nine was the year of the California gold rush.

Not two decades later Alexandre Dumas—who was not just a popular French writer of his generation but also the foremost gastronomic authority of his time—would write that, after Paris, San Francisco was the greatest culinary city in the world. While others had written of San Francisco in the same effusive vein, Dumas's words established the city's international renown as a place of gastronomic greatness—a renown earned in breathtakingly little time.[12]

Today, California is as renowned for its wines as San Francisco is for its food, though the former arrived much more slowly.

The history of wine in California—of wine-grape growing and winemaking—is a story of five beginnings. The middle three beginnings were dashed by one calamity after another. The fifth beginning—the least promising, ironically—has taken California wine to the celestial success it enjoys today.

The first beginning was effected by the first non-native population: the Franciscan padres, who established and ran the California missions, were the region's first winemakers, though for domestic and sacramental purposes only. Their vineyard at Mission San Gabriel became known as the Vina Madre, the "mother vineyard." Accordingly, one could be justified in considering them the fathers of California wine. But, as their vintages weren't produced for sale, perhaps that honorific should instead go to a Frenchman named Jean Louis Vignes, California's first commercial winemaker. Indeed, his name itself says as much: in French it means "vines" or "vineyards." But it was a later vintner who earned the honorific. Agoston Haraszthy de Mokesa—a Hungarian who called himself both "Colonel" and "Count" Haraszthy, each title resting on equally dubious grounds—was long after his death lionized as the "Father of California Wine."[13] The winery he established in Sonoma in 1862 became Buena Vista; still operating today, it touts itself as California's oldest premium winery.

But any claims regarding the rightful bearer of the title "Father of California Wine"—whether the padres, Vignes, Haraszthy, or even a prominent later vintner named Charles Kohler—require a fundamental qualification. Regardless of these figures' prodigious contributions to the state's winemaking, after this first "beginning" California's grape growers and winemakers suffered four devastating setbacks. From each they had to start virtually anew, with new fathers. Only after overcoming these hardships has the region's wine industry attained the successes and recognition of recent years, pinnacles not likely dreamed of in the early days.

The first setback, which occurred late in the nineteenth century, was the infestation of California vines by phylloxera, a louse that attacks the roots. The second was the San Francisco earthquake and fire of 1906, in which the state lost perhaps three-fourths of its wine supply. The third setback occurred during the Panama-Pacific International Exposition of 1915, which had been planned in large measure to showcase California's wine industry, among many other jewels, to the French, German, and Italian wine aristocracy. But, as it happened, the ravages of World War I kept many of the intended audience from attending. The industry received its most grievous blow from the bludgeon of Prohibition. (It is hoped that Prohibition was the industry's ultimate—last—insult.) And, of course, Prohibition ended in 1933, in the midst of the Great Depression, which in turn ended only with the outbreak of World War II.

Those four setbacks were inauspicious times for California's grape growers and winemakers. Yet subsequent generations haven't just thrived; with the vision and drive of new leaders, California wines have attained world recognition. These new leaders who achieved the vision of Vignes, Haraszthy, Kohler, and others include Robert Mondavi, Ernest and Joseph Gallo, Martin Ray, André Tchelistcheff, and, most recently, Bill Harlan. The story of the attainment of that vision—the vision of California as one of the great wine regions of the world—is told in the third part of this book. The second part tells of the four calamities. The first part, to which we turn next, offers the beginnings. ∎

Notes

1. "Scorpion I's wines predate the advent of Egyptian vineyards and were imports from the Jordan River valley," http://news.nationalgeographic.com/news/2009/04/090413-scorpion-king-wine.html, accessed December 16, 2016.

2. Wilford, "Wine Cellar, Well Aged," A5.

3. Homer, *Iliad,* trans. Robert Fagles (London: Penguin Books, 1990), 1:264.

4. Ibid., 6:297–311.

5. In one depiction, a wine goblet has been knocked over and another is raised in a toast. *Wedding of Peleus and Thetis* by Abraham Bloemaert (1564–1651).

6. Gen. 9:20–29.

7. Gen. 19:24–35.

8. John 2:3–10, Mark 14:23–25, and Matthew 26:27.

9. Simon, *Noble Grapes,* 1–2.

10. Simon, *History of the Wine Trade,* vol. 1.

11. Lewis, *San Francisco,* 46–47.

12. How that happened is explored in another book: John Briscoe, *Tadich Grill: History of San Francisco's Oldest Restaurant.*

13. Hutchison, "Northern California," 30, 31.

CRUSH

PART ONE

❧

Beginnings

Mission Vines, Vignes, and Buena Vista

The entire story of wine in California is indeed a rich
pageant of continuities and associations between
the Old World and the New. . . . Wine upgrades
California, . . . urging it onwards to further civilization.
In wine, in the wine country, the American-as-
Californian becomes, not only the pioneer coaxing
virgin soil to fruition, but the heir to the ages, bent
upon an immemorial task of translation and care.

—KEVIN STARR, *Land's End*

CHAPTER 1

Early California, the Missions, and Their Eponymous (and Tasteless) Grape

1769–1833

> The greater part of our vast country—but more especially
> the Pacific slope—abounds with soil and climate congenial
> to the culture of the grape, which is its natural home,
> foreign as well as native. And, therefore, all classes
> of wines can be made there, more particularly the
> potent wines, like Port, Sherry, and Madeira, in greater
> abundance and of as good quality as in any country.
>
> —MATTHEW KELLER, "California Wines"

WE KNOW THAT WINE first found its way to the New World via Christopher Columbus's ships. Historian Samuel Eliot Morison writes: "For drink they had wine, while it lasted, and water in casks, which often went bad."[1] In this context, wine was an essential beverage. As for the first *vintage* produced in the New World: it was also essential, but for an entirely different purpose. The Spaniards who settled Santa Elena, South Carolina, in approximately 1568 are generally thought to have been the first vintners. Their purpose was primarily sacramental: wine was used in mass. As for more established winemaking, that wouldn't occur for another sixty-odd years, produced by Franciscan missionaries across the continent in the Southwest, in what is now New Mexico.

The first grapes of that region took root around 1626, planted along the Rio Grande at the Mission Socorro. One leading authority on the subject, Thomas Pinney, writes that the grapes the missionaries cultivated there were vinifera, the Mediterranean grape used in Europe for winemaking for thousands of years. In which case, the Spaniards and Indians of the Southwest drank wine "as it had been known in Europe since the first apparition of Dionysus."[2] Frank Schoonmaker defines *vinifera* thus:

Vinifera (vine-*if*-er-ah): By all odds the most important of the 40-odd species that make up the genus *vitis*. Appropriately named "the wine bearer," *Vitis vinifera,* which originated in Transcaucasia in prehistoric times, is responsible for virtually all of the world's wines (the rest are made from hybrids and from a number of native American varieties). There are more than a thousand varieties of *vinifera*—black, purple, blue, red, pink, amber, yellow, green—of which the most famous include Cabernet Sauvignon, Pinot Noir, Zinfandel, Nebbiolo, Chardonnay, Riesling, Sauvignon Blanc, Semillon, Chenin Blanc, and Grenache.[3]

Note that the grape planted in the vineyards of southwestern missions may or may not have been the grape later planted at the California missions, thusly called the Mission grape.[4]

And where the missionaries went, so, in time, would wine. Franciscan hands also planted the first grapes on the Pacific coast, in both Alta and Baja California. To paraphrase another authority, Vincent P. Carosso: the history of the first viticulture in California is essentially the history of the missions. Ergo, the first period of California viticulture was thus the mission period, from 1769 until 1833.[5]

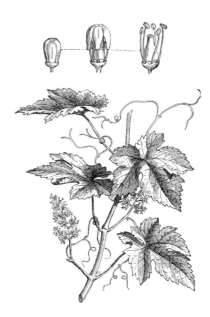

Vintage illustration of the common grape vine (*Vitis vinifera*), from *Meyers Konversations-Lexikon,* 1897.

The Discovery(ies) of California

The first colonizers could just as easily have been English, or Russian—in which case Lord knows what we'd be drinking today. But they were Spanish.

Fifty years after Columbus landed on the New World's shores, Europeans discovered and, for reasons that are not entirely clear, named the region California. Spain, though, had acquired "legal title" to California long before any of her explorers or conquistadors even saw the place. On May 4, 1493, less than six months after Columbus discovered the Americas, Pope Alexander VI divided the so-called New World between Spain and Portugal. He assigned to Portugal all lands she might discover east of an arbitrary meridian of longitude, the Line of Demarcation (the eastern "bulge" of the future Brazil, for example), and to Spain all lands west of that line. By this decree, California—if Spain could find it—belonged to the Spanish.

In 1513, the Spaniard Vasco Núñez de Balboa reached the west coast of Panama and named the ocean he saw there the Pacific. Twenty-two years later, in 1535, another Spaniard, Hernán Cortés, discovered an "island" (in fact a peninsula) that he named California (today called Baja California). Later still, in 1542, the

Spanish viceroy for New Spain, Don Antonio de Mendoza, sent Juan Rodríguez Cabrillo—a navigator (likely a Spaniard long said to have been Portuguese)[6]—to further explore the coastline. On September 28, 1542, in San Diego Bay, Cabrillo noted in his log: "We discovered a port closed and very good," which he decided to call San Miguel.[7] Sailing north from San Diego, they next encountered Santa Monica Bay and the Santa Barbara Channel, ultimately exploring as far north as today's Point Reyes. But, just as others had done, Cabrillo's ships missed the Golden Gate altogether. (This is an understandable oversight, as it's often enshrouded in fog.)

After Cabrillo's death in January 1543, thrashing winter winds and spoiled supplies forced his crew to return to Mexico. His voyage was the end of the first phase of Spain's limited exploration of the California coast. Having lost their faith in the prospect, Spanish officials decided that the New World north of Mexico contained "neither wealth nor navigable passage . . . between the Atlantic and Pacific Oceans."[8] And so they ignored the region altogether, for more than two hundred years.

THE JESUITS AND THE BAJA CALIFORNIA MISSIONS: 1697–1767

A hundred and fifty years after Cabrillo's death, in 1697, the Roman Catholic Society of Jesus—better known as the Jesuits—was granted permission to establish missions in Baja California. This sort of endeavor, of course, concerns the fervent desire to share the teachings of God with native peoples. And, as we have seen, since the Catholic mass requires sacramental wine, with missionaries comes winemaking. The first vineyard in Baja might have been planted by Father Juan de Ugarte, at Mission San Francisco Xavier, which was founded circa 1699. Later a number of the other Jesuit missions developed their own vineyards and wineries.

Accounts differ as to whether the wine produced at the missions of Baja California was ever offered for sale. In his 1789 book *The History of Lower California,* historian and teacher Father Don Francisco Xavier Clavigero writes: "The missionaries of [lower] California never sold their wine. . . . They used it for mass, the table, and the sick; and what was left over they sent as a gift to their benefactors or exchanged for those provisions which they received from Sinaloa and Sonora." In addition: "There was wine at only five or six of the existing missions, and all that was made did not amount to one hundred casks, as I well know from the very ones who made it."[9] Add to this the following from Father Jacob Baegert:

> Five of the missions had vineyards; and the grapes were sweet and delicious. For wine-making the berries were pressed out with the hands and the must collected in large stoneware jars brought from Manila. The wine was excellent. There was no want of cellars; but the difficulty was to find such as were cool enough; and it was not infrequent to have the wine overheated and spoiled. As, however, *very little was used except for church purposes,* there was enough to supply all the missions of the peninsula and a number of those on the other side of the gulf.[10] (Emphasis added.)

The above text, which appeared in the first volume of Theodore H. Hittell's 1898 *History of California,* was translated from a 1773 German text, *Nachrichten Von Der Amerikanischen Halbinsel Californien* (Account of the American Peninsula of California). That German work was later published by the University of California Press, providing more of the original text in a translation that is intriguingly different in parts:

> It was not necessary to buy sacramental wine elsewhere. The land produces it, and without doubt it could become an excellent and generous product if cool cellars, good barrels, and skilled vintners were available, because the grapes are honey-sweet and of superior flavor. Five missions have vineyards. The juice is merely pressed from the grapes by hand and stored in stone jars. These jars hold approximately fifteen measures (one measure is two quarts, approximately) and are left by the ship which makes a yearly visit to California on her way from the Philippine island of Luzón to Acapulco in Mexico. The storage cellar for the wine is an ordinary room on level ground and—in California—necessarily warm. Therefore usually half of the grape juice, or even more of it, turns to vinegar. Ten or fifteen jars full of sacramental wine were sent each year to the missions across the California Sea and to the four or six missions in California which had no vineyards. When it left the cellar, the wine was good, but it did not always arrive in the same condition because it had to be carried on muleback in the hot sun for fifty or more hours. As a result, the wine often turned sour, sometimes on the way, sometimes soon after it was delivered.
>
> It was not permissible to give wine to the Indians. Some of the missionaries never tasted any except during Mass. *One measure of it sold for six florins,* so that neither soldier nor sailor could

Early image of three coastal inhabitants. Its original caption reads: "1. (*left*) Wahla, chief of the Yuba tribe—civilized and employed by Mr. S. Brannan. 2. (*middle*) A partly civilized Indian. 3. (*right*) A wild Indian. From a daguerreotype by Mr. W. Shaw." Printed in *The Annals of San Francisco,* by Frank Soulé, John H. Gihon, and James Nisbet, D. Appleton, 1855.

afford to get drunk frequently. Yet there was no aged or choice wine in California.

From these facts it can be seen that only a small quantity of wine was successfully produced. It was not surprising that many times I and my colleagues had no wine, even for the Holy Mass. Yet *it has been claimed that the missionaries of California sold much wine and sent it to other lands.*[11] (Emphasis added.)

In 1767, following the lead of Portugal (in 1759) and France (in 1764), a Spanish court opted to force the Jesuits from the New World—that is, from South America, from Central America, and from western North America. Exactly why the Jesuits were expelled remains a mystery to historians; one lasting theory—or, as Caughey puts it, "wild rumor"—is that the Jesuits were suspected of operating for personal gain, perhaps—again from Caughey—"hoarding vast treasures from secret mines [or] pearl fisheries," or simply extorting from the natives.

Next began the process of transitioning oversight of the missions from the Jesuits to the Franciscans; regarding that endeavor, Father Junípero Serra was named president of all California missions. Six months later, on July 16, 1769, the Franciscan padres dedicated Mission San Diego de Alcalá, the first of a string of California missions that would begin European colonization of California, as well as incubate the California wine industry. The Franciscans established twenty-one missions in all, the last in Sonoma in 1823. Some missions had presidios (military garrisons) and pueblos (towns) established nearby as well, as befit Spain's colonization approach for all its "far-flung" possessions.

The Franciscans and the Alta California Missions: 1767–1833

The missions were the centerpiece in a system of colonization that was the reverse of the English system on the eastern coast of North America—notwithstanding the use of violence on both coasts. Some have said that the Spanish did not look upon the native Californians as enemies or savages that had to be subdued or eradicated, but rather as fellow human beings, to be given the word of God, converted to Christianity, and taught the arts and industries of "civilization," the fruits of which they were to share. But the subsequent maltreatment of many of the native Californians seems to belie, or at least shade, this outlook. The mission, which was never replicated—nor even approximated—on the eastern frontiers of Anglo-America, was the most prominent institution of Spanish America. The center of a mission was the church. Clustered around it were the housing quarters: for the missionaries, for the Indians, and for the soldiers—garrisoned there to protect from without and preserve order from within. There were also granaries and storerooms. There were shops used for carpentry, blacksmithing, and weaving, as well as for the making of pottery, candles, soap, and wine. Beyond were corrals for horses, vegetable gardens, irrigated fields, grazing lands for cattle, and vineyards.[12]

The mission system never fully worked. The "natives" did not wish to be subjugated, and the soldiers intended to keep them in order were underpaid and ill-disciplined. In 1821 Mexico won its battle for independence from Spain. Then, in a series of decrees starting in 1833, the new Mexican authorities in California ordered the "secularization" of the missions, stripping most of the mission lands from the Franciscans. This secularization gutted the mission system, effectively emancipating the neophytes and making a majority of the most valuable coastal land in California—from San Diego to the Sonoma Coast—available for distribution to favored grantees of the new government. When Mexico lost its war against the United States in 1848, it lost all its "Alta" states, including California.

The overall effect of this history on the native Californians was dire. European disease and a harsh, unaccustomed mission life proved fatal for many (as did the "homemade brandy" sometimes given in payment for their labor). Add to this consideration the ways white incursions of lands reduced food resources. In his 2016 book *An American Genocide: The United States and the California Indian Catastrophe*, Benjamin Madley offers the following sobering figures: in 1542 (at first European "contact"), there were approximately 350,000 native Californians; from then until the end of the mission period (1834), the population dropped to approximately 150,000. In the fifty years following secularization, the native population plummeted far more dramatically—to approximately 18,000. Over the course of just two and a half centuries, foreigners managed to annihilate 95 percent of the native population.

Those native Californians who lived within the mission system, and survived it, provided the bulk of the labor for the planting and tending of the mission vineyards—not to mention the olive groves and fruit orchards—the harvesting of the grapes, and the making of wine. And, fortunately, there were at least a few white settlers whose eyes and hearts were open to the plight of the Indians.

THE FIRST CALIFORNIA VINTAGES

It was mentioned previously that where the missionaries established roots, so, in time, would wine. As for when California winemaking specifically began, some have asserted that the first vineyards were planted at the first mission, Mission Basilica San Diego de Alcalá, in 1769. Three formidable "witnesses" attest to this assertion. The first is no less than General Mariano Vallejo.

In 1833 Mariano de Guadalupe Vallejo, the military commandant of Alta California, was dispatched to locate sites for outposts to ward off any Russian expansion of its 1812 settlement at Fort Ross—not to mention the English settlement farther north on the Columbia River. With a handful of settlers, Vallejo established communities at Petaluma and Santa Rosa.[13] He later became one of the first wine-grape growers in Northern California, as well as a friend of his pioneer neighbor, Agoston Haraszthy.

In 1874, General Vallejo wrote that California pioneers—including his father, a Spanish soldier among the first sent to California—had told him that Father Serra had brought wine grapevines from Baja California and planted them at Mission San Diego in 1769. Of course, we can't know if this report originated from Father Serra himself or in fact from someone else.

The second "witness" to the planting of wine grapevines in

1769—or, more correctly, witness once or twice removed—was Arpad Haraszthy, the son of Count or Colonel Agoston Haraszthy. Like General Vallejo, Arpad Haraszthy was reporting what *his* father had told him, or, perhaps, what his father-in-law, General Vallejo, had told his father.[14]

The third witness was California's early in-depth chronicler of its wine industry, Frona Eunice Wait. A professional writer who had worked as a reporter for the *San Francisco Examiner,* Wait published *Wines and Vines of California* in 1889. In it she states that Franciscan padres had planted the first wine grapes at Mission San Diego in 1770, and that by 1774 "these holy fellows had pipes of piquant inspiration in their mission cellars."[15] But, since Wait had interviewed Arpad Haraszthy at length for her book, it's highly likely all three witnesses rely on the putative statement of one man: General Vallejo's father.

It so happens that Father Serra himself seems to have contradicted these accounts. As Thomas Pinney notes in his first volume of *A History of Wine in America,* Serra complained throughout the mission-founding process of how wine for mass was so hard to come by in Alta California—and what wine he did get came from Spain or Mexico.[16] If San Diego was indeed producing wine in 1774, as Frona Wait reported, it's hard to imagine that Serra would go to the trouble of importing wine as well.

The first unmistakable mention of the planting of grapes at a California mission concerns Mission San Juan Capistrano. It occurred in 1779, and perhaps yielded a small crop as early as 1781. This assertion derives from Roy Brady, who more than suggests that the first vines were brought to San Diego in 1778, aboard the supply ship *San Antonio* under the command of Don Jose Camacho:

> Careless writers are in the habit of saying that Father Junípero Serra brought the grapevine with him when he arrived in 1769. As spiritual leader of the Gaspar de Portolá expedition that came to plant the first European settlement in California, he needed wine to celebrate the Mass. It's a pretty story, the beloved father carefully tending the vine cuttings through the arduous trek up Baja California and putting them gently in the earth of San Diego with his own hands. The story was pretty enough to cause the California wine industry, or some of its less scholarly sectors at any rate, to observe the bicentennial of California wine prematurely in 1969.[17]

Supporting his statement, Brady cites an obscure letter to

The Making of Mission Wines

A number of scholars have offered information regarding just how wines were produced at the missions. Ruth Teiser and Catherine Harroun write that "mission winemaking was done in the traditional Spanish way," which included growing vines unsupported by stakes or trellises, planted customarily in haphazard rows, "but with different dramatis personae." Regarding the "Spanish way," Thomas Pinney adds that one mission had a copy of a 1777 edition of a winemaking guide written in 1513, the second part of Alonso de Herrara's *Agricultura general*.

Of winemaking at Mission San Gabriel, author Frances Dinkelspiel shares: "the Native Americans. . .did virtually all the work to make the wine. They cleared the ground of shrub and chaparral. They planted Mission grapes and tended the vines. They picked the grapes and carried them to the vine house, where they crushed them." The process of crushing involved piling the grapes onto some sort of cowhide-covered sloped or inclined crushing platform; or, at least at San Gabriel, onto a cowhide sort of hammock tied to four poles. The Indians would then crush the grapes with their feet—though recall that earlier Father Jacob Baegert is quoted as saying the grapes were pressed by hand. The juice was caught in leathern bags and then stored in stone jars or wooden tubs, where, according to Hubert Howe Bancroft, "the liquid was kept two or three months, under cover of the grape-skins, to ferment. Such as did not flow off [the cowhides] was put into wooden presses, and [then] the juice into copper jars and covered with a kind of hat. Through two or three inserted tubes heat was conveyed to the mass to aid evaporation and condensation. These jars served as a still for brandy. For white wine the first juice only was taken and stored."

In a passage quoted earlier Father Jacob Baegert noted that, though the native Californians tended the process from planting to "decanting," so to speak, they were not allowed to even taste the fruits of their labor. This is curious, given that the wine's raison d'être was for the sacrament of Mass. Since the Indians had been baptized, wouldn't they participate in communion? One wonders if perhaps the good Father chooses his own interpretation. Teiser and Harroun point out that, though the native Californians ate the native *Vitis californica* grapes, they had long before learned that these grapes did not make good wine.

Sources: Teiser and Harroun, *Winemaking in California*, 1, 3, 20; Pinney, *History of Wine in America*, 1:241, citing Webb, *Indian Life at the Old Missions*, 98–99; Dinkelspiel, *Tangled Vines*, 74–75, citing McKee, "Beginnings of Los Angeles Winemaking"; Baegert, *Observations in Lower California*, 130–31; Bancroft, *California Pastorat*, 371–72.

and of its "abundance" of grapes.[28] It would appear that, at least by 1829, the mission supported a *commercial* winemaking enterprise—though we must keep in mind the fact that foreign commerce was illegal under Spanish rule, thereby limiting what could feasibly be sold, at least up until the secularization of the missions began in 1833.

THE MISSION GRAPE

And what of the Mission grape itself? This plant is an exotic whose place of origin (as well as the precise time when it acquired its name) long remained a mystery. Professor Harold P. Olmo, a renowned plant detective from the University of California, found similar grapes in other parts of the world. He posited that the Mission grape was related to the Negra Criolla of Venezuela—*creole* meaning a New World descendant of an Old World ancestor.[29] Indeed, the Mission grape is very much like the Criolla of Mexico and South America. More recently, however, the mystery has been solved. Researchers have determined the Mission grape is in fact Listán Prieto, an old Spanish variety—so old it's no longer grown in Spain, though it can be found in vineyards in the Canary Islands.[30] As prolific California historian John S. Hittell describes: "The berry is bluish-black in color; is covered, when ripe, with a grayish dust, which brushes off, leaving a glossy, smooth skin; is about half an inch in diameter at its largest size; [and] has a thin, sweet juice, with more meat and a little fruitiness of a flavor."[31]

As we have seen, California's first viticulture could only begin once the Mission grape was brought by the Franciscan fathers. This is because, though the state's soil and climate definitely helped establish its wine industry, its native grapes did not. Two grape species are native to California: *Vitis californica* and *Vitis girdiana*. Early Californians, like John Sutter, were disappointed when neither produced a wine of decent quality. The species fared no better in the hands of University of California scientists seeking pest-resistant rootstock. And though they remain uncultivated, these grapes can still be found growing wild, often in woodsy areas or near streams.[32]

In thus greatly improving upon the native grapes, the Mission grape was perfectly suitable for its intended role at the altar. Since it favors the hot California climate, it grows prolifically. That it can be made into a decent sweet wine suited the era, since early California lacked the ideal cellars of today's industry so necessary for preserving low-alcohol dry wines. And it was certainly not without its fans, well past the era of secularization. Julius Dresel claimed that his brother Emil's Mission wine was "pure of taste, ripe, and unctuous," "of a marked Burgundy flavor," with a "sweetness and high percentage of genuine alcohol."[33] (Even today the Mission grape has its fans; located east of Sacramento, Story Winery makes wine from an acre of Mission vines planted in 1894.)

And yet, this sort of praise notwithstanding, many consider the Mission grape woefully mediocre as a table wine. As Thomas Pinney describes, it "lacks distinctive varietal character" on account of its inherent low acidity; given that, any dry wines attempted from the grape are destined to underwhelm.[34]

Another reason the Mission grape failed to impress likely stems from the fact that many California winemakers didn't know how to either properly grow the grape or make wine from it. And so, California wines in the decades immediately after the mission era attained a deserved disrepute. Even the winemakers who had the wit to make good wine from the Mission grape nonetheless contributed to the problem by selling too much of the product before it had sufficiently aged.

All the same, for decades after the demise of the missions, their eponymous grape continued to dominate the California wine industry.

THE WANING OF MISSION VINICULTURE GIVES WAY TO THE EMERGENCE OF COMMERCIAL VITICULTURE

To summarize the distance we've travelled so far: the Spanish decree of 1767 banishing the Jesuits from New Spain ushered in the era of the Franciscan missions in what is now the American state of California. During that mission period—from 1769 until 1833—the cultivation of the wine grape took root, leading to a flourishing viticulture. At the end of that period, viticulture extended as far as the missions extended—from productive San Diego in the south to the sleepy (at the time) town of Sonoma in the north.

The secularization of the California missions in the 1830s ushered in the era of the grand California ranchos—roughly six hundred of them legal and two hundred more of them not[35]—the era romanticized by writers like Helen Hunt Jackson. Subsequently there was a marked decline in mission wine production—as well as a gradual abandonment of their vineyards and winemaking equipment. This demise receives a poignant mention in English captain Edward Belcher's account of his round-the-world voyage of the 1830s: "These were the only places of resort for travellers throughout California, and even in their palmy times were only tolerable; but now a meal cannot be procured without difficulty, and travellers must rely upon their own resources." In 1839 Captain Belcher put in at San Diego. There, he wrote, "little wine is made since the virtual death of this mission, and that little of very inferior quality."[36]

Of course, as one industry wanes, another can take root. And, as it happened, Southern California winemaking in that era hadn't been solely a mission enterprise. The decline of the missions and their viticulture roughly coincided with the rise of commercial winemaking, first in Los Angeles. Thus began the second period in California viticulture.

Notes

1. Morison, *Christopher Columbus.* The menu for Spanish seamen on Columbus's ships in his 1492 voyage included the following: water, vinegar, wine, olive oil, molasses, cheese, honey, raisins, rice, garlic, almonds, sea biscuits (hardtack), dry legumes (such as chickpeas, lentils, and beans) salted and barreled sardines, anchovies, dry salt cod and pickled or salted meats (beef and pork), and salted flour (http://www.christopher-columbus.eu/food.htm).

2. Pinney, *History of Wine in America,* 1:233.

3. Schoonmaker and Bespaloff, *New Frank Schoonmaker Encyclopedia of Wine,* 544.

4. Pinney, *History of Wine in America,* 1:233–34.

5. Carosso, *California Wine Industry,* 3. See also Teiser and Harroun, *Winemaking in California,* 5.

6. University of San Francisco professor Christopher O'Sullivan has noted that, although great pains have been taken to maintain the premise that Cabrillo was Portuguese, there is insufficient evidence to support the claim. Huntington Library research scholar Harry Kelsey convincingly argues in his 1986 biography *Juan Rodríguez Cabrillo* that Cabrillo was Spanish.

7. Miguelito, "The Voyage with Cabrillo: The Adventures of a Pajé," San Diego harbor, September 28, 1542. Website of the Cabrillo National Monument, San Diego, accessed December 22, 2016, nps.gov/cabr/forteachers/upload/JR%20Cabrillo%20Teacher%20Packet.pdf.

8. Federal Writers' Project, *California,* 42–43.

9. Clavigero, *History of (Lower) California,* 6.

10. Text from Hittell, *History of California,* 1:283, citing Father Jacob Baegert, *Nachrichten Von Der Amerikanischen Halbinsel Californien,* pt. 3, sec. 5, 241–45.

11. Baegert, *Observations in Lower California,* 130–31. Available via the UC Press E-Books Collection, 1982–2004, http://publishing.cdlib.org/ucpressebooks/view?docId=ft5r29n9xv.

12. Federal Writers' Project, *California,* 45–46.

13. Soulé, Gihon, and Nisbet, *Annals of San Francisco,* 771; Caughey, *California,* 191.

14. Pinney, *History of Wine in America,* 1:238, citing McKee, "Beginnings of California Winegrowing," 59–60. In an article published in 1871, however, Arpad claims the year was 1771, and the mission was San Gabriel. Arpad Haraszthy, *Wine-Making in California,* 15.

15. Wait, *Wines and Vines of California,* 33. Scholar Thomas Pinney has traced that the above quotation was actually written by Ben C. Truman and published in the *New York Times* on January 16, 1887.

16. Pinney, *History of Wine in America,* 1:238.

17. Brady, "Alta California's First Vintage," 10, 15.

18. Ibid., 12, 14.

19. Leggett, *Early History of Wine Production,* 15–17, 21, and references cited.

20. Muscatine, *Old San Francisco,* 208–9.

21. Leggett, *Early History of Wine Production,* 17.

22. Vancouver, *Voyage of Discovery,* 2:17.

23. Bancroft, *History of California,* vol. 7, *1860–1890,* 46; Carosso, *California Wine Industry,* 3; Gregory, *History of Sonoma County,* 30.

24. Davis, *Seventy-Five Years in California,* 5.

25. Carosso, *California Wine Industry,* 3. According to the California State Board of Agriculture report for 1912, prior to perhaps 1833 the missions collectively produced 700 to 1,000 gallons of wine per acre, and "practically all was consumed in the neighborhood." George Robertson, state statistician, "Statistical Summary of the Production and Resources of California," *Report of the California State Board of Agriculture* (Sacramento, 1913), 183.

26. Pinney, *History of Wine in America,* 1:239, citing, in part, Alfred Robinson, *Life in California* (New York: Wiley & Putnam, 1846).

27. Ibid., 1:241; for Harrison Rogers quotation, Pinney cites Harrison Clifford Dale, ed., *The Ashley-Smith Explorations,* rev. ed. (Glendale, CA: Arthur H. Clark Company, 1941), 195.

28. Captain John Hall, "Appendix 1: Remarks on the Harbours of California, with Directions for Navigating Them—Extract of a Letter to the Editor," in Forbes, *California,* 330.

29. Teiser and Harroun, *Winemaking in California,* 5.

30. Robinson, Harding, and Vouillamoz, *Wine Grapes,* 551–52.

31. Hittell, *Resources of California,* 194–95.

32. Teiser and Harroun, *Winemaking in California,* 5.

33. Julius Dresel, writing to the editors of the *Daily Alta California,* 1872, qtd. in Mobley, "Mission Revival," L6.

34. Pinney, *History of Wine in America,* 1:234.

35. Robinson, *Land in California,* 105–7.

36. Belcher, *Narrative of a Voyage,* 1:118, 327.

CHAPTER 2

"City of Vineyards"—
Commercial Winemaking Takes
Root in Southern California

1790s–1890s

Within "the whitewashed walls of the winery...were
the vats, coils, and cooperage of my new calling,
awaiting the late summer's harvest and the crush of
fall. Inhaling deeply, I convinced myself that I could
smell a suggestion of new wine already on the air."

—KEVIN STARR, *Land's End*

TODAY, CALIFORNIA WINES are most often thought of as
Northern California wines: from Napa, of course, the best-
known wine-producing region in the state, but also from
Sonoma—not to mention Mendocino and a host of other "wine
counties." But in the early nineteenth century, Los Angeles was
California's incontestable "city of vineyards." Even the city's first
official emblem was simply a cluster of grapes.

EARLY ROOTS OF THE LOS ANGELES COMMERCIAL
WINE INDUSTRY—1790s–1830s

The first Los Angeles vintner whose name we know was a Spanish Californian soldier named Antonio María Lugo, who planted
a vineyard soon after he received a circa 1810 land grant of Rancho San Antonio.[1] Less than a decade later—once others, like
Manuel Requena, had followed his lead—Los Angeles boasted
fifty-three thousand vines in an area of fifty-three acres. (For a
sense of that volume, note that if a parcel of land in the shape of
a square were exactly one-quarter mile on a side, its area would
be forty acres.) Lugo remained engaged in his property well into
his twilight years. Even as an octogenarian he could be seen riding "into town on horseback, erect, with his sword strapped to his
saddle beneath his left leg."[2]

Just as the first settlers of the pueblo of Los Angeles were Spanish and Mexican, so too were the first vineyardists. This is partly because initially foreigners were forbidden from living in Alta California, not to mention owning land. *California: A Guide to the Golden State* tells us that, "even before 1800, the Spanish Court had instructed the colonists that no foreigners were to land at California's ports or cross its borders." But, starting in 1824, the Spanish and then Mexican governors of Alta California began loosening such restrictions.[3] Following the wandering spirit that has long led to ever-westward expansion, before long the English, French, Irish, and Dutch were drawn to the region, as were those from the eastern United States. Unfortunately, as Teiser and Harroun point out, these Anglo-Saxon arrivals ultimately "replaced" the pioneer vineyardists.[4]

———— ❧ ————

IN 1824, JOSEPH CHAPMAN—who was notably aboard Bouchard's *Argentina* when it landed in Monterey—became the first American (that is, U.S.–born) winegrower in the Los Angeles pueblo in the by-then Mexican province of Alta California. Hubert Howe Bancroft relates that Chapman was

> impressed into that service at the Sandwich Islands, as he claimed —taken prisoner at Monterey, and soon finding a home in the south. . . . In '20 [he] was employed at Mission Santa Inés, where in '21 he built a grist-mill and obtained from Governor Sola the king's amnesty to Anglo-American prisoners. Then he went to Mission San Gabriel to build another mill and was baptized at San Buenaventura in '22 as José Juan, being married the same year . . . to Guadalupe Ortega. . . . In '24 he bought a house at Los Angeles and got a piece of land, where he planted a vineyard of 4,000 vines.[5]

Thomas Pinney points out that Chapman likely learned the winemaking trade from his time at Mission San Gabriel.[6] A Dutchman named Johann Groningen, a ship's carpenter whose vessel had wrecked in San Pedro Bay on Christmas Day, 1828, also settled in Los Angeles, planting vines a few years after Chapman.

Soon other "Yanquis" arrived. Other vineyardists of this era include carpenter William Logan, New Yorkers William Hill and William Chard, and Lemuel Carpenter of New Mexico, all of whom planted vineyards and prospered. French cooper Louis Bouchet also caught the vintner bug; his holdings in time led to the name Bauchet Street.[7] Hill joined Bouchet in the latter's business. Chard and Carpenter joined forces as well, planting a vineyard together near the Los Angeles River.

Not every visitor to the region felt the calling to stay. One was young Harvard student Richard Henry Dana, who decided to sail as an apprentice seaman in the trade along Mexico's Alta California coast. His bunk on the ship was "before the mast," meaning more forward in the ship, and subject to more pitching at sea. His account of his experiences would become a classic of California and American history: *Two Years Before the Mast*. After a voyage of 150 days from Boston harbor, the brig *Pilgrim* reached Santa Barbara, which he later described as a "large bay without a vessel in it; the surf roaring and rolling in upon the beach; the white mission, the dark town, and the high, treeless mountains."[8] In time the *Pilgrim* sailed up the coast to Monterey to trade, principally in "hide-droghing." His account of Monterey and their wine was less than flattering: "The Californians are an idle, thriftless people, and can make nothing for themselves. The country abounds in grapes, yet they buy bad wines made in Boston and brought round [Cape Horn] by us, at an immense price, and retail it among themselves at a *real* (12½ cents) by the small wine-glass."[9]

INDUSTRY LEADERS EMERGE—1830S–1850S

The Los Angeles viticulture begun by the friars and expanded by the pioneer vintners soon flourished into a bona fide industry: by the 1830s Los Angeles alone (including what is now Orange County) produced nearly half the total wine-grape crop of Alta California. Before long, it became clear just who most influenced and contributed to this culture.

Jean Louis Vignes

Jean Louis Vignes was California's first full-time professional winemaker. Born in the Bordeaux region of France, where he trained as a distiller and cooper—coopers build and repair wooden casks and barrels—Vignes brought to the rough Mexican province of Alta California a knowledge of the great wine estates of his birthplace. He arrived in Los Angeles in the early 1830s, when he was in his early fifties. He soon saw that California could be the equal of Bordeaux, and by 1833 was well established as a grape grower and winemaker.

Some details about Vignes's life are not definitive. One source states he had been married and had children; another

Always cognizant of the fact that the quality of his product would in the long run determine the quantity of his profit, Don Luis felt it was not too much expense to send his wines for an ocean trip—usually from California to Boston and back—to improve their quality before putting them on the market. The practice of improving choice wines by sending them on long sea voyages was customary and was also practiced by Eastern wine merchants.

Roughly fifty years later, Sonoma's Oliver W. Craig did the same with his hock, which he "sent on a round trip to China for mellowing."

Sources: Carosso, *California Wine Industry*, 9; Teiser and Harroun, *Winemaking in California*, 74.

asserts he was a lifelong bachelor. We don't even know why he left Bordeaux.[10]

What little we know about Vignes's early years in the Americas we know from a letter of a priest, Father Alexis Bachelot, written to his order's headquarters in Paris. In 1826, Father Bachelot and Vignes left France for the Sandwich Islands—the priest on a religious mission, Vignes an agricultural one. In this letter, the priest wrote that Vignes "had been forced into exile as a result of troubles caused by his loyalty, his misplaced tenderness, and his over-zealous desire to be of service." (To whom, the priest doesn't say.) In the Sandwich Islands, which is to say Hawai'i, Vignes grew sugarcane as well as grapevines, and distilled rum from the sugarcane. In about 1831 or 1832 Vignes sailed to California and took up residence in the pueblo of Los Angeles. There he practiced his trades of cooper and distiller, and bought a 104-acre tract of land for a vineyard and orchard.[11]

William Heath Davis, born in Honolulu of a second-generation Yankee trader, was a boy of nine when he sailed on the ship, the *Louisa,* that had borne Vignes from the Sandwich Islands to Monterey, California. In his *Seventy-Five Years in California,* Davis wrote of Vignes:

Don Luis, as the Californians called him, was a Frenchman, who came to Monterey in the bark *Louisa* with me in 1831. . . . From Monterey he went to San Pedro, shortly afterward established himself at Los Angeles, and before long had the largest vineyard in California. At that early day he imported cuttings of different varieties of grapes, in small quantities, which were put up with great care and sent from France to Boston; thence they came out in the vessels trading on this coast, to be experimented with in wine producing.[12]

Davis, who later became a wine merchant, described a visit to his older friend's home about two years after Vignes had established himself in Los Angeles:

In 1833 I called to see him at his house and found him well established. . . . He said to me most warmly, "William, I only regret that I am not of your age. With my knowledge of vine and orange cultivation and of the soil and climate of California, I foresee that these two are to have a great future; this is just the place to grow them to perfection." He was then about fifty years old [fifty-four, in fact], full of zeal and enterprise. He was one of the most valuable men who ever came to California, and the father of the wine industry here.[13]

Nine years later, in 1842, Davis visited Vignes again:

[Vignes] asked me if I remembered what he had said to me when I was last there, about the California wine, its importance and value, and remarked that he would now prove to me that his predictions were correct. . . . [H]e had written home to France representing the advantages of California for wine making, telling them that he believed the day would come when California would rival "la belle France" in wine producing of all varieties, not only in quantity, but in quality, not even excepting champagne; and that he had also induced several of his relations and a number of his more intelligent countrymen to come to California to settle near Los Angeles, and engage in the business.[14]

By then the Frenchman Vignes had come to be called Don Luis del Aliso, Aliso being the name of his winery.[15]

William Wolfskill

That William Wolfskill ranks among the most notable vintners of this era is somewhat surprising, given that he began as a quintessential swashbuckling American frontiersman. In 1821 he left behind his Kentucky roots for a trading expedition to New Mexico; from there he encountered many who shared his love for hunting, trapping, fishing, and trading. Having taken to the region and its ways, in 1830 he converted to Christianity, chose the name José Guillermo, and became a Mexican citizen.[16] That same year a beaver-hunting expedition enticed him ever westward, this time toward what is now Northern California. (One of the members of his party was George C. Yount, who would later be a pioneer settler in the Napa Valley.)

En route, prevented from crossing snowed-in mountain passes, they rerouted south,[17] and were hosted for a time by Don Antonio María Lugo—noted earlier as the first Los Angeles wine-grape grower whose name we know—at his Rancho San Antonio. By then Lugo had been a vintner for more than twenty years. Through him the group—or Wolfskill and Yount at least—also visited Mission San Gabriel, where Father José Sanchez continued their incipient exposure to California viticulture.[18]

Soon thereafter Yount moved on to Northern California, while Wolfskill, realizing that hunting and trapping weren't lucrative pursuits, chose to give up his frontiersman trades and settle in Los Angeles. First working as a carpenter, he steadily moved toward his goal: buying a vineyard, which he did with his brother John in 1838. He continued to expand their operation—buying additional land, developing a large wine cellar and distillery—over time rivaling Vignes in running one of the most significant winemaking operations in the city.[19] He did this by seeking innovation in various aspects of the business, including exploring beyond the boundaries of viticulture. One expansion: growing citrus fruits as well as grapes. (A region south of the City of Vineyards later developed into Orange County.) Vincent Carosso writes how, from 1841, Wolfskill "built a nursery and carried out many experiments to determine what fruits were the most adaptable to the soil and climate of California." Later, his "grapes and wines sold throughout California"; in the San Francisco market, he sold fruit as well.[20] In other words: throughout his life, Wolfskill strove to determine exactly what would work best in a given situation; this approach is to be credited for his impressive and varied successes.

In its October 24, 1857, issue, the *Los Angeles Star* noted that "his grounds are well stocked with peach, pear, apricot, fig, and apple trees." "We also saw in his garden quite a number of citron trees, heavily laden with their fragrant fruit." The portrait continues, sharing a bit about Wolfskill's winemaking process:

> The grapes, as they come from the vineyard, are thrown into a large shallow vat, where half a dozen persons rapidly mash the grapes by treading them. The vat is slightly inclined, so that the liberated juice rapidly flows into a cistern, from which it is removed to larger fermenting tubs. If intended for white wine, the juice is fermented by itself. If for red wine, the grape skins and pulp are added to the wine, and all fermented together. After it is sufficiently fermented, the wine is drawn off and the "rest" is placed in a still, water is added, and grape brandy is the product.
>
> Angelica is a sweet liquor, or wine, admirably designed to please the palate, but producing the "largest-sized" headache on those who indulge in its use too liberally. It is made by one gallon of grape brandy to three gallons of unfermented juice. A slight fermentation takes place, and if bottled, it becomes somewhat sparkling. It is a most palatable and agreeable drink, but woe to him who drinks too deeply.[21]

Edwin Bryant, in his book *What I Saw in California,* regarding his "tour . . . through California in the years 1846–1847," had the following to say about William Wolfskill:

> The quantity of wines and *aguardiénte* produced by the vineyards and distilleries, at and near Los Angeles, must be

Kohler & Frohling Pure California Angelica wine label, San Francisco. Courtesy of the Early California Wine Trade Archive.

considerable—basing my estimate upon the statement of Mr. Wolfskill, an American gentleman residing here, and whose house and vineyard I visited. Mr. W.'s vineyard is young, and covers about forty acres of ground, the number of vines being 4,000 or 5,000. From the produce of these, he told me, that last year he made 180 casks of wine, and the same quantity of *aguardiénte*. A cask here is sixteen gallons. When the vines mature, their produce will be greatly increased. Mr. W.'s vineyard is doubtless a model of its kind. It was a delightful recreation to stroll through it, and among the tropical fruit-trees bordering its walks. His house, too, exhibited an air of cleanliness and comfort, and a convenience of arrangement not often met with in this country. He set out for our refreshment three or four specimens of his wines, some of which would compare favorably with the best French and Madeira wines. The *aguardiénte* and peach-brandy, which I tasted, of his manufacture, being mellowed by age, were of an excellent flavor. The quantity of wine and *aguardiénte* produced in California, I would suppose, amounted to 100,000 casks of sixteen gallons, or 1,600,000 gallons. This quantity, by culture, can be increased indefinitely.[22]

Given all this praise, it should be no surprise that the industrious Wolfskill's impressive vineyards were twice (1856 and 1859) awarded the top prize at the state fair.[23]

Later Vintners in a Shifting Industry—1860s–1880s

In just one paragraph, Harris Newmark lays out a veritable Who's Who and What Was What of the late Los Angeles era. This passage follows his description of how Jean Louis Vignes's vineyard was taken on by his nephews in 1855:

This lithograph of Los Angeles was drawn from nature and on stone circa 1857 by Kuchel & Dresel (Charles C. Kuchel and Emil Dresel). The third image down on the left border depicts the vineyard of "Frohling & Kohler" [*sic*]. From the Robert B. Honeyman, Jr. Collection of Early Californian and Western American Pictorial Material (BANC PIC 1963.002:1457—D). Courtesy of The Bancroft Library, University of California, Berkeley.

The activity of these Frenchmen reminds me that much usually characteristic of country life was present in what was called the city of Los Angeles, when I first saw it, as may be gathered from the fact that, in 1853, there were a hundred or more vineyards hereabouts, seventy-five or eighty of which were within the city precincts. These did not include the once famous "mother vineyard" of San Gabriel Mission, which the padres used to claim had about fifty thousand vines, but which had fallen into somewhat picturesque decay. Near San Gabriel, however, in 1855, William M. Stockton had a large vineyard nursery. William Wolfskill was one of the leading vineyardists, having set out his first vine, so it was said, in 1838, when he affirmed his belief that the plant, if well cared for, would flourish a hundred years! Don José Serrano, from whom Dr. Leonce Hoover bought many of the grapes he needed, did have vines, it was declared, that were nearly a century old. When I first passed through San Francisco, en route to Los Angeles, I saw grapes from this section in the markets of that city bringing twenty cents a pound; and to such an extent for a while did San Francisco continue to draw on Los Angeles for grapes, that Banning shipped thither from San Pedro, in 1857, no less than twenty-one thousand crates, averaging forty-five pounds each. It was not long, however, before ranches nearer San Francisco began to interfere with this monopoly of the South, and, as a consequence, the shipment of grapes from Los Angeles fell off. This reminds me that William Wolfskill sent to San Francisco some of the first Northern grapes sold there; they were grown in a Napa Valley vineyard that he owned in the middle of the fifties, and when unloaded on the Long Wharf, three

Wine label for Sainsevain's California Wine Bitters, Sainsevain Bros., San Francisco. Courtesy of the California State Archives.

or four weeks in advance of Los Angeles grapes, brought at wholesale twenty-five dollars per hundred weight![24]

In 1855, Don Luis Vignes sold his Aliso winery—which included an orange grove and an extensive and prolific vineyard—to his Bordeaux nephew Jean Louis Sainsevain for $42,000. Jean Louis's brother Pierre joined him in the enterprise, and thus began one of the pioneer wine establishments of California, Sainsevain Brothers.[25]

In a short time they greatly augmented Vignes's operations, becoming notable and successful wine merchants selling others' products as well as their own—still with the Aliso label. Also, no doubt sensing where the wine industry was headed, in 1857 they began both manufacture and retail operations in San Francisco.

Unfortunately, not all entrepreneurs reach the apex they desire. Pursuing a dream of creating their own sparkling wine, the Sainsevains incurred a heavy investment—which proved fatal to their bottom line, ultimately forcing them to close operations in 1862. Thomas Pinney attributes this unfortunate end to two factors: the Mission grape's low acidity, and the brothers' insufficient methods. El Aliso was sold in 1865, and in time subdivided into an unidentifiable part of the present-day inner city of Los Angeles.[26]

Neighboring William Wolfskill's vineyard was that of "Don Mateo," as Irishman Matthew Keller came to be known. Like many fortune seekers before and after, Keller came to Los Angeles by way of gold country in 1849. By 1853 or so, having bought

Pedro Sainsevain in 1886 Recalls

In 1886 Arpad Haraszthy wrote Pierre Sainsevain inquiring about the origins of El Aliso. Pierre, who by then went by the Spanish "Pedro," sent the following reply.

San Jose, June 22nd, 1886
Mr. Arpad Haraszthy,
Dear Sir:—

I have the pleasure to receive your letter of yesterday and hasten to answer. The vine, as you know, was first introduced into California by the Spanish Missionaries, each Mission possessing a certain quantity. The products of each were used by themselves, but in 1830, my uncle, Mr. Jean Louis Vignes, bought a property at Los Angeles, where he immediately planted vines for a speculation. As soon as the vines produced, he made wines and brandies from them, which he sold, not only in Los Angeles but along the entire Coast. When I re-joined my uncle in July 1839, he possessed in the neighborhood of 40,000 vines, a very good cellar, and good casks, which he had constructed right on the place from the oak of the country which he had himself, cut. In 1840, I started out on the ship "Moosoon" [*sic*], with a cargo of his wines and his brandies, for the ports of Santa Barbara, Monterey, and San Francisco; and sold them at the good price of $2.00 per gallon for the white wines, and $4.00 for the brandies. My uncle always remained in this business up to the year 1855, at which time my brother and myself bought from him the above property. It was named "El Aliso," and we have continued the business. In 1855, Messrs. Kohler & Frohling bought grapes at Los Angeles and made wine, and in 1857, they established a depot in San Francisco, under Montgomery Block; and we, my brother and myself, established our depot in the same year, in the cellars on the corner of Jackson and Montgomery. In this same year, 1857, I bottled 50,000 bottles of champagne; and the year following, 1858, I bottled 150,000 bottles. I continued to bottle champagne at different times in small quantities since, here in San Jose. In 1860, I sent a cargo of our different wines to New York, and in Jan. 1860, I established my cellar at No. 81 Cedar St. in New York. A few months afterwards, the agent of Messrs. Kohler & Frohling likewise established a cellar in Broadway. As you see, Kohler & Frohling were not the first merchants in the California wine business, neither here nor in Los Angeles. Mr. John L. Vignes began 25 years before them. That was his only occupation, and my brother and myself continued the business. Mr. Manuel Requena, a Mexican at Los Angeles, as well as Don Guillermo Wolfskill of the same place, an American, made and sold wines and brandy, beginning in 1840, the produce of their vines. Mr. Louis Rouchet, a Frenchman at Los Angeles, proprietor of a vineyard, must have begun to make wine in 1837. I can also cite to you, Don Antonio Coronel, Don Tibulcio Tapia, and several other Californians, who had vineyards at Los Angeles, made and sold their wines 10 or 12 years before the Messrs. Kohler & Frohling. Therefore you see that they are very wrong to think themselves pioneers in this industry. Mr. Jean Louis Vignes was the first, and the others followed him.

—Pedro Sainsevain

Source: Arpad Haraszthy, "Haraszthy Family," 46–48.

did love the whole human family; and Don Benito seemed to have a special love and regard for the red branch thereof—the poor Indian. He always had a smile, a kind word, and was wont to manifest his love for his charge in substantial gratuities."[33]

Indeed, such benevolence could be seen even in Wilson's earliest days in California. He'd arrived in 1841 with the intention of heading to China, a destination he never reached. But, as he later reported: "Receiving so much kindness from the native Californians I arrived at the conclusion that there was no place in the world where I could enjoy more true happiness and true friendship than among them, there were no courts, no juries, no lawyers, nor any need for them. The people were honest and hospitable, and their word was as good as their bond."[34] Later in life Wilson wrote of his experiences working with the California natives in *Indians of Southern California in 1852*.[35]

As the appointed subagent of Indian Affairs, it was Wilson who saw to all Indian concerns. What were these concerns? In *California,* historian John Caughey starts off his chapter "Liquidating the Indians" by noting that, after secularization in 1833, "the annals of Los Angeles for the late forties and fifties abound with mention of the Indians reduced to starvation, beggary, and petty crime, of their hopeless addiction to drink, of Indians caught like cattle for the work season, and of the Monday slave mart at which their services for the week were auctioned off to cover the fines for their inevitable drunkenness." In addition, "the prevailing attitude seemed to be that [killing an Indian] was by no means a crime."[36]

Author Frances Dinkelspiel fills in a few pertinent details:

When California became a state in 1850, it immediately legalized a practice of short-term indentured servitude for the Native Americans, a practice of which winemakers took advantage. One of the first acts passed by the California Legislature was a law nicknamed the Indian Indenture Act. It stripped Native Americans of most of their rights, including the right to vote or testify against whites in court. The law also made it easy for vineyardists and farmers to use the pretext of vagrancy to obtain cheap Indian labor. Any Indian who appeared to be drunk or loitering, or was seen in a place where liquor was sold, could be arrested. Sometimes just the word of a white man could lead to an arrest. A justice of the peace could order that the Indian be hired out for up to four months to the highest bidder to pay off his fine.[37]

Fortunately, some native Californians evaded the reservations. In *Beasts of the Field: A Narrative History of California Farmworkers, 1769–1913*, Richard Steven Street writes that in this era many Indians worked in the Los Angeles wine industry, "where a core group of field hands mastered virtually every task associated with winemaking." Matthew "Don Mateo" Keller concurs: "Most of our vineyard labor is done by Indians, some of whom are the best pruners we have—an art they learned from the Mission fathers."[38] Vintner and subagent Don Benito Wilson adds: They "understand the mysteries of irrigation, the planting season, and the harvest . . . planted all the fields and vineyards." "Without [them] a *rancho* [*sic*] would eat much less bread and vegetables!"[39]

Don Benito Wilson's son-in-law, James de Barth Shorb, joined him in making wine. Among their holdings was a portion that derived from the San Pascual Rancho, one of many land grants resulting from the secularized San Gabriel Mission property. As is noted in *Los Angeles in the 1930s: The WPA Guide to the City of Angels:* "In 1874 they laid out a subdivision and called it the Alhambra Tract, so-called because someone in the Shorb family was reading Washington Irving's *The Alhambra* at the time, and convinced the subdividers that the Spanish countryside described by Irving ('a stern, melancholy country, with rugged mountains and long, sweeping plains, destitute of trees') was similar to the surroundings of the tract."[40]

Another prominent, perhaps the most prominent, vintner of this later period was Bavarian Leonard J. Rose, who began his tenure purchasing land from Benjamin Wilson. By 1869 his enterprise was so expansive that he welcomed wine orders from both coasts. As Charles Sullivan notes in *A Companion to California Wine,* Rose's "great Sunny Slope estate eventually covered 1,960 acres on the foothill land that would become the city of Pasadena. When he sold the property and his name to an English syndicate in 1889, he was producing 750,000 gallons of wine and 100,000 of brandy."[41]

In his history *Los Angeles Wine,* Stuart Douglass Byles relates the following about the *second*-generation L. J. Rose:

> The [1884] publication of Helen Hunt Jackson's best-selling novel *Ramona* was a sensation and caused a renewed—but mainly romantic—public interest in the mission period. Business owners took advantage of this nostalgic dream, often twisting the actual

facts out of proportion. L. J. Rose Jr., in the biography of his father, relates an example of this fabrication. A tavern owner in San Gabriel, abutting the old mission, had a huge grapevine shading the patio of his restaurant. On it he posted a placard that read: THIS VINE WAS PLANTED BY FATHER SERRA IN 1771. Not only was the mission not even there. . . at the time, . . . its extensive vineyards [were] not planted until much later, but L. J. Jr. also derisively writes that the vine was originally a cutting from one planted by his father in 1863.[42]

Possible apocrypha abound in the history of wine in California, as in all history, but about wine in Los Angeles there are some solid accounts to offset the dubious.

A VITICULTURE WITHERS

In their book *Winemaking in California,* Ruth Teiser and Catherine Harroun note that in 1863 there were roughly two hundred fifty grapevines for each resident in the city of Los Angeles: namely, four thousand people and a viticulture of a million vines. The lion's share of these had been cultivated by William Wolfskill and Matthew Keller, with 85,000 and 64,600 vines, respectively.[43] If you expand the consideration to include Los Angeles County, then Benjamin Wilson heads the list with the 100,000 vines of his Lake Vineyard.

For all its glory, in the mid-nineteenth century the viticulture of Southern California saw its lights fading in favor of its upstart competitor to the north, San Francisco. For one thing, the port facilities of San Francisco are among the best in the world, let alone on the Pacific Coast. But, of course, the largest factor was

This 1880 lithograph shows vineyards and orchards along the eastern bank of the Los Angeles River, in present-day Boyle Heights. Courtesy of the Los Angeles Public Library Photo Collection.

Bacchus Wines, Gundlach-Bundschu Wine Co., San Francisco directory advertisement, circa 1894. Courtesy of the Early California Wine Trade Archive.

the growing market caused by the Gold Rush of 1849. From that point forward, San Francisco became the primary market of the wine industry. By 1859, just ten years later, twenty-three Los Angeles winemakers—including Kohler and Frohling and the Sainsevains, to name just a few—had established wine "depots" in San Francisco.[44]

In part illustrating that trend, the partnership of German immigrants Kohler and Frohling begins and ends in San Francisco—though it first took root in Los Angeles. And though the two men joined forces in wine, it was music that originally brought them together—and which kept them going, at least for a time.

Their interesting partnership begins with an interesting story. Historians tell how three German immigrant musicians, Charles Kohler, John Frohling, and John Beutler, often took long walks together in Gold Rush–era San Francisco. On one outing either Kohler or Frohling had brought grapes for them to eat, grapes recently imported from Los Angeles (perhaps from William Wolfskill's estate). Beutler admired the cluster, deeming it superior in size and quality to any he'd seen in Germany—at which point he declared that a country that produced such fine grapes could be destined to create great wine. He then, perhaps apocryphally, pronounced: "We will build an altar to the god Bacchus, and introduce the wine business on this coast!"[45]

Recognizing the wisdom of that pronouncement, they lost no time in following it through. They raised funds and bought a small Los Angeles vineyard, which Frohling managed, producing the young firm's first vintage in 1854. In the meantime, Kohler remained in San Francisco, running the merchant end of the business, including establishing a small cellar and, later, delivering wine. (John Beutler didn't remain with them, as it happens.) Part of their resulting success stems from the fact that for the first several years the two musicians kept the operation going by the power of their instruments. As Thomas Pinney puts it: with fiddle and flute, they made "up by night the money the firm may have lost by day."[46]

And so, with one foot in Los Angeles and another in San Francisco, the team Kohler & Frohling built a firm that would significantly contribute to the California wine industry. Their ambition is cogently summarized in a comment Kohler wrote in 1857, regarding the challenge of breaking into the established global wine market: "On the long run we will beat Europe anyhow."[47]

THE WINE INDUSTRY in Southern California did not die all at once; it suffered a long moribundity. Thomas Pinney attributes this decline to three main factors. The first was the "much-complained-about practice" whereby eastern dealers finagled "adulterations" to Los Angeles wines that increased the profit for the former while lessening the reputation of the latter. As for the second and third factors, the region as a whole suffered from ill-timed circumstances in the 1870s: overproduction in times of financial crisis.[48]

One stalwart player during this late period was Anaheim. Just south of the city of Los Angeles, Anaheim began as a German viticultural colony in 1855. The vineyardists and vintners of the cooperative—most of whom learned on the vine, so to speak—produced several types of wines, sparkling and still, dry and sweet, including Santa Ana, a "white sweet wine" much like the Italian Lacryma Christi. But, for all that, only so much quality can be pressed from their mainstay, the Mission grape. In quantity, though, they were not lacking, and produced 1,250,000 gallons of wine in 1884, what would prove to be their last fruitful year.[49]

As the nineteenth century drew to a close, the decline of Los Angeles as the state's major wine producer was well advanced. But that didn't stop Frona Eunice Wait, enthusiastic writer on California wines, from championing the region. Her 1889 book notes how "Los Angeles County, long the leading county in the production and exportation of all kinds of wines, [is] now the leading one in the production of what are known as sweet wines and still a close second to either Napa or Sonoma County in its production and sales of red and white wines."[50]

One might see this as the praise of a proud parent who can speak no ill of a favorite (if lesser-performing) child. And yet, in her chapter on Los Angeles vineyards, Wait seems to take a rather complacent view of what was by then a serious concern: "So far in the history of grape cultivation in Southern California, it has been comparatively free from all diseases and pests; and coulure or blight is hardly known. . . . Three or four years ago [1884] a disease appeared among the vines in the neighborhood of Orange and Anaheim. This disease, a species of fungus, has been made the subject of careful examination on the part of our scientific men, but they have not yet arrived at any definite conclusion as to [its] nature."[51] This point is curious given that, though her book was published in 1889, she failed to include the fact that by 1887—a mere three years from the first observation of the

A vineyard of Mission grapes in Los Angeles County killed by the Anaheim disease. From Newton B. Pierce, *The California Vine Disease,* 1892.

fungus—a vast majority of the region's vines had been killed by "the Anaheim disease."

Historian Thomas Pinney sheds light on Wait's rosy-hued assessment, and it's not a flattering one. It would appear that, as much as Wait loved her words, they weren't in fact all hers: fellow scholar Charles Sullivan discovered that she "plagiarized large parts of her book from letters written to the *New York Times* by Major Ben Truman."[52] One could say she was a bit too enthusiastic in her vocation. The so-called Anaheim disease has since been named Pierce's disease, to which the Mission grape was particularly susceptible; by 1891, only fourteen acres of vineyards remained in Anaheim. In the wake of the disease, much of the colony became the home of Knott's Berry Farm (1920) and Disneyland (1955). The rest of the former vineyards of the colony are today just buildings and ballparks.[53]

For all of the promise and history of the region, for all the vigor and innovation of its agents—Vignes, Wolfskill, Keller, Wilson, and Rose most notable among them—Southern Californian viticulture was not destined for longevity. Once the world started rushing toward the gold fields of 1849, many in the Los Angeles region packed up their vine cuttings and coopers' barrel staves and headed north to the once sleepy pueblo of San Francisco and its impressive, beckoning port. And from San Francisco it was only a day's travel to the idyllic Napa and Sonoma Valleys, where an ideal climate and soil would help winemakers truly realize California's viticulture potential. In the wake of this desertion, Los Angeles was left to developers, filmmakers, and freeways, and the grapevine became an oddity in the once-idyllic "city of vineyards."

Notes

1. Robinson, *Land in California*, 55.

2. Teiser and Harroun, *Winemaking in California*, 16.

3. Federal Writers' Project, *California*, 49; Robinson, *Land in California*, 65–66. Robinson writes: as of 1822, "Mexican authorities continued to give vague cattle-grazing permits." "The first step toward clarification came on August 18, 1824, when the Mexican Congress established rules for the colonization of national lands. . . . They promised security to foreigners who wished to establish themselves in Mexican territory, but prohibited colonization of territory within twenty leagues of the boundaries of a foreign nation or within ten leagues of the seacoast. . . . They encouraged the entry of foreigners, but in the distribution of lands Mexican citizens were to be given preference."

4. Teiser and Harroun, *Winemaking in California*, 16.

5. Bancroft, *History of California*, vol. 2, *1801–1824*, 757. The formatting of the passage has been slightly modified: abbreviations have been spelled out, capitals made lower case, commas made into periods, etc.

6. Pinney, *History of Wine in America*, 1:245.

7. Ibid., 1:245–46; Teiser and Harroun, *Winemaking in California*, 16–17.

8. Dana, *Two Years Before the Mast*, 28.

9. Ibid., 24.

10. Compare Teiser and Harroun, *Winemaking in California*, 17, with McKee, "Jean Paul Vignes," 176, 177.

11. Teiser and Harroun, *Winemaking in California*, 17.

12. Davis, *Seventy-Five Years in California*, 91.

13. Davis, *Sixty Years in California*, 170.

14. Ibid., 170–71.

15. Newmark, *Sixty Years in Southern California*, 197. In this book, Harris Newmark noted that the name Aliso had emerged from the fact that an old sycamore tree on the property has been confused for an alder; the Castilian word for alder is *aliso*.

16. Carosso, *California Wine Industry*, 10; Teiser and Harroun, *Winemaking in California*, 20.

17. Carosso, *California Wine Industry*, 10–11; Teiser and Harroun, *Winemaking in California*, 20.

18. Teiser and Harroun, *Winemaking in California*, 20.

19. Carosso, *California Wine Industry*, 11; Teiser and Harroun, *Winemaking in California*, 20.

20. Carosso, *California Wine Industry*, 11–12; Bancroft writes: "Wolfskill appears to have been the first in 1849 to ship wine to S.F.," Bancroft, *History of California*, vol. 7, *1801–1824*, 46n8.

21. Section headed "Our Vineyards—The Vintage," *Los Angeles Star*, vol. 7, no. 24 (October 24, 1857).

22. Bryant, *What I Saw in California*, 412.

23. Teiser and Harroun, *Winemaking in California*, 20.

24. Newmark, *Sixty Years in Southern California*, 199.

25. Ibid., 198–99; Teiser and Harroun, *Winemaking in California*, 19.

26. Teiser and Harroun, *Winemaking in California*, 18–20; Pinney, *History of Wine in America*, 1:253–54, in which he cites McKee, "Jean Paul Vignes," 179.

27. Pinney, *History of Wine in America*, 1:250–51; Teiser and Harroun, *Winemaking in California*, 64–65.

28. Teiser and Harroun, *Winemaking in California,* 64–65.

29. Pinney, *History of Wine in America,* 1:296. Regarding Wilson trying out additional grape varieties, Pinney offers: "Wilson's winemaker sent him a thousand cuttings from General Vallejo's vineyards in 1864. Wilson Flint sent him Muscat of Alexandria in 1866; and Wilson's San Francisco manager sent him 10,000 cuttings of Frontiniac in 1869" (Wilson Papers, February 23, 1864; February 16, 1866; January 29, 1869).

30. Teiser and Harroun, *Winemaking in California,* 66

31. Ibid., 64–66.

32. Wilson, *Indians of Southern California in 1852,* 77.

33. Horace Bell, *Reminiscences of a Ranger,* 28.

34. Byles, *Los Angeles Wine,* 28.

35. Wilson, *Indians of Southern California.*

36. Caughey, *California,* 319–20.

37. Dinkelspiel, *Tangled Vines,* 88. See also Dinkelspiel, "When LA's Vineyards Ruled California by Abusing Native Americans," *LA Observed,* October 26, 2015, http://www.laobserved.com/intell/2015/10/violence_in_the_vineyards.php.

38. Keller, "Grapes and Wine of Los Angeles," 347, cited in Pinney, *History of Wine in America,* 1:253n87.

39. Street, *Beasts of the Field,* 143, quoting from Wilson, *Indians of Southern California,* 23, 60.

40. Federal Writers' Project, *Los Angeles in the 1930s,* 322.

41. Sullivan, *Companion to California Wine,* 291.

42. Byles, *Los Angeles Wine,* 58.

43. Teiser and Harroun, *Winemaking in California,* 64–65.

44. Muscatine, *Old San Francisco,* 208–9.

45. Teiser and Harroun, *Winemaking in California,* 58; Pinney, *History of Wine in America,* 1:254, citing in part Charles Kohler, Bancroft dictation, n.d. (MS, Bancroft Library, University of California).

46. Sullivan, *Companion to California Wine,* 172; Teiser and Harroun, *Winemaking in California,* 58–59; Pinney, *History of Wine in America,* 1:254nn93–94.

47. Ibid.

48. Pinney, *History of Wine in America,* 1:250.

49. Teiser and Harroun, *Winemaking in California,* 66–67.

50. Wait, *Wines and Vines of California,* 172.

51. Ibid., 172–73.

52. Thomas Pinney, correspondence with the author, July 28, 2016. See also Pinney, "Strange Case of Frona Eunice Wait and Major Ben C. Truman," 17–19, www.waywardtendrils.com/pdfs/vol.23_2013.pdf. In a note for that article, Pinney specifies that it was Charles Sullivan who happened upon the plagiarism in the course of his research; Sullivan referenced it in note 22 of his article "Wine in California: The Early Years—The Great Valley and Its Foothills—The Sierra Foothills 1849–1900, Part 1: El Dorado County," *Wayward Tendrils Quarterly* 22, no. 4 (October 2012), 19–24.

53. Pinney, *History of Wine in America,* 1:292, citing Gardner and Hewitt, *Pierce's Disease of the Grapevine,* 5–31; Teiser and Harroun, *Winemaking in California,* 67.

CHAPTER 3

Northern California—The Gold Rush, Agoston Haraszthy, and the Roots of the Modern California Wine Industry

1836–1869

> A basking inclination, and stones, to be a reservoir
> of the day's heat, seem necessary to the soil for wine;
> the grossness of the earth must be evaporated, its
> marrow daily melted and refined for ages; until at
> length these clods that break below our footing, and
> to the eye appear but common earth, are truly and
> to the perceiving mind, a masterpiece of nature.

—Robert Louis Stevenson, *The Silverado Squatters*

As we've seen, the Franciscan missions brought winemaking to Northern California. Of the eleven northern missions, the vineyards and vinting at San Jose, Santa Clara, and Sonoma laid the foundations for what would come to be a storied viticulture.

The first figure outside the mission system to grow grapes in Northern California was the original commandant of Alta California, later governor of the province, Pedro Fages. He planted a small vineyard in Monterey around 1783, in part to please his wife. But she hated California and connived to secure his recall to Mexico City.[1] And so, it seems his was a bit of a false start.

Quite a few years passed before the next winemaker planted roots, but those fared much better. General Mariano de Guadalupe Vallejo had originally founded both Petaluma and Sonoma in 1834, as part of both Mexican secularization of the missions and measures against Russian encroachment in Northern California. It was then that Vallejo took over the vineyards at the Mission San Francisco Solano and planted his own vineyard, from which he made wine and brandy—all solely from the Mission

Wine label for General Vallejo's Lachryma Montis Vineyard, Sonoma Red Wine, 1858. From Mariano Guadalupe Vallejo miscellany, MS 2204. Courtesy of the California Historical Society.

grape. He welcomed newcomers to his estate in Sonoma, Lachryma Montis ("Tears of the Mountain"); he generously shared his grape cuttings too, and so spread the region's viticulture all the more. Historian Charles Sullivan notes that Vallejo was the father of Sonoma Valley's commercial wine industry.[2]

We first met George Yount when he accompanied William Wolfskill from New Mexico to Los Angeles, where they were introduced to winemaking by Don Antonio María Lugo and Mission San Gabriel. Whereas Wolfskill remained to ply the wine trade in Los Angeles, in 1833 Yount headed north. Since he was skilled as a carpenter and blacksmith, he found work with both the pre-secularization Mission San Francisco Solano and General Vallejo. In 1836 the Mexican government granted him 11,814 acres (roughly eighteen and a half square miles) of land in the Napa Valley, so named for the indigenous people there, the Nappa Indians. (Since Mexico wasn't keen on granting land to foreigners, Yount was baptized Jorge Concepcion by Padre Quijas of Mission Solano.)[3] On his Caymus Rancho, Yount planted that valley's first vines in 1838—in what is today the town of Yountville—with cuttings from General Vallejo's vineyard in Sonoma. And so Napa Valley viticulture descended from Sonoma County winemaking, a point of little amusement to Napa Valley winemakers today.[4] Yount produced an undistinguished product at first. But, twenty years after he planted his first vine, in 1857 the Napa County Fair awarded his wine second prize, and his brandy first prize.[5]

Across the Carquinez Strait from Napa Valley, Dr. John Marsh was the first permanent American-born settler in Contra Costa

County, having in 1837 purchased Rancho Los Meganos. He made wine from the Mission, Isabella, and Catawba grapes of his small vineyard at the foot of Mount Diablo.[6] During his travels through California in 1836 and 1837, Edwin Bryant stayed for a time with Marsh, and later wrote of the visit:

> The residence of Dr. M[arsh] is romantically situated, near the foot of one of the most elevated mountains in the range separating the valley of the San Joaquin from the plain surrounding the Bay of San Francisco. It is called "Mount Diablo," and may be seen in clear weather a great distance. The dwelling of Dr. M. is a small one-story house, rudely constructed of adobes, and divided into two or three apartments. The flooring is of earth, like the walls. A table or two, and some benches and a bed, are all the furniture it contains. Such are the privations to which those who settle in new countries must submit. . . .
>
> I noticed near the house a vegetable garden, with the usual variety of vegetables. In another enclosure was the commencement of an extensive vineyard, the fruit of which (now ripe) exceeds in delicacy of flavor any grapes which I have ever tasted. This grape is not indigenous, but was introduced by the padres, when they first established themselves in the country. The soil and climate of California have probably improved it. Many of the clusters are eight and ten inches in length, and weigh several pounds. The fruit is of medium size, and in color a dark purple. The rind is very thin, and when broken the pulp dissolves in the mouth immediately. Although Dr. M. has just commenced his vineyard, he has made several casks of wine this year, which is now in a state of fermentation. I tasted here, for the first time, aguardiente, or brandy distilled from the Californian grape. Its flavor is not unpleasant, and age, I do not doubt, would render it equal to the brandies of France.[7]

John Marsh wasn't judged warmly by all, however; ten years after Bryant's visit Marsh was brutally murdered. For whatever reason, his winemaking was not carried on by heirs or successors, and so what he might have contributed to California winemaking, and to making Contra Costa County a major wine region, was cut short just as he was.[8]

The World Rushed In, Bringing Its Appetites

Until 1849, San Francisco was a loose agglomeration of three settlements: the Presidio, a military garrison at the entrance to San Francisco Bay; the old Spanish mission, Mission San Francisco de Asís (commonly called "Mission Dolores"); and the village of

Pueblo of Yerba Buena (which had changed its name to San Francisco in only 1847). Together these settlements amounted to little more than a hamlet or village, and a pretty somnolent one at that. In his *Two Years Before the Mast*, Richard Henry Dana offers an account of sleepy San Francisco as he observed it on Sunday, December 6, 1835:

> This large bay...was discovered by Sir Francis Drake, and by him represented to be (as indeed it is) a magnificent bay....About thirty miles from the mouth of the bay...is a high point, upon which the presidio is built. Behind this is the harbour in which trading vessels anchor, and near it, the mission of San Francisco, and newly-begun settlement, mostly of Yankee Californians, called Yerba Buena, which promises well.[9]

Had Dana visited again but thirteen years later, he might have barely recognized it.

In 1840, five years after Dana's ship continued on its course, John A. Sutter was given a parcel of land situated at the junction of the Sacramento and the American Rivers, where much of downtown Sacramento now lies. He built a substantial walled fortress that still stands, just north of L Street between Twenty-Eighth and Thirtieth Streets. He named the place New Helvetia, after his native Switzerland, and built an inn, granaries, warehouses, and general store. More than forty miles upstream, in a valley called Coloma, Sutter ordered the building of a sawmill on the south fork of the American River, to be constructed under the supervision of James Marshall.

The sawmill was powered by the flow of water. Water, diverted by means of a millrace, a channel excavated in a side of the river, turned the millwheel, which in turn powered the giant sawblades. Marshall had the millrace deepened so as to increase the water flow. On January 24, 1848, inspecting the progress of their efforts, Marshall observed a tiny object that would soon have gargantuan effect: "My eye was caught by something shining in the bottom of the ditch. . . . I reached my hand down and picked it up; it made my heart thump, for I was certain it was gold. The piece was about half the size and shape of a pea. Then I saw another. . . ." Marshall's men, digging in the rushing winter waters of the American River, had loosened bits and nuggets of gold that had lain there for centuries.[10]

Two months later, on the Ides of March, as it happens, the San Francisco newspaper the *Californian* reported the story in a brief paragraph on the back page. Two weeks later, the editor of the rival weekly newspaper, Edward C. Kemble, who had visited Sutter and his mill, wrote in the *California Star* that any report regarding the significance of the finding was "a humbug." How curious, then, that in May 1848 the founder of the *Star,* the hard-drinking Mormon Sam Brannan—having since stocked his Sutter's Fort and Coloma general stores with most of the picks, shovels, pans, and other handy supplies the region had to offer— strutted down Montgomery Street, brandishing a vial of glittering gold and shouting, "Gold! Gold on the American River!"[11]

The Gold Rush that followed transformed California to an inexpressible degree. No other comparable state or country has ever been changed so much in so short a time, save cities like Troy, sacked and burned upon conquest. As a historical event, its sweep and scope are not fully apprehensible even today. For more than 150 years, writers and historians have tried to convey a sense of the force of the Gold Rush. The historian J. S. Holliday writes in *The World Rushed In:* "Everything about California would change. In one astonishing year the place would be transformed from obscurity to world prominence. . . . The impact of that new California would be profound on the nation it had so recently joined."[12] Novelist Wallace Stegner called the Gold Rush a "universal mass trespass that shortly created laws to legitimize itself."[13] One particularly remarkable characterization of the Gold Rush was written during its first flush. In an article published in Germany in early 1850, Karl Marx and Friedrich Engels predicted that the discovery of gold in California "will have much greater consequences than the discovery of America itself."[14]

The population growth in California as a result of the Gold Rush is difficult to exaggerate. At the end of 1848, California was estimated to have had a population, not counting Indians, of about 14,000 (though some think the number was not nearly that large). In 1852, the official state census recorded a population of 224,000.[15] By 1880, that was the population of San Francisco alone.[16]

Historian John Walton Caughey writes:

When gold was discovered, San Francisco was a village boasting two hotels, two wharves nearly completed, and 812 persons. Early in the summer of 1848, the population shrank almost to zero; everyone had gone to the mines, and the town was dead. It revived rapidly under the impetus of hundreds of thousands of dollars in gold pouring in from the diggings. The miners wanted supplies,

Trademark for French Colony Vineyard Company, including the seal of California. California secretary of state's office, "Old Series Trademark No. 3400," 1899. Courtesy of the California State Archives.

The French in California

Of course, the Gold Rush attracted all nationalities, in great numbers. As for the French: in as early as 1850 there was a need for San Francisco to have not just one but two French-language newspapers: the *Californien* and the *Gazette Republicane;* a third, the *Courrier du Pacifique,* followed in 1852. In October 1950 the French consul, Patrice Dillon, estimated there being twenty-five thousand French citizens in California; his final tally judged that, over time, thirty thousand gold-seekers had hailed from La Belle France. Some present-day place-names identify congregating immigrant inhabitants, such as French Camp (in San Joaquin Valley), French Corral (in Nevada County), and French Gulch (in Shasta County).

Many French stayed, and prospered. In 1850, Emile Verdier founded the City of Paris department store in San Francisco. Twenty years earlier in Los Angeles, as we have seen, Jean Louis Vignes established the impressive Aliso Winery, followed by the Sainsevain brothers. Later, in 1852, Etienne Thee acquired land south of San Jose where his son-in-law, Argonaut Charles LeFranc in 1858 founded Almaden Valley Vineyards south of San Jose; later still, Paul Masson joined LeFranc, and forged his own legacy.

Sources: www.foundsf.org/index.php?title=San_Francisco_Newspapers; Rohrbough, *Rush to Gold*, 177, 269; Rawls, *Dr. History's Whizz-Bang*, 14–15; Sullivan, *Companion to California Wine*, 7–8 and 188.

and San Franciscans assumed the twin responsibilities of providing supplies and an outlet for the miners' gold. Business flourished during the last months of 1848, but the next year saw the real boom, with 40,000 Argonauts avalanching upon the town.[17]

It didn't take distant contemporary writers like Marx and Engels—or much later American writers like Wallace Stegner and Jim Holliday—to recognize that something remarkable was happening in San Francisco. Three men privy to how the Gold Rush transformed the city chronicled its history from its Spanish beginnings until the spring of 1854. They were Frank Soulé, John H. Gihon, and James Nisbet. Their work, *The Annals of San Francisco,* published in 1855, consists of more than eight hundred pages of rigorous historical research peppered with amusing anecdotes. In their opening chapter they write of what San Francisco "almost already is, but which it will more plainly soon become, the

In his book *Sonoma Wine and the Story of Buena Vista,* Charles L. Sullivan writes:

> The Sonoma phenomenon in that period was part of a statewide movement that was equally rapid in Santa Clara County, the East Bay, the Sacramento area, and Los Angeles County. By 1855 it had become increasingly obvious that grape crops had a multiplicity of money-making outlets. Most obvious then were the profits from fresh fruit. And there were also table wine, fortified sweet wine, brandy, and even raisins. If anything triggered the post-1855 wave of vineyard plantation it was Col. [James] Warren's continuous advocacy of viticulture in his influential *California Farmer,* then the state's only periodical devoted to agriculture. He set off his campaign with his articles in 1855, headed "Cultivators of California! Plant Your Vineyards. Begin now. . . . No better investment can be made."[25]

And begin they did, as we shall soon see. But this isn't to say that quality and quantity increased in tandem. As Doris Muscatine points out in *Old San Francisco:*

> In an attempt to fill the Gold Rush demand, many amateurs turned out wines of questionable character. It was a common practice to bottle the juice well before it had had a chance to age, to adulterate it, and to falsify labels. Grape growing was big business, and many of the new viticulturists, knowing little of the conditions of soil and climate, in their haste frequently planted in the wrong location. Further, the Mission grape, the principal variety in use for more than eighty years, although a hearty producer, was rough and of generally poor quality, often made worse by the blunders of amateur horticulturalists. The European immigrants, many experienced in grape culture and winemaking, became the nucleus of the industry, at first preserving it from disaster, and eventually bringing it into full, quality production.

All this wine production also made for significant employment, especially San Francisco's cooperage (barrels) and glass industries (bottles).[26]

Where and by whom did all this planting and aging and bottling occur? Just as vines can become entwined or be grafted, Northern California vintners entwined with each other, whether by buying and selling land or by sharing cuttings and knowledge. They even entwined family members; many a daughter or niece, son or nephew begat the next generation's winegrowers.

Robert Louis Stevenson on the "Prospecting" Wine-Grower

Wine in California is still in the experimental stage; and when you taste a vintage, grave economical questions are involved. The beginning of the vine-planting is like the beginning of mining for precious metals: the wine-grower also "prospects." One corner of the land after another is tried with one kind of grape after another. This is a failure; that is better; a third best. So, bit by bit, they grope about for their Clos Vougeot and Lafite. Those lodes and pockets of earth, more precious than the precious ores, that yield inimitable fragrance and soft fire; whose virtuous Bonanzas, where the soil has sublimated under sun and stars to something finer, and the wine is bottled poetry: these still lie undiscovered; chaparral conceals, thicket embowers them; the miner chips the rock and wanders farther, and the grizzly muses undisturbed. But there they bide their hour, awaiting their Columbus; and nature nurses and prepares them. The smack of California earth shall linger on the palate of your grandson.

Source: Stevenson, *Silverado Squatters,* 22–23.

General Mariano de Guadalupe Vallejo with his daughters Maria Luisa and Maria Ignacia and his granddaughters, 1867. Photograph courtesy of the Sonoma County Library.

To start we return to General Mariano Vallejo in Sonoma County, who first took over established vineyards in 1834. By 1850, Vallejo's Mission grape wines brought in $6,000; by 1854, that figure had jumped to $20,000. Then, when Agoston Haraszthy shared superior cuttings from European stock, perhaps in 1857,[27] Vallejo's wines fared even better. The entwining continued when, on June 1, 1863, two of the general's daughters, Natalia and Jovita, married Haraszthy's sons Attila and Arpad, respectively.[28]

In the early years of the Gold Rush, fortune seeker Etienne Bernard Edmond Thée decided that viticulture held more promise than did either the gold fields or his native Bordeaux. And so in 1852 he established Almaden Valley vineyard south of San Jose. Though he at first planted Mission grapes, in 1857 his son-in-law, fellow Frenchman Charles Lefranc, brought in superior European varieties. By 1860 Lefranc had expanded operations into what would become the first successful large-scale commercial winery in the Santa Clara Valley.[29]

Dr. Edward Bale had married General Vallejo's niece, María Ignacia Soberanes. Their daughter Carolina married Charles

Krug on December 26, 1860. Before then, the German immigrant had taught school in Philadelphia and worked for San Francisco's first German newspaper, *Staats Zeitung*. Then he decided to venture into agriculture. This he did in San Mateo, where he met the Hungarian Agoston Haraszthy, who guided his course thereafter. First he followed Haraszthy to work at the San Francisco Mint in 1855; in 1857 he moved with him to Sonoma to work as a vineyardist. He also purchased thirty acres of land from Haraszthy, on which he planted European varieties. He made wine for other regional pioneers, including General Vallejo, John M. Patchett, Edward Bale, brother-in-law Louis Bruck, George Yount, and others. (Given this freelancing, writer John Olney notes that "Charles Krug can lay claim to being the 'first consulting winemaker in Northern California.'") When he married Carolina he moved to St. Helena in Napa Valley and planted a vineyard on her dowry, a parcel of Edward Bale's Rancho Carne Humana. By 1861 he had established the storied Charles Krug Winery.[30]

Bavarian Jacob Gundlach was drawn to San Francisco in 1850, where the same year he established the Bavarian Brewery. Later he met fellow German Emil Dresel. After forming a partnership, Dresel & Co., in 1858 they planted eighty-five acres on their Rhine Farm in Vineburg, just east of the town of Sonoma, on gently sloping hillsides between the Napa and Sonoma Valleys. There they produced German-type white varietal wines, establishing a grape-growing and winemaking enterprise that continues to this day—likely the second-oldest operating winery in California. Charles Sullivan notes that the two partners each contributed expertise to the partnership: Dresel the winemaking and Gundlach the business undergirding. (Dresel even took over operation of Buena Vista in 1866 when the oft-mentioned Agoston Haraszthy was otherwise detained.)[31]

Of course there were those who dabbled in grape growing as well. One was James Marshall, who established a vineyard in Coloma, the remote outpost where he'd made his momentous discovery. Many another forty-niner put down grape-vine stakes in the Mother Lode country, designated as the west side of the Sierra Nevada mountains due east from San Francisco. Some worked their vineyards between stints in the "diggins"; others cultivated their lands in lieu of the risky and backbreaking work of prospecting for gold.[32]

One from the latter camp was John Sutter. He'd started even before the discovery; at his New Helvetia land in as early as 1840

Advances in Viticulture: John Sutter's Hock Farm

When the visiting committee of the California State Agricultural Society inspected Hock Farm in 1858, it found a vineyard that represented a significant advance over those planted in the Mission tradition. On some thirty acres there were thirty-four thousand vines planted only five to six feet apart, compared to the traditional seven feet. A five-foot stake was "set by the side of each vine, to which the branches are brought up from near the ground forming a symmetrical pyramid," a contrast to the unstaked vines of the old mission vineyards. From the twelve thousand bearing vines that year, Sutter made four hundred gallons of wine, which, the committee reported—apparently without tasting it—"was said to be of excellent quality."

Sources: Teiser and Harroun, *Winemaking in California*, 29; *Transactions of the California State Agricultural Society*, 167–68.

he'd experimented using wild grapes to make brandy. Then, when beset by hordes of squatters on his gold-central property, he escaped to the Feather River and his Hock Farm, where he, and his wine, fared better. Indeed, as Ruth Teiser and Catherine Harroun put it, Sutter "always believed that agriculture, not gold, would be the source of California's prosperity.[33]

AGOSTON HARASZTHY: ENTREPRENEUR

Of all the vintners who helped to plant and nurture the roots of the modern wine industry in California, one has been singled out as being the most influential: Agoston Haraszthy. In 1946, nearly a century after he first arrived in the Golden State, Haraszthy was formally lionized by state officials as being the "father of California viticulture," an honor not all historians endorse.[34] Regardless, it is undeniable that Haraszthy made an enormous impact on the business. John N. Hutchison states that "no other figure [was] so able to excite his contemporaries to plunge into winemaking in the early years of statehood."[35] To consider this one man's details is to consider the "stuff," as Kevin Starr might have phrased it, of California.

In 1849, Agoston Haraszthy arrived in California from Hungary, by way of Wisconsin. But he came not for the Gold Rush; while the Argonauts sought gold, Haraszthy's quest was wine. By the time he arrived winemaking was fully established in the state, and efforts to improve both grape varieties and wine were well under way. Though some might question some of Haraszthy's motives, it seems fair to say that he always sought to improve upon what had come before him.

John N. Hutchison describes Haraszthy thus:

> A man so energetic that in a sense he finally outran his own destiny, he engaged in enough occupations in his fifty-seven years to supply both the governmental and commercial needs of an entire town. In those in which he failed or lost interest, he seemed not to be more than briefly dismayed. By the time he began to exert a major influence on the California wine industry, he had already shaken off a long series of reverses, moving on to each new venture with scarcely a pause.[36]

According to accounts, in 1840, at the age of twenty-eight Haraszthy left Hungary for the United States settling in Wisconsin. Within the next decade he made his first attempt at grape growing, but the effort apparently failed. He attempted quite a few other endeavors as well. As Thomas Pinney notes:

With a partner he set about developing a town—at one point it was called Haraszthy—and he took a hand in all sorts of pioneer enterprises: a brickyard, a sawmill, a general store, a hotel. He sold lots; he operated a ferry across the Wisconsin River and a steamboat on it; he held a contract for supplying corn to the soldiers at Fort Winnebago, and raised large numbers of pigs and sheep; he planted the state's first hop yard (prophetic of Wisconsin beer). He also published *Travels in America,* a two-volume account of his American impressions, in Hungary in 1844, partly in order to stimulate immigration to his Wisconsin lands. . . . Haraszthy seems to have spent much of his time as an enthusiastic outdoorsman, riding and hunting with a flamboyance that amazed the simple Wisconsin settlers. . . . He was tall, dark, fiercely mustached, and given to wearing aristocratic boots and a green silk shirt with a red sash. It is no wonder that the natives always called him "Count."

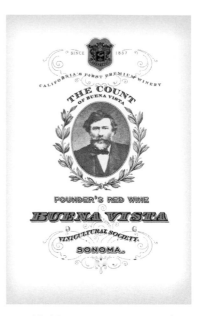

Wine label for Buena Vista Winery, The Count Founder's Red Wine. The image is of Agoston Haraszthy. Courtesy of Buena Vista Winery, Boisset Collection.

As if all that weren't enough, in Wisconsin Haraszthy also began a career in public service when he was appointed state director of emigration. He continued in this vein after he and his family moved to California in 1849. For a time they shared the Santa Fe Trail with other fortune seekers before heading in different directions: while most continued on to Gold Country, the Haraszthys headed south.[37] As biographer Brian McGinty writes: "In the two years he lived in San Diego [Haraszthy] not only planted a vineyard, he also operated a stable and omnibus line, participated in the operation of a butcher shop, took at least two mineral-prospecting trips, took the lead in subdividing a major stretch of the San Diego bay shore, built the first San Diego city jail, held two important public offices [including sheriff] and waged a successful campaign for a third, and played a leading role in a short but bloody 'Indian War' that sent waves of fear through settled communities throughout southern California."[38] Benjamin Hayes later wrote that Haraszthy's Mission grapes were "not very sweet, probably because they were the first, quite small, with rather a rough taste."[39] In 1851 Haraszthy was elected to the new State Assembly as a representative of San Diego, and so they moved to the equally new capital in Sacramento. He soon after planted a third vineyard, the nursery and horticultural garden he named Las Flores, in San Francisco just south of Mission Dolores; and then another about twenty miles down the peninsula, on his Crystal Springs property in San Mateo County.[40]

In the meantime, Haraszthy had forged connections with fellow Hungarians in San Francisco who worked as private assayers of the gold and silver eked out of the region. He joined forces with the Wass, Molitor, and Uznay firm of assaying and refining. Then in 1854, once San Francisco opened a U.S. Mint—which alleviated the need to transport gold and silver to the mint in Philadelphia—Haraszthy became its first assayer, by appointment of no less than President Franklin Pierce. Just over a year later, in August of 1855, he was promoted to overseeing the melting and refining of gold.

Separate from his work at the mint, Haraszthy continued his pursuit of winemaking. In 1856, obviously impressed with his expertise, the California State Agricultural Society asked Haraszthy to write a treatise on the science and mystery of wine growing in the state, a task he accepted with aplomb. As for his personal holdings, given that the two sites Haraszthy had chosen for his latest vineyards didn't fare much better than had his vineyard in Wisconsin, he opted to follow the lead of General Mariano Vallejo, who by then had already earned prizes for his Sonoma wines. In 1856, Haraszthy bought a small vineyard in Sonoma, and thereafter began the process of transplanting vines from his other properties. In time he would hire Charles Krug as his winemaker and establish the estate and winery he called Buena Vista, "beautiful view."[41]

Haraszthy's Agricultural Contribution to Viticulture

Haraszthy's contributions to viticulture fall into a few categories: agricultural, intellectual, and promotional. Concerning the agricultural, put succinctly, in Sonoma Haraszthy planted, for himself and for fellow vintners, hundreds of different varieties of grapevines planted in the tens of thousands, both those he'd imported and those he'd grown in his nurseries. Thomas Pinney writes: "By the end of 1857 Haraszthy and others had more than tripled the total grape acreage of Sonoma County."[42] In 1860, the Visiting Committee of the California State Agricultural Society reported that Buena Vista was "the most extensive vineyard enterprise yet undertaken by one individual in the state."[43]

During this period, Haraszthy's zeal for the wine business was hampered by his position overseeing the melting and refining at the San Francisco Mint. As part of his work investigating federal financial facilities in the region, agent J. Ross Browne, in surveying the mint's operations, assessed that at least $130,000 worth of gold had flown up the flue on Haraszthy's watch. This triggered a long investigation of the facilities, its processes, and its actors. When Browne considered Haraszthy's business associations with a private melting and refining firm, and appraised Haraszthy's landholdings as far surpassing his *visible* financial means, he ultimately concluded that Haraszthy had stolen the gold. In October 1856, he reported that he considered Haraszthy an "unsafe man" and recommended his removal.

While Haraszthy was building out his Sonoma vineyard, in June 1857 Agent Browne filed formal charges against him for the mint's losses; anticipating this, Haraszthy had two months earlier resigned from the mint. Faced with a hefty bond, in order to maintain his freedom Haraszthy was forced to deed over his property to the government. After several months' consideration, in September 1857, a federal grand jury indicted him on the charge of embezzlement of $151,550 in gold.[44]

Haraszthy's Intellectual Contribution to Viticulture

In addition to expanding his winemaking business—part of his tangible contribution to California viticulture—Agoston Haraszthy also made a significant scholarly contribution via both his explorations and study of the field and the writings that study produced. An early example of this was the treatise on grape growing that the California State Agricultural Society had requested of him—which he undertook while under investigation from the federal government. In February 1858 he presented his "Report on Grapes and Wine of California"; historian Thomas Pinney notes this may have been the first written treatment of the subject. Much can be said about Haraszthy's discourse, but on one point he was, if not original, prophetic nonetheless: the California winemaking industry would do well to not rely solely on the Mission grape—indeed, to not rely solely on any one variety.

> To illustrate this more to every man's mind, I will compare the winemaking with the cooking of a vegetable soup. You can make from turnips a vegetable soup, but it will be a poor one; but add to it also potatoes, carrots, onions, cabbage, etc., and you will have a fine soup, delicately flavored. So it will be with your wine; one kind of grapes has but one eminent quality in taste or aroma, but put a judicious assortment of various flavored grapes in your crushing-machine, and the different aromas will be blended together and will make a far superior wine to that manufactured from a single sort, however good that one kind may be.[45]

The treatise also provided detailed information about ideal conditions for climate, locality, and soil:

> The California climate, with the exception of the sea coast, . . . is eminently adapted for the culture of grape vines. . . . The production is fabulous, and there is no doubt in my mind that before long there will be, accidentally, localities discovered which will produce as noble wines as Hungary, Spain, France, or Germany, ever have produced. Vineyards planted in various counties, from San Diego to Shasta, have proved magnificent results, and leave no doubt in the mind that the north is as favorable and productive as the south.[46]

The treatise also specifies best practices for plowing, laying out the vineyard, digging, planting, cultivating, and pruning; for the gathering, crushing, and pressing of grapes; and for the considerations of barrels, cellars, and the treatment of wines—plus approximate costs and yields. It also offers instructions on making Tokay, champagne, port, and brandy.

Haraszthy's treatise was praised as being the "first American explication of traditional European winemaking practices."[47] As Teiser and Harroun state: "It served to bring viticulture in California—where in some vineyards grapes were still being trampled in hides slung from poles—into the mainstream of the nineteenth century."[48]

Haraszthy's methods also proved their mettle when, in 1859, he claimed first prize for the best exhibit of wines at the California State Fair, "with reference to the number of varieties, vintages, and quality,"[49] among them a Tokay.

The Political Climate of the Day—A Nation Divided

Though California operated at some remove from much of the nation, it was hardly impervious to the political concerns gathering throughout the states. Indeed, storm clouds in California mirrored the larger, national debate and fervor regarding secession and slavery. In the late 1850s emerged a movement to divide the state in two, a movement that very nearly succeeded.

In 1859, pro-slavery sentiment was high in California, its forces potent. Wittingly or not, the pro-slavery forces, the Lecomptonites, allied themselves with the largely agrarian southern part of California; the anti-Lecomptonites, opponents of the expansion of slavery, tended toward the north of state.[50] In a letter to President James Buchanan dated January 12, 1860, incoming California governor Milton Latham wrote of the passage of California

Assembly Bill 223, which by overwhelming majority favored cleaving California in two along the line of San Luis Obispo County. (The region above this line was to be the state of California; all below would be a new territory of the United States.) Latham explained that the bill's origin was "to be found in the dissatisfaction of the mass of people, in the southern counties of this State, with the expenses of a State Government. They are an agricultural people, thinly scattered over a large extent of country. They complain that the taxes upon their land and cattle are ruinous [particularly as] the policy of the State, hitherto, having been to except mining claims from taxation. . . . In short, . . . the union of Southern and Northern California is unnatural."[51] Underneath this lurked an additional factor: the looming Civil War, and whether most Californians were loyal to the Union or the emerging Confederacy.

The historical authorities are not clear about what precisely happened other than that Congress took no action.[52] This political split in California over the question of slavery would spill over and affect the course of winemaking in California, setting it back by decades, maybe longer.

Haraszthy's Promotional Contribution to Viticulture

In February 1861, Haraszthy was fully exonerated of all charges made against him. (Many more months would pass before he secured a full settlement with the government, and a return of the deeds to his lands.)[53] Through all his draining and expensive legal troubles, he still managed to advance his viticulturalist standing. It was at this juncture that his efforts in promoting California's wine industry—his third major contribution—stepped to a higher stage. In his capacity serving on the State Board of Agriculture and the legislative Committee on Vines, he continued his dogged endorsement of the value and significance of the state's stake in the business. As John Hutchison puts it, Haraszthy "had with his own hands and wit done more by 1860 than any other individual to point the world of wine toward California."[54] Wanting to further the cause, he recommended to the Agricultural Society that they authorize a fact-finding mission to research the best practices and materials of successful vintners in Europe and South America. According to a Haraszthy family manuscript, Haraszthy was "convinced that it was necessary to import the very finest varieties of vines and to make with them a series of experiments to see which were best adapted for this country; . . . and that to obtain the quickest and most satisfactory result, it would be advisable to introduce all the varieties at the same time."[55] With the support of the state legislature, in May of 1861 Governor John Downey appointed Haraszthy to a state commission to report "upon the Ways and Means best adapted to promote the Improvement and Growth of the Grapevine in California."[56] Note that the terms of the commission speak only to fact-finding, not acquisition.

So Haraszthy and his son Arpad left for Europe on a journey that was to bring him both opprobrium and approbation. They spent five months traveling through Spain, Portugal, Hungary, Italy, Germany, Switzerland, Rhenish Prussia, Bavaria, Nassau, Baden, and France. Throughout they gleaned and recorded all viticultural information they could, sending home periodic reports that were printed in San Francisco's daily newspaper *Alta California*. They also purchased for shipment back to California, in Arpad's conjecture, "nearly 200,000" rooted vines and cuttings of approximately three hundred varieties of wine grapes, "though they came catalogued under 492 different names."[57]

After their return to California, Haraszthy presented his findings. He touted the California climate as being particularly well suited to the growing of grapes. He noted how California's long dry summers allowed for the ripening of the grapes, whereas the heavy rains and hailstorms of Europe's summers often damaged grape crops. He believed that

> California is superior in all the conditions of soil, climate, and other natural advantages to the most favored wine-producing districts of Europe, and that it actually has yielded considerably more per acre. All this State requires to produce a generous and noble wine is the varieties of grapes from which the most celebrated wines are made, and the same care and science in its manufacture. . . . Frequent consultations with many eminent men in Europe . . . assured me that the quality of the grapes governs, in a great measure, the quality of the wine.[58]

All but about 5 percent of the purchased vines and cuttings arrived in good condition. Haraszthy urged that the state take charge of them immediately for cultivation, propagation, distribution, and study. And with his report he submitted his bill, for his "travelling expenses" and for the cost of the 100,000 vines "embracing about 1,400 [*sic*] varieties" plus their freight charges.[59] Arpad and his father gave wildly different figures for the number of vines they purchased in Europe. He then met his opprobrium. The California legislature was not pleased with either the submission of his bill or its total: $12,000. Biographer McGinty notes: $12,000 was "a very substantial sum in 1862, as [Haraszthy] no doubt realized, for he added: 'The sum...will be but a trifle to the real value of said vines...to the people of this State it will in time be worth as many millions." Haraszthy had also specified: "I ask no remuneration to my personal services as Commissioner."[60] Thomas Pinney explains this latter point: "The resolution of the assembly authorizing the commission contained this explicit proviso: 'Such commissioners who may accept the office shall not ask, or receive, any pay or other compensation for the performance of the duties of their offices."[61] And yet, McGinty proposes that Haraszthy submitted his bill with the understanding that Governor Downey would appeal to the legislature for reimbursement; indeed, Downey did so—in his farewell address, before newly elected Republican Leland Stanford replaced him as governor of California.[62] Accordingly, the legislature took their time in presenting their response.

As for approbation, rightly or wrongly the knowledge and lore with which he returned from Europe were such that the story of winemaking in the United States has ever after been divided into two parts—the part before Haraszthy's European tour, and the part after.

In January 1862 Haraszthy wrote a second treatise on winemaking in which he reasserted his conviction that California had more natural advantages as a winemaking region than any European district. He also advocated for the creation of a state agricultural experiment station, state support of plant exploration, and the appointment of a state agency to handle the commerce of wine in California to eliminate unsavory business practices. He soon after published commercially, through Harper's in New York, a book based on his European tour: *Grape Culture, Wines, and Wine-Making, with Notes upon Agriculture and Horticulture*, a work that greatly contributed to viticulture.[63]

While Haraszthy's book certainly promoted the wine industry in general, his dealings with the legislature did not. Some would say that his personality (perhaps even hubris) conspired with the politics of the day to severely set back the industry in California. John Hutchison suggests it wasn't just Haraszthy's excessive request for reimbursement that put him out of favor with the California legislature; given that its members as of just that year were predominantly Republican, and as Haraszthy was the chair of the State Democratic Committee, his support of secession in the midst of the Civil War could easily have been more than they could abide.[64] (The Haraszthy family manuscript states that he had been "falsely accused of being a Secessionist.")[65] In any case, in April 1862, the legislature officially refused to reimburse any of Haraszthy's expenses, both personal and viticultural.

Thomas Pinney offers a different view, judging as excessive the painting of Haraszthy as a "martyr to political fashion." He writes: "Before [Haraszthy] left for Europe he was advertising a scheme for buying vines and other plants in Europe for subscribers: $25 would buy twenty-five varieties of vine, $50, fifty varieties, and so on up to $500, in return for which the subscriber would receive 'two cuttings of every variety of grape now in cultivation in the civilized world.'"[66] Now, that seems pretty damning. But then again, Haraszthy had long been selling such items. For example, the advertisement below dates from 1858, three years before his European tour. And it's also true that Haraszthy kept the imported vines and cuttings for a year in hopes of the legislature reversing their decision.

The state's refusal to purchase and make productive use of at least some of the vast number of European vines and cuttings offered them definitely set back the industry. But Haraszthy is equally at fault, and not just for the sense of entitlement he displayed. In the time that the vines and cuttings were in his care he could have seen to their being properly tended, classified, and identified (as by tags with indelible ink). Indeed, the

Agoston Haraszthy advertised GRAPE VINES & FRUIT TREES FOR SALE AT LOW PRICES even before his 1861 European tour. This advertisement appeared in *California Culturalist*, November 15, 1858.

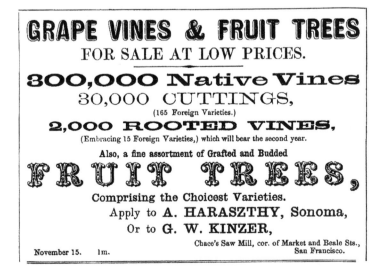

GRAPE VINES & FRUIT TREES
FOR SALE AT LOW PRICES.

300,000 Native Vines
30,000 CUTTINGS,
(165 Foreign Varieties.)
2,000 ROOTED VINES,
(Embracing 15 Foreign Varieties,) which will bear the second year.
Also, a fine assortment of Grafted and Budded
FRUIT TREES,
Comprising the Choicest Varieties.
Apply to A. HARASZTHY, Sonoma,
Or to G. W. KINZER,
November 15.   1m.   Chace's Saw Mill, cor. of Market and Beale Sts., San Francisco.

family manuscript—again, likely written by Arpad Haraszthy—states that with the submission of his report he'd noted how "the vines were perishable articles and needed taking care of." To this the legislature had "directed him to plant them and give them the needed attention." But he did not do this; nor did he take much care in distributing them once he offered them for sale. Many buyers were ignorant of the proper care of vines and cuttings, and few were interested in, say, cultivation in an experimental vineyard. Identification tags fell off the vines, or the writing on them became smudged or obliterated, all adding to the confusion about just what vines had been purchased and planted.[67]

Arpad Haraszthy, who would himself become one of California's principal wine men, believed the legislature's refusal to pay for the vines and cuttings caused an untold loss to the state, and set back the development of the wine industry in California by many years, even decades.[68] In this light, the Civil War can be said to have been the cause of one of the first setbacks for the California wine industry. On the other hand, Haraszthy's European tour introduced a fair number of choice foreign vines into the state—vines that soon replaced the Mission grape—even if no one knew what had been planted.

Haraszthy Continues On—
Buena Vista, Zinfandel, and Nicaragua

In a stroke that in many ways epitomizes the Haraszthy story, on April 23, 1962, just "a week after the state senate rebuffed him (and in the same room in which they had done so), he was elected to the presidency of the State Agricultural Society."[69]

And so Haraszthy continued on. He further expanded Buena Vista by employing Chinese laborers to both plant vines and excavate wine cellars out of stone.[70] (As it happens, just a month after his election as president the legislature imposed a tax on Chinese residents: $2.50 a month.) While this regular employment could be seen in a positive light for the Chinese, on the other hand, Haraszthy's motives weren't exactly charitable, since he paid the Chinese laborers $8 a month plus board—a quarter of the going rate of $30 plus board for white workers. (Vincent Carosso argues that "the Chinese at Buena Vista, although not slaves, were in many respects the American counterpart to the pre-1848 serf and agricultural field labor of eastern Europe.")[71]

Doris Muscatine offers a succinct summation of Haraszthy's progress during this period:

Chinese laborers secured work, such as at Agoston Haraszthy's Buena Vista vineyards, through Ho Po (*pictured*), a San Francisco labor contractor. Photograph courtesy of the California Wine Institute.

Haraszthy's liberal employment of the Chinese enabled him to expand his Sonoma vineyard until its large-scale production of wine and brandy brought general prosperity to the surrounding area. Land values increased twenty-five times over. Further, Haraszthy's methods and his writings on viticulture favorably affected the whole industry. He demonstrated by his prizewinning wines that irrigation was not necessary to produce superior grapes; he showed that hillside cultivation was practical and gave good results; he substituted redwood for oak casks when oak was in short supply; his lobbying efforts on behalf of the industry for years avoided prohibitive taxation; [and] in 1862 he was instrumental in establishing the first California Wine Growers' Association in San Francisco.

In addition, and perhaps ranking among his greatest achievements: Haraszthy's "importation of foreign root stock and cuttings constituted the foundation of the modern vineyard."[72]

Regarding that last point is the consideration of exactly which vines Haraszthy imported. When Haraszthy turned to selling what the legislature wouldn't buy, he prepared a catalog of the 492 varieties available. The ones most highly regarded in California today are the Cabernet Sauvignon, Carignane, Gewurtztraminer, Pinot Noir, Riesling, Sauvignon Blanc, Semillon, Sylvaner, and possibly Chenin Blanc (if that is what his "Pineau Blanc" was). Missing from his listing are a number of grapes one would expect to find, including Chardonnay, Grenache, Syrah, and Zinfandel. That Zinfandel doesn't appear is perplexing because Haraszthy has long been credited with bringing Zinfandel to California from his native Hungary. Indeed, this legend runs as strong as does the assertion that Haraszthy is the father of California winemaking. San Gabriel winegrower L. J. Rose writes in the 1879 *Transactions of the California State Agricultural Society* that Zinfandel was "introduced by the late Colonel Haraszthy from Hungary."[73] In 1880 Charles Wetmore on the Board of State Viticultural Commissioners writes of the "princely gift to this State made by Col. Agoston Haraszthy in 1860, who brought us hundreds of varieties of valuable grapes from Europe, including our now famous Zinfandel."[74] And in her 1889 *Wines and Vines of California*, Frona Eunice Wait claims the "father of the wine industry in this state" in 1852 "received his first importation, consisting of six varieties from Hungary, among which was our present world-renowned Zinfandel." She also wrote that he produced the first vintage of Zinfandel in 1862.[75] But if he had, why was it not mentioned in his catalog? The answer to that will have to wait.

By 1863, Haraszthy's plans for expansion had crashed up against state law restrictions on the total acreage of a corporation's farmland: 1,440 acres. So as to work around this regulation, in March he and "nine silent backers"—including William C. Ralston, the Comstock financier who in the following year founded the Bank of California—created the Buena Vista Vinicultural Society. Haraszthy then sold Buena Vista to the society, staying on as general manager in pursuing an ambitious plan to produce millions of gallons of wine per year, including champagne, on a six-thousand-acre vineyard.[76]

This was the point when, to borrow John Hutchison's phrasing, Haraszthy in a sense finally outran his own destiny. He lost a second battle with California authorities, this time regarding taxing Chinese labor. He suffered great financial losses from his son Arpad's first venture in making champagne. He also had difficulties working with Ralston. Prophetically, around this time a distillery boiler exploded. In the end Haraszthy resigned, and in 1868 the family headed to Nicaragua, where with new partners Agoston started a distillery on a large sugar plantation. Within months of their arrival, in July 1868, Haraszthy's wife died of yellow fever; a year after that, Haraszthy himself disappeared, in circumstances that have remained a mystery.[77] One account states "his footsteps were traced to a tree leaning over a river on his plantation. One of the limbs on the tree was broken and it was concluded that he had been drowned, though his body was never recovered."[78]

Whether or not Agoston Haraszthy deserves the official title of "father of California wine," the extent of his influence cannot be disputed. In his wake, grape growers and winemakers in California slowly but steadily produced ever-better wines, in time fulfilling the vision for California that Haraszthy had held so dear.

Notes

1. Teiser and Harroun, *Winemaking in California,* 8–9.

2. Sullivan, *Companion to California Wine,* 377–78.

3. Heintz, *California's Napa Valley,* 12–13.

4. Thompson and Johnson, *California Wine Book,* 64; Pinney, *History of Wine in America,* 1:259.

5. Pinney, *History of Wine in America,* 1:259; Sullivan, *Companion to California Wine,* 404.

6. Lyman, *John Marsh, Pioneer,* 212, 291.

7. Bryant, *What I Saw in California,* 303–4. Note that the home Bryant describes was an early iteration; Marsh later built a magnificent stone Gothic-Revival style house that is now on the National Register of Historic Places.

8. Pinney, *History of Wine in America,* 1:259. Also: William Mero notes that "a legal dispute with Ygnacio Sibrian led to a rumored contract on Dr. Marsh's life," which may have been enacted when he was brutally murdered in Pacheco and left in a roadside ditch. http://johnmarshhouse.com/bandits-brentwood-wild-frontier.

9. Dana, *Two Years Before the Mast,* 72–73.

10. Holliday, *World Rushed In,* 33–34.

11. Lewis, *San Francisco,* 47–49; Holliday, *World Rushed In,* 34, 41. Holliday notes: "Brannan had purchased almost $12,000 in supplies" (41). By this means Brannan became the first millionaire of the Gold Rush.

12. Holliday, *World Rushed In,* 26.

13. Stegner, "Gift of Wilderness," 164.

14. Marx and Engels, "Review: January–February 1950," 265.

15. Bancroft, *History of California,* vol. 7, *1860–1890,* 698 and n6.

16. The population of the City and County of San Francisco in 1880 was 233,959, www.bayareacensus.ca.gov/counties/SanFranciscoCounty40.htm.

17. Caughey, *California*, 303. Oscar Lewis has written that the 1847 census put the population at 469, but that figure excluded residents of the Mission and the Presidio. Lewis, *San Francisco*, 46.

18. Soulé, Gihon, and Nisbet, *Annals of San Francisco*, 22.

19. Ibid., 640.

20. Dumas, *Alexandre Dumas' Dictionary of Cuisine*, 22.

21. Muscatine, *Old San Francisco*, 229–30.

22. Soulé, Gihon, and Nisbet, *Annals of San Francisco*.

23. Brewer, *Up and Down California*.

24. Thomas, "On Agricultural Statistics," table x x v, 343; Pinney, *History of Wine in America*, 1:262.

25. Sullivan, *Sonoma Wine*, 144, for which Sullivan cites *California Farmer*, January 11, 1855.

26. Muscatine, *Old San Francisco*, 209.

27. McGinty, *Strong Wine*, 300–301.

28. Register of Marriages, St. Francis Solano Church, Sonoma, June 1, 1863; "Married," *San Francisco Alta California*, June 6, 1863, 4.

29. Johnson, *Hugh Johnson's Modern Encyclopedia of Wine*, 421; Muscatine, *Old San Francisco*, 210; Sullivan, *Companion to California Wine*, 7.

30. Muscatine, *Old San Francisco*, 210; Teiser and Harroun, *Winemaking in California*, 82–83; Sullivan, *Companion to California Wine*, 175; John Olney, "Part One: The Krug Estate—The Charles Krug Era," Napa Valley Winery Histories, The Wine Country Club blog, April 5, 2005, http://twcchistories.blogspot.com/2005/04/part-one-krug-estate-charles-krug-era.html.

31. Muscatine, *Old San Francisco*, 210; Sullivan, *Sonoma Wine*, 145; Teiser and Harroun, *Winemaking in California*, 75.

32. Teiser and Harroun, *Winemaking in California*, 73.

33. Ibid., 29; Muscatine, *Old San Francisco*, 210.

34. Pinney, *History of Wine in America*, 1:269.

35. Hutchison, "Northern California," 30.

36. Ibid., 30–31.

37. Pinney, *History of Wine in America*, 1:270–72.

38. McGinty, *Strong Wine*, 183.

39. Hayes, *Pioneer Notes*, 131, qtd. in McGinty, *Strong Wine*, 183.

40. Teiser and Harroun, *Winemaking in California*, 36; McGinty, *Strong Wine*, 241, 243, 245.

41. Pinney, *History of Wine in America*, 1:273; Teiser and Harroun, *Winemaking in California*, 82.

42. Hutchison, "Northern California," 30–36; Sullivan, *Companion to California Wine*, 38; Pinney, *History of Wine in America*, 1: 269–73 and references cited: *Transactions of the California State Agricultural Society During the Year 1858*, 242–43; *Alta California*, September 21, 1863; and *First Annual Report of the Board of State Viticultural Commissioners*, 2nd ed. (San Francisco: 1881), 110. The quotation about the tripled acreage appears in Pinney, *History of Wine in America*, 1:273, citing *Transactions of the California State Agricultural Society During the Year 1858*, 242.

43. "Notes of Visiting Committees," *Transactions of the California State Agricultural Society During the Year 1860*, 78; qtd. in Leggett, *Early History*, 70.

44. Muscatine, *Old San Francisco*, 211; McGinty, *Strong Wine*, 278, 282–83.

45. Agoston Haraszthy, "Report on Grapes and Wine of California," 326. Haraszthy's report also appeared as "Grape-Growing and Wine-Making in California" in *The California Culturist: A Journal of Agriculture, Horticulture, Mechanism and Mining*, vol. 2, *June 1859 to May 1860*, ed. W. Wadsworth (San Francisco: Towne & Bacon, 1860).

46. Haraszthy, "Report on Grapes and Wine of California," 313.

47. McGinty, *Strong Wine*, 311, and reference cited: David Darlington, *Zin: The History and Mystery of Zinfandel*, 72.

48. Teiser and Harroun, *Winemaking in California*, 37.

49. Pinney, *History of Wine in America*, 1:274, citing *Transactions of the California State Agricultural Society, 1859*, 269–70.

50. Bancroft, *History of California*, vol. 7, *1860–1890*, 254–55.

51. Milton Latham, "Communication of Governor Latham," January 12, 1860, in *Journal of the Proceedings of the Assembly of the State of California* (Sacramento: C. T. Botts, State Printer, 1860), 125.

52. Bancroft, *History of California*, vol. 7, *1860–1890*, 255–60; Senate Misc. Document No. 2, 36th Cong., 1st Sess., p. 1. After another attempt in 1881 to divide the state, according to one historian, "the question of division fell into a state of innocuous desuetude." Guinn, "How California Escaped State Division," 233.

53. McGinty, *Strong Wine*, 290–91.

54. Hutchison, "Northern California," 33.

55. Leggett, *Early History*, 70n29; 69n27. For the first quotation Leggett cites Agoston Haraszthy, *Grape Culture*, xv; the second quotation cites the "Haraszthy Family" ms., 9.

56. Teiser and Harroun, *Winemaking in California*, 38.

57. Muscatine, *Old San Francisco*, 212; Teiser and Harroun, *Winemaking in California*, 38; Arpad Haraszthy, *Wine-Making in California*, 26. Note that other sources, including Teiser and Harroun and Agoston himself, give the number of vines and cuttings as one hundred thousand.

58. Agoston Haraszthy, "Report of Commissioners," xv–xvi.

59. Haraszthy, *Grape Culture*, xx, 33. Regarding the "1,400" figure: Pinney suggests this bloated tabulation resulted from numerous vines of the same variety being given different names, an oversight later remedied by closer inspection. Pinney, *History of Wine in America*, 1:279, 280.

60. McGinty, *Strong Wine*, 361–62, citing Haraszthy, "Letter from Mr. Haraszthy," dated Buena Vista Ranch, February 8, 1862, in Appendix to Journals of State and Assembly (1862); original in California State Archives, Sacramento.

61. Pinney, *History of Wine in America*, 1:279.

62. McGinty, *Strong Wine*, 359.

63. Muscatine, *Old San Francisco*, 212; Teiser and Harroun, *Winemaking in California*, 38–39.

64. Hutchison, "Northern California," 35.

65. Muscatine, *Old San Francisco*, 212; "Haraszthy Family," 9–10; Pinney, *History of Wine in America*, 1:279, citing *Journal of the Senate*, 13th sess., 1862 (Sacramento, 1862), 570.

66. Pinney, *History of Wine in America*, 1:279, citing an advertisement in *California Farmer*, May 24, 1861, and after.

67. Muscatine, *Old San Francisco*, 212; Teiser and Harroun, *Winemaking in California*, 39; Arpad Haraszthy, "Haraszthy Family," 9–11.

68. Arpad Haraszthy, "Haraszthy Family," 10.

69. Hutchison, "Northern California," 35; McGinty, *Strong Wine,* 376; Fredericksen, "Haraszthy's Busy Last Years," 22.

70. Muscatine, *Old San Francisco,* 212.

71. Carosso, *California Wine Industry,* 71.

72. Muscatine, *Old San Francisco,* 213.

73. L. J. Rose, *Transactions of the California State Agricultural Society, 1879* (Sacramento, 1880), 146, qtd. in Pinney, *History of Wine in America,* 1:282 and n39.

74. California Board of State Viticultural Commissioners, *First Annual Report,* 26, qtd. in Pinney, *History of Wine in America,* 1:282 and n40.

75. Wait, *Wines and Vines of California,* 91–94. In this account Wait relies exclusively on Arpad Haraszthy's version of the early days of winemaking in Sonoma County, "Early Viticulture in Sonoma." And see generally Hutchison, "Northern California," 30–36. Professor Jim Rawls, "Dr. History," makes the same assumption about Haraszthy as have so many others. Rawls, *Dr. History's Whizz-Bang,* 91–92.

76. Hutchison, "Northern California," 35.

77. Muscatine, *Old San Francisco,* 213; Hutchison, "Northern California," 30, 35; Teiser and Harroun, *Winemaking in California,* 39; Arpad Haraszthy, "Haraszthy Family," 12–13.

78. Leggett, *Early History,* 61.

CHAPTER 4

After Haraszthy—Sonoma, Napa, and the Confluence of Wealth and Wine

1860s–1890s

It may be set down as a fact that Napa and Sonoma
Counties produce the most satisfactory dry red and white
table wines that are made in California. These two great
wine-making counties lie side by side, Sonoma being
nearest the ocean. Both front on the bay of San Francisco
and have navigable estuaries; both are set in a spur of
the Coast Range, and both possess the topography;
that is, gentle sloping hills and the saline atmosphere
demanded by nature for the production of a dry wine.

—Frona Eunice Wait, *Wines and Vines of California*

Had Agoston Haraszthy lived one more decade, he would
have seen Northern California overtake the south in wine production, largely by producing wines from scores of varieties other
than the Mission grape—just as he and others had urged. In the
1870s, Northern California's production of grapes and wine exceeded that of Southern California.[1] This was a remarkable feat.
By 1857, Haraszthy's son Arpad later wrote, Los Angeles County
alone "possessed fully one-half of all the grape vines" in California.[2] And yet, by 1874 Sonoma County bested Los Angeles
County in wine production—and every other county in the state
as well.[3] Indeed, both Sonoma and Napa Counties led the state in
wine production in the 1870s.

SONOMA COUNTY VITICULTURE

It's not surprising that Sonoma County became the leading edge
of Northern California's eclipse of Southern California's wine industry. Given that Sonoma was where Agoston Haraszthy established his Buena Vista vineyard and winery in 1857, it was thus

the site of his pioneering work and the center from which he der-vishly promoted California wine. But other factors contributed to the northward shift as well. One was the northern climate, since very few grape varieties can flourish in the semidesert heat of Southern California. And then there is, again, the limitations—the mediocrity—of the Mission grape as a wine grape. Once the Mission was replaced by superior varieties, the confluence of factors almost inevitably brought about the reign of Northern viticulture.

John S. Hittell writes as much in 1867:

> The Mission grapes are hardy, healthy, long-lived, productive, and early in coming into bearing; but they are surpassed in flavor, hardi-ness, productiveness, earliness of ripening, and earliness of bearing, by many foreign varieties, which, so far as is known, are not inferior in any respect. . . .
>
> The superiority of the foreign grapes is so great, that no reason-able man, acquainted with the subject, doubts that they will drive the Mission grapes out of the market. Flavor is a matter of vast importance in fresh fruit, and the want of it is the great defect of the Mission grape, which will not command more than six or eight cents per pound in the San Francisco market, at the very time that fine foreign varieties bring twenty-five and thirty-seven cents. Cut-tings of the Mission grapes can now be had for ten dollars per thou-sand, a price that will not more than pay for preparing them for market; while those of the foreign cost from forty to one hundred and fifty dollars per thousand. For wine, the foreign grape has an equal or still greater advantage. Flavor and fruitiness are not less needed there than in fruit to be eaten fresh at the table. The lack of fruitiness is the great misfortune of the wine made from the Cali-fornian grape, and the evil can only be remedied by the use of the foreign grape.[4]

Charles Kohler and Zinfandel

We now return to the firm of Kohler & Frohling, who prospered just as they'd planned. A manuscript in the Bancroft Library, "Wine Production in California: An Account of the Wine Busi-ness in California, from Materials Furnished by Charles Kohler," offers a glimpse into their aspirations, and achievements, as winemakers.

> From the beginning of the enterprise Messrs. Kohler & Frohling sought to produce an article that should compete in quality, quan-

tity, and price with the wines of the old world, and by perseverance and hard work and close attention to the business, in a few years they established quite a reputation for their wines, and showed the public that good wine could be made in California, and sold, and even old European [illegible] had to acknowledge their enterprise and success.

They exported wine to some extent from 1858 to 1862, when they commenced sending large quantities abroad, and have continued to do so from that time to this, and are now the most extensive exporters of the State. In 1868 a California German, familiar with their excellence, ordered some cases of the various kinds of Kohler & Frohling's wine to be sent to Mechlenburgh [*sic*], and having removed the labels from the bottles, invited his friends to try them, informing them only that they were from a new vineyard. They were delighted, and pronounced them superior to any German wines, but supposed they came from some other part of Europe, and were astonished exceedingly when told that they came from California. The long voyage and constant motion of the vessel had imparted to them a flavor and mellowing which they would not have acquired in long years of lying still in a wine cellar, if at all.[5]

When John Frohling died in 1862, the enterprise had a New York agency, customers on both coasts, and half a million gallons of wine with which to fill their orders. In 1865, seeing that future prosperity lay in Northern rather than Southern California, Charles Kohler bought land in Sonoma County. Though he later expanded in this northern county, developing his Tokay Vineyard in 1874, he also knew there was still a market for sweet wines and brandy, for which reason he also purchased in Fresno County, where he planted the six-hundred-acre Sierra Vista Vineyard.[6]

Kohler's wisdom about the preferable climate and terrain of Northern California went hand in hand with his belief that the future of the state's viticulture stemmed not from the Mission grape but from Zinfandel. In committing his own vineyards to Zinfandel, he promoted—à la Haraszthy, both father and son—the bounty to be reaped from planting rugged, northern vineyards with this superior variety. Kohler demonstrated to the small ranchers and vineyard owners of the more temperate regions of Northern California the success that could be had growing wine grapes other than the Mission grape—especially ones, like Zinfandel, that would produce pleasing dry wines. Indeed, landowners of the region were avidly told of the wisdom of planting vineyards on land that is not easily irrigated or that is too rugged for agriculture such as truck crops or nut orchards. This is because stressed vines produce grapes of more intense flavor than vines planted in rich, loamy, well-irrigated soil.[7]

Arpad Haraszthy and the Buena Vista Vinicultural Society

One of those figures advocating for expanding northern viticulture was Agoston Haraszthy's son Arpad Haraszthy, who shared his father's passion for California wines and his knack for publicizing his convictions. In May 1872 Arpad described how wine grapevines flourish in steep and rocky terrain, as well as how the state could reap the economic windfall of this fact:

> The State derives the great benefits from the plantation of vineyards, as they have been planted during the last ten years—that is, on the hill-sides and on those lands too steep to cultivate with any thing else, or so poor that nothing else will grow. Thus the vineyards of the future will all be planted upon the mountain-sides, and interfere in no manner with the grain-lands. Millions of acres that are now covered with *chaparral* and *manzanita*-bushes will become utilized; for just those spots where these bushes grow, if there is any soil at all, are the very finest for vineyards. Nothing else will generally grow in such places, except these bushes and a short, tufted grass, that here and there seems to cling to the ground for dear existence. The vine, however, not only thrives, but actually luxuriates upon it. If the roots are only nourished with enough moisture during the first twelve months, all is right and sure; thereafter they push forward and downward where the moisture never fails, even through the most minute crevices of rocks or cement, in a manner most wonderful to behold.
>
> In gravelly soils the roots of vines seven years old have been found thirty feet below the surface, and they have been found half that distance in crevices of the most compact cement. . . . It is by this culture that our thousands of now idle steep and rugged hills and mountains will become transformed into producers of value, and the laborious and patient owner will reap from them harvests of gold.[8]

In addition to pitching optimal land use, Arpad also furthered his father's advocation for the Mission grape being abandoned in favor of superior varieties. Picking up where his father had left off, in 1872 he wrote four articles on "Wine-Making in California" that appeared in Bret Harte's *Overland Monthly*. The first of these conveyed that Colonel Haraszthy had brought back from his 1861 European trip two hundred thousand [*sic*] rooted vines and cuttings of hundreds of different varieties of grape, which were then "planted in many varied localities" in California. As for those, "not a single variety in this vast collection has not done well, and raised and matured its fruit to perfection." He goes on to add, "these varieties of grape-vines, in every case, have not only been found to produce a finer wine than the Mission grape, but, also, when properly trained and pruned, to yield a greater crop to the acre. They possess still another advantage—and that is, a much greater uniformity from year to year in their bearing qualities." And as for the objections of naysayers, he points out that "time and facts have given these assertions the most emphatic denial."

One naysayer, though writing nearly a decade later, handily sums up the long-standing resistance to change. Quoted in the *Los Angeles Times* in 1883, former California governor John Downey notes: "We may and do want other varieties of vines, but be slow in your changes. Stick to your so-called Mission. We have not yet found its substitute, its equal, or peer. It is an old friend; cling to it with affection, and let our friends at the north follow that vagary of jumping from one thing to another."[9] (Never mind that it was Downey who, as governor two decades earlier, had appointed Agoston Haraszthy to report "upon the Ways and Means best adapted to promote the Improvement and Growth of the Grapevine in California.") Indeed, the willingness to change was slow in coming. As Charles Sullivan notes of this era, "growers were unwilling to rip up established vineyards and plant a new grape, because the Mission was neither unsuccessful nor unprofitable."[10]

Arpad Haraszthy concludes his essays with a brash prophecy, one that scarcely more than a century later proved to be true:

> We have endeavored to lay before the reader the true value, actual merit, and real qualities of our wines, without the slightest exaggeration....
>
> It has taken ages to discover and make known to the world the qualities of those grand wines produced from hardly more than a dozen vineyards [in Europe], and we have not yet placed the name of a vineyard among this select few; but we will and the day draws nigh. Every season brings us better wines, the product of some newly discovered locality, planted with choicer varieties of the grape, and entirely different from any thing previously produced. And thus the circle will continue to narrow until California will proudly place the name of that future-discovered vineyard among

those of the choicest of the earth. It will not be overshadowed by the crumbling walls of castle or monastery, whose very dampness is replete with memories of past violence and torture; nor will it require any of these auxiliaries to make its merits known. It will be the modest home of an American, surrounded by all the civilizing influences of our bright age, and with no past history but that of the peaceful, patient, and noble toils of its founder![11]

In chapter 3 we learned how California prohibited any corporation from holding more than 1,440 acres of land. So to expand his operation, in March 1863 Agoston Haraszthy, funded by financial backers, formed the Buena Vista Vinicultural Society—and then secured special legislation that would exempt the Buena Vista Society from that restriction. Haraszthy then sold his vast winery assets to the society, including a four-hundred-acre vineyard planted with 150,000 foreign vines, plus the most modern equipment, including a steam-operated crusher capable of extracting juice from 50,000 pounds of grapes a day. Besides the large stone cellars and capacious storage and fermentation tanks, the society acquired "inexhaustible quarries of white and red stone" and five sulfur springs. In 1862, Haraszthy had produced 30,000 gallons of wine; in 1863, the society's production amounted to about 100,000 gallons. Given this bounty, the society was primed to be a top producer of California's wine.[12]

Following several years of study abroad, Arpad Haraszthy, all of twenty-three years of age at the time, was put in charge of champagne-making at the society in 1863. Paul Frederickson notes that his initial, small batches showed promise: "Samples shown at the 1863 State Fair . . . won an honorary diploma." (Note,

Lithograph of the vineyards and vaults of the Buena Vista Vinicultural Society (BVVS), Sonoma, California, circa 1870. Courtesy of Buena Vista Winery, Boisset Collection.

though, that his was the only champagne under consideration.) But his larger-scale efforts were failures. Of this outcome scholar Vincent Carosso cites two culprits: the Mission grape—which he considers to be "totally useless as a champagne variety"—as well as lack of experience with the tricky process of fermentation in bottles. (Sometimes the carbonation process can bring bottles to explode.) Though Arpad resigned in 1864, the society, which then employed the expertise of French P. Debanne, managed to earn honorable mention for their "Sparkling Sonoma" at the Paris Universal Exposition of 1867. In time they became the state's first successful large-scale manufacturer of champagne, producing nearly 120,000 bottles in 1868 and 1869.[13]

Though the Buena Vista Vinicultural Society ultimately failed as a business enterprise, it nonetheless accomplished much for the future of the California wine industry. The publicity it garnered induced many farmers to try viticulture. Following the lead of Arpad Haraszthy's assertions on the merits of hilly terrain, lands in Sonoma and elsewhere, previously considered worthless for agriculture, had been planted with grapes. As the society declared in their own 1866 report: "How far we have succeeded in establishing the fact that planting vines, raising grapes, and manufacturing wines and brandy may be a lucrative business, let the figures show; and remember, gentlemen, that this was accomplished under the most unfavorable beginning." The Vinicultural Society also implemented use of the dug-out hillside cellar, the redwood tank, and unirrigated vineyards—the latter an option that could never be employed farther south. In addition, the society identified all the problems of inexperience that can plague large-scale viticulture in California, both in the field and in the market.[14] In later years the estate itself suffered the indignities of phylloxera, the 1906 earthquake, and Prohibition, but restoration to structures and vineyards begun in 1942 brought it back into production. It's changed hands twice since.[15]

Other Sonoma County Vintners

The long, slow demise of the Buena Vista Vinicultural Society notwithstanding, Sonoma County was ascendant in California winemaking in the 1870s. Many of its vintners came to Sonoma to grow grapes and make wine inspired by the still-infant winemaking tradition that had been founded by General Vallejo and Agoston Haraszthy. One was Jacob Rink Snyder, an easterner in his early thirties who began his western existence at Sutter's Fort in

1845. At first his tenure was in the military: after serving as a major in Frémont's California Battalion, he was later a delegate to the 1850 constitutional convention alongside General Vallejo. Then he took a turn at the San Francisco mint during Haraszthy's tenure there. In the end, he was inspired to follow them to Sonoma to also grow grapes and make wine. (He was also one of the backers of the Buena Vista Vinicultural Society.) His own winemaking aspiration was a successful one: in 1872, the State Agricultural Society reported that his cellar held from 35,000 to 40,000 gallons of wine. At the time of his death in 1878 he was the president of the Wine Growers Association of California.[16]

Three other Sonoma wine-grape growers of that era were Oliver Craig, William McPherson Hill, and Leonard Goss. Craig made white wines, including "hock," produced from Riesling, Muscat, and "Tramina" [Traminer]. Craig and Goss made sturdy but unspectacular wines, but Hill would achieve a bit of fame, particularly with wines made from his Zinfandel grapes. Dreamers among his contemporaries, in part because of the quality of Hill's wines, thought the Zinfandel would be the varietal to lift a California wine to the level of Bordeaux.[17]

Having learned winemaking from his French-born father, Isaac De Turk settled in Sonoma's Bennett Valley in 1859. Given his background, it didn't take him long to embark on the enterprise of winemaking, which he did with zeal. By the early 1870s De Turk had become the leading grape grower and winemaker in Sonoma, and, in time, the largest; by 1888 his winery had a capacity of a million gallons. A lifelong bachelor, De Turk became active as a member of the Board of State Viticultural Commissioners formed in 1880. His winery continued in operation until the earthquake of 1906.

De Turk contributed to the region's industry with innovation as well as capacity. Foremost, he aged his wines with care. He also shipped his wines in bottles, not casks, and urged other winemakers to do likewise, with the winemaker's label glued to each bottle. This practice rather irked those unscrupulous wine merchants and brokers accustomed to adulterating barrel wine for their financial gain.[18]

Agoston Haraszthy's Buena Vista Winery claims to be the oldest winery in California, dating its establishment to 1857. A few miles down the road, Gundlach-Bundschu claims to be the second oldest, by a mere two months, established in 1858.[19] We met Bavarian Jacob Gundlach in chapter 3; under the name Dresel &

Co., he and partner Emil Dresel ran Rhine Farm. In 1866, after Agoston Haraszthy resigned from Buena Vista and was drawn to his end in Nicaragua, Dresel took over operations at Buena Vista. (He was also one of the backers of the Buena Vista Vinicultural Society.) In 1868, German Charles Bundschu joined Gundlach. They produced wines under the Bacchus label. Two major changes occurred in 1875: Jacob formed J. Gundlach & Co., and Jacob's daughter Francisca married Charles Bundschu.[20] Though Emil Dresel died in 1869, his brother Julius Dresel stepped in to continue his share of the enterprise. Another changing of the guard occurred at Jacob Gundlach's death in 1894, at which point they operated under the name Gundlach-Bundschu. Today, the winery is run by descendants of the Bundschu family.[21]

In 1857, a committee of the State Agricultural Society predicted that the Russian River Valley would become a major wine-growing region in California. And indeed it did, particularly once the Korbel brothers made their mark.[22] The three brothers—Francis, Josef, and Anton—hailed from Bohemia, the western Czech region of the Austrian Empire. Francis had worked in the tobacco industry; his brothers were skilled mechanics. Soon after they arrived in California in the early 1860s, Francis—beholding the forests of the region, and having a background in tobacco—was inspired to launch a cigar box factory, and then a full-scale sawmill, for which they bought land in Sonoma County. Years later, once they'd denuded their property, they made a wise move: they consulted the University of California on how best to utilize their land. The answer: cultivate grapes—which they did, the rows of vines interrupted by enormous redwood stumps. But by the time their first crop was harvested in 1881, there was no money to be made selling grapes, so they determined to make wine instead. Consider the contrast between this and the approach of others in this narrative. Many set out with the distinct desire to make wine, but then too quickly invested resources in an inopportune location. Whereas the brothers Korbel sought how best to work with what they had.

Their standards of excellence can be seen throughout the Korbel realm. As Joan Goodlett writes, they "made their own brick for the building; they designed machinery for pressing the grapes; they supervised the building of magnificent oak cooperage for the storage vaults which are in use today; they even made the huge, hand-forged hinges on the doors of the winery. They built solidly, imparting the flavor of castles in Bohemia. Today the winery and the turreted buildings that surround it are an echo of the Old World set on the Sonoma slopes."

Their dedication to their enterprise was recognized in their wines, which were admirably received at the 1893 Columbian Exposition in Chicago. Once fellow Czech Franz Hazek joined them in 1896, Korbel produced champagne as well as wine and brandy. Approaching the venture with the now characteristic Korbel aplomb, Hazek developed champagne using imported vines from Champagne, France, produced in the celebrated European manner. By 1899, as Goodlett describes, the Korbel name became nearly synonymous with fine champagne.[23]

Another Sonoma County success story was that of the Italian Swiss Colony. Much of their success derived from their ability to adapt as necessary to whatever befell them.

The Italian Swiss Colony was begun by Genovese Andrea Sbarboro, who in 1881 formed a winemaking operation with a mind to helping struggling Italian immigrants. The enterprise, designed along the lines of his profitable work organizing building and loan societies, originally involved a few Swiss members, so they took the name Italian Swiss Colony. They purchased 1,500 acres in Sonoma County near Cloverdale and founded a village named Asti, after a Piedmont town famous for its wines. Thomas Pinney specifies that, though the venture was intended to be both profitable and self-sustaining, it was also heartfully intended to benefit workers: an entity of "genuine social philanthropy" that provided "steady, dignified work for the many Italians who had . . . sunk to the bottom of the labor pool" in San Francisco. In addition, their work benefits included "as much wine as a man could decently drink."[24]

While the Colony's initial efforts in vinting proved feeble, the hiring in 1887 of first-class winemaker Pietro C. Rossi produced immediate results, beginning with the next year's vintage. Similarly, though Italian Swiss had been founded as a "self-help cooperative" for struggling immigrants—as Bob Thompson and Hugh Johnson put it—they reformed it into a commercial venture, which they ran frugally and wisely.[25]

By 1893, the Colony's one thousand acres of wine grapes included Italian varieties like Barbera, Neggiolo, and Sangiovese. Indeed, it was from the Sangiovese grape that they made their top-selling wine, Tipo Chianti. Their Golden State Champagne also earned a distinctive reputation. By the end of the nineteenth century, theirs was a household name: the largest source

Korbel in Later Years

After the repeal of Prohibition, Korbel resumed winemaking, producing again one of California's best sparkling wines. In 1939, Frank Schoonmaker urged the Korbels, now a second generation of owner-operators, to make a drier sparkling wine. That they did, and Korbel Brut became perhaps the standard dry California sparkling wine for decades. In 1954 the winery was sold to the Heck family, which increased production from 10,000 cases in 1954 to a million cases of sparkling wine a year by the 1990s, and half a million cases of brandy. Seeing a good thing, Anheuser-Busch bought Korbel in 1991.

Sources: Sullivan, *Companion to California Wine*, 173–74; Teiser and Harroun, *Winemaking in California*, 81.

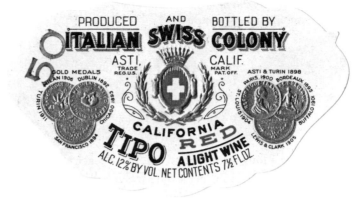

Wine label for Italian Swiss Colony, Tipo California Red. From the California Wine Label and Ephemera Collection, Kemble Special Collection 07-013. Courtesy of the California Historical Society.

Italian Swiss Colony in Later Years

After the Colony's gifted wine-maker Pietro Rossi died in 1911, his twin sons, Robert and Edmund Rossi, took over as winemakers. After the repeal of Prohibition in 1933, they brought the Colony to still-impressive heights, in terms of both volume and quality. Sullivan notes how by 1937 theirs was the largest table-wine operation in the states. And, as Thompson and Johnson put it, "their blend of Tipo Chianti was a wine of enough style to see M. F. K. Fisher and other seasoned palates through the Great Depression of the 1930s." However, during World War II the Asti winery was sold to National Distillers Products Corporation; it later changed hands again and again, to United Vintners, and then to Heublein, Inc. The further from the intentional heart and practiced hand the wine went, the lower fell both its quality and esteem.

Sources: Thompson and Johnson, *California Wine Book*, 75; Pinney, *History of Wine in America*, 1:327–29; Sullivan, *Companion to California Wine*, 161–62.

of table wine in California, perhaps in the country. The operation was certainly national: all major cities had company depots at which the Asti-produced wine was bottled and distributed. By 1910 the vineyards had grown fivefold, to more than five thousand acres, and the stock, originally worth $150,000, was valued at twenty times that much. Charles Sullivan credits their "high quality, good leadership, and a growing immigrant population" for making them "the most successful independent winemaker before Prohibition."[26] That leadership included shareholder and auditor Charles Kohler.[27]

One example of good leadership was Andrea Sbarboro's prescience regarding the dangers of the growing temperance movement, which he avidly worked to temper, as it were, as demonstrated in this May 1909 issue of the National Temperance Society's monthly publication *The National Advocate*:

> The latest literature [of the California Wine Makers] is full of plausible argument in regard to their alleged "sympathy" with the Temperance Movement, and presents in a little different style the old falsehoods about drunkenness in Southern Europe and other wine-drinking countries.
>
> One reason for this sudden enthusiasm over the alleged "light wine" theory . . . is revealed in the recent address of their president, Andrea Sbarboro, who said: "The Prohibitionists are encroaching on our territory, and unless we begin at once to offer some resistance, they will put us out of business and eventually ruin one of the State's greatest industries. Throughout this country there is a movement on foot that will in time do away with all alcoholic liquors, and of course, our industry will be killed if this is not checked. This campaign (to extend the market for wine) will

One vintner of this ilk was Clement Colombet. A native of Nice, France, Colombet settled in Alameda County's Fremont in 1851. A mere five years later, his claret had the honor of being the first California wine to win a prize awarded by the San Jose fair of the California Agricultural Society. Boosted by his success, in 1856 he bought the Warm Springs–region 9,500-acre Agua Caliente ("hot water") Rancho, which soon thereafter boasted sixty thousand vines and a winery. Taking full advantage of the agua caliente, he also built a resort hotel, which became a notable destination in its day. But then an act of God intervened; the damage to the hotel from the earthquake of 1868 prompted Colombet to sell to Leland Stanford in 1869. In 1886, spurred by the "consideration of love and affection," Stanford deeded the Agua Caliente Rancho to his brother Josiah. Josiah's vision was not of a world-class winery, but rather a world-class resort intended to best the Hotel Del Monte, which Charles Crocker had opened in 1880 in Monterey. But luck was not to be Josiah's, who died in 1890, just four years after the purchase. Afflicted by the phylloxera, the Colombet vineyards soon met the same fate.[32]

Historian Charles Sullivan deems Julius Paul Smith's Olivina Vineyard, begun in 1881, the "greatest" of the valley. It would appear Smith applied to winemaking the same acumen that earned him a fortune in the borax business, as he succeeded spectacularly in both. One point of advantage: Smith enhanced his venture by studying European expertise in the trade; another advantage: his choice of terroir. A scant decade after starting, in annually producing three hundred thousand gallons of wine, Smith had become the valley's leading vintner.[33]

Vintners of Santa Clara County

Santa Clara County also experienced a blossoming of viticulture and winemaking in the latter part of the nineteenth century. The 1860 U.S. Census listed twenty-six grape growers and winemakers in Santa Clara County that year, just one shy of the number listed for Sonoma.[34] That should be no surprise; until the latter half of the twentieth century, the Santa Clara Valley was known as the "Garden Spot of the World,"[35] so fertile were its soils and hospitable its climate. (Now, developed with office buildings and the corporate campuses of some of the largest corporations in the world, it is known as Silicon Valley.)

The most prominent name among the vineyardists and vintners of Santa Clara County was Charles Lefranc, considered the

Alameda's Earliest Viticulture

The cooler regions of Alameda County made wine early. The 1860 census lists the county as having produced in that year over 8,000 gallons of wine—almost eight times as much as Sonoma—and all of it in Washington Township. One of six large areas of the county of Alameda, today Washington Township consists of Fremont, Newark, and Union City.

The Fremont portion of the township in particular grew rapidly at the time of the Gold Rush. Agriculture dominated the economy, with grapes, nursery plants, and olives as leading crops. But in 1868 the 6.8-magnitude Hayward earthquake on the Hayward Fault collapsed buildings throughout Washington Township, leaving Mission San Jose and its outbuildings in ruins. Similarly, Fremont's Palmdale Winery was one of the largest in California—until the 1906 San Francisco earthquake. The ruins of the winery are still visible near Five Corners in Irvington.

Source: Peninou and Greenleaf, *Directory of California Wine Growers*, 1–2.

Advances in Viticulture: Wine and Redwood

George M. Taber writes: "The French have aged wine in oak [barrels] since Roman times, and for a good reason. Oak imparts subtle tastes, texture, and aroma that lift a good wine to a whole new level of enjoyment." But what if oak is in short supply? Agoston Haraszthy advocated redwood as an excellent substitute, and the Korbel brothers advertised redwood vats for fermenting. But it was Charles Lefranc who received grand praise for the practice. In visiting New Almadén in 1872, the California Agricultural Society reported: "We saw fully demonstrated the important fact the redwood is equally as good as the best of oak for the storage of wine." The butts (large casks) "are made on the place, from split staves obtained in the redwoods nearby. Before shaving they are steamed for two or three days, and while steaming are brought to the proper shape, then seasoned, shaved, and put together. . . . Half as costly, they will last longer than casks made from the best of oak. Worms never touch them, and they impart neither taste nor color to the wine. . . . The wine growers of California are indebted for a discovery that adds millions to the value of their industry."

Sources: Taber, *Judgment of Paris*, 139; Pinney, *History of Wine in America*, 1:363 and n73, citing Agoston Haraszthy, "Wine-Making in California," 28 (Korbel reference on p. 365); California State Agricultural Society, *Transactions*, 200–201.

Wine label for Paul Masson Champagne Company, Oeil de Perdrix. From the Paul Masson Papers, MS 1421-001. Courtesy of the California Historical Society.

father of commercial winemaking in Santa Clara. He was one of a community of Frenchmen who had come to California during the Gold Rush but who settled instead in the fertile Santa Clara Valley—preferring, at least during their generation, to refer to themselves as "nurserymen" or "gardners," not "vineyardists" or "viticulturalists." Arriving in 1850, Lefranc first worked with Etienne Thée on his Almaden Valley vineyard south of San Jose; in 1857 he'd married Thée's daughter Marie Adèle and become Thée's business partner. A year later he facilitated for New Almadén Vineyards what would be the winery's masterstroke, replacing the established Mission grapes with various superior French varieties. With these grapes Lefranc produced California's first commercial Bordeaux. His efforts made New Almadén Santa Clara's top winemaking enterprise.[36]

Lefranc's history in part replayed itself when fellow Frenchman Paul Masson, from Burgundy, came to work for him in 1878. A decade later, Masson married Lefranc's daughter Louise, thirty years after Lefranc had married *his* employer's daughter. But unlike Thée, Lefranc was not witness to the wedding, having been trampled to death by horses in a freak accident in 1887 at the age of sixty-three. Thereafter the winery, then called simply Almaden, was taken over by his son Henry in partnership with Masson.[37]

In 1892 Lefranc and Masson released a bottle-fermented sparkling wine that, as wine scholar Charles Sullivan puts it, "took the California market by storm." Then, in 1896, Masson purchased an old vineyard and winery two miles west of Saratoga where he established the Paul Masson Winery and Vineyards. There he produced wines considered the "Pride of California." His sparkling Oeil de Perdrix (eye of the partridge) was generally acclaimed as the finest of its kind produced in America.[38]

Outsized Wallets with Personalities to Match

The synergy of wealth and winemaking in Northern California also took root in Napa Valley. One of the state's first millionaires was Sam Brannan, an early promoter of San Francisco, and the earliest promoter of the Gold Rush. Charles Sullivan describes Brannan as "a famous Mormon apostate who had his hand in almost every aspect of California's early state history." A little more than ten years after the Gold Rush, Brannan bought a parcel of land in northern Napa Valley that he named Calistoga, a whimsical portmanteau of *California* and *Saratoga,* the latter being a resort spa in New York. He planted two hundred acres of French grapevines from among the twenty thousand cuttings he'd acquired in France—a full two years before Agoston Haraszthy's European jaunt. He produced his "Calistoga Cognac" in the distillery he built in 1868. But his luck ran out in the 1870s when his finances collapsed; by 1875 his Calistoga holdings were no longer his. It would seem the career that began with a shout ended with but a whimper.[39]

Brannan may have failed in Calistoga, but he firmly helped establish grape growing and winemaking in the upper Napa Valley. By the last decade of the nineteenth century, the area boasted about fifteen hundred acres of vines managed by about seventy growers, thirteen of which produced commercial quantities. One of the large-scale vintners was A. L. Tubbs. A New Englander made wealthy by his San Francisco cordage firm, Tubbs planted 110 acres of vines north of Calistoga in 1882; within five years he produced 75,000 gallons of wine a year. Charles Sullivan notes that, also by 1887, Tubbs was experimenting with rootstock resistant to pests and pestilence. During Tubbs's reign the vineyard and winery was known as Hillcrest; after Prohibition, the estate lived again as Chateau Montelena. In a mere forty years after repeal, Chateau Montelena would produce one of the most famous wines in history.[40]

Like William Ralston and Sam Brannan, Leland Stanford was a man of prodigious wealth. Governor of California, U.S. senator from California, founder of Stanford University, and one of California's illustrious Big Four, Stanford had early evinced an interest in wines and winemaking. He also vividly demonstrated that not

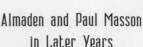

Almaden and Paul Masson in Later Years

The wineries born of Charles Lefranc and Paul Masson continued to have similar histories even to their ends. In the wake of Prohibition, San Francisco businessman Louis Benoist acquired Almaden in 1941, joining forces with wine expert Frank Schoonmaker. Together they brought Almaden to new heights, ranking among the leading commercial wine enterprises of the day. But financial problems having nothing to do with the winery forced Benoist to sell Almaden in 1967 to National Distillers, which sought to capitalize on the name. But National only cheapened it by affixing the Almaden label to inexpensive jug wines. National sold to Heublein in 1987, and the degradation of the name continued.

The same fate met the Paul Masson winery, though more than two decades earlier. In this case it was the giant distiller Seagram, who after its 1943 acquisition sullied the mystique of the Masson name on yet more quantities of jug wine. Thus were desecrated two of the most celebrated names in the history of California wine.

Source: Sullivan, *Companion to California Wine,* 8, 204.

This Vina Distillery Pure Grape Brandy advertisement reads: "Pure Grape Brandy, Senator Leland Stanford's Vina Distillery—The Largest Vineyard in the World, Vina, Tehama County, California." Courtesy of the Stanford University Print Collection (SC 1039). H. H. Bancroft reported that, in 1888, Vina—with 3,575 acres (almost six square miles) and 2,860,000 vines—was the largest vineyard in the world. Bancroft, *History of California*, vol. 7, *1860–1890*, 48n8.

all who rise always succeed. We learned earlier how in 1868 he had bought Clement Colombet's vineyard and earthquake-damaged winery and resort hotel at Warm Springs in southern Alameda County. Soon after, a second winery emerged from the rubble of the old hotel, producing mostly bulk wines. Then, after being inspired from visiting French chateaus, Stanford shifted course: he planned to produce wines that would impress even the French. Deeding the Colombet property to his brother Josiah, in 1881 Stanford bought in Tehama County in the Sacramento Valley, first a ranch, then a mature vineyard with thriving winery that he named Vina Vineyard.[41]

Historian Thomas Pinney offers a detailed account of Stanford's unfolding vision:

> In one year a thousand acres of new plantings were added . . . ; vast arrangements of dams, canals, and ditches for irrigating the ranch were constructed, fifty miles of ditch for the vineyards alone; a number of French winegrowers were brought over and housed in barracks on the ranch; a winery, storage cellar, brandy distillery, warehouses, and all other needful facilities were built, no expense spared. The new-fangled incandescent lights were installed in the fermenting house so that work could be carried on night and day during the critical time of the vintage. All the while Stanford continued to add to the acreage of his ranch; . . . [By 1885], Vina Ranch spread over 55,000 acres of foothill pasture and valley farmland.

The moral of this enterprise, larger and more costly than anything else ever ventured in California agriculture to this point, was

This image was the frontispiece to E. H. Rixford's *The Wine Press and the Cellar: A Manual for the Wine-Maker and the Cellar-Man,* published in San Francisco in 1883. It depicts the California bear, holding a champagne glass, awaiting Lady Liberty's sparkling wine. An overturned wine barrel offers the seal of the state of California. Wine boxes in the foreground read: MISSION, PINEAU, RIESLING, and ZINFANDEL.

not long in appearing: size and wealth are not enough to make up for lack of experience. The circumstances were all wrong for what Stanford wanted to do, and though the Vina property was lovely to the eye and richly productive in all sorts of crops, it did not and never could have made fine table wines.[42]

Vina "never could have made fine table wines" because the grapes used to make the unrivaled French wines wither in the hot summers of the upper Sacramento Valley. Nor can they thrive in the region's rich soil; they prefer the rugged terrain Arpad Haraszthy so emphatically endorsed for wine growing. In short, the fertile, fecund soil of the Sacramento River Valley is good for peasant produce like carrots, tomatoes, and peppers, but not for fine wine grapes.

Upon Stanford's death in 1893, Vina became part of the endowment of Stanford University. This proved to be rather ironic, given that the university's first president, David Starr Jordan, was an ardent teetotaler and prohibitionist. He oversaw the dismantling of the vineyard and winery even before passage of the constitutional amendment that mandated Prohibition.[43]

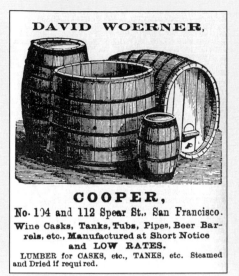

San Francisco, Heart of the Wine Market

By the 1880s the state annually produced fifteen to twenty million gallons of wine from scores of wineries. Such significant operation called for a central hub, and San Francisco provided that nicely. For one thing, the city's world-class seaport well served both the industry and its market. Also, being the state's largest city at the time, San Francisco possessed a muscular labor force ready and able to work where needed. For example, David Woerner's cooperage business employed one hundred workmen making barrels and casks.

And then consider the climate; though Mark Twain is erroneously credited with saying "the coldest winter I ever spent was a summer in San Francisco," he certainly should have, as anyone who has summered there can tell you. Though less ideal for tourists, the city's fog well served the millions of gallons of wine stored there at the time. That construction was under way to hold millions more gallons—providing even more opportunities for employment—indicated just how broadly, and confidently, those in the know anticipated ever-increasing demand.

Source: Hutchison, "Northern California," 46.

On February 20, 1875, *Pacific Rural Press* ran the following advertisement: "David Woerner, Cooper, No. 104 and 112 Spear St., San Francisco. Wine Casks, Tanks, Tubs, Pipes, Beer Barrels, etc., Manufactured at Short Notice and Low Rates. Lumber for Casks, etc., Tanks, etc. Steamed and Dried if required." Courtesy of the University of California, Davis, Library.

Two of Stanford's fellows in the U.S. Senate shared his interest in wine. One was James Graham Fair, a forty-niner who became a millionaire through investment in the Comstock mines. (He had a San Francisco hotel venture as well, the Fairmont.) In the 1880s he bought a large vineyard and winery on the Petaluma River. In 1894 his Fair Ranch, which boasted the first brandy distillery on the Pacific Coast, produced 300,000 gallons of wine and brandy a year. Fair believed "there will always be a market for wine."[44]

Our third senator is George Hearst. He was the husband of Phoebe Apperson Hearst, monumental benefactress of the University of California, and father of William Randolph Hearst. Like Fair, George Hearst was a successful Argonaut-turned-entrepreneur: in 1877 he was a founding member of the Homestake Mining Company; in 1880, he purchased the *San Francisco Examiner*. He too held Fair's belief about the future of California wine. In about 1885, Hearst acquired the 350-acre Madrone Vineyard and small stone winery at Glen Ellen, near Agua Caliente in Sonoma County. He later replanted the vineyard, grafting Medoc and Gironde vines onto disease-resistant rootstocks. Hearst also added two cellars with a capacity of a quarter-million gallons; in addition, a new brandy distillery sought to set the record for capacity. The esteemed Professor E. W. Hilgard of the University of California pronounced Madrone "capable of growing the finest wine grapes in the world." Between 1887 and 1891 when a lethal combination of overproduction and low prices for grapes threatened the California wine industry, Hearst became an early champion for improved quality in California wine. He particularly encouraged each wine-grape grower to bottle and market his or her own wine as the means to overcome the economic doldrums.[45] A large broadside in the *San Francisco Examiner* in 1890 would drive this point home—one year before Senator Hearst died. In 1905, Phoebe Apperson Hearst sold the Madrone Vineyard and winery to the California Wine Association.[46]

NAPA VALLEY VITICULTURE

In 1860 Napa Valley had but half the number of grape growers and winemakers of Sonoma: Napa fourteen, Sonoma twenty-seven.[47] And yet, "half-pint" Napa produced nearly nine thousand gallons of wine that year, seven and a half times Sonoma's nearly twelve hundred gallons. Napa's star was ascending.[48] Frona Eunice Wait adds: "From Yountville to St. Helena is one vast vineyard."[49]

In their book *Winemaking in California* Ruth Teiser and Catherine Harroun offer a picturesque description of how Napa Valley viticulture descended from that of Sonoma County. In 1838 Kentuckian George Yount "crossed the western Mayacamas range separating the two parallel valleys" carrying wine cuttings from General Vallejo's Sonoma Valley vines. Just over twenty years later, Krug repeated Yount's trek, settling in Napa in 1860 on the dowry land of his new bride, Carolina Bales—the land a parcel of Rancho Carne Humana north of George Yount's Rancho Caymus. Planting those vines and building a winery, he soon made a name for himself and for Napa.[50]

Charles Sullivan writes:

> [Krug is] remembered today for his great estate and its wines, but his friends, neighbors, and associates in the industry knew and loved him for qualities not measured in gallons or acres. He was the conscience of his winemaking community, a pillar of constant integrity, and a steady voice in favor of higher standards and better quality. . . . He organized the growers and producers in Napa Valley and showed the rest of the state how to do it. He demonstrated how

to take an issue affecting local interests and publicize it through broader agencies. A member of the State Viticultural Commission, he was a voice of reason among what was often a cacophony of egocentric showoffs. Along with Charles Kohler, Krug must be considered as one of the best-loved Californians of his time.[51]

The organizing and promoting and sharing that Sullivan describes is reminiscent of Agoston Haraszthy's efforts on behalf of California viticulture. But then, this should not be surprising, since young Charles Krug had been inspired by Haraszthy from the time they first met. Just as Krug had tended their respective vineyards in Crystal Springs, he tended Haraszthy's vines in Sonoma as well.[52]

Inglenook is the most celebrated name in California winemaking. Or rather, it was. Even its beginnings touch on both familial and thematic story lines. Here George Yount appears again, as it was his son-in-law, W. C. Watson, who in 1871 established Inglenook, which began as a vineyard adjoining a resort/sanitarium estate. In 1879 he sold to wealthy Finnish fur trader Gustave Niebaum. At the 1891 completion of his winery, Niebaum set out, like contemporary Leland Stanford in Sacramento Valley, to create wines to rival the best in the world. And, like Stanford, he spared no expense in the undertaking. But unlike Stanford, Niebaum considered terroir before committing to his venture. Niebaum's dedication to excellence—not the veneer thereof, but studied, practiced excellence, ever seeking innovations that would improve the quality of his wines—transformed Inglenook, bringing it the reputation and success that Stanford dearly sought but never reached.

One practice served the industry as much as it did Inglenook. Niebaum for the most part sold his wine in bottles rather than casks—just as Isaac De Turk had begun earlier in Sonoma, urging others to the same. In thus making adulteration by merchants and wine brokers almost impossible, bottling didn't just protect the "sanctity" of any winery's product; it also protected the reputation of winemaking as a whole. Niebaum managed both, producing in the 1890s about fifty thousand gallons of wine per year.

As much as nineteenth-century wine enthusiast Frona Eunice Wait praised many California wineries in her 1889 *Wines and Vines of California*, she wrote of none so glowingly as Inglenook:

> The Inglenook Vineyard is situated in the heart of Napa County, which, with Sonoma, is justly named the "Bordelaise of California."

This Inglenook Vineyard promotional piece reads: "The standard of excellence & purity—California old table wines grown and bottled at the Inglenook Vineyard, Rutherford, Napa County, California." It also specifies: "None genuine unless bearing [the Inglenook Vineyard] trade mark on cork or seal." Trade card or price list cover, circa 1895, courtesy of the Early California Wine Trade Archive.

Frona Eunice Wait on the Care and Time Necessary to Produce a Good Wine

[In that Inglenook is situated with] its rear sheltered by a solid hill of stone, Nature has assisted Science in maintaining in the vaults a uniform temperature, so necessary to the care and the development of wines. . . .

. . . Steam and water pipes are to be found in every part of the immense [winery] building, with conduits to carry off the waste, preventing stagnant water and those disagreeable odors which often offend the senses.

It is in the picking and assorting of the grapes that the quality of the wine can be assured. On the approach of the harvest the grapes are tested daily as to their perfect maturity, and if not found thoroughly ripe by the development of the saccharine and normal acid they are abandoned, or distilled into brandy. In order to insure perfection of the grapes the second crop is sacrificed, thus benefiting the first growth. On the reception of the grapes at the winery they are placed in the cellar to cool off. Before passing to the crusher and stemmer the grapes are carefully assorted, all broken, rotten, or unripe grapes being thrown aside. The grapes are then placed upon the elevator, which has a gradual ascent, are again assorted by a man on each side of the apron of the elevator, and then dropped to the second apron, where a strong draught from a Sturtevant Blower cools the grapes and frees them from dust and vermin, and from which the grapes pass into the crusher perfectly free of impurities. Passing into the crusher the grapes are stemmed and the mass is passed to press, where the juice runs off into the fermenting-tanks, where it lies during the process of fermentation, and when

perfectly dry or free from sugar it is racked off in storage cooperage, where it goes through its rackings from time to time, and is held until bottle-ripe, which takes from two to five years.

In order to avoid the sub-fermentation by the wine coming in contact with any metal that will produce an acetic acid, all the vessels are of hard wood, the forks and shovels used in handling the grapes must be nickel-plated, and, in order to preserve the utmost cleanliness and to prevent any sub-fermentation, the crushers, press, aprons, and even the grape-boxes are thoroughly scoured with soda and steamed, and the floors scrubbed at the end of each day's work.

Having thus assisted Nature by the most scrupulous cleanliness in producing a pure grape juice (the must), the experienced palate is brought to bear in the delicate task of blending the different varieties to make a perfect wine. No one kind of vine possesses all the different constituents that go to make a perfect whole, and it is in the blending of homogeneous qualities that has made a wine fit "even for gods to sip." In France this blending is poetically named "Le Mariage des Vins," the Marriage of Vines, and like its connubial patronymic it must be a congenial and perfect union to be a happy one. All the famous "crus" of the old world are the result of perfect blends, and, to give an idea of the difficulty of attaining this perfection, over one hundred blends of the Inglenook red wines were made before the present blends were selected. I have dilated on this head to explain the care and time necessary to produce a *good* wine.

Source: Wait, *Wines and Vines in California*, 112–14.

Surrounded by the majestic foothills of the Coast Range, sheltered from the strong winds and coast fogs, it nestles among the towering forest-covered hills, deserving well its name of the "Inglenook" (Scotch word for fireside). . . .

. . . There are at present about three hundred acres in vines, embracing the finest varieties of foreign grapes culled from every part of the world, cuttings of which have been grafted on old Mission and Zinfandel stocks. . . . [Having] taken very kindly to the soil, [these cuttings] produce wine which will compare favorably with its namesakes in the old country both as to delicacy of flavor and bouquet. . . . The reputation of Inglenook wines amply prove that, with perfect cultivation, a thorough knowledge of the soils, and the most rigid cleanliness in the vineyard and cellars, good and drinkable wines can be produced in this State.

Wait specifies that "perfect cultivation" includes the "thoroughly examined" Inglenook soils having their "excessive productiveness [eliminated] by a liberal deposit of sweet water gravel and fertilizers."[53]

———— ✵ ————

NAPA'S GREATNESS in wine, in Frona Wait's mind, hardly lay only in Inglenook, or only in Napa's "demanded" topography. She also praises others' efforts in striving for excellence. One was Henry W. Crabb, as she called him, though modern historians name him either Hiram W. Crabb or Hamilton Walker.[54] She writes: "Nestled cosily back from the county road, and half hidden by a wilderness of vines and trees, is the celebrated To-Kalon Vineyard, belonging to Mr. Henry W. Crabb. The fact that Mr. Crabb is an Ohio man may have something to do with his phenomenal success as a vigneron, but his confrères seem to think that study and much practical experience are the qualifications which have crowned To Kalon products with success. 'The name To-Kalon,' said Mr. Crabb, 'is Greek, and means the highest beauty, or the highest good, but I try to make it mean the boss vineyard.'"[55]

When he first arrived in Napa in 1865 Crabb began planting vineyards with the energy of a young man, though young he wasn't.

White wine presses used at the To-Kalon vineyard of H. W. Crabb, Napa Valley. Printed in Wait, *Wines and Vines of California*, 1889.

He approached his particular passion, experimenting with different varietals, with equal zeal. Teiser and Harroun write how by the 1880s he had "some four hundred [varieties]. It was said that, after the phylloxera hit the vines in the Luxembourg Gardens in Paris, and before it hit those of Mr. Crabb...he had the largest collection of *Vitis vinifera* varieties in the world." They also note that he was not one to keep the bounty to himself; he "enriched" the state's vineyards with the many cuttings he sold.[56]

The Nineteenth Century Heads into the Twentieth

In wrapping up this first third of the history of California wine, we note that, despite the growing concern about phylloxera, the state's wine industry enjoyed a robust prosperity in the 1870s. Some of this success can be attributed to the concerted efforts of those figures discussed here. Of course, replacing the Mission grape with superior varieties of wine grapes was an essential improvement, as was choosing terrain conducive to the optimal development of the vine. Other innovations to be credited include standards of quality regarding the perfection of grape, the material of storages, even the cleanliness of the facility.

By 1870 California's viticulture held great promise, in large part due to legislation at both the state and federal levels that greatly favored the industry. The earliest legislation, in 1850, was the so-called "Indian Indenture Act," which made it easy for vineyardists and farmers to use the pretext of vagrancy to obtain cheap Indian labor. Note its deceptive proper title: "An Act for the Government and Protection of Indians."[57] In 1859, California passed the "Act to provide for the better encouragement of the culture of the Vine and the Olive," which, in exempting from taxation vines younger than four years old, meant that growers didn't have to pay taxes on their investments until they had an actual crop to speak of. Then 1861 saw the establishment of the "Commission upon the Ways and Means best adapted to promote the Improvement and Growth of the Grape-vine in California," under whose auspices the Haraszthys studied European viticulture.[58] And at the federal level, in 1864 the U.S. Congress passed a tariff act that mandated increased import taxes on foreign wines. Needless to say, this was a tremendous boon to California's industry, spurring, as Vincent Carosso puts it, "enthusiastic planting," citing that three million vines were planted annually in the 1860s.[59]

Furthering the great promise of wine, by 1870 the state's vicultural investment was estimated at more than $30 million in gold.

Carosso notes that California readily encouraged the grape-grow-ing industry because "it attracted 'honest, industrious, and moral immigration.'" In addition, the California "press advocated more wine farms because grapes and grape products commanded higher prices, required less labor, and yielded substantially more profits than any other agricultural pursuit."[60]

It wasn't just the California press that promoted the industry; in 1886 the *New York Times* ran a series of articles on the "fruit and raisin culture" of California written by Major Ben C. Truman. These made a big impression on our California wine advocate Frona Eunice Wait—so much of an impression that she opted to weave Truman's words into her own. One page from *Wines and Vines of California* reads:

> Wine-drinking is largely on the increase among Americans, and as it is an acquired habit, only traveled and cultivated Americans know how to drink wine. . . . If they could secure good, wholesome California wines they would appreciate and have the courage of their convictions. Unfortunately, that class were largely induced to try the first shipments of California wines and alas! They have never quite recovered from that experience. That was in the days when the Mission and Zinfandel were considered the only grapes for wine-making on this coast, when every kind of wine was made from one variety of grape and when cellar practice was on a par with these preposterous notions. The depression of 1876 taught the growers a severe lesson. . . . Inquiry and study soon corrected imperfect cellar arrangements, and to-day California has some of the finest as well as the largest cellars in the world.[61]

Though we've been discussing notable wineries, and have highlighted the better wines, note that during the 1870s su-perior California wine was in the minority. This oddity re-sults in part from the fact that the promise of the industry was so great, and the market so large, that many an entre-preneur tried his hand at the trade. As Victor Carosso states, "Many vintners were convinced the industry could not be overdeveloped, and as long as there was a demand for wine new areas were planted with grapes. Thirty-five of the for-ty-four counties of the state planted vines on a large scale." But as we've seen, producing a good wine calls for not just fi-nancial investment but also time, patience, method, experi-ence, and care—attributes often not found in those seeking a quick buck. And so, much of the wine produced during this era was "strong, heady, and lacking in the finer qualities of its European counterpart."[62]

In addition, there was the age-old problem of fraudulent merchants. John Hutchison writes: "Americans were developing an appetite for wine faster than they were learning to tell the good from the bad." In the early 1870s, the eagerness "to appease [the demand] encouraged unscrupulous people to adulterate wine, mispresent its origins, and even to make it without any grapes at all."[63] In his 1876 *Handbook of Grape Culture,* Thomas Hart Hyatt lamented how the "good reputation to which the wines of California are entitled from the innate fine qualities, the rich saccharine properties, [and] the delicious aroma which characterize our pure wine, has been greatly impaired by the impositions practised [*sic*] by jugglers in the business, who have attempted to improve upon Nature, or rather to improve their pecuniary condition by palming off upon the public the bogus, doctored adulterations which are so often met with in the wine markets, especially in the Eastern States."[64] The effect of spoiled reputation can be long term, as the subsequent decades would show.

But let us isolate the minority good from the majority bad in considering California wines in the century's latter two decades. How did the better wines fair? Some quite well, apparently. Quoting again from *Wines and Vines of California*:

> For more than thirty years improvements have been made (and are being made) in the cultivation of the vine and in the improvement of the wines of California. . . .
>
> As an illustration of the growing popularity of California wines at home (here in California), it is not too much to say that not ten gentlemen in San Francisco, twenty years ago, ever placed native wines or brandies upon their tables; partly because they were inferior and cheaper. Gradually, however, the white and red acid wines of Napa, Sonoma, and Los Angeles Counties improved and were trusted, and at present no Californian is ashamed of entertaining his guest with either the Sauterne, Hock, muscatel, Zinfandel (Claret), Riesling, or burgundy of his own native land. These wines are all becoming favorites in the East and in England, and particularly among connoisseurs who know pure wines from adulterated ones.[65]

California also maintained its high levels of wine production. Another point of note: California was home to the largest vineyard in the world. That was in Sacramento Valley—Leland

Stanford's Vina Vineyard, which boasted nearly four thousand acres and more than three million vines. As the largest vineyard, Vina receives particular mention in *Wines and Vines,* which also cites California as possessing the smallest vineyard in the world, a single "monster" grapevine in Santa Barbara County.[66]

But with expansion can come disruption too. Recall that the 1870s were rife with financial upheaval, starting with the Panic of 1873. By 1876, California agriculture took a huge hit. Growers were overwhelmed with grapes that cost more to pick than they got on the market, and a gallon of wine sold for just ten cents. Only one winery in three weathered the storm: of the 139 wineries in 1870, only 45 remained in 1880. But as with the thinning of a herd, the hardship proved beneficial as well: many who went under were those who used lesser grape varieties—or were just lesser vintners themselves.[67]

Regardless of the ebbs and flows of production, an old prejudice persisted about California wines, even in California. Consider the plight of European wine and its market. Starting in 1865, phylloxera had been ravaging the vineyards of France and Spain, a calamity that cut vintages in half—all while consumption of French and Spanish wine in America had more than doubled. And yet, as Frona Wait lays out, wines masquerading as being of "illustrious" 1870s European vintages were included on wine lists in San Francisco, and likely on many more throughout the country. But, she writes, "there is not a single gallon of any of it genuine, and if it were, it would be on the market in America." Marshalling statistics with the precision of a trial lawyer, Wait proves that all these supposed French and Spanish, Italian and Hungarian wines in truth hailed from California. "The fact that the fraud is not detected," she concludes, "speaks well for the quality of the wine itself."[68]

———— ❧ ————

ON SUNDAY, APRIL 6, 1890, the *San Francisco Examiner* ran a fourteen-page feature section on California wine offering "A Complete History of the Wine Industry of California–Where to Buy Fine Wines–How to Avoid Fraud and Sophistication–Wine-Growers Who Are Prepared to Supply Customers Direct–The Leading Vineyards—Facts About Wine and Raisin Lands–Famous Wine-Growing Counties." It begins: "California is soon to be the great wine-producing country of the world. Already she is making wines that equal, if not excel, any European vigneron's

This image appeared in the fourteen-page feature section on California wine that ran in the *San Francisco Examiner* on April 6, 1890.

skill, but she and her products are kept back by that abominable and superstitious worship of all that is foreign which finds its commonest expression in contempt for all that is made near home."[69]

As the nineteenth century drew to a close—even as perfectionist vintners bottled ever better product, even as it seemed that soon California wines would indeed attain the greatness prophesized by early extravagant predictions—four ominous events loomed, each of which nearly doomed the California wine industry. They are the topics of part 2.

Notes

1. Teiser and Harroun, *Winemaking in California,* 73.

2. Arpad Haraszthy, *Wine-Making in California,* 23.

3. Teiser and Harroun, *Winemaking in California,* 73.

4. Hittell, *Resources of California,* 195.

5. Kohler, "Wine Production in California," 9–10.

6. Sullivan, *Companion to California Wine,* 172; Teiser and Harroun, *Winemaking in California,* 58–60; Pinney, *History of Wine in America,* 1:315.

7. Kohler, "Wine Production in California," 9–11; Pinney, *History of Wine in America,* 1:315.

8. Arpad Haraszthy, *Wine-Making in California,* 61.

9. Mobley, "Mission Revival," L7.

10. Sullivan, "Viticultural Mystery Solved," 124.

11. Arpad Haraszthy, *Wine-Making in California,* 25–27, 68–69.

12. Carosso, *California Wine Industry,* 68–69, citing *Alta California,* September 21, 1863.

13. Fredericksen, "Haraszthy's Busy Last Years," 22; Carosso, *California Wine Industry,* 67–74.

14. Carosso, *California Wine Industry,* 73; Fredericksen, "Haraszthy's Busy Last Years," 22; Buena Vista Vinicultural Society, *Reports of the Board of Trustees and Officers,* 6.

15. Peninou and Greenleaf, *Directory of California Wine Growers,* 63–65.

16. Teiser and Harroun, *Winemaking in California,* 73–74; Northern California Historical Records Survey Project, "Calendar," 6.

17. Teiser and Harroun, *Winemaking in California,* 74.

18. Ibid., 73–75.

19. Sullivan, *Companion to California Wine,* 38, 143.

20. Muscatine, *Old San Francisco,* 210; Teiser and Harroun, *Winemaking in California,* 75.

21. Teiser and Harroun, *Winemaking in California,* 75; Sullivan, *Companion to California Wine,* 143.

22. Teiser and Harroun, *Winemaking in California,* 75.

23. Goodlett, "Korbel," unnumbered pages 1–2.

24. Pinney, *History of Wine in America,* 1:327–28.

25. Thompson and Johnson, *California Wine Book,* 75; Pinney, *History of Wine in America,* 1:327–29; Sullivan, *Companion to California Wine,* 161–62.

26. Ibid.

27. Pinney, *History of Wine in America,* 1:328.

28. National Temperance Society, *The National Advocate* 44, no. 5 (May 1909): 74.

29. Keller, "California Wines," 137–38.

30. Stevenson, *Silverado Squatters,* 24.

31. Sullivan, *Companion to California Wine,* 244; Pinney, *History of Wine in America,* 1:320–21, and references cited.

32. Peninou and Greenleaf, *Directory of California Wine Growers,* 1–2.

33. Pinney, *History of Wine in America,* 1:326.

34. Peninou and Greenleaf, *Directory of California Wine Growers,* 48–57, 60–70.

35. Teiser and Harroun, *Winemaking in California,* 48–50; Sullivan, *Companion to California Wine,* 7, 188.

36. Teiser and Harroun, *Winemaking in California,* 48–50; Sullivan, *Companion to California Wine,* 188.

37. Sullivan, *Companion to California Wine,* 8, 188, 204.

38. Ibid., 188, 204; Muscatine, *Old San Francisco,* 210.

39. Sullivan, *Companion to California Wine,* 35.

40. Ibid., 63–64.

41. Muscatine, *Old San Francisco,* 210–11; Pinney, *History of Wine in America,* 1:321–22.

42. Pinney, *History of Wine in America,* 1:322–25 and n34.

43. Ibid., 324.

44. McKee, "Three Wine-Growing Senators," 15.

45. Ibid.

46. Sullivan, *Companion to California Wine,* 150.

47. Peninou and Greenleaf, *Directory of California Wine Growers,* 32–37, 60–70.

48. Ibid., 32, 60; Teiser and Harroun, *Winemaking in California,* 82.

49. Wait, *Wines and Vines of California,* 106.

50. Teiser and Harroun, *Winemaking in California,* 82–83; Sullivan, *Companion to California Wine,* 175–76.

51. Sullivan, *Companion to California Wine,* 175.

52. Teiser and Harroun, *Winemaking in California,* 82.

53. Wait, *Wines and Vines in California,* 111–12. (The last sentence of the main quotation re: Inglenook's reputation appears on page 111.)

54. Sullivan, *Companion to California Wine,* 78–79. To complicate

matters further, Teiser and Harroun insist that Mr. Crabb was "Hamilton Walker Crabb" (*Winemaking in California,* 83). We'll just call him "Crabb."

55. Wait, *Wines and Vines of California,* 108.

56. Teiser and Harroun, *Winemaking in California,* 83.

57. Dinkelspiel, *Tangled Vines,* 87–88. See also Street, *Beasts of the Field,* 119.

58. "An Act to Provide for the Better Encouragement of the Culture of the Vine and the Olive," California Statutes of 1859, 10th Sess., 210; and "Commission upon the Ways and Means Best Adapted to Promote the Improvement and Growth of the Grape-vine in California," Concurrent Resolution No. 25, California Statutes of 1861, 12th Sess. of the Legislature, 677. See also Pinney, *History of Wine in America,* 1:263.

59. Carosso, *California Wine Industry,* 76, citing in part H. D. Dunn, "California: Her Agricultural Resources," *Report of the United States, Commissioner of Agriculture,* 1866, 608.

60. Carosso, *California Wine Industry,* 86, citing San Francisco *Bulletin,* June 17, 1870, in "Bancroft Scraps," *California Agriculture* 1: 142.

61. Benjamin C. Truman, *New York Times,* January 16, 1887, borrowed and partially credited in Wait, *Wines and Vines of California,* 10. Historian Charles Sullivan originally discovered the liberal use of Truman's *Times* text in *Wines and Vines of California;* Thomas Pinney later tracked which portions derived from which of Truman's different articles. Wait did state the following in the first paragraph of her preface: "It is my privilege to acknowledge assistance from other workers who have scattered fragments of much needed information along the way. First among these is Major Ben C. Truman in a series of letters about California Wines to the *New York Times.*" Wait, *Wines and Vines of California,* 3. See also Pinney, "Strange Case," 17–19.

62. Carosso, *California Wine Industry,* 90, citing Hittell, *Resources of California,* 255.

63. Hutchison, "Northern California," 37.

64. Hyatt, *Hyatt's Handbook of Grape Culture,* cited in Hutchison, "Northern California," 37.

65. Wait, *Wines and Vines of California,* 10, 13, attributed in part to Ben C. Truman, in articles printed on January 16 and January 30, 1887, *New York Times.*

66. Ibid., 35–36, attributed in part to Truman's articles printed on January 16, 1887, *New York Times.* The text reads: "California also has the smallest vineyard in the world—the monster (one) grapevine in Santa Barbara County, which is about 68 years old, has a diameter one foot from the ground of 12 inches, and whose branches cover an area of 12,000 feet. This one vine produces from 10,000 to 12,000 pounds of grapes, and for many years these grapes were made into wine, the process being the treading out of the juice by naked Indians. I have picked bunches of grapes from this vine many a time that weighed five, six, and seven pounds. This vine was planted by a Mexican woman named Maria Marcilina Felix, who died under her own vine and fig tree in 1865, aged 107."

67. Hutchison, "Northern California," 39.

68. Wait, *Wines and Vines of California,* 5–9.

69. "California Wines," *San Francisco Examiner,* Sunday, April 6, 1890, 37–50, courtesy of Bancroft Library and Charles Faulhaber.

PART TWO

A Bug, a Temblor, a Sunken Liner, and One Bummer of a Law

Four Setbacks

Wine has a rich cultural background, covering
religion, covering literature, covering politics,
covering economics. . . . Wine has a cultural appeal
as a science, it has a cultural appeal as an art.

—Louis Gomberg,
"Analytical Perspectives on the California Wine Industry"

CHAPTER 5

Phylloxera and Other Perils

1873–1900s

> The phylloxera have made fearful ravages . . . whole
> vineyards have been destroyed. This [is the] most
> dreaded of all depredators upon the vine.
>
> —Frona Eunice Wait, *Wines and Vines of California*

In many ways, for California viticulture the transition from the nineteenth century to the twentieth was like the transition from childhood to adolescence. It was caught in two intertwining phases of self-assessment and inquiry. One was sheer survival; its leaders asked: *How can we weather the storms? How can we overcome our long-term dangers?* Another concerned identity: *What is California wine? What should it be?* Throughout the transition, a sometimes contradictory multiplicity of factors both propelled and hindered, discouraged and inspired.

The first great crisis to be visited upon the wine industry in California was an infestation of the phylloxera. Native to the eastern United States, the tiny phylloxera is a plant louse or aphid whose reputation in France earned it the French name *Phylloxera vastatrix*—"the destroyer" or "devastating dry leaf creature"— though its official name is *Dactylasphaera vitifoliae*.[1] Whatever its name, its effect was substantial: Frona Wait noted that, by 1890, the French and Spanish "vintages have fallen off nearly one-half."[2] George Ordish, who as author of *The Great Wine Blight* is essentially phylloxera's biographer, goes further, stating that the insect phylloxera "slowly and surely killed any European vine to which it gained access. It would thus have wiped out the wine grape throughout Europe and eventually the whole world."[3] This is not hyperbole; John N. Hutchison notes that the "louselike aphid" found its way to Greece, Algeria, South Africa, Russia— even Australia.[4]

It seems the aphid-like phylloxera was first noticed in England in 1863, when Oxford entomologist Professor O. Westwood examined a shipment of new insects. But the occurrence was no more eventful than that at the time. What was noticed was the effect on the grapevine once the insect got established:

> A vine or two, usually in the center of a vineyard, would start to sicken, the leaves yellowing at first, the edges then turning red, the leaves finally drying up and dropping. The next year the symptoms would be worse and could be seen spreading to neighbouring vines; the extension growths were weak, the dried-up tips being easily broken in winter. If any fruit set it might ripen if the attack was slight, but would be of poor quality, watery, acid[ic], and with no bouquet. The [normally] black grapes stayed clear red or pink in colour. Wine made from them was very poor and did not keep. With heavier attacks the bunches of grapes just dried up and usually fell off. The third year the vine was dead, and when dug up the external tissues of the roots were black and rotting.[5]

The above was what happened to vineyards in France in 1863, when it was considered an "unknown disease." This was a reasonable assumption, since France's viticulture had nearly been wiped out by the fungus disease oidium in the 1840s. Indeed, even the fact that phylloxera-stricken grape leaves reddened brought to mind the red flush of victims of tuberculosis.[6]

Five years passed before the true culprit was identified: the tiny phylloxera. In a strange twist, the louse was introduced to Europe by means of vines imported from eastern America. The phrase "carrying coals to Newcastle" comes to mind—American vines shipped to Europe?[7]

Since American vine cuttings had first been sent to Europe as early as 1629, one might think the American phylloxera could have travelled anytime thereafter. Indeed they might have—it's just that in the age of sail any infected vine cuttings would have died during the long voyage. But with the nineteenth-century invention of the steamship, the length of the journey across the Atlantic was greatly reduced, just as the railroad shortened the inland passage of the journey. George Ordish believes the steamship "undoubtedly led to the spread of pests around the world as the pace of international commerce quickened."[8]

After reaching Europe by ship, the louse phylloxera reversed course, so to speak; it came to California on vines from Europe or the eastern United States or both.[9] It was first discovered in 1873, in a Sonoma County vineyard.[10] That it was found then and there suggests that perhaps Agoston Haraszthy brought the American

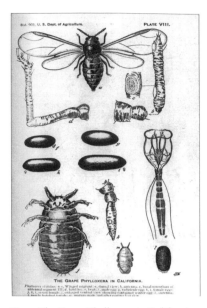

From *The Grape Phylloxera in California*. Bulletin 903, U.S. Department of Agriculture, plate VIII. Courtesy of the Wine Institute.

émigré to the West Coast via the tens of thousands of vines and cuttings he brought back to Buena Vista in 1861. If so, what a bitter irony—that in striving to advance the state's viticulture Haraszthy might have unknowingly facilitated its near demise.

Note that this theory is plausible if we go by the repeated claim that phylloxera likely reached Europe in the 1850s—even though it wasn't noticed until 1863—and that, similarly, it arrived in California in the 1850s and 1860s, well before its first notice in 1873. Such is what historians Thomas Pinney and Charles Sullivan have indicated, in part quoting others.[11] And yet, in *The Great Wine Blight* George Ordish states that the "insect is so destructive that a long interval between its presence and its discovery is unlikely, so that its successful establishment [in France] cannot have been much before 1863."[12] According to these terms, the phylloxera similarly could not have arrived in California much before 1873. That Haraszthy's imported vines arrived nearly a decade earlier, in 1862, could suggest he is not to blame for the state's scourge. It's a pity we can't ask the now-deceased Ordish just how long he considered a "long interval" to be.

On the other hand, we don't need additional evidence of just how the "insect is so destructive." Once introduced to Europe, phylloxera wreaked a terrible and quick devastation. In less than a decade, the microscopic marauder had laid to ruin thousands of acres of French vineyards. The speed of this destruction resulted from the fact that the winged form of phylloxera survives well in humid climates, where it literally travels with the wind—and France is a land of summer rain.

By contrast, the winged phylloxera was not so much a factor in dryer California. There the spread was facilitated by various carriers: cuttings, wagons, even workers' boots, much as how sudden oak death can be transmitted in Northern California today. (That the insect cannot spread in sandy soil explains why some regions, such as can be found in Southern California, have managed to avoid infestation.) But regardless of the pace of its progress, the infestation's effect on the state's viticulture was devastating all the same.[13] Frona Wait wrote in 1889: "When there have been small rains during the winter months and correspondingly short natural grasses during the summer months following—[then] the bearing power of the vine has been entirely destroyed in the northern counties, and especially in Sonoma county. The phylloxera have made fearful ravages at times and whole vineyards have been destroyed."[14] Indeed, within seven years after its first identification, phylloxera had laid waste to six hundred acres of Sonoma vines, and had been found in every wine-growing region in California except Los Angeles.

That the scourge had hit Europe a decade earlier meant that Europe had a head start in quelling the blight—the various methods of which California's wine industry applied in earnest. It could be argued that one of those methods—that of simply "wait and see"—is less method and more procrastination, or even denial. Certainly, Thomas Pinney notes, many Californian growers were slow to come around to acknowledging the extent of the danger phylloxera posed.[15] This is a curious stance, given the tremendous hit Europe's vineyards had experienced by that time. As it happens, we copied denial of the wine pest as much as we aspired to copy—nay, improve upon—European wine itself. In his circa 1895 report to the state on phylloxera, A. P. Hayne declares:

> We in California behaved, in regard to the pest, just as did the inhabitants of other countries. At first we made light of it; then we refused to allow it to be known how serious the trouble was, regarding it as an insult to be told that the pest had infected our vineyards. . . . [I]n . . . the Champagne region in France . . . , the peasants resented the imputation so strenuously that it took regiments of soldiers to enforce the quarantine rules. . . . In California, though we have had no bloodshed, there was much ill feeling engendered; so much so that even to this day some refuse to accept the inevitable, or to listen to those who would assist them.[16]

A second approach involved assaulting the phylloxera in some manner, whether by flooding the vineyards or spraying with chemicals—or, surprisingly, electric shock. Peninou and Greenleaf offer the following: "Some of the remedies or treatments tried by the French were: tobacco leaves, fresh or dry, dug in near the vines; crushed garlic mixed with salt water; discharges of electricity; chips of soap at some depth around the roots which the rains would dissolve and wash down; and a bed of plaster around the roots of the vines to prevent the descent of the phylloxera. No comment is necessary on the results of these treatments, which would seem comic if they were not pathetic."[17] Indeed, nothing proved effective; to this day no such remedial approach has been found.

To best understand the next two attempted methods, it helps to know something of how and why phylloxera attack their prey. Though some strains of the insect feed from grape leaves, most

Hand-drawn illustration of grapes by Victoria Novak.

The Propagation of Grapevines from Wine Grapes

In their book *Wine Grapes,* Jancis Robinson, Julia Harding, and José Vouillamoz offer the following on the propagation of grapevines.

Every single grape variety is the result of a single vine grown from a single seed, and this seed is the result of sexual reproduction between two parent varieties. The following set of conditions has to be fulfilled for a new variety to be born:

- a flower in a grape bunch is fertilized, resulting in the formation of a berry;
- the berry falls to the ground or is eaten and carried away by an animal, very often a bird;
- the grape seed from that berry falls onto the soil and germinates, producing a seedling;
- the plantlet has to survive at least three years in order to bear fruit and to be identified as an interesting grapevine. . . .

Like most plants, flowers of almost all cultivated grape varieties are hermaphroditic and have both male organs (stamens that produce pollen) and a female organ (a pistil that contains the ovary to be fertilized). . . .

The pollen that reaches the pistil of a grape flower, thanks to the wind or to insects such as flies, may come from the same flower, from another flower on the same plant, or from a flower of another plant of the same grape variety. In each case, this is known as self-pollination or selfing. Cross-pollination occurs when the pollen comes from a flower of another plant of another grape variety. In modern regimented, monovarietal vineyards, self-pollination is far more common, ensuring fruitful harvests every year, and thus the economic well-being of the grape grower and wine producer.

Source: Robinson, Harding, and Vouillamoz, *Wine Grapes,* xiv.

favor the sap of grapevine roots. Their feeding process can deform the roots to the extent that nutrient flow to the vine is diminished. To that insult are added two injuries: the insect's poisonous spittle can be injected into the roots, and the vine can develop fungal infections at the feeding sites. Altogether, the insect is formidable against the defenseless European vinifera. But the grapevines in the valleys of the Mississippi and Missouri Rivers, where the aphidlike "sap suckers" originated, are not susceptible: in the course of adapting over time, they developed defenses against the voracious insect. First, these vines have a sticky sap that can choke the biting nymph phylloxera. Second, even if the nymph succeeds in securing a "feeding wound," the vine can form a protective tissue that fends off potential secondary infection.[18]

So a third attempted remedy was a primitive form of genetic engineering: to produce a hybrid grapevine by cross-pollinating European grape varieties with resistant American varieties. Unfortunately, extensive efforts using this approach in Germany and France produced inferior fruit.[19] Singular grape varieties are best propagated from cuttings rather than seeds, since cuttings preserve one parent's DNA, whereas seeds contain two sets of DNA. In essence, the hybrid fruit was inferior because the resistant variety's fruit was inferior.[20]

The fourth approach to addressing the phylloxera scourge hit upon the genetic engineering concept via a different method, this time grafting superior vinifera varieties onto American resistant rootstock. With this approach, a cutting is physically fused into the secondary rootstock, often held in position with twine. In time, the two grow into a viable, fruiting vine.[21]

By 1880 in the United States, phylloxera had fully demonstrated that its destructive capacity called for greater opposition than could be provided by individual grape growers tending their stricken vines. To address the situation, in April 1880 the California legislature created two institutions of authority: the Board of State Viticultural Commissioners and the Department of Agriculture at the University of California, Berkeley. Though the two entities were often rivalrous, they equally considered the use of resistant rootstock of native American varieties to be the only solution to the phylloxera problem—and fervently advised as much. But most vineyardists were slow to follow suit; by 1888, fewer than two thousand acres had been planted to resistant rootstock, leaving phylloxera free to expand its devastation.[22] For example, on January 27, 1893, the *Napa Register* published a letter by George Husmann that reads: "I venture to predict that there will be but little left of all the vines in Napa Valley, except those on resistant root, within two years." This view proved to be all too prophetic: in 1890, Napa had eighteen thousand acres of bearing vines;[23] by 1900, only two thousand remained in the county. By one estimate, ten thousand acres were destroyed by phylloxera between 1889 and 1892.[24]

By the 1890s the solution of grafting fine vinifera onto resistant rootstock was becoming the accepted remedy. But the fight against phylloxera was still a protracted process—and not merely because of the obstinacy of winegrowers or the cost of replanting vineyards. Many questions remained: *Precisely what rootstocks are most resistant to the louse? Which rootstocks are best for which varieties of vinifera? And for which particular soils?* These answers took years to determine. A significant amount of that determination resulted from the work of German vintner and horticulture professor George C. Husmann, whom we shall properly meet later on.

Fortunately, the state wasn't lacking in figures dedicated to both saving and advancing the industry. The trouble was, they often didn't agree on the best approach. There was great agreement, however, on the significance of the death of Charles Kohler in 1887, which inspired an uncommon outpouring of grief. Hubert Howe Bancroft memorializes his legacy in sharing how "the wine manufacture of California today is a monument to the wisdom, the enterprise, and the industry of Charles Kohler."[25] An unpublished manuscript from 1878 states that "the discovery of the peculiar fitness of California for vine growing may in the future prove to have been quite as important as the discovery of gold."[26] Charles Wetmore, whom we'll also meet later on, deems him "the pioneer and founder of the present wine trade in California." He also aptly sums up the feelings of many in proclaiming, as if about the industry as a whole as much as about Kohler himself: "I feel lost now because I do not see where his successor can be found."[27]

AMID GROWING PAINS, NEW LEADERS EMERGE

The many angles considered in confronting the scourge of phylloxera, and the best means of eradicating it, stand as a microcosm to the macrocosm of California viticulture, the foundation of which in the 1890s was rocky at best—and not just on account of phylloxera. Additional concerns also vexed the industry: uneven winemaking, poor marketing, and wildly vacillating volume—especially overproduction, even within the phylloxera era.

As for the overproduction of wine, recall that, though Southern California's wine-growing glory days began to fade with the rush to gold, it remained viable for a time. Thomas Pinney notes how starting in the late 1870s several vintners of the "Southern Vineyard"—James de Barth Shorb, E. J. "Lucky" Baldwin, and L. J. Rose—took advantage of the phylloxera's advances in Europe by expanding their enterprises to fill the vacuum in the global wine market.[28] And though they couldn't have known it at the time, their region was essentially immune to the tiny phylloxera. And so, even with the insect of the north wreaking its havoc there, annual production in California as a whole rose, from fifteen million gallons in 1887 to twenty million in 1891. The resulting glut in the market caused prices to plummet, which led some stricken farmers to rip out their vineyards in the race to cultivate something else and fast. John Hutchison sums it up handily: the state's viticulture rose and fell in fits and starts, "riding from shortage to surplus and battered by calamities. Overproduction in some districts, phylloxera and Pierce's in others, and prices that fell as low as ten cents a gallon drove many growers to the wall." In some years, the culprit of overproduction was clement weather, which produced bumper crops; in 1897 production rose to thirty-four million gallons, more than twice that of the vintage of ten years before, but that uptick was but a blip, and of wine of poor quality.[29]

It was a similar state of overproduction that spurred the *San Francisco Examiner* on July 23, 1889, to scream how "Wine Is Too Cheap." This pronouncement headed a series of articles on California viticulture, expounding on the likes of "California Industry Threatened with Destructive Low Prices" and "Sold at Less Than Cost; What Prominent Winemakers Say Must Be Done to Rescue the Industry." Two wine merchants and more than one hundred vineyard owners and winemakers had been consulted for the series. The overwhelming majority were of the view that poor quality and overproduction were at the heart of the malaise in the industry. Several solutions were proposed on how to address overproduction, including reducing vineyards and making raisins rather than wine. But another, flip-side consideration emerged as well: increasing consumption, the idea being to encourage the drinking of wine over whiskey or beer, or even nonalcoholic drinks. One respondent, Charles Detoy of Santa Clara, wrote of grape growers who served their workers and family tea and coffee instead of wine. His solution: "People who are afraid to use their own product [should] quit raising grapes." It was proposed that hotel keepers and restaurant owners be encouraged to serve more California wines, and to charge less for them than for foreign wines. Many thought Californians should be encouraged to drink wine with meals at home. Mr. B. Ehlers of Napa County found the latter suggestion futile: "The majority do not like wine, or are afraid to use it in the house on account of the women."[30]

Several years after the *Examiner* series, a report by Charles Wetmore, "Treatise on Wine Production," reiterated the difficulties of expanding the domestic market for wine: "Americans are slow to adopt wine-drinking customs at the family table," Wetmore writes, "or in hotels and restaurants, because good foreign wines are too expensive, ordinary foreign wines too low in quality, Eastern domestic wines from native grapes too peculiarly flavored, and California wines too strong. Light beers and ales are very popular and rapidly becoming the national beverage."[31]

The series identified a fourth perceived bogeyman: a sinister combination of merchants who preyed upon the growers and winemakers, referred to as the "Frisco dealers" or a "dealers' ring." (Again, more than one hundred vineyard owners and winemakers had weighed in on the subject, whereas just two merchants had contributed.) Isaac De Turk, the successful and respected Santa Rosa vintner, had much to say on the subject. He saw no point in attempting to depress production, because he felt the entire concern resulted from "an unnatural condition of the wine market, caused by a combination of dealers." In essence he said, "the middleman is making all the profit, while the grape grower is sustaining a heavy loss." He detailed how the wine dealer netted a minimum of fifty-three cents for selling a gallon of bottled wine, and yet he paid only seven cents to the winegrower; for superior wines such as a "good claret," the dealer netted two dollars, though he paid the grower just ten cents. De Turk notes: "One would think that dealers would hesitate to kill the business that was making them rich, but they do not seem to have any care for the future." Of the two wine merchants interviewed for the series, one, Isaac Landsberger, not only adamantly asserted there was no combination of dealers, he also considered that such would, in fact, benefit the entire California wine industry, especially in times of "excessive supply." He states: "A combination now would relieve each merchant from fears of rivals' competition in buying cheaply, and make the dealers feel more confidence in their ability to meet the demands of the producers."[32]

A month later, on August 8, 1889, the *Examiner* published a follow-up to the series, an open letter called "Plain Talk to the Winemen." Its author, Eugene Woldemar Hilgard, was the dean of the University of California College of Agriculture. From 1880 onward he had conducted extensive viticultural studies—complete with a vineyard and wine cellar right on campus.[33] In his "Plain Talk" Hilgard offers his expertise on the subject, particularly regarding the market concerns of overproduction. He deplores both "the poor quality of the larger part of the wines made and their immaturity when put on the market." He laments that "the foreign guest at our principal hotels might be aghast at having the claret cork fly at him, followed by a significant puff of smoke, and a liquid resembling sauce rather than wine and of uncanny odor." And yet, nonetheless, "the label assured him that it was all right and that such was the nature of California wine." In no uncertain terms, Hilgard lays the brunt of the blame at the feet of the winemakers who engage in various sloppy practices. Included in his excoriation are those who "promiscuously" crush together grapes in all states, whether "sound, moldy, green, [or] sunburnt." He also addresses the winemaker who "allows his fermenting tanks to get so hot as to scald the yeast, and then wonders why the wine has 'stuck'"—meaning the fermentation process stopped too soon—as well as the winemaker who "permits the 'cap' to get white with mold and swarming with vinegar flies, and then cheerfully stirs it under so as to thoroughly infect the wine with the germs of destruction."[34]

It was noted above that California had two institutions dedicated to the study of its viticulture. Hilgard was the dean of the second, at the University of California College of Agriculture. His numerous publications reflect the precision of his numerous experiments—and he wasn't one to mince words regarding the perpetrators of the industry's villainies. One report reads: "It is high time that the haphazard methods even yet so commonly pursued in this State, should be discarded, and that the experience had, whether in the winery or in the laboratory, should be gathered into a definite form, as a guide to the rational wine-maker; so that hereafter California wines may appear on the world's market under their own labels, instead of being, as has heretofore been too largely the case, disguised under foreign ones, when of good quality; while the poorer qualities were sure to be placed upon the market with the true statement of their California origin."[35]

In his position in academia, Hilgard's purview necessarily included the highest aspirations worth striving toward. And yet, most aspirations must work within the reality of their environment. Perhaps it is for this reason that the State of California funded two viticultural institutions. The other, the Board of State Viticultural Commissioners, approached the field from a commercial perspective: all nine members were winegrowers or vintners—including Arpad Haraszthy, its first president. Given their makeup, it should be no surprise that the board viewed viticulture with a mind to what was practical and possible.

At its inception, the Board of State Viticultural Commissioners was headed by executive officer Charles Wetmore. He was also an acclaimed winemaker in his own right; his Livermore Valley vineyard, Cresta Blanca, produced award-winning wines.[36]

Though oftentimes Wetmore and Hilgard were at odds, on certain topics they did agree. Wetmore's 1894 "Treatise on Wine Production," for example, reports no better news than Hilgard would have proclaimed. In it Wetmore lays out the unfortunate combination of factors that winegrowers of the day faced. First: "Much misconception of our vintages and their possibilities springs from lack of knowledge of the circumstances under which growers work. As a rule, the wine maker is not rich; generally he is in debt. He is not in a position to develop a wine market." Wetmore also notes the unfortunate economics of the business, one where "quality and quantity are inversely related," and where "quantity has paid the best." For this reason, many winegrowers were resorting to what had worked previously: "grafting back to more prolific varieties." He also had strong words about the extensive loss of vineyards—nearly thirty thousand acres in the previous six years—on account of "no efforts [being] made to check the ravages of diseases."[37]

Given that the California winegrower was "not in a position to develop a wine market," of additional concern was the fact that the "New York market knows little of our best wines." California wines lacked the cachet of European wines, French in particular, and so the East Coast merchants sought West Coast wine only for the profitable—cheap—market. And though Wetmore liked to complain that the New Yorkers were wine snobs who had never bothered to taste the finer California wines, he had to concede that these merchants didn't often travel to California. And though Wetmore was enough aligned with the winegrowers to point out the difficulties they faced, he wasn't reluctant to blame the guilty either. To his mind, easterners knew nothing of the excellent wines California could produce in large part because of vintners' overall slipshod methods, including uncontrolled fermentation, insufficiently cool storage, and aging too long in wooden casks. Given such standards, it was no surprise that California wine, once shipped to its destination, often arrived well below par. In brief: for the "gentlemen connected with the trade in foreign wines," he said, "small places in Europe occupy, in their

The Phenomenon of the International Exposition

The trend of hosting a large, lavish "international exposition" began in London in 1851, at the Great Exhibition of the Works of Industry of All Nations. As the name suggests, the idea was to provide a showcase where nations could celebrate their culture and display their achievements in agronomy, industry, and the arts. (Some would say it was the opportunity to demonstrate its technical and industrial prowess that was Britain's true motive in hosting the grand display.) The smashing success of Britain's venture, nicknamed the Crystal Palace Exposition, inspired other cities to hold their own extravagant exhibits.

Wine was featured at the Paris Exposition of 1889—as well as at subsequent expositions in Dublin, Bordeaux, Berlin, Ghent, and Paris again in 1900. At the wine competition at the Exposition Universelle of 1889, the Grand Prix was awarded to Charles Wetmore for the first vintage of his Cresta Blanca Winery, a dry white wine. At the 1900 Paris Exposition, two California wines took gold medals for Cabernet Sauvignon: Howell Mountain and Monte Bello. So as not to be left behind, the United States also hosted international expositions—in Philadelphia, Atlanta, Buffalo, St. Louis, Portland, and Seattle. All had wine competitions, and all had entrants from California wineries.

Sources: Sullivan, *Companion to California Wine*, 107–8; Auerbach, *Great Exhibition of 1851*, 23; Williams, "How the Great Exhibition of 1851 Still Influences Science Today." *Guardian*, August 28, 2015.

Cresta Blanca California Red Pinot wine label. The text curved around the gold medals at the top of the label reads: "Gold medals awarded Cresta Blanca wines since 1889," accompanied by the listing of six different expositions, from 1894 to 1909. Courtesy of Olivina, LLC, of Livermore, California.

of Viticultural Commissioners at the time. Putting the value of Commissioner Gos's glowing endorsement aside, the board was unsatisfied with California's showing at the fair. And so they decided San Francisco needed to hold its own wine exhibition.[41]

Michael de Young, the energetic, scandalmongering publisher of the *San Francisco Chronicle,* was commissioner of the California Exhibits at the 1893 Columbian Exposition in Chicago. There he'd seen how a well-planned world's fair could financially and civically invigorate a city—two benefits that San Francisco sorely needed. Adrift in the doldrums of an economic recession, San Francisco at the time was also riven with strife, including bitter union strikes. And so de Young proposed that San Francisco host a world's fair. This was an astonishing prospect. For one thing, San Francisco was in effect a mere girl of a city—forty-four years old, reckoning from its formative birth in 1849. Even more astonishing was the fact that de Young conceived of the fair opening just six months later, on January 1, 1894. The Chicago fair, a success by virtually all measures, had been seven years in the planning, whereas bad planning had helped to doom the 1884 New Orleans World's Fair to fiscal failure. But de Young had a method to his seeming madness: he believed the exhibitors at the 1893 fair, particularly those from overseas, could be enticed to ship their exhibits from Chicago to San Francisco for a second world's fair, which would garner them additional exposure. The proposed date had another benefit: showcasing California's extraordinary, year-round clement weather. Open the fair on New Year's Day, Michael de Young exclaimed, and call it a Midwinter Exposition. The pitch worked; de Young convinced enough San Francisco financiers to back his idea, and the plan was afoot. The city would host a world's fair in its beautiful Golden Gate Park.[42]

But the idea was not embraced by all. It was fiercely opposed by John McLaren, the legendary superintendent of Golden Gate Park; also opposed was millionaire W. W. Stow, a conservationist and friend of the park (for whom Stow Lake—which was part of the site of the 1894 exposition—is named). But de Young and his idea won out, and miraculously the fair came together with but six months of planning. The exposition's chief engineer—and it required a lot of engineering—was William O'Shaughnessy. (He would later play a pivotal role in the rebuilding of San Francisco after the 1906 earthquake and fire, as well as in the much larger and grander 1915 world's fair.)[43] In the latter six months of 1893, San Francisco raised the needed money, solicited bids from architects and builders, awarded contracts, invited exhibitors, cleared almost 180 acres of Golden Gate Park, and built on those acres 180 structures. And the fair opened, almost on time.[44]

The California Midwinter International Exposition became the official title of the San Francisco world's fair of 1894. It ran from January 27 through July 8 in Golden Gate Park. The center of the expo was the Electric Tower, affectionately known as "La Petite Tour Eiffel de San Francisco," which rose from the middle of the Court of Honor, itself part of what is now the park's Music Concourse. The concourse, an immense sunken outdoor auditorium, was encircled by the various buildings of the expo. Of these, the Fine Arts Building housed an exhibit that became the foundation of today's de Young Museum, and the Japanese exhibit remains today as the Japanese Tea Garden.[45]

Included in the Midwinter Expo were exhibits from thirty-six California counties, five states, and thirty-eight foreign countries. The wine industry also had an exhibit, but there is little mention of it in the historical record. Even the major historian of California

This illustration of the building for a United Viticultural Display appears in a handsome souvenir booklet, *California Midwinter International Exposition, San Francisco, California*. (Published in Portland, Maine, by the Leighton & Frey Souvenir View Company, 1894.)

wine between 1830 and 1895, Victor Carosso, wrote nothing about the industry's showing at the 1894 Midwinter Expo. He saw interest in only the fair that had inspired it.[46]

A hard-bound souvenir booklet of the exposition includes a drawing of an elegant "Building for a United Viticultural Display."[47] And yet, interestingly, the building depicted was not in fact the Viticulture Building, the entrance to which was a massive oak barrel. In *The Fantastic Fair,* Arthur Chandler and Marvin Nathan paint an illustrative scene, noting its interior was "designed like a traditional German *Weinstube* with vine-covered rafters, large written inscriptions on the wooden walls of the tasting room, and plaster casts of Bacchus and Mercury." The wine exhibit itself seemed to taunt European winemakers to match California's wines for quality. It included an engraving of a tall and strong though "aged" man (symbolizing Europe), his bowed head "wreathed with a circlet of grape leaves," handing his thyrsus (the staff carried by Bacchus, god of wine) to a young man standing beside a lady wrapped in the American flag. Given that the young man obviously represents California, the message is less than subtle, never mind presumptuous.

In addition, the Viticultural Building's "shelves featured the finest wines from throughout the world, including such California vineyards as Inglenook, Cresta Blanca, and Buena Vista. Indeed, over three dozen local wineries had displays, and several of these vintages won awards."[48]

In the end, de Young and company pulled off a miracle; everyone considered the Midwinter Expo a success. From this experience the leadership would be prepared a mere two decades later to host a much grander international exposition. As fabulous as it was, the 1894 Midwinter Exposition in San Francisco was just a warm-up.

The California Midwinter International Exposition closed on July 8, 1894. In that same year, the *Report of State Viticultural Commissioners* estimated that the wine production of France had jumped to "thirteen hundred million," perhaps double its volume at the start of the decade. As William Heintz puts it: "Through careful management of vineyards and the widespread introduction of resistant rootstock, France's vineyards were rebounding."[49] Although it was tremendous news that a viable solution to phylloxera had been found, that news came with a terrible blow as well. Recall that the vast new export markets created by the European phylloxera had triggered a vast increase in the production of California wine: from ten million gallons in 1880 to eighteen million gallons in 1886. But by 1892, Zinfandel grapes, for example, were selling for ten dollars per ton—less than the cost of picking them. Wine at wholesale fetched a mere ten cents a gallon.[50] And with French wine production now on the rise, the market in Europe for California wine began to close—by which time California's volume was so great that even other potential markets, such as in South America and across the Pacific, could hardly absorb it. The upshot: California wine was demoted back down to "runner-up" or substitute status. (The irony is that it was American rootstock that saved France; so, though French experimentation helped save California from phylloxera, the States also contributed to the closing of this valuable market.)

In a move to keep themselves in the game, in August 1894, the month after the Midwinter Exposition closed, seven of the state's most prominent wine dealers joined to form the California Wine Association (CWA). Each of the seven companies contributed its assets and received shares in the new entity, whose initial capitalization was valued at $3 million. The companies were S. Lachman & Company, the Napa Valley Wine Company, B. Dreyfus & Company, Kohler & Frohling, Kohler & Van Bergen, C. Carpy & Company, and Arpad Haraszthy & Company. All were based in San Francisco.[51]

This joint-effort organization functioned via well-appropriated shared resources that centralized the production, packaging, distribution, and marketing of its members' wines. Production (receiving, storing, then blending) took place in the Kohler & Frohling plant. Packaging (bottling, labeling) and distribution (packing and shipping, plus accounting) took place in the S. Lachman & Company plant. As Thomas Pinney puts it, the

The California Wine Association trademark; from the "California Wine Association, Winehaven" promotional pamphlet, 1909. Courtesy of the Sonoma County Library.

CWA was a "fully integrated enterprise, beginning with the grape and ending at the retail shelf, and this on a scale without precedent." As a centralized entity, the CWA could pool its resources in promoting its products; and, as it happens, this one-stop setup benefitted the dealers as well. Another essential plus was quality control, as well as the reputation earned from providing a consistently reliable product: dealers knew they'd never get stuck with a bad wine. Unfortunately, CWA wines' reputation had a flip side as well: *Never a bad wine, yet never a great wine either.*[52]

All wines produced by the CWA were bottled under the CALWA brand. Its trademark depicts a young Bacchus on the prow of a ship, which is itself emblazoned with the seal of the state of California. The California grizzly bear and, of course, luscious bunches of grapes add to the scene.[53] One promotional piece declared that CALWA-brand California wines were "fine, matured, reliable wines." It's perhaps rather telling that they also distinctly mentioned their capital of "ten million dollars."[54] In other words, the CWA was very much about industry—and not about individual vintages, let alone the individual wine consumer.

As could be expected, the association quickly assumed dominance over the California wine industry. Ruth Teiser and

Frona Eunice Wait on Wine Blends

Frona Eunice Wait's 1889 publication *Wines and Vines of California* shares the following on the art of blending wine:

Cabernet Sauvignon, which is everywhere recognized as infinitely the best grape for claret that grows, may be blended with Cabernet Franc, or Merlot, or some other grape less charactistic for vinosity. Sometimes there are four or five blends before an aggregation of body, tannin, color, bouquet, and aroma is secured. The consumer wants all of these. Without body there would be no exhilaration; the tannin is nutritive and regulating; the commonest claret-drinker as well as the most critical one demands color. This is the most unfortunate item of all, for this same imaginary desideratum often times forces producers to introduce cherry juice, which is expensive, or aniline dyes, which are not expensive but are poisonous, into their clarets to give them that superb color which a good, properly aged red vine should possess. Bouquet is the soul of wine, while an agreeable aroma unfailingly imparts a delicious sensation.

Source: Wait, *Wines and Vines of California*, 104, attributed in part to Ben C. Truman, *New York Times*, March 13, 1887.

Catherine Harroun provide a tidy assessment: "That [the CWA] was able to control the market was perhaps an indication of the need for such an organization, as well as a testimonial to the evenly good quality of its wines. That it was able to operate without running afoul of antitrust laws was undoubtedly an indication of its careful management."[55] Indeed, it was very carefully managed by Percy T. Morgan, who is largely credited with the initial concept of the CWA.

The key to uniformity—that "evenly good quality"—was blending. The critical work of blending and tending to the CWA cellars was in the hands, and nose, of founding member Henry Lachman. Lachman, along with fellow founder Charles Carpy, was considered among the best wine tasters in California.[56]

All seven members of the CWA were wine merchants; a few produced wine as well. This setup proved to be a concern to outsiders, since many in the industry were alarmed at the prospect of contending with such a powerful entity. (Recall that in the July 23, 1889, "Wine Is Too Cheap" *Examiner* series, the contributors had widely blamed the industry's difficulties on the merchants—the middlemen "Frisco dealers.") And so, in an effort to counter the CWA with the clout of their own, power-in-numbers entity, several wine producers—led by Pietro Rossi and Andrea Sbarboro of the Italian Swiss Agricultural Colony—formed the California Wine Makers Corporation (CWMC). The CWMC was managed by John H. Wheeler, formerly secretary of the Board of State Viticultural Commissioners. As historians Peninou and Greenleaf tell us: "The Corporation was composed of growers and winery owners who either did not want to deal directly with the Association or were not invited to do so." This way they didn't have to function at the mercy of the whims of the association.[57]

Though at first the CWA elected not to challenge the CWMC, as years passed they played much less nicely, to the extent that by 1897 they were bona fide enemies clashing in price wars. With repeated instances of slashing its prices, by 1899 the CWA's tactics had vanquished the CWMC. With the dissolution of the CWMC, the California Wine Association, the largest organization the wine world had ever seen, had the field to itself.[58]

The CWA soon sought to expand its power by commanding more aspects of the winemaking process. Soon it was a fully vertical enterprise, controlling the growing of grapes, the making and storage of wine, and its sales and distribution—worldwide. From the beginning the association had a number of prime properties, including the Glen Ellen Vineyards in Sonoma County, the Orleans Hill Vineyards in Yolo County, the Cucamonga Vineyards in San Bernardino County, and Greystone Cellars in the Napa Valley. At the turn of the century, the association welcomed investment from three of the state's principal bankers, including Isaias W. Hellman of the Farmers and Merchants Bank of Los Angeles. This infusion of capital and the subsequent acquisition spree resulted in the CWA controlling the production of more than fifty wineries in the state by 1902, producing in that year thirty million of California's forty-four million gallons of wine. And it had achieved these heights in just eight years.[59] By 1910, a CWA brochure crowed that it "cultivates more vineyard acreage, crushes more grapes annually, operates more wineries, makes more wine, [and] has a greater wine storage capacity than any other wine concern in the world."[60]

Since at the turn of the century the California Wine Association handled approximately 70 percent of the state's wine production, it essentially set the California wine standard—which means its inventory indicates some of the prevailing tastes of the day. Of note is the fact that the association consciously did not claim to offer wines known to be European; instead, it offered California wines, its particular blends thereof, with California names—alongside helpful descriptions of "type." Among the reds sold under the CALWA label were Winehaven, a "matured table Claret," La Loma, a "fine Burgundy type," and Hillcrest, the "finest old Cabernet Claret." These ranged in price from four to eight dollars per case. Among the white wines were Greystone, a "good light hock type," Rockdale, a "Chablis type," Cerrito, a "fine dry Sauterne type," Glenridge, a "fine haut-Sauterne type," and Vine Cliff, the "finest Reisling." They also sold sparkling wines, brandies, and dessert wines like sherry, port, Tokay, Malaga, and Madeira "types." Curiously, missing from this catalog were Zinfandel and Chardonnay.[61]

Even though Clarence Edwords's *Bohemian San Francisco* was published in 1914, the only California wine Edwords mentions is Italian Swiss Colony, and even then only obliquely.[62] The fact that the San Francisco–based entities CALWA and CWMC, even with their extensive moneyed promotion, garnered just one wine mentioned in this entirely relevant book on San Francisco illuminates just how tricky the wine market was at the time.

From Edwords's "hints" in *Bohemian San Francisco* on how to serve wines, it is plain that today's conventional wisdom—red

Bon Vivants and Bohemians on Wines

However fine they were, California wines had not by the turn of the century become the wines of choice for the San Franciscan bon vivant. Consider *Joe Tilden's Recipes for Epicures,* written by the city's most renowned gourmet and bohemian of his day, Major Joe Tilden, and published posthumously in 1907 by an anonymous friend. In a chapter on "Wine Cups and Punches," despite repeated mentions of champagne, Claret, and sherry, not a single California wine is mentioned.

Similarly, in his 1914 *Bohemian San Francisco,* Clarence Edwords wrote a "few hints" for serving wines. The hints are telling in several respects, not the least being the almost total absence of reference to California vintages.

How to Serve Wines

A few hints regarding the proper serving of wines may not be amiss, and we give you here the consensus of opinion of the most noted gourmets who have made a study of the best results from combinations:

- Never drink any hard liquors, such as whisky, brandy, gin, or cocktails, with oysters or clams, as it is liable to upset you for the rest of the evening.

- With the hor d'ouvres [*sic*] serve vermouth, sherry, marsala, or madeira wine.

- With soup and fish serve white wines, such as Rhein wine, Sauterne, or White Burgundy.

- With entrees serve Clarets or other red wines, such as Swiss, Bordeaux, Hungarian, or Italian wines.

- Burgundy may also be served at any of the later courses.

- With roasts serve champagne or any of the sparkling wines.

- With the coffee serve kirsch, French brandy, or fine champagne.

- After coffee serve a liqueur. Never serve more than one glass of any liqueur.

Sources: Joe Tilden, *Joe Tilden's Recipes for Epicures,* 125–31; Edwords, *Bohemian San Francisco,* 127.

wine with red meat, white wine with fish or fowl—is but today's conventional wisdom. His phrasings are also intriguing. For example, he distinguishes between Claret and Bordeaux ("with entrées serve Clarets or *other* red wines, such as...Bordeaux"). But the English, who coined *Claret,* use it as a synonym for Bordeaux.[63] Also, what is the "Burgundy" he says may be served "at any of the later courses"? Does he mean red wine made from

Pinot Noir grapes in the Burgundy region of France? Assuming that is what Edwords meant, why is "Burgundy" not among "the other red wines" that may be served "with entrées"? If on the other hand he meant *white* Burgundy, why didn't he say so, as he had when he wrote of wines that may be served "with soup and fish"?

THE NINETEENTH CENTURY HEADS
INTO THE TWENTIETH, REPRISE

As California entered the twentieth century, the devastating effects of the industry's first major crisis were still being felt. In 1904, deeming that "all efforts to check the devastation of the phylloxera had failed,"[64] the federal Department of Agriculture undertook a program to study the menace. It was headed by German vintner and horticulture professor George C. Husmann, whose father had been a pioneer grape grower in Missouri. The breadth of Husmann's interest and dedication can be seen in the titles of his various publications, including *The Cultivation of the Native Grape, and Manufacture of American Wines* (1866), *American Grape Growing and Winemaking* (1880), and, with Eugene W. Hilgard as part of the University of California Agricultural Experiment Station, *Grafting and Fruiting of Resistant Vines* (1885). Arriving in California in the early 1880s, Husmann applied his extensive viticultural knowledge and experience to the particular needs in Northern California. Perhaps most notably, he had been instrumental in guiding Europe out of its phylloxera era by sending them resistant rootstock from Missouri—the place of origin,

This advertisement, wherein George Husmann offers phylloxera-resistant vines so as to "make your vineyards permanent," appeared in *Pacific Rural Press,* December 29, 1883.

as it happens, of both phylloxera and Husmann. In time, Pacific winegrowers followed his lead, but slowly.[65]

When he delivered his report to the International Congress of Viticulture in 1915, Husmann did not mince words on the molasses pace of progress:

> The waste of money spent in reestablishment of vineyards in California from the first appearance of phylloxera to the present time cannot even be approximately estimated. It is more than likely, however, that at least two hundred and fifty thousand acres of once flourishing vineyards have been destroyed by phylloxera and other agencies during the last decades. The claim is made that there are but few vineyards in California that are more than ten years old at the present time, and we are sorry to say a large percentage of these are not on resistant stock.

And yet he had good news to report as well, proclaimed with no particular modesty: "America in her native grapes has not only given the world new fruits but, because of their resistance to the phylloxera, has through them saved the viticultural industry of the world."[66] Indeed, Thomas Pinney considers George Husmann a "pioneer winegrower . . . one of the most devoted proselytizers in the cause of the grape in the nineteenth century."[67]

This pioneer's work, as well as that of many others, undoubtedly saved the viticulture of California. Once all rootstocks had been newly grafted, phylloxera faded as a concern—well into the twentieth century. But in the 1980s a new infestation renewed alarm when a previously reliable rootstock proved undependable, requiring massive replantings in Napa and Sonoma. In fact, since no "cure" has been found, to this day phylloxera is still a problem to be reckoned with in some regions, and so the grafting continues.[68]

As for the rest of the industry, the dawn of the new century found the California Wine Association, possessor of enormous warehouses and storage facilities in San Francisco, in control of as much as two-thirds of the wine produced in the state. But even the might of the CWA could not avert the industry's second crisis, which hit in 1906.

Notes

1. Sullivan, *Companion to California Wine*, 262; Pinney, *History of Wine in America*, 1:27.
2. Wait, *Wines and Vines of California*, 7.
3. Ordish, *Great Wine Blight*, 1.

4. Hutchison, "Northern California," 39.

5. Ordish, *Great Wine Blight*, 1, 6.

6. Ibid., 6.

7. Sullivan, *Companion to California Wine*, 262.

8. Ordish, *Great Wine Blight*, 5, citing in part J. C. Loudon, *An Encyclopedia of Plants* (London: n.p., 1829).

9. Sullivan, *Companion to California Wine*, 262.

10. Pinney, *History of Wine in America*, 1:344–45, and references cited.

11. Ibid., 1:27–28, 95, n11.

12. Ordish, *Great Wine Blight*, 5.

13. Sullivan, *Companion to California Wine*, 262; Pinney, *History of Wine in America*, 1:343.

14. Wait, *Wines and Vines of California*, 34.

15. Pinney, *History of Wine in America*, 1:343–44, citing in part *Southern California Horticulturist* 2 (November 1878): 16.

16. Hayne, "Phylloxera," 376–77.

17. Peninou and Greenleaf, *Winemaking in California*, vol. 3, *The California Wine Association*, 29.

18. Wine & Spirit Education Trust, *Wine and Spirits*, 2–5.

19. Sullivan, *Companion to California Wine*, 262.

20. Robinson, Harding, and Vouillamoz, *Wine Grapes*, xiv.

21. For more, see ibid., "Vine Breeding," xvi–xvii, and "Pests and Diseases," xvii–xviii.

22. Pinney, *History of Wine in America*, 1:344–45, citing in part California Board of State Viticultural Commissioners, *Annual Report, 1887* (Sacramento, 1888), 88.

23. Heintz, *California's Napa Valley*, 173–74.

24. Pinney, *History of Wine in America*, 1:345.

25. Sullivan, *Companion to California Wine*, 172–73.

26. Kohler, "Wine Production in California, 11.

27. Sullivan, *Companion to California Wine*, 172–73.

28. Pinney, *History of Wine in America*, 1:310–11.

29. Hutchison, "Northern California," 46–47.

30. Teiser and Harroun, *Winemaking in California*, 155–56.

31. Wetmore, "Treatise on Wine Production," 37.

32. Teiser and Harroun, *Winemaking in California*, 156–57.

33. Hutchison, "Northern California," 41.

34. Pinney, *History of Wine in America*, 1:355, n49, wherein he cites Hilgard, "Plain Talk to the Winemen."

35. Hilgard, "Letter of Transmittal," 1–2.

36. Hutchison, "Northern California," 42–43.

37. Wetmore, "Treatise on Wine Production," 35, 36, cited in Pinney, *History of Wine in America*, 1:355–56.

38. Wetmore, "Treatise on Wine Production," 5, 35, 37–38, cited in Pinney, *History of Wine in America*, 1:355.

39. Carosso, *California Wine Industry*, 162.

40. Commissioner François Gos, *San Francisco Call*, October 17, 1893, cited in Carosso, *California Wine Industry*, 164–65.

41. Carosso, *California Wine Industry*, 165, and references cited.

42. Chandler and Nathan, *Fantastic Fair*, 1–7; *Official History*, 30–35.

43. Chandler and Nathan, *Fantastic Fair*, 5–6.

44. Ibid., 6.

45. Federal Writers' Project, *San Francisco,* 338.

46. Carosso, *California Wine Industry,* 165.

47. *"California Midwinter International Exposition,"* souvenir pamphlet of the 1915 San Francisco Exhibition.

48. Chandler and Nathan, *Fantastic Fair,* 26–28.

49. Heintz, *California's Napa Valley,* 174.

50. Adams, *Wines of America,* 172; Peninou and Greenleaf, *Winemaking in California,* vol. 2, *From the Missions to 1894,* 1; Pinney, *History of Wine in America,* 1:356.

51. Teiser and Harroun, *Winemaking in California,* 156–57; Pinney, *History of Wine in America,* 1:356.

52. Pinney, *History of Wine in America,* 1:356; Peninou and Greenleaf, *Winemaking in California,* 3:19. Peninou and Greenleaf note: "The S. Lachman & Company plant was . . . connected by a pipeline laid under the streets with the Kohler and Frohling cellar. The Eagle Wine Vaults of B. Dreyfus & Company handled the dessert wines and brandies; the Kohler and Van Bergen cellar, the surpluses and the wines for the local jobbers. The wines of the Napa Valley Wine Company were transferred to the Kohler and Frohling cellars."

53. Pinney, *History of Wine in America,* 1:356.

54. www.collectorsweekly.com/articles/california-wine. The promotional piece is the seventh image on the webpage. Its caption reads: "The C.W.A.'s logo featured Bacchus, the god of wine, sailing with a grizzly bear like the one on California's state flag."

55. Teiser and Harroun, *Winemaking in California,* 155. Some authorities give the date as 1892; the correct date is 1894.

56. Pinney, *History of Wine in America,* 1:356; Peninou and Greenleaf, *Winemaking in California,* 3:19.

57. Teiser and Harroun, *Winemaking in California,* 156–57; Pinney, *History of Wine in America,* 1:356, 358–59; Peninou and Greenleaf, *Winemaking in California,* 3:19–20. Generally, see also Peninou and Greenleaf, *Winemaking in California,* 3:1–29.

58. Teiser and Harroun, *Winemaking in California,* 156–57; Pinney, *History of Wine in America,* 1:358–59; Peninou and Greenleaf, *Winemaking in California,* 3:19–20.

59. Teiser and Harroun, *Winemaking in California,* 157–58; Pinney, *History of Wine in America,* 1:356.

60. "The California Wine Association," company brochure (San Francisco circa 1910) (Huntington Library), cited in Pinney, *History of Wine in America,* 1:493n54.

61. Pinney, *History of Wine in America,* 1:360.

62. Ibid. On page 128 Edwords writes: "Italian wines are mostly red, the most noted in California being Chianti, and its California prototype, Tipo Chianti, made by the Asti Colony."

63. Schoonmaker and Bespaloff, *New Frank Schoonmaker Encyclopedia of Wine,* 147.

64. Husmann, "Resistant Vines," 49.

65. Hutchison, "Northern California," 41; Pinney, *History of Wine in America,* 1:346.

66. Husmann, "Resistant Vines," 46, 47.

67. Pinney, *History of Wine in America,* 1:181.

68. Sullivan, *Companion to California Wine,* 263.

CHAPTER 6

The San Francisco Earthquake and Fire

1906

> The streets were humped into ridges and depressions, and
> piled with the debris of fallen walls. The steel rails were
> twisted into perpendicular and horizontal angles. The
> telephone and telegraph systems were disrupted. And the
> great water-mains had burst. All the shrewd contrivances
> and safeguards of man had been thrown out of gear by
> thirty seconds' twitching of the earth-crust.
> Not in history has a modern imperial city been so
> completely destroyed. San Francisco is gone.
>
> —Jack London, *Collier's*, May 5, 1906

WINE HISTORIAN Charles L. Sullivan writes: "California is earthquake country; California is wine country. The inevitable outcome of these two situations has been a series of vinous mishaps and one disaster." As for the vinous mishaps: the Fort Tejon earthquake in 1857 "smashed barrels and sent bottles flying" along the San Andreas Fault in central California. In 1868, the Hayward Fault earthquake completely wrecked the winery of French vintner Clement Colombet, approximately forty-five miles from San Francisco.[1]

But on April 18, 1906, the earth quaked in a slippage along the longest fault line of two of the world's most vast tectonic plates, the North American and the Pacific. The two plates had strained for years to move in opposite directions, the Pacific to the north and the North American to the south, but had been locked like two grappling wrestlers unable to budge the other—until at once the grip was lost, convulsing the city of San Francisco in one of the most violent earthquakes in recorded history. Had there been a Richter scale then, the quake would have measured about 8.3 according to modern estimates. (Note that the Richter scale is logarithmic. An 8.3 earthquake releases roughly seventy-five times the energy of a 6.9 tremor, which was the strength of the 1989 San Francisco quake. The Japanese earthquake of 2011 was an unthinkable 9.1.) In Olema, just north of San Francisco, the earth west of the San Andreas Fault jerked twenty feet to the north of the land to the east.[2] (While Olema was long thought to have been the epicenter of the 1906 quake, today that spot is considered to be in the Pacific Ocean, about two miles west of the city.[3])

Alexander McAdie, head of the San Francisco office of the U.S. Weather Bureau, meticulously recorded the details of the 1906 earthquake and aftershocks. The first shock wave, he reported, lasted "approximately forty-five seconds." It also stopped the clock of the Ferry Building. When the pitching and shuddering subsided, fires broke out as ruptured gas mains ignited. Additional ruptures in the water mains rendered the city's firefighters mostly helpless to stop the fires—which raged for four days. The last of the fires was extinguished on Saturday, April 22, at the corner of Francisco and Montgomery Streets, near North Point.[4] Combined, the earthquake and fires destroyed virtually all of San Francisco. As contemporary writers Charles E. Banks and Opie Read put it: "The earthquake, with its gigantic undulations that cause an indescribable sickness, passed, and fear was giving place to returning hope when the whole city seemed to burst into flames. . . . What the quake had spared the flames devoured."[5] The earthquakes in 1857 and 1865 had rattled the California wine industry, but the 1906 earthquake and fire brought it to its knees.

"VIBRATION AND FIRE JOINED TO WORK THIS AWFUL DESTRUCTION"

At nearly a quarter past five on the morning of April 18, *San Francisco Examiner* reporter Fred. J. Hewitt was at the intersection of Larkin Street and Golden Gate Avenue when the first shock wave passed beneath him.

> It is impossible to judge the length of that shock. To me it seemed an eternity. I was thrown prone on my back and the pavement pulsated like a living thing. Around me the huge buildings, looming up were terrible because of the queer dance they were performing, wobbled and veered. Crash followed crash resounded on all sides. Screeches rent the air as terrified humanity streamed out into the open in agony of despair. Affrighted horses dashed headlong into ruins as they raced away in their abject fear. . . .
>
> The first portion of that shock was just a mild forerunning of

This souvenir postcard fuses two extraordinary details of the April 18, 1906, earthquake in San Francisco. First, the city's three daily newspapers jointly published a single issue that day, using *The Call-Chronicle-Examiner* as its masthead. And second, behind the "torn" front page stands what remained of the recently completed City Hall. Postcard printed in Switzerland for Victor W. Bauer of San Francisco.

what was to follow. The pause in the action of the earth's surface couldn't have been more than a fraction of a second [it was actually ten or twelve] . . . then came the second and most terrific crash.

The street beds heaved in frightful fashion. The earth rocked and then came the blow that wrecked San Francisco from the bay shore to the Ocean Beach and from the Golden Gate to the end of the peninsula. . . .

[After wind dispersed obscuring dust clouds,] the dome [of City Hall] appeared like a huge birdcage against the morning dawn. The upper works of the entire building [lay] . . . in the street below.[6]

The phrasing "the dome appeared like a huge birdcage" beautifully captures the wreck that remained of City Hall. Simon Winchester tells us that the building, only recently completed, "had taken twenty-six years to build, had cost $6 million, and was by far the biggest and grandest structure west of the Mississippi." And yet, the splendor lay in ruins, its "shoddy construction"—the product of "graft, corruption, swagger, and show"—"dramatically revealed by its spectacular collapse."[7]

The destruction wrought in those two convulsing minutes was

|

mirrored in its people. Hewitt wrote of an "excited-crazed populace...herds of huddled creatures...each and every person I saw was temporarily insane. Laughing idiots commented on the fun they were having. Terror marked other faces. Strong men bellowed like babies in their furor. No one knew which way to turn, when on all sides destruction stared them in the very eye. A number of slight tremors followed the first series of shocks. As each came in turn fearful agony spread...on every brow."[8] To this, from nearby at City Hall, police officer Edward J. Plume adds: "Then the quaking stopped, and we could hear screams in all directions."[9]

Hewitt was right about there being a number of tremors following the main quake, but they were hardly "slight." Alexander McAdie reported twenty-seven earthquakes. The first aftershock hit just two minutes after the initial two-part quake. By the end of the tyranny of terror, the seismograph at the University of California recorded 120 separate shocks.[10]

In their book *Denial of Disaster*, Gladys Hansen and Emmett Condon write:

> Everyone searched for a simile to describe the shaking. [Reporter James] Hopper said, "It pounced on the earth like a bulldog." Others felt the city was in the grip of a giant fist or like a rat shaken by a terrier. A musician sensed the violence of the sound more than anything else, "like a thousand violins playing off key." The Metropolitan Opera's Alfred Hertz contemplated professionally on the way the disaster was scored. "Something comparable to the mezzo forte roll on a cymbal or gong." It was left to Mr. Hopper's imagination to describe how human silence was the true measure of the terror.[11]

Scientists of the day used the simply descriptive Rossi-Forel scale, which rated earthquakes from one to ten, ten meaning simply "complete destruction." The Weather Bureau classified the 1906 San Francisco earthquake as a Rossi-Forel No. 9, described by the bureau's Alexander McAdie as "an earthquake which throws down badly built buildings and will give in the streets of the city a large amount of debris. It is about as severe an earthquake as can be experienced without total destruction, without great yawning chasms and complete destruction of life and property. The effect is more pronounced upon filled-in ground, loose soil, made land, and alluvial soil than upon rock formation."[12]

The earthquake wrought a devastation that even today is hard to apprehend. As McAdie describes above, filled or "made" land fares worst in earthquakes; the shock of the passing seismic waves causes a phenomenon known as liquefaction—the ground literally liquefies. At the site of the Valencia Street Hotel, a four-story wood-frame building with a brick foundation, the filled-in ground beneath became quicksand—at which point the hotel sank three stories, collapsing into itself, leaving but one crumpled story above ground level. Most of the victims trapped in the lower three floors of the hotel no doubt drowned.

Wooden structures can withstand, if creakily, an earthquake's shocks, but fireproof brick buildings often cannot. In some parts of the city, virtually all of the brick structures collapsed.

Later collected accounts suggest that the grand Palace Hotel, for thirty years the largest hotel in the world, experienced some of the quake's worst pitching and shaking. Cora Older described the "sensation of the earthquake as resembling the roaring of a monstrous train." She recalled: "The Palace Hotel turned on its axis; the building twisted and moaned. The sound of the earth grew more ominous, then in the living room of our suite a crash as if the walls had collapsed. I found myself out of bed kneeling in the passageway between the bedroom and the living room." Famous tenor Enrico Caruso, staying in the hotel as well, reported how "everything in the room was going round and round. The chandelier was trying to touch the ceiling, and the chairs were all chasing each other. *Crash—crash—crash!* It was a terrible scene. Everywhere the walls were falling and clouds of yellow dust were rising. The earth was still quaking. My God! I thought it would never stop."[13]

THOUGH THE EARTHQUAKE did wreak a terrible destruction on San Francisco, that destruction was not nearly so terrible as what was done by the ensuing fires, which became known collectively as the Great Fire. Writer Jack London noted: "Within an hour after the earthquake shock the smoke of San Francisco's burning was a lurid tower visible a hundred miles away. And for three days and nights this lurid tower swayed in the sky, reddening the sun, darkening the day, and filling the land with smoke." (London, who had felt the earthquake at his ranch in Glen Ellen, fifty miles away, headed straight to San Francisco to record the event.)[14]

The havoc wreaked was compounded by two factors noted earlier. One, the earthquake and its initial aftershocks created breakages of the major water mains, one thirty inches and another forty inches in diameter—thus destroying two of the key sources of water needed to fight the fires. A later municipal report for the city states: "Several of the fires thus caused could not be subdued in their early stages, and soon passed beyond the means of control. Had not the water supply been destroyed, it is probable that no serious loss by fire would have resulted. As it was, the City's Fire Department was rendered practically useless."[15] Jack London witnessed this throughout the beleaguered city: "Time and again successful stands were made by the fire-fighters, and every time the flames flanked around on either side or came up from the rear, and turned to defeat the hard-won victory."[16]

Compounding the disaster, in short order the entire commercial telephone system was left abandoned, its terrified telephone operators unwilling to return to their switchboards. (This is not surprising given that there were so many aftershocks; one could easily imagine just one more small tremor finally toppling the remaining buildings.) The earthquake had wrecked underground telephone and telegraph works, knocked down telephone poles, and tossed overheads to the ground. Banks and Read describe how "the electric wires, torn from their fastenings, had the loose ends flung high in the air to fall in a tangle, like lightning falling out of the sky." For the time, San Francisco's only means of communication was a military telephone circuit, two unreliable telegraph lines to Oakland, and the trans-Pacific cable to Manila, in the Philippines.[17] Word was sent out, however, and before long outside military and civilian assistance arrived to join the relief effort.

Though the conflagration triggered by the earthquake is often referred to as the Great Fire of 1906, in truth it was fifty-two fires, and it was unlike anything the world had ever seen.[18] In addition to the fire itself, its rising heat then created its own wind, a firestorm not unlike that which in the latter days of World War II would engulf Dresden following bombing by British and American air forces. John B. McGloin describes the city ablaze that night as the sixth circle of Dante Alighieri's *Inferno*. Witnesses to this inferno were the remaining, homeless citizens of San Francisco—those who could not afford to pay the princely charges for boat passage across the Bay—who could only helplessly gather on hilltops to watch their city burn.[19]

In all, the fire consumed 514 city blocks, or nearly five square miles of San Francisco's total of seven square miles—thus, about 70 percent of the city. One report listed that 28,188 buildings burned, with the assessed loss of structures costing $52,504,000.

Insurance experts greatly revise that amount, reckoning the total loss as being between $350 and $400 million—four-fifths the property value of San Francisco.[20] Of San Francisco's population of about 410,000, between 200,000 and 250,000 people were left homeless.[21]

What of loss of life? In 1978 John McGloin wrote that the "most accurate figures" were 667 dead, plus 352 "listed simply as missing," attributing the figures to Gladys Hansen, then the archivist of the City and County of San Francisco. Some years later, Hansen and Emmet Condon, a former fire chief of San Francisco, published *Denial of Disaster*—released, as it happens, just days after the earthquake of 1989. Hansen's extensive research established two significant findings: that the loss of life was much greater than those earlier "most accurate figures," and that the death count was deliberately falsified. Going by a revised concept of what constitutes a casualty—not just injury or death resulting directly from the earthquake and fire, but also indirect or collateral casualty—Hansen's project determined that three thousand men, women, and children had lost their lives on account of the 1906 earthquake and fire.[22] (Today the Library of Congress cites the same figure.[23])

FROM THE CELLAR TO THE BOTTLE, LITTLE WAS SPARED

The wine industry was hardly spared the cataclysmic destruction the earthquake wrought, which sprawled from Santa Clara County northward through Sonoma County. In the south, the industry suffered its most severe loss with the destruction of the Gallegos Winery near Mission San Jose, in the Irvington District of what is now the city of Fremont. (This is also where Colombet's winery was hit in the 1868 earthquake.) The vineyards of the Gallegos firm, once part of the lands now referred to as "ex–Mission San Jose," were sold in 1881 to Juan Gallegos, a Costa Rican who formed the Palmdale Company and built the Gallegos Winery. In 1893 the firm boasted six hundred acres in vineyards, annually produced 2,400 tons of grapes, and held 1,250,000 gallons of wine in cooperage. In 1905 Henry Lachman, the famed "nose" of the California Wine Association, purchased the estate and winery—only to lose it to the 1906 earthquake, along with nearly two million gallons of wine.[24]

In San Francisco, though, the loss of wine in the 1906 earthquake and fire—never mind damage to wineries, cooperage, and equipment, which was a "chaos of hoops and debris"—was im-

Why Not Oakland Too?

Bret Harte was once asked why Oakland was always spared the destruction that earthquakes wreaked on San Francisco. Citing as his authority "Schwapplefurt, the celebrated German geologist," Harte responded that there are some things the earth simply cannot swallow.

Source: Federal Writers' Project, *San Francisco*, 56–57.

mense. The California Wine Association alone lost eight million gallons of wine. As for the state's industry as a whole, records indicate that about fifteen million gallons had been lost, though some think the figure twice that.[25] Nearly a century later, wine historian William Heintz researched a more complete tally, one that also includes the wine kept in public establishments, such as hotels, restaurants, and saloons, as well as that of home winemakers and the well-stocked wine cellars of the elite. He concludes that the total was more on the order of fifty million gallons lost in San Francisco—two-thirds of the wine in California.[26]

Given that San Francisco was the center of the state's wine industry, it's not surprising that the disaster resulted in such heavy industry losses. First, consider the climatic conditions of Northern California: wine needs to be stored in consistently cool facilities, which are not plentiful throughout the region. In Sonoma, Napa, and San Joaquin Valleys, summer daytime temperatures often exceed one hundred degrees Fahrenheit—which essentially roasts wine. Whatever caves exist in a region can be used

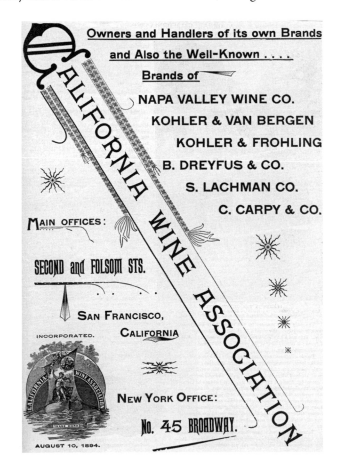

This California Wine Association advertisement appeared in *Pacific Wine & Spirit Review* in the late 1890s. The ad notes that the California Wine Association are the "owners and handlers of its own brands and also the well-known brands of Napa Valley Wine Co., Kohler & Van Bergen, Kohler & Frohling, B. Dreyfus & Co., S. Lachman Co., C. Carpy & Co." Courtesy of the San Francisco History Center, San Francisco Public Library.

for storage, but their capacity is limited. And though the first mechanical air conditioner functioned as of 1902, it was just one, and it was in Buffalo, New York.[27] But San Francisco, where summer high temperatures rarely exceed seventy degrees, has the perfect climate for wine storage. Second, San Francisco is an optimal hub of transit, as it has the Bay's principal port, plus access to the railheads of the transcontinental railroads. And so most large winery owners stored wine in San Francisco—as did the many unaffiliated wine warehouses, which held the new vintages of numerous small wineries so that they wouldn't spoil in the summertime heat. These vast wine-warehouse complexes held millions of gallons of wine.[28]

Swift thinking, swift feet, and swift sailing—plus teamwork and ingenuity—salvaged two million of the CWA's ten million gallons of wine. This was made possible by the fact that the lowest floor of its cellars at Third and Bryant Streets had solid concrete walls and floors. Though wine spilled out from bursting and burning wooden casks, the room itself served as a vast impervious vat. The swift thinking can be credited to Louis Wetmore (son of Charles Wetmore), who managed the association's George West & Son winery in Stockton. Wetmore chartered three river steamers and several grain barges from outside San Francisco and dispatched them to the Third Street wharf. Then men from the El Pinal Winery in Stockton laid a line of pipe from the wharf along Third Street, circuitously avoiding the fire, to the association's cellars at Third and Townsend Streets. Wetmore then somehow cajoled San Francisco firefighters into assisting in the operation. Using fire-engine pumps, they pumped the cellars' wine into the pipeline—and into the holds of the grain barges.[29]

But to salvage the *quality* of this wine, one had to address the fact that it tasted smoky, mixed as it was with bits of charred wood. It was not potable as a table wine, and so the only option was to make it into brandy. That task was assigned to CWA employee Charles Ash, who with some experimentation came through in spades. He recalled: "I was told not to return until I could produce brandy good enough for fortification. I was lucky. I observed that, when wine was made alkaline and then distilled, the smoky taste in the resulting distillate was accentuated. When made acid, the reverse took place."[30] And so he tinkered until he found the right balance—and was allowed to return with his prize.

It's rather remarkable that Ash succeeded, especially given the tremendous journey that had taken place. Two million

Where Did Those Millions of Gallons of Wine Go?

We know San Francisco lost a tearfully prodigious thirty million gallons of wine—but where did it go? As William Heintz points out, according to the series of eyewitness accounts published in 1926 in the *San Francisco Argonaut*, "there is not one mention of red wine flowing ankle deep in the gutters."

So where did the wine go? Ruth Teiser and Catherine Harroun suspect that some was likely "thrown on flames to quench them," and "a certain amount was undoubtedly gulped down in the terror of the moment. But most of the City's wine simply sank into the ground beneath the buildings where it was quietly aging, making San Francisco soil surely the winiest in the world, unequalled even by that of Pompeii."

Sources: Heintz, *California's Napa Valley*, 215; Teiser and Harroun, *Winemaking in California*, 166.

gallons of wine had flowed in cascading cataracts from its bursting casks through seams and drains in upper floors into the massive cement lower floor of the California Wine Association's Bryant Street warehouse. A few days later, it was then pumped out and piped along several streets to waiting grain barges at the Third Street wharf, where it was unceremoniously poured into the holds of the barges to be ported upstream. There it was pumped out again and this time poured into tank cars, in which the wine journeyed by rail to wineries, principally the West winery in Stockton. There it was pumped out again into holding tanks, where it endured laboratory experimentation before finally being alchemized into something drinkable. The final chemistry was to treat this beleaguered wayfarer with sulfuric acid and potassium permanganate, then to distill it into a solid fortifying brandy. As the initiator of this protracted rescue mission, Louis Wetmore became a wine-industry hero.[31]

As for the means by which this cellar's wine was spared, one might wonder why the firefighters, rather than pumping the wine to safety, didn't demand to use it to thwart the fires. William Heintz suggests that the "largely untrained" firefighters likely thought to do so would have only fed the flames. As it happens, experienced vintners and their ilk actually used wine—which has an alcohol content of just 10 to 12 percent—to put out their own occasional fires; indeed, a decade previous a large fire at the Korbel winery had been quenched in precisely this manner.[32]

Just as firefighters helped save CWA wine, men in uniform helped save whiskey too. Indeed, author Philip Fradkin notes (wryly) that the whiskey was saved in part because it "piqued the interest of the military."

One of the methods used to curb the progress of the Great Fire was to remove or destroy flammable items in the fire's path. This could be as simple as tearing down curtains in windows or clearing away wooden fences. But it also often involved dynamiting buildings that would otherwise have simply spread the fire—especially buildings near structures deemed too important to lose. One scenario concerned the Appraiser's Building—known as the U.S. Customs House—located at Sansome, Washington, and Jackson Streets. This building happened to be adjacent to the warehouse of A. P. Hotaling and Company, the city's largest distiller and liquor wholesaler. At first the plan was to save the Customs House by blowing up Hotaling's, but that proposal was deterred by pleas regarding the likely consequential "immediate combustion of all this vast amount of highly inflammable spirit, which would flow. . . in a liquid wave of flame." (The alcohol content of whiskey is close to 60 percent.) Various small fires that sprang up were kept at bay via diligent attention, but given the vagaries of the wind, an all-consuming fire was never far away. They needed to move the "highly flammable spirit"—and so men were hired to roll barrel after barrel of Old Kirk whiskey to safety. A. P. Hoteling's manager, Edward M. Lind, noted that these hires, paid one dollar an hour, were supplied with "ale and stout 'for their sustenance. In this way [the] force was maintained intact and enthusiastic.'"[33]

Accounts vary as to just how Hoteling and its neighboring structures were saved. We do know that credit goes in large part to Navy Lieutenant Frederick Newton Freeman. It was mentioned above that fireboats and engines at the waterfront—and in some cases, "civilian" tugboats—were used to pump seawater directly into firehoses. Freeman and the men in his command were instrumental in saving several structures thanks to the fire tug *Leslie* moored at Meiggs' Wharf. Some claim that the fire threatening the buildings at Sansome and Jackson Streets was stopped thanks to a mile-long firehose slung from *Leslie* over the brow of Telegraph Hill down into what is now called Jackson Square. But Freeman's own report of the day's events tells us that, "owing to the dilapidated condition of the hose. . ., [and] owing to the great pressure carried for two days, numerous lengths became porous and a large stream could not be carried." Another plan was conceived to run hose from the tug *Active* at the Jackson Street Wharf, but their connectors were the wrong size.[34]

In *The Great Earthquake and Firestorms of 1906: How San Francisco Nearly Destroyed Itself*, Philip L. Fradkin offers a very different, much less savory whiskey-saving scenario. He relates how, with the help of two wine pumps, Hotaling employees pumped up from a nearby construction site a combination of sewage and seawater that, delivered by bucket brigade, was then used to coat the "roasting woodwork" of the barrels of whiskey still in the warehouse, effectively saving them from the fire.[35]

From May 1926 to August 1927, the weekly newspaper the *Argonaut* ran a sixty-nine-part series featuring eyewitness reports of the disaster. The narrator of that series credits Hotaling manager Edward Lind with saving the only stock of whiskey in the city, noting: "Thus it happened that while millions of dollars' worth of normally non-inflammable material was reduced to ashes, some three thousand barrels of highly inflammable whiskey were preserved intact in the very heart of the tremendous holocaust."[36]

After the fact, playwright and author Charles Kellogg Field penned the following:

> If, as they say, God spanked the town
> > For being over-friskey—
> Why did He burn all the churches down
> > And spare Hotaling's Whisky?[37]

While Freeman's report doesn't convey just how their work was effected, he did proclaim: "In summing up the work done by the Mare Island fire tugs I particularly lay claim to the work done in saving... that section of the city: ... the North by Jackson Street, including the Appraisers' building, the Hotaling and Company, the Bank of Italy, which is far from the water front; and the saving of the large storehouses in the lee of Telegraph Hill, including... the Italian-Swiss Colony Warehouses, etc.; and the stopping of the fire abreast Lombard Street wharf."[38] Indeed, Freeman and others were responsible for saving the precious stock of the Italian Swiss Colony.[39]

But the tremendous loss of wine wasn't the only setback the disaster wreaked upon the industry. Given that the rupture of the earthquake was nearly three hundred miles long—from Monterey County in the south to Mendocino in the north—its effect was extensive. Wine operations in both Napa and Sonoma sustained significant damage, in some parts complete destruction. Postquake fires erupted in Sonoma as well. The Brun and Chaix cellars in Napa Valley's Oakville lost 100,000 gallons of wine.[40] And the earthquake wrought nearly total destruction on the venerable Buena Vista Winery.[41]

An additional, less-immediate indignity suffered by the industry was, of all things, the loss of its stores of sulfur, which is normally dusted on grapevines in autumn so as to inhibit powdery mildew. The lack of preventative treatment in the fall of 1906 resulted in a widespread spoilage of grapes from the bacterium that causes what the French call Tourne disease. According to the CWA's great charred-wine saver, Charles Ash, the *tourne* caused a gas in the 1906 vintage that could lead to bottles exploding under the pressure, even for years afterward.[42]

Scholar Thomas Pinney deems that the greatest setback to the industry resulted from the loss borne by the California Wine

Association's cellars, and not just for the loss of drinkable wine itself. With the goal of crafting exquisite wine, the CWA had been incubating select vintages so as to demonstrate, in time, what particular care and attention could produce. Hiram S. Dewey, president of the American Wine Growers' Association, pronounced the following as part of the International Congress of Viticulture in 1915:

> Many of you remember how your former president, Mr. Percy T. Morgan, spent years in selecting choice wines and had them given the most careful and watchful care, then had them bottled and stored away in one of your cellars . . . in San Francisco, to age in the bottle, when your dreadful fire destroyed all of his years of labor. That was one of the greatest calamities that ever visited the California wine business. . . .
>
> It was our privilege only a month ago . . . to drink some white and red wines which Mr. Morgan had bottled before the fire, and I want to state that they would grace the table of any gentleman. Make such wines and then ask a price to justify the expense and you will have a great market.[43]

Though the devastating effects of the disaster of 1906 lingered for years after, the day came when Dewey's words proved to be prophetic—but not before a great deal more time, money, and effort had been expended in the pursuit of viticultural excellence. That which managed to rebound from the disaster did so on account of luck, brilliance, and the exertion of many. In the meantime, amid catastrophic loss and ruin, the CWA, the California wine industry, and San Francisco itself began the long process of rebuilding.

Notes

1. Sullivan, *Companion to California Wine*, 97.

2. Hansen and Condon, *Denial of Disaster*, 13–14.

3. "The Northern California Earthquake, April 18, 1906," U.S. Geological Survey, U.S. Department of the Interior, page last modified April 7, 2016, https://earthquake.usgs.gov/regional/nca/virtualtour/earthquake.php.

4. Hansen and Condon, *Denial of Disaster*, 13–14; McGloin, *San Francisco*, 133–40.

5. Banks and Read, *History of the San Francisco Disaster*, 28. The subhead following this note derives from this source as well; Banks and Read write how "the two greatest forces known to man, vibration and fire, were joined and let loose to work this awful destruction."

6. Fred. J. Hewitt, "Wreck of City's Buildings Awful," *San Francisco Examiner*, April 20, 1906, http://www.sfmuseum.net/1906/ew4.html.

7. Winchester, *Crack in the Edge of the World*, 281.

8. *San Francisco Examiner,* April 20, 1906, http://www.sfmuseum.net/1906/ew4.html; see also Winchester, *Crack in the Edge of the World,* 20.

9. As quoted in Hansen and Condon, *Denial of Disaster,* 16, from the account of Officer Plume in the San Francisco Archives, San Francisco Public Library.

10. McGloin, *San Francisco,* 136.

11. Hansen and Condon, *Denial of Disaster,* 36.

12. McGloin, *San Francisco,* 132–36; Hansen and Condon, *Denial of Disaster,* 14.

13. Older, *San Francisco,* qtd. in Hansen and Condon, *Denial of Disaster,* 27.

14. London, "Story of an Eyewitness."

15. *San Francisco Municipal,* 702–3, https://archive.org/stream/sanfranciscomuni56sanfrich#page/702/mode/2up.

16. London, "Story of an Eyewitness."

17. Hansen and Condon, *Denial of Disaster,* 47.

18. McGloin, *San Francisco,* 137–38, citing in part *San Francisco Municipal Reports,* 702–3.

19. Ibid., 139.

20. Ibid., 140–41; *San Francisco Municipal Reports,* 703.

21. Fradkin, *Great Earthquake,* 179, citing U.S. War Department, "Earthquake in California," 107, 114, 129; O'Connor, *San Francisco Relief Survey,* 69.

22. Hansen and Condon, *Denial of Disaster,* 153. Hansen's guidelines included psychological trauma such as suicides and severe depression; long-term illnesses resulting from unsanitary conditions caused by the earthquake; and injury or death related to the enforcement of laws by members of the military or civilian law enforcement agencies, or death by homicide.

23. Finefield, "San Francisco," https://blogs.loc.gov/picturethis/2012/04/san-francisco-before-and-after-the-1906-earthquake-and-fire/. This webpage offers photographs and video footage of the disaster, as well as a slideshow of "San Francisco's growth and transformation from 1851 to 1922."

24. Sullivan, *Companion to California Wine,* 97–98; Singleton, "Lost Wineries and Vineyards."

25. Peninou and Unzelman, *California Wine Association,* 97; Teiser and Harroun, *Winemaking in California,* 166.

26. Heintz, *California's Napa Valley,* 213–15.

27. Gajanan, "Who Invented Air Conditioning?"

28. Heintz, *California's Napa Valley,* 214–15.

29. Peninou and Unzelman, *California Wine Association,* 97–98; Teiser and Harroun, *Winemaking in California,* 166–67. The following webpage offers four photographs of this ingenious wine-saving operation: http://cf.collectorsweekly.com/uploads/2015/12/11083317/CWA1906Pumping-Wine4.jpg; see also Marks, "Forgotten Kingpins."

30. Teiser and Harroun, *Winemaking in California,* 167.

31. Peninou and Unzelman, *California Wine Association,* 97–100; Teiser and Harroun, *Winemaking in California,* 166–67.

32. Heintz, *California's Napa Valley,* 215.

33. Fradkin, *Great Earthquake,* 169–70.

34. Report by Lieutenant Frederick Newton Freeman (commanding USTBD *Perry* at Mare Island) concerning the U.S. Navy's efforts to save the San Francisco waterfront in the aftermath of the earthquake. National Archives and Records Administration, Pacific Region, San Bruno, California. See also http://www.sfmuseum.org/1906/usn.html.

35. Fradkin, *Great Earthquake,* 171.

36. Ibid., 168.

37. Muscatine, *Old San Francisco,* 225.

38. Report by Lieutenant Frederick Newton Freeman.

39. Teiser and Harroun, *Winemaking in California,* 167.

40. Heintz, *California's Napa Valley,* 216–17.

41. Thompson and Johnson, *California Wine Book,* 84.

42. Teiser and Harroun, *Winemaking in California,* 167.

43. Pinney, *History of Wine in America,* 1:360, citing Hiram S. Dewey, "Intelligent Blending of Wines," 302. Note that this is the same conference at which George Husmann lamented the industry's loss to phylloxera.

CHAPTER 7

A City Rebuilt, a "War-Ending" War, and an Underattended World's Fair

1906–1915

> Our California wine producers, without any attempt
> at imitation, have tried to approach the general good
> qualities of. . . European types of wine by careful handling
> and the planting of the most renowned varieties of
> grapes; and it will remain for you to determine how
> near our wine growers have approached the general
> type claimed or how far they may be away from it.
>
> —ARPAD HARASZTHY,
> "Instructions for the Jury of Awards, Midwinter Fair," 1894

WHEN THE DUST from the earthquake had settled, and the last embers of the four days of fires had cooled, San Francisco put its shoulders, some forty thousand of them, to the work of rebuilding itself.

REBUILDING—UP FROM THE ASHES

As we saw in the previous chapter, prevailing through desperate times requires resolve and leadership. Those two million gallons of California Wine Association vintage wouldn't have been saved if Louis Wetmore hadn't had the inspiration and gumption to salvage the smoky liquid contents of the CWA Bryant Street basement-turned-wine vat. Nor would the West Coast's largest supply of whiskey have been saved if it weren't for the dedication and ingenuity of Edward M. Lind and Navy Lieutenant Frederick Newton Freeman. In times of crisis, a bewildered populace can be simultaneously soothed and braced by visionary, galvanizing leadership. Or, it can receive notices like the following, which was presented to stunned San Franciscans on the morning of April 18, 1906, just hours after the earthquake had struck:

The Federal Troops, the members of the regular police force, and all special police officers have been authorized to KILL any and all persons found engaged in looting or in the commission of any other crime. I have directed all the gas and electric lighting companies not to turn on gas or electricity until I order them to do so; you may therefore expect the city to remain in darkness for an indefinite time. I request all citizens to remain at home from darkness until daylight of every night until order is restored. I warn all citizens of the danger from fire from damaged or destroyed chimneys, broken or leaking gas pipes or fixtures, or any other like cause.

—E. E. SCHMITZ, Mayor[1]

It should be no surprise to learn that the mayor's proclamation, ostensibly made only with a desire to prevent yet more destruction, was vigorously enforced. Author Philip Fradkin notes that "innocent people were shot or dealt with summarily for minor offenses." Add to that policy the prominent presence of the U.S. Army under General Frederick Funston, called in to help maintain order among the remaining beleaguered residents. Though martial law was never declared in San Francisco, the populace was certainly under the impression that it had been.[2] But it was assistance and comfort that the people needed, not stern threats, especially given the breadth of the destruction that had befallen the city. As we shall soon see, it wasn't the needs of San Franciscans that the mayor was particularly concerned about.

Though Mayor Schmitz took charge from the start, he had to find a new spot from which to do so, since City Hall, though virtually new, had all but collapsed in the earthquake, its records consumed by fire. So Schmitz set up his mayor's office in the majestic Hall of Justice. When flames advanced on the hall just a few hours later, the mayor retreated to the Fairmont Hotel. That too was soon overtaken by fire, and so the mayor's office repaired to Franklin Hall. He would move yet again a few weeks later to the Whitcomb Hotel on Market Street.

Schmitz appointed a "Committee of Fifty" to assist in rescue and rebuilding, and asked former mayor and political opponent James D. Phelan to head it. (That Phelan accepted demonstrates just how different politics was then.) And though these leaders kept their eye on the view ahead—regrouping and rebuilding—relief was the first order of business. At least half of the city's four hundred thousand–plus residents were homeless, most of them almost overnight. For a while thereafter, the only homes to be found were in the temporary villages quickly constructed in the city's parks.

Once immediate relief was provided, the next job was to rebound anew—beginning with cleanup. In the months to come, San Francisco would clear tons of debris and haul away masses of twisted steel. Some ruins were laid to waste; others were pillaged for reusable bricks and wood. Just these initial efforts cost an estimated $20 million.[3]

San Francisco Politics and the Burnham Plan

On June 15, 1906, not two months after the earthquake, Mayor Schmitz issued a statement in which he exhorted San Franciscans to pull together:

> Let us therfore [*sic*] put aside all partisan feeling, all feeling of antagonism from whatever cause, and let us determine to lend what aid we can toward the rebuilding of the greater San Francisco, a city second to none and equal to any in the world. We can do this because, in the trying times of the past few months, the courage, perseverance, and determination of the people have been proven beyond a doubt; with that courage, perseverance, and determination properly directed, we cannot fail, but we must and will see the rebuilding of San Francisco greater, grander and more beautiful than ever—a city that will stand for generations to come as a standard for others to follow.

One might wonder why Schmitz included in his motivational announcement mention of partisan feeling and antagonism. He also called for "a great deal of sacrifice"—within references to erecting "fire and earthquake proof" buildings in the burned districts, and to widening streets and reducing grades. In so doing he was referencing the specifics of a rebuilding plan that had by that date roused both endorsement and opposition from among the city elites. Schmitz made his point unequivocally: "The plan of Mr. D. H. Burnham should be the ideal for which we strive."[4]

Daniel H. Burnham was one of the greatest architects and urban planners of his or any day, a protégé of Louis Sullivan and the foremost exponent of the Chicago School of architecture. He was one of the contributors to the design of Washington, D.C., including the extension of the Mall, the design and location of Union Station, and the creation of the Lincoln Memorial. Just these examples alone demonstrate that Burnham did not think small.

Of course, the largest pressing concern after the disaster was facilities. A new building under construction at the time, Casa Calwa, had survived partly intact; in short order it became the CWA's bottling plant, and functioned through to Prohibition. But the cellars needed to be replaced. As it happens, Morgan had long planned to consolidate the cellars of the association's seven members, and so the need to start anew was put to good use. Wisely, Morgan opted to rebuild in a less disaster-prone region. (Similarly, Lachman and Jacobi reestablished its cellars and workhouses in Petaluma.) The CWA relocated to a cove that would have been a bootlegger's delight, on the shore of Contra Costa County near the city of Richmond, today known as Point Molate. They built in essence a company town, consolidating wine production, storage, and distribution—including even handsome living cottages. Named Winehaven, and built of steel, concrete, and red brick, it resembled a German fortress. It began operations in late 1907; in 1908, it produced 675,000 gallons of wine. The "largest and most up-to-date winery plant in existence," Winehaven also became a treasured marketing tool of the California wine industry, offering chartered boat tours and hosting an annual Recreation Day for customers and friends.[17] A promotional pamphlet released in 1909 boasted that Winehaven cultivates "more vineyard acreage, crushes more grapes annually, operates more wineries, makes more wine, [and] has a greater wine storage capacity than any other wine concern in the world."[18]

The California Wine Association maintained its dominance of the California wine market and, in turn, of California wines in the

"California Wine Association, Winehaven" promotional pamphlet, 1909. Courtesy of the Sonoma County Library.

American wine market up until Prohibition. Vintner Frank Swett credited Percy Morgan for much of this stature, proclaiming that the "strong, intelligent, and far-seeing management of Mr. Morgan has been one of the predominant factors in the prosperity of both growers of wine grapes and makers of wine. He is entitled to a vote of thanks from every California grower and from every competitor who is making honest wine."[19]

Cooperage had also been a casualty of the earthquake and fire. Millions of gallons of barrel capacity had been destroyed, barrels valued at half a million dollars. This loss led to high demand and prices for Eastern white oak, which was considered best for cooperage. So in 1907 the California Wine Association offered a prize for the best substitute material; among those proffered were fir, spruce, and hemlock. In the end the prize went to redwood. Some likely thought no contest was needed, since redwood had proven its viability in viticulture long before, promoted by both Agoston Haraszthy and the Korbel brothers. It was also specifically touted by the California Agricultural Society in 1872, when they openly praised Charles Lefranc's use of it at his New Almadén vineyard, noting how redwood, "half as costly, . . . will last longer than casks made from the best of oak." And yet, despite the twice-deemed superiority of plentiful California redwood, in 1907 the California Wine Association also invested in white oak to replenish supply.[20] This decision mirrors the wisdom and foresight with which Morgan ran the CWA—which in turn demonstrates how the CWA weathered the 1906 disaster as well as it did.

The California wine industry was recovering, rebuilding, and looking to the future with great optimism. In early 1910 Charles Oldham, president of the Calwa Distributing Company—formed in 1909 for the purpose its name suggests—proclaimed, "At no period in the history of the California wine trade was there a time when the future of the best class of California wines had a more promising outlook than the present."[21]

Anticipating Celebrating the Panama Canal

In May 1904, with the building of the Panama Canal under way, notable figures in San Francisco had set their sights on staging an event to celebrate its eventual completion. After all, the canal would do for San Francisco's oceangoing commerce what the 1869 transcontinental railroad had done for its overland commerce. It would cut the time of sea passage from the U.S. East Coast ports to San Francisco, the principal West Coast port, by more than half—as well as make the voyage quite a bit safer than the hazardous journey around the Cape. Since the canal was scheduled to open in 1914, it was thought that San Francisco should host an international exposition in 1915.[22]

The rebuilding of San Francisco that had taken place by the end of 1906 made it clear that the exposition could also celebrate the estimable rebirth of the nearly obliterated city. Fortunately, the U.S. Congress in essence agreed with this view: in 1911 it selected San Francisco as the official site of the country's celebration of the canal. This result was a remarkable promotional and lobbying feat on the part of the reviving city, especially since older and more established cities—including Baltimore, Boston, New Orleans, and Washington, D.C.—had been vying for the honor.[23] Thrilled by the selection, the various authorities in San Francisco began the process of choosing a site, planning landscapes, designing structures, and considering artistic themes. San Francisco sought to celebrate the opening of the Panama Canal, and its own rebirth, with impressive grandeur.[24]

The Politics of Rebuilding

The rebuilding continued, notwithstanding some recalcitrant insurance companies, and notwithstanding San Francisco's mayor, E. E. Schmitz, being convicted for graft and spending nearly a year in jail. (Dr. Edward R. Taylor served as mayor in the interim.) But there was an obstructive issue smoldering under the surface. Given the extent of the disaster, the wisest course would have been to rebuild with full acknowledgment that a future disaster was always possible—indeed, likely—and to design a San Francisco capable of withstanding earthquake, or fire, or both. But there were strong influences afoot that strove to downplay, or even obliterate altogether, the concept of earthquake. Why? Because many believed that openly acknowledging the city's high likelihood of future temblors doomed it as a thriving metropolis; the only way to ascend to greatness was to convince local and foreign investors alike that San Francisco was a good bet. And that meant attributing the vast majority of the damage to the fire, not the earthquake. One can plan for and prepare to defend against future fires; the assault of fire feels somewhat tangible, manageable—the devil you know. But violent, unpredictable earthquakes, which emerge from unknown depths underground—that devil you don't want to acknowledge. Donald L. Miller refers to this phenomenon in relation to Chicago rebuilding after its 1871 fire, noting that their recovery effort "induced the temporary amnesia one often needs in order to get on with life after a searing loss."[25] Philip Fradkin adds to the Chicago discussion: "The emphasis was on forgetting, or not remembering exactly. Nine years [after the fire], *Harper's Weekly* stated that no one had died in the fire," whereas in fact about three hundred had died.[26]

In the several years following the 1906 earthquake and fire, Stanford geology professor John Casper Branner and Andrew Lawson, chair of the geology department of the University of California, both decried the lack of official information from the City and County of San Francisco about the earthquake. Professor Lawson wrote: "The commercial spirit of the people fears any discussion of earthquakes for the same reason as it taboos any mention of an occurrence of the plague in the city of San Francisco. It believes that such discussion will advertise California as an earthquake region and so hurt business."[27]

In *Denial of Disaster*, Gladys Hansen and Emmet Condon describe how the Southern Pacific Company, the largest business in California in 1906—and the publisher of the tony *Sunset Magazine*—put its mighty public-relations machine to work to minimize the idea of the earthquake, or even to erase it from the public's mind. In the two years following the fire, the "disinformation campaign" of *Sunset Magazine* widely published, in Hansen and Condon's words, "sanitized, simplistic, and, in many cases, grossly inaccurate versions of the earthquake's effects." "'It wasn't the earthquake—it was the fire,' they said—at real estate conferences, at community meetings, and in the offices of the companies listed on the New York Stock Exchange. . . . The real problems were the tenements, the flimsy, poorly built rooming houses, [the] old brick structures on made ground, and the poor water supply."[28] Such echoes Mayor Schmitz's tactic in the first hours after the earthquake: dare to control what you can; ignore what you can't. Philip Fradkin sums up the effects of the "disinformation campaign": "Although the eastern money men were not deceived, San Franciscans believed the locally generated propaganda. Lines portraying earthquake faults were struck from state maps, the number of casualties was downplayed, geologists were discouraged from probing for explanations, a history of the earthquake was never published, and the city was rebuilt as quickly as possible with scant regard for future cataclysms."[29]

———— ❧ ————

As it turned out, building "as quickly as possible" did not involve bringing the Burnham plan into beautiful reality. Many considered this to be a missed civic opportunity; some would call it an architectural sin. Of the rebuilt San Francisco, art historian and professor Eugen Neuhaus writes how the "terraced city, on the south, without a doubt looks best on a densely foggy day. With its fussy, incongruous buildings—I hesitate to call them architecture—it serves hardly as a background for anything, let alone a group of monumental buildings. The opposite side, where nature reigns, atones for multitudes of sins that man committed on the city's hills. But how great an opportunity there was lost!"[30]

As for "regard for future cataclysms," it should be noted that, although the Burnham and Root Chronicle Building withstood the 1906 quake, Stephen Tobriner, architectural history professor and author of *Bracing for Disaster: Earthquake-Resistant Architecture and Engineering in San Francisco, 1838–1933,* says of the Burnham design: "As a visual plan it's cool and beautiful, but as a real thing imposed on the city it would have been so totally wrong. It's a total misreading of what was necessary for San Francisco."[31]

Notwithstanding opinion regarding the Burnham plan or lack thereof, the rebuilding of San Francisco required prodigious feats of engineering—particularly given the deadline for the Panama-Pacific International Exposition of 1915.[32] By the time of the exposition the city had a wholly reconstructed sewer system, a network of firefighting pipelines and reservoirs, a completely new city-owned transit system, and the most ambitious and elaborate water-supply system ever designed and built for an American city. The (re)building of San Francisco's infrastructure was directed largely by one man, City Engineer Michael O'Shaughnessy—who was also responsible for the transportation system for the world's fair.

World War I and the 1915 Panama-Pacific International Exposition

While San Francisco tended to its plans for the future, large-scale concerns simmered well beyond its city limits. In 1914, the promise of the Hague Peace Conference of 1899 was pitched into an unprecedented abyss when, on June 28, 1914, a Serbian teenager named Gavrilo Princip fatally shot the Archduke Franz Ferdinand, heir to the throne of the Austro-Hungarian Empire. In short order, a chain of events deriving from "mutual defense" clauses in alliances forged by secret treaties unfolded to launch World War I.[33]

When the Great War broke out in Europe, anxiety arose in San Francisco about the exposition. What if the warring nations wouldn't send their promised exhibits? Or forbid their people from attending the fair? Or what if the people themselves balked at the trans-Atlantic ocean voyage to reach San Francisco?[34]

All fears aside, the fundamental celebration underlying the world's fair—its raison d'être, the completion of the Panama Canal—still existed even with the war. And its existence was highly significant to the Western Hemisphere, for whom life continued as usual, regardless of the horrific rumblings to the east. On the occasion of the Panama-Pacific Historical Congress, one of the canal's most enthusiastic promoters, Theodore Roosevelt, put it this way:

> There is not one action of the American government, in connection with foreign affairs, from the day when the Constitution was adopted down to the present time, so important as the action taken by this government in connection with the acquisition and building of the Panama Canal. I am here to-night to speak to you, and I have come to see this Exposition, because I know that in the course of that action every step taken was a step not only demanded by the honor and the interest of my country, but one taken with scrupulous regard to the nicest laws of international morality, and fair and upright dealing.[35]

In addition, it could be noted that the exposition celebrated the fact that unity among diverse countries and continents was still possible—even while on the Western Front French soldiers took the woods north of Perthes, Germans advanced southeast of Alsace, and Dardanelles forts were bombarded on the Southern Front.[36]

Despite the various apprehensions, the Panama-Pacific International Exposition opened February 20, 1915. Officially it was held "to Commemorate the Discovery of the Pacific Ocean and the Construction of the Panama Canal," phrasing that forms part of the subtitle of Frank Morton Todd's five-volume *Story of the Exposition*.[37] To others, including President Roosevelt, it was the Panama Canal that brought them there. To most of the visitors, however, the fair was a celebration of a city that had returned to greatness.

Just after dawn on the morning of February 20, 1915, 150,000 people walked through the Scott Street gates to the exposition. It was launched with opening words by Secretary of the Interior

Panama Pacific International Exposition 1915, San Francisco, California. This postcard depicts both ruined and new buildings in San Francisco, with the California bear in the foreground. The two buildings shown at the bottom were built for the exposition. F. Koch copyright 1911 Edward H. Mitchell. Library of Congress Prints and Photographs Division.

Franklin K. Lane. Once he'd finished his rousing speech, President Wilson flipped a switch in the White House that tripped a galvanometer in San Francisco, opening the doors of the Palace of Machinery. Frank Morton Todd, the exposition's historian, writes, "The wheels of the great Diesel engine began to rotate, bombs exploded, flags fluttered, whistles and sirens screamed. . . and the waters of the Fountain of Energy gushed forth." The long-planned exposition ran until December 4, 1915.[38]

A quarter million people would visit the fair on just that first day; during the nearly ten-month run, upwards of nineteen million attended. These visitors were received by fairgrounds covering approximately seventy-five city blocks. While the dreamily beautiful Palace of Fine Arts anchored the western end, the exposition was graced by eleven other palaces as well, ornate exhibit halls dedicated to Education, Social Economy, Liberal Arts, Manufacturing, Machinery, Transportation, Agriculture, Food Products, Live Stock, Horticulture, and Mines and Metallurgy. Of particular significance was the five-acre scale model of the Isthmus of Panama, complete with canal and all its locks. In addition there were five Courts, the Column of Progress, the Tower of Jewels, and scores of other structures,[39] including the foreign pavilions of some twenty-five nations and the state buildings of forty-three U.S. states and territories. The breadth of the displays was as impressive as they were educational. Turkey offered a replica of the mosque of Sultan Ahmed I; Japan, the sacred temple Kin Ka Ku Ji in Kyoto. California was represented by a Spanish mission.[40]

Though the plan for the design of the exposition was a collaborative effort, its final form was largely the work of Chicago architect Edward H. Bennett, with Willis Polk as the chief of the architects of the twelve palaces. Incidentally, both men had assisted in Burnham's plan for San Francisco.[41] In his 1915 book about the architecture and art of the Panama-Pacific International Exposition, art historian and critic Eugen Neuhaus writes that the exposition "was a typically big western idea, an idea that as a rule never gets any farther than being thought of, or possibly seeing daylight as an 'esquisse'—but seldom any farther than that. The Burnham plan for San Francisco was such an unrealized dream, but here the dream achieved concrete form. The buildings as a group have all the big essential qualities that art possesses only in its noblest expression. Symmetry, balance, and harmony work together for a wonderful expression of unity, of oneness, that buildings devoted to profane purposes seldom show."[42]

The Wine Industry at the Panama-Pacific International Exposition

The California wine industry saw in the 1915 San Francisco exposition an unprecedented three-part opportunity: the chance for their products to take the stage with the world's finest wines. For one thing, California wines could be tasted by visitors throughout the exposition's run—tasted alongside the more acclaimed foreign vintages also on display. Those in the industry, of course, believed those visitors would be pleasantly surprised—indeed, greatly impressed—by the quality of the domestic wines. Of equal importance was the fact that, after much persuasion, the prestigious Permanent International Viticultural Commission had authorized a convening to be held at the 1915 exposition. (Nearly a thousand other "congresses" were held.) This decision on its own was a great honor, but in addition it meant that the foremost vineyardists and winemakers, and the great wine judges of the world, would all be in attendance at the exposition—and would participate in the final golden opportunity: hosting a Wine Day tasting and competition.[43]

For this 1915 tasting, planners turned to the "Instructions for the Jury of Awards" that Arpad Haraszthy had prepared for the 1894 Midwinter Fair. Even the merest glance at his precise instructions demonstrates the seriousness with which the leaders of California viticulture took their calling.

The wine industry's California Viticultural Exhibit Association built a massive display in the Palace of Food Products. Exposition historian Frank Morton Todd describes how the exhibit had "an enclosure like a trellis of vines supported by columns formed of casks painted white, with gilt hoops."[44] And of course there was a popular sampling room. William Heintz notes: "Fairgoers tasted freely of the wine and ate tons of fresh grapes."[45]

Two international wine contests were held: the first in May, and the second in July, as part of the International Congress of Viticulture. The international jury included three Californians: Henry Lachman, generally considered to be the finest wine taster in the United States; Charles Carpy, whom some (including himself) considered to be Lachman's equal; and Kanaye Nagasawa. (Nagasawa, though technically the representative of Japan on the wine jury, had developed his wine expertise in California's Fountain Grove.)

In 1872, when Henry Lachman was still a boy, his wine merchant father, Sam Lachman, founded S. Lachman and Company. In 1894, two years after Sam Lachman's death, Henry and his brother Albert folded the Lachman company into the newly formed California Wine Association. Years later Charles Ash of the CWA described Henry Lachman as the "greatest wine man we have ever had in California. He could go through a hundred samples like lightning and classify them with uncanny accuracy."[46] For the Paris Exposition of 1900, Lachman wrote "A Monograph on the Manufacture of Wines in California," in which he describes wine tasting thus: "In tasting there is the 'first taste,' the 'second,' and the 'good-bye,' after the wine has left the mouth. On the 'first

This image of Arpad Haraszthy & Co. Eclipse Extra Dry sparkling wine appeared in the *Official Guide to the California Midwinter Exposition in Golden Gate Park, San Francisco,* published in San Francisco by G. Spaulding & Co. in 1894. Courtesy of the San Francisco History Center, San Francisco Public Library.

Arpad Haraszthy's "Instructions for the Jury of Awards"

It is exceedingly important to have each class of wine tried in its proper glass. All of these should be thin, perfectly white, and every exhibitor should have his wine tasted from glasses of the same shape and size as that of his competitor, and no variation shall be permitted; all are treated alike. . . .

The wines should be tasted in a moderately cool room where the temperature is about 60°; otherwise full justice could not be done to the delicacy of many wines presented.

All bottles submitted to the Jurors must be carefully wrapped, so as to prevent any identification whatever. This will enable the Jurors to arrive at a decision based only upon the merits of the wine tried. The competing wines should be wrapped with the same kind of paper, without any mark or number thereon. Complete uniformity must be impartially maintained for every exhibitor. The removal of corks and capsules should be done by an attendant, so that none of the Jurors may notice or recognize any mark tending to indicate who the exhibitor is, thus giving the most convincing proof of absolute impartiality. . . .

The points guiding the Jurors to reach conclusions of comparative merit will be the following: (1) Brightness of the wine; (2) Beauty of color or shades of color; (3) Perfection of bouquet; (4) Purity and delicacy of taste; (5) Quality of body; (6) Quality of savor; (7) Proper alcoholic strength; (8) harmonious perfection of the whole.

In trial for sparkling wines the two following additional points must be considered: (9) Vivacity of sparkle; (10) Duration of sparkle. Each of these, if perfect, would be given 100. . . .

. . . Our California wine producers, without any attempt at imitation, have tried to approach the general good qualities of . . . European types of wine by careful handling and the planting of the most renowned varieties of grapes; and it will remain for you to determine how near our wine growers have approached the general type claimed or how far they may be away from it. . . .

While trying California wines the Jurors should also consider whether the same are bottled in bottles properly belonging to the type it is claimed they represent. . . . The more or less neatness of label, capsule, and general get-up should also be considered, and remarks favorable or otherwise made note of.

Source: Haraszthy, "Instructions for the Jury of Awards," 86–87.

taste' the body or extract is detected; on the 'second taste,' the acids, free and acetic; and on the 'good-bye' the tannin, flavor, and defects are caught." Another tidbit: Lachman never *drank* wine, he only tasted it; he feared that drinking wine would dull his senses of taste and smell.[47]

French-born Charles Carpy, who arrived in California in his late teens, was also a founding member of the California Wine Association, as well as its first president. He'd established C. Carpy and Co. in 1886; it had two wineries in Napa and two cellars in San Francisco. In 1894 he had also acquired the Greystone winery.[48]

At the Viticultural Congress banquet in July of 1915, Charles Carpy gave a speech entitled "How Do I Know Good Wine?" In it he proffers:

> First, it should be brilliant. Second, it should appeal to the sense of taste; it should be clean; its vinosity should be pronounced; after tasting, it should leave upon the palate the clear, definite impression of cleanliness. Third, it should appeal very strongly to the sense of smell; the bouquet should be unimpeachable. Fourth, it should be served and tasted under proper conditions.
>
> A wine may have passed every qualification . . . and still leave the man who has drunk two or three glasses sated or cloyed. This is a fatal defect. Any wine that leaves the drinker in the condition of "Oh, I don't want any more," or leaves him heated up like a furnace, is not a fine wine, no matter how much it may appeal to the senses of sight, taste, and smell.[49]

A few months into the exposition, attendance at the wine exhibit had been plentiful and the praise gratifying. But, just as many of the planners had feared, the travails of war reduced, perhaps greatly, those who would attend the fair and experience California wines for themselves. On May 7, 1915, a German torpedo fired from a U-boat hit and sank the *Lusitania*, a Cunard liner that had sailed from New York the week before. Nearly twelve hundred of the nearly two thousand passengers and crew were killed, all presumably civilians.[50] Needless to say, after the sinking many chose to not brave the Atlantic Ocean. And so the European wine experts did not come to the International Congress of Viticulture, held on July 12–13, and the European judges, mostly the same men, did not arrive for Wine Day, July 14. One of the more anticipated would-be participants was Frenchman Prosper Gervais, the "Perpetual Secretary" of the Permanent Viticultural

Commission, who was to have presided over the Congress. Gervais sent his regrets: "My son, my only son, is dead on the plains of Flanders. I cannot come." Baron von Buhl, president of the German Wine Association, declined as well, writing: "We cannot leave the Fatherland now; it is impossible."[51]

The *Official Report of the International Congress of Viticulture* gives a sense both of the expectations of the Americans and the disappointment that the Europeans did not attend. Its introduction reads:

> The International Congress of Viticulture of 1915 was held at San Francisco under the authority of the Permanent International Commission.... At that time no one anticipated that by reason of a world-wide war the European members would be unable to attend.
>
> ... The members attending the Congress and the papers presented were almost entirely American. The absence of most of the active members of former Congresses, and the lack of their valuable papers and discussion, were serious deficiencies. The Congress, however, was valuable as an indication of the progress and extent of viticulture in the United States and the report should be of interest to the viticulturists of the world as a symposium of American viticulture.[52]

The Europeans who did not attend included the viticulture or agriculture ministers, or leading academics, of Austria, France, Germany, Hungary, Italy, Portugal, Russia, Spain, and Switzerland. President of the Congress William B. Alwood lamented: "For four years I have been laboring over the preliminaries of this Congress. Many of the best men of Europe interested in viticulture were anxious to come to California, the land of wonder." Some simply couldn't make the journey; others had by then left this world altogether.[53]

And so the California Viticultural Exhibit Association proceeded without their distinguished European members. Following the two-day Congress of July 12–13, the second wine-tasting competition took place on July 14, Wine Day. An earlier competition had been held in May, and California wines fared well at both. Secundo Guasti won a gold for his Grignolino. A Korbel wine called Zernosek (a Czech word for the Bavarian grape) won a grand prize. A Kunde Estate Zinfandel also took a gold. Charles Krug was awarded a grand prize for its Sauvignon Vert. And Claus Schilling's Lomas Azulas wines took home a grand prize as well as several gold medals.

One big winner was Carl Dresel. (Carl was the son of Julius Dresel, who had taken over Dresel & Co. on the death of his brother Emil Dresel, who had run Rhine Farm with Jacob Gundlach.) At the 1915 exposition Dresel won gold medals for his Traminer and his Johannisberg, Granken (Sylvaner), and Kleinberger Rieslings. Carl Dresel was also a pioneer in labeling wines by variety—he sold wines labeled SEMILLON, CABERNET SAUVIGNON, and ZINFANDEL—a custom not adopted industry-wide until after Prohibition.[54]

CODA TO THE PANAMA-PACIFIC
INTERNATIONAL EXPOSITION

Carl Nolte in the *San Francisco Chronicle,* quoting in part the great historian Kevin Starr, offers a coda to the 1915 Panama-Pacific International Exposition. He notes that Starr viewed the fair as "a bit of a farewell to the city's past as well as show of the future, mixed together. 'One city gone and another born.'"[55]

A few years following its close, the official history of the Panama-Pacific International Exposition was published, in five large volumes of florid, prolix prose. In its approximately two thousand pages of text—plus magnificent photographs—the exposition's ordinarily exuberant historian Frank Morton Todd gives a somewhat strange, minimalist description of the wine industry's exhibit:

> It is easy to fall into the habit of using the word "comprehensive" in characterizing an exhibit. Most exhibits aim to be comprehensive, and at the Panama-Pacific International Exposition a great many were. . . . But there was no exhibit that deserved the adjective more than that of the California Viticultural Exhibit Association. It epitomized the whole wine industry of the State, as far as that could ever be done under a roof.
>
> The setting and framing were in character, with an enclosure like a trellis of vines supported by columns formed of casks painted white, with gilt hoops. Everywhere were garlanded casks and clambering vines, and famous old California wineries reproduced in miniature, with pictures of the juicy berry, and processed examples of fifty of the leading varieties of grape used in wine making in California. . . .
>
> The outer part of the space was devoted to small booths of contributing members supporting the exhibit: the California Wine Association, . . . Korbel & Brothers, Lachman & Jacobi, the Gundlach-Bundschu Wine Company [etc.]. . .; and there were interesting exhibits, along the wall of the interior chamber, by [several others]. . .
>
> In the center of the booth was a moving-picture theater in which more than 100,000 people during the Exposition saw the beautiful wine country of California, with all the scenes of cultivation and the vintage. The working plant of every important firm was shown. Champagne making and the interesting process of "disgorging" were depicted. Scenes from the Vintage Festival at St. Helena added variety. Champagne making was illustrated in detail. About 15,000 feet of film was projected here. The cost and upkeep of the exhibit ran over $75,000.[56]

This description of the wine exhibit, appearing in a chapter entitled, oddly, "Salmon, Clams, and Wine," does not exactly engender longing to have experienced the splendor in person. In some ways it is emblematic of the effect the 1915 exposition had on the California wine industry as a whole: it occasioned valuable attention to be sure—indeed, substantial praise in the awards won—but something was still left wanting, a flag left unwaved.

But others have offered rather tantalizing descriptions of the California Viticultural Exhibit Association's efforts. In *Empire of*

Vines: Wine Culture in America, Erica Hannickel shares charming details, beginning with how the grape and wine display carried a "domesticated Mission theme," and that its nicknamed "Grape Temple" "was thus something of a miniature of the larger fair itself, which included several buildings in the Spanish Colonial Revival, or Mission Revival, style." She notes how "wine casks formed the pillars for the room, and pictures and Victorian furniture were set among the dangling vines, evoking domestic elegance." Of particular mention:

> The displays were designed and funded by the all-male Viticultural Exhibit Association, but men in vineyards (other than Greek gods in statues and pictures) were conspicuously absent from the display. The picture of the Italian-Swiss Colony booth within the California Wine Exhibit also reveals that the wine on display at the fair was set within a domestic, feminine atmosphere. Such displays forwarded the feminine pastoral ideal surrounding grape cultivation, an aesthetic similar to much high-Victorian homemaking. Positioning wine as a beverage used in moderation with meals in the home perhaps helped dislodge it from association with beer and spirits in saloons. This domestic context seems an effort to further separate wine from other forms of alcohol in a time of growing prohibitionist fervor.[57]

But, of course, given that she published in 2013, Hannickel has the benefit of hindsight of the century that passed between then and now. Frank Morton Todd only spoke of then. In his five-volume collection, our underwhelmed chronicler of the viticulture exhibit concludes the matter of wine in eight short words: "This is history—closed by the Eighteenth Amendment."[58]

Had Gavrilo Princip not shot the Austrian Archduke Franz Ferdinand in June 1914, or had the European alliances not deemed it necessary to go to war, or had the German U-boat *U-20* not torpedoed the *Lusitania* in May 1915, perhaps Prosper Gervais and the other members of the European wine elite might have made the voyage to San Francisco for the Panama-Pacific Exposition: to attend their Congress, and to taste and judge California's wine. If they had made the voyage, would they have passed favorable judgment on the wines of the Golden State? If they had, this third setback of the California wine industry would have been averted. And what if they had made a favorable judgment? To leave speculation for the moment, and simply imagine, perhaps, just perhaps, the fourth crisis for California wine might have been averted. For if by the time of Prohibition wine had been fully established as an essential part of sophisticated culture—apart from and superior to beer and mere liquor—the Volstead Act, though inevitable, just might have excluded wine.

Notes

1. A copy of the Schmitz proclamation is in the historical archives of the University of San Francisco (in the Schmitz Papers).

2. Fradkin, *Great Earthquake,* 6–7.

3. McGloin, *San Francisco,* 144–45, 149.

4. Ibid., 150.

5. Winchester, *Crack in the Edge of the World,* 356–57; Fradkin, *Great Earthquake,* 13, 18.

6. Tobriner, *Bracing for Disaster,* 86.

7. Winchester, *Crack in the Edge of the World,* 356–57; Brechin, *Imperial San Francisco,* 151–53.

8. Winchester, *Crack in the Edge of the World,* 356–57.

9. Brechin, *Imperial San Francisco,* 151–53.

10. Winchester, *Crack in the Edge of the World,* 358; Brechin, *Imperial San Francisco,* 153.

11. Scott, *San Francisco Bay Area,* 115 and n19, citing Michael de Young, *San Francisco Chronicle,* May 23, 1906, 6 and n21, *San Francisco Bulletin,* May 24, 1906, 4.

12. Ibid., 115.

13. E. Schmitz, article written for the *San Francisco Independent,* quoted in McGloin, *San Francisco,* 150–51 and n10.

14. Peninou and Unzelman, *California Wine Association,* 98.

15. Sullivan, *Companion to California Wine,* 98.

16. Peninou and Unzelman, *California Wine Association,* 98, 101.

17. Ibid., 103–4, and references cited.

18. "California Wine Association, Winehaven, 1909," promotional pamphlet, Sonoma County Library, http://heritage.sonomalibrary.org/cdm/singleitem/collection/p15763coll13/id/856/rec/1.

19. Peninou and Unzelman, *California Wine Association,* 106, citing *Pacific Wine and Spirit Review* 49, no. 10 (August 31, 1907): 16.

20. Ibid., 101–5; California State Agricultural Society, *Transactions,* 200–201.

21. Ibid., 107, quoting in part from Charles Oldham, *California Fruit Grower* 41, no. 1127 (February 12, 1910): 13.

22. McGloin, *San Francisco,* 156–57.

23. Ibid.; Lewis, *San Francisco,* 221.

24. McGloin, *San Francisco,* 158–59.

25. Miller, *City of the Century,* 142; also quoted in Fradkin, *Great Earthquake,* 18.

26. Fradkin, *Great Earthquake,* 18.

27. Hansen and Condon, *Denial of Disaster,* 107–8.

28. Ibid., 106–10.

29. Fradkin, *Great Earthquake,* 7.

30. Neuhaus, *Art of the Exposition,* 7.

31. Stephen Tobriner, qtd. in King, "Great Quake."

32. The Library of Congress offers an excellent photographic journey through "San Francisco's growth and transformation from 1851

to 1922," including a panorama of the Pan-Pacific Exposition grounds three months before opening day. https://www.loc.gov/pictures/related/?va=exact&fi=id&sg=true&op=EQUAL&st=slideshow&q.

33. Davies, *Europe,* 877.

34. McGloin, *San Francisco,* 159.

35. Theodore Roosevelt, "The Panama Canal," qtd. in Stephens and Bolton, *Pacific Ocean in History,* 150. His speech begins on page 137.

36. Michael Duffy, "On This Day: 20 February 1915," August 22, 2009, *FirstWorldWar.com,* A Multimedia History of World War One, www.firstworldwar.com/onthisday/1915_02_20.htm.

37. Todd, *Story of the Exposition.* See also Ackley, *San Francisco's Jewel City.*

38. Brechin, *Imperial San Francisco,* 245–48.

39. McGloin, *San Francisco,* 159–60; James, *Palaces and Courts of the Exposition,* 7–8.

40. Federal Writers' Project, *San Francisco,* 308–10. See also Newhall, *San Francisco's Enchanted Palace.* Note that different sources give different figures for the "twenty-five" nations that took part.

41. See generally Newhall, *San Francisco's Enchanted Palace; Todd, Story of the Exposition;* and Maybeck, *Palace of Fine Arts and Lagoon.*

42. Neuhaus, *Art of the Exposition,* 4.

43. Pinney, *History of Wine in America,* 1:369; Stephens and Bolton, *Pacific Ocean in History,* 3–4.

44. Todd, *Story of the Exposition,* 4:301–2.

45. Heintz, *California's Napa Valley,* 235.

46. Teiser and Harroun, *Winemaking in California,* 168, quoting in part Charles Ash, "Reminiscences of Pre-Prohibition Days," *Proceedings of the American Society of Enologists* 3 (1952): 42.

47. Ibid., 169, quoting in part Henry Lachman, "A Monograph on the Manufacture of Wines in California," published with H. W. Wiley, "American Wines at the Paris Exposition of 1900: Their Composition and Character," U.S. Department of Agriculture, Bureau of Chemistry, Bulletin No. 72 (Washington: Government Printing Office, 1903), 36.

48. Teiser and Harroun, *Winemaking in California,* 169.

49. Ibid., 169.

50. Brechin, *Imperial San Francisco,* 275–76.

51. *Official Report of the Session of the International Congress of Viticulture,* 14–15.

52. Ibid., 5.

53. Ibid., 14–15.

54. Sullivan, *Companion to California Wine,* 92, 107, 140, 173, 318, 320.

55. Nolte, "Panama-Pacific Fair."

56. Todd, *Story of the Exposition,* 4:301–2. Thomas Pinney makes a similar observation in *History of Wine in America,* 1:370.

57. Hannickel, *Empire of Vines,* 183–85.

58. Todd, *Story of the Exposition,* 4:302.

CHAPTER 8

The Ignoble Experiment
of Prohibition

1920—1933

In all ages, intoxicating liquors have been the
fruitful sources of crime, misery, and death.
Notwithstanding . . . efforts . . . made to reclaim men
from the dreadful habits engendered by the frequent
use of many poisonous compounds, the practice is
still indulged in to an immense extent. In consequence
of it, men are daily tottering towards a drunkard's
grave; . . . mothers are suffering in agony for their
offspring; . . . and orphans are weeping bitter tears.

— "God Speed to the Dashaways,"
San Francisco Daily, 1859

NOTWITHSTANDING the lessened heights of what might have
been achieved on Wine Day at the 1915 Panama-Pacific International Exposition, the California wine industry had much to
take pride in by the fair's end. In less than a decade, the industry
had dusted itself off from the near-total destruction of the 1906
earthquakes and fires to compete against the finest winemakers
in the world—and it did so with flair. And though at the 1915 International Congress of Viticulture George Husmann lamented
how slowly California was attending to its phylloxera concerns,
nonetheless, he boasted how the state had saved the viticultural
industry of the world.[1]

But dark days lay ahead for the wine industry. Proponents of
temperance had been preaching and wheedling and cajoling for a
hundred years in America. But proponents of prohibition,[2] something far different, had been steadily gaining adherents, popularity, and power.

Since the pilgrim and pioneer days Americans had been
drinkers of alcohol, whether moderately, exuberantly, or profligately. Indeed, many colonial laws referred to liquor as "the good

creature of God." Some English colonists subscribed to the opinion proffered in Andrew Boorde's 1542 book of dietary health, that alcohol is a more healthy beverage than water: "Water is not holesome, sole by it selfe. . . . If any man . . . drynke water with wyne, let it be purely strayned; and then [boil] it, and after it be cold, let hym put it to his wyne." In other words, if you *must* dilute your wine, then be sure to purify your water first. (He also speaks of "ale, bere, and cyder.")[3]

By the end of the seventeenth century, rum had become the preferred drink. In 1699 Edward Ward describes how rum is "adored by the American English. . . . 'Tis held as the comforter of their souls, the preserver of their bodies, the remover of their cares, and promoter of their mirth; and is a sovereign remedy against the grumbling of the guts, a kibe-heel, or a wounded conscience, which are three epidemical distempers that afflict the country."[4] In the eighteenth century, it was customary for all to stop business and have a drink at 11:00 AM; the shop doors closed in the interim. This custom was known as "Leven O'clock Bitters"— whereas today the dictionary definition of *elevenses* connotes teetotaling coffee or tea. Alcohol was also traditionally a part of communal work, such as haying, reaping, or barn-raising. As Herbert Asbury describes it, "On these occasions liquor was free to all, and enormous quantities were consumed." In addition, "Workmen commonly received part of their wages in . . . spirits. . . . It was well-nigh impossible for a farmer who didn't provide plenty of liquor to get farm hands to work for him; it was generally agreed that no man could do a day's work on a farm without alcoholic stimulation."[5] Historian W. J. Rorabaugh sums it up tidily: "Alcohol was pervasive in American society; it crossed regional, sexual, racial, and class lines. Americans drank at home and abroad, alone and together, at work and at play, in fun and in earnest. They drank from the crack of dawn to the crack of dawn."[6]

Given the wide consumption, some conducted studies on just how alcohol affects the human organism. One study was published in 1784 by physician Benjamin Rush in an essay titled "An Inquiry into the Effects of Spirituous Liquors on the Human Body." As Thomas Pinney puts it: "With zealous exaggeration, Rush attributed almost every physical malady and social problem to the abuse of strong drink: falsehood, fraud, theft, uncleanliness, and murder, as well as yellow fever, jaundice, dropsy, diabetes, gout, epilepsy, gangrene, and madness." However decided Rush's views were about *spirits*, he did not apply these concerns to wine. Indeed, he "encouraged the whiskey-riddled to consider a transitional beverage: wine mixed with opium or laudanum." Even for those who weren't liquor-riddled, Rush explained, "It must be a bad heart, indeed that is not rendered more cheerful and more generous by a few glasses of wine."[7] Sixteenth-century "physycke" Andrew Boorde would agree, as he claimed that wine, moderately drunk, quickens the wit, comforts the heart, and scours the liver. And if it be white wine, then add that it also nourishes the brain and body and cleanses wounds and sores. "Furthermore, the better the wyne is, the better humours it doth ingender."[8]

While regular drinking together had long been a mainstay of social culture, the early nineteenth century saw an appalling rise in public drunkenness in America, the reasons for which are many and varied. With this development, for the first time men of the cloth weighed in—heavily—railing against the "liquor evil." The Reverend Lyman Beecher was one of the first American clergymen to take up the pulpit against demon alcohol. He proclaimed, with a mastery that filled his offering baskets, that Americans were "a generation of drunkards."[9] All hyperbole aside, drinking was on the rise. In 1810, per capita consumption of hard liquor in America was about 4.7 gallons per year; in 1823, the amount had risen to 7.5 gallons. Compare those figures to a more modern-day tally: in 1985 the per capita consumption of distilled spirits in America was about 2.5 gallons per year.[10]

Regardless of the motivations for drinking in this era, there was the sheer availability of liquor: in the 1820s, rum and whiskey, the drinks of choice, were everywhere available, and everywhere cheap.[11] David Brion Davis writes: "Beginning in the eighteenth century, improvements in distillation, transportation, and distribution had made spiritous liquor cheap and universally accessible (by the 1820s, the price of whiskey had fallen to 25 cents a gallon)."[12] Even then that was cheap.

THE BEGINNINGS OF THE TEMPERANCE MOVEMENT IN THE UNITED STATES

The rise in public drunkenness in America led inexorably to what was called the "temperance movement," a name that stuck long after the movement was no longer about temperance. The first "temperance" groups were advocates of drinking temperately—not advocates of abstinence, as in not drinking at all. For example, the Union Temperate Society, founded in 1808, didn't speak to the drinking of beer or wine, just distilled spirits; it also had no religious underpinnings.[13] Similarly, though the Washingtonian Temperance Society, formed in 1840, encouraged confession, it was "a gift for self-dramatization" they sought, not religious adherence.[14]

Another angle in the changing opinion about liquor concerned the association of rum with slavery. Rum was distilled in New England, from molasses made from cane harvested from the labors of slaves in the southern states. The fury that arose against "demon rum" thus found a common cause with the abolition movement, which had been gaining traction since the late 1700s.[15] In 1845, when addressing an audience about intemperance and slavery, Frederick Douglass said: "If we could but make the world sober, we would have no slavery. . . . All great reforms go together."[16]

At some point the taking of a pledge became a significant feature in meetings of temperance groups such as the Sons of Temperance and the Templars of Honor and Temperance.[17] And while there were variations, they all derived from a singular intention: "I hereby pledge myself, God being my helper, to abstain from the use of intoxicating liquors."[18] The advent of the ritual pledge coincided with temperance groups seeking support: since societal drunkenness had not been solved with previous temperance efforts, clearly more stringent measures were called for. And call for them they did; the trouble was, they couldn't agree on just how to proceed. In 1833, dozens of state and local temperance groups joined forces as a national organization: the American Temperance Union. But they struggled to reach consensus. When those with more moderate views pulled out, control fell into the hands of the radical wing, which wanted nothing less than total abstinence, preferably federally mandated.[19]

Local efforts continued as well. In 1843, Portland, Maine, became the first city to declare itself "dry." A law against the sale of alcohol passed the following year in the far-off Wild West of the Oregon Territory. But it was the 1851 "Maine (Liquor) Law" that became the model for subsequent legislative efforts; by 1855, twelve eastern and midwestern states had similar laws.[20]

Despite these legislative victories, the Drys soon learned that laws on the books didn't always mean enforcement of those laws—and of course it was compliance that was sought, not mere governmental stance. John Kobler notes in *Ardent Spirits* how prohibitionists were hugely successful in expanding their political reach in the decade leading up to the Civil War; and yet, during this same period the "per capita consumption of beer, wine, and whiskey *increased*," from almost five gallons to well over six (italics added).[21] In addition, historian Daniel Okrent points out that by the end of the 1850s, "states that had enacted versions of the Maine Law had repealed them—Maine included."[22] The Drys needed to rethink their strategy.

THE TEMPERANCE FEVER in California paralleled the movement in the rest of the country. Even in wide-open Gold Rush San Francisco, Bible-shaking preachers could be found on street corners railing against the evils of liquor and drunkenness. By 1854 no fewer than four temperance organizations had sprung up—the Temperance Society, the Cadets of Temperance, the Daughters of Temperance, and the Sons of Temperance. The Dashaway Association, so named for its members' "pledge to 'dash away' from their lips 'the cup that intoxicates,'" soon joined the cause. Its members employed the tactic of dragging public drunkards to meetings in the hopes of reforming them.[23]

At the end of the Civil War, California continued its Dry trajectory, particularly in Southern California. Two towns were founded as abstaining communities: Compton and Long Beach. Long Beach was particularly dedicated to the cause; there the original deeds to lots contained clauses providing that if the owner of the property ever engaged in liquor traffic the property would revert to the original owner (or heirs). By 1890, almost fifty cities and towns in Southern California had dry laws.[24] These efforts were furthered when, in 1912, the state of California enacted a "local option" statute, which expressly allowed local communities to enact their own levels of prohibition, partial or total, as they wished. In the subsequent seven years, several wine-producing regions denounced their vinting history and voted dry, most of them in Southern California.[25] And yet, though many other states prior to 1919 enacted state laws prohibiting alcoholic beverages, California only did so *after* passage of the Eighteenth Amendment.

Meanwhile, the temperance movement was gaining steam. Emboldened, the Drys formed the National Prohibition Party in 1869. At its 1876 convention in Cleveland, Ohio, the party introduced its most radical stance yet: to abolish alcohol at the constitutional level—a countrywide legal mandate. In the cause the party was aided by the nascent Women's Christian Temperance Union, founded in 1874. The WCTU sought prohibition as "protection of the home" against alcohol's corrosive effect on families.[26]

The histories of the women's movement and the temperance movement dovetail almost poetically, each aiding the other's cause. For starters, from its inception in 1869 the Prohibition Party became the first to accept women as not just party members, but also "shapers of the party agenda."[27] In *Last Call: The Rise and Fall of Prohibition,* Daniel Okrent relates how critic Gilbert Seldes

> believed that the most urgent reasons for women to want to vote in the mid-1800s were alcohol related: They wanted the saloons closed down, or at least regulated. They wanted the right to own property, and to shield their families' financial security from the profligacy of drunken husbands. They wanted the right to divorce those men, and to have them arrested for wife beating, and to protect their children from being terrorized by them. To do all these things they needed to change the laws that consigned married women to the status of chattel. And to change the laws, they needed the vote.

Okrent adds that the WCTU was "undoubtedly, the nation's most effective political action group in the last decades of the nineteenth century."[28]

Of even greater aid to the National Prohibition Party was the Anti-Saloon League. Founded in 1895, the league became the real muscle of the Dry cause, especially in terms of propaganda and politics; it is likely due the credit for the actual enactment of national prohibition in 1919.[29]

In *The Great Illusion: An Informal History of Prohibition,* Herbert Asbury states that "the Anti-Saloon League always called itself 'the [Protestant] church in action against the saloon.'" "During the formative years when it was still wooing the church," officials claimed that the league was not a political organization, a pretense it maintained without so much as a smirk until 1913. The league's original strategy was to dry up the country in portions—cities and towns here and there, then states, then at last the nation.[30] And while it ran no candidates for public office as a party (again, pretending to not be a political organization), it would, as Thomas Pinney puts it, "support any candidate who could stay sober long enough to vote Dry."[31] This pragmatism,

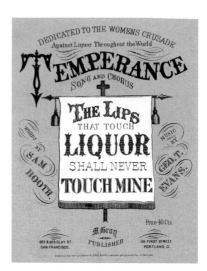

This temperance song and chorus, "The Lips That Touch Liquor, Shall Never Touch Mine," was dedicated to the "Womens Crusade Against Liquor Throughout the World." Words by Sam Booth, music by George T. Evans. Published by M. Gray in San Francisco, California, in 1874. Courtesy of the Lester S. Levy Sheet Music Collection, Sheridan Library, at Johns Hopkins University.

in addition to the league's from-the-ground-up strategy, opened a schism between the league and the Prohibition Party, which wanted adherence to principle, and nothing less than a constitutional amendment banning alcoholic beverages from coast to coast. The estrangement between the Anti-Saloon League and the National Prohibition Party was healed, however, when in 1913 the two joined in openly advocating a constitutional amendment to effect national prohibition.[32] What proceeded involved a conscious plan of patience, weighing member fervor against the practicalities of biding one's time until the Dry winds blew in their favor.

In the words of historian Herbert Asbury, while the "political *modus operandi* of the Anti-Saloon League . . . didn't necessarily include the outright purchase of a politician," neither "did it preclude such a buy if the situation warranted." Their procedure was a mastery in "swarming into a contested area and bringing every imaginable sort of pressure to bear upon the candidates and officeholders; in saturating the country with speakers and literature; in laying down a barrage of abuse, insinuation, innuendo, half-truths, and plain lies against an opponent; and in maintaining an efficient espionage system which could obtain reliable knowledge of the enemy's plans." Of all the league's agents, secret and otherwise, the most notorious was William E. "Pussyfoot" Johnson, who later "boasted that he had lied, bribed, and drank—'gallons'—to put over Prohibition." For some the cause justifies the means.[33]

The Anti-Saloon League fanatically outworked and outwitted the liquor interests opposed to prohibition. And while their methods could be shameful, even shocking, the league and its allies were never charged with crimes—whereas the similar attempts of the Wets didn't fare so well. The brewer groups in particular behaved like the Keystone Cops in clumsy, often bungled attempts to buy elected officials and newspaper editors, rig elections, and intimidate businesses—bumblings the league's propaganda apparatus was all too ready to publicize. In perhaps one of its crowning feats, in 1918 the league broadcast two incidents of brewing industry corruption involving conspiracy and political-contribution laws—just when the Eighteenth Amendment was being considered in thirty-four states.

Through its various tactics, the Anti-Saloon League and its allies won over dozens of state legislatures, at a rate that only accelerated as the years passed.

By March 1917, the German navy had just resumed unrestricted submarine warfare in the Atlantic, and that month had sunk seven American merchant vessels. On April 2, President Woodrow Wilson, who had previously opposed America's entry into the conflict, urged Congress to declare war against Germany, pleading "the world must be made safe for democracy." On April 6, Congress approved the call to arms and declared war.

Since it was imperative they not be perceived as exalting their cause over wartime concerns, the Drys once again practiced patience in their quest for a constitutional amendment. But they still seized every opportunity to advance the Dry cause by other means. An early example of this involved the food control bill, which was written to conserve foodstuffs for the war effort. The Drys succeeded in getting the House of Representatives to amend the bill to prohibit the use of grain (or any other food) in the manufacture of alcoholic beverages—beer and wine included. This development so panicked the beer lobby that it abandoned its allies in the hard-liquor industry, an exodus that divided and weakened the Wet front. As rewritten in the Senate, and signed by the president on August 10, 1917, the Food and Fuel Control Act prohibited the manufacture of distilled liquor, leaving to the president the question of whether to ban beer or wine—with the general "understanding" that beer would be included soon enough.

The California Wine Industry Opposes Prohibition

California's grape growers and wine producers fought hard against Prohibition—or at least against the prohibition of wine. Like the Drys they employed their own propaganda, lobbying, and lawsuits. One early success was achieved in 1913: the passing of legislation establishing a State Board of Viticultural Commissioners. (The previous entity, the Board of State Viticultural Commissioners, had ceased in 1895.) The board then became the third prominent entity of the wine industry, joining the California Grape Protective Association in standing with the vintners and vineyardists themselves.[34]

Of course, the primary angle in the argument against prohibition concerned the livelihood of all who benefitted from the fermentation of the grape. This argument was cogently conveyed in Walter V. Woehlke's October 1916 article in *Sunset: The Magazine of the Pacific* entitled "The Grape and Prohibition: A Survey of the Effect of Morality Legislation on the Economic Status of California's Vineyards":

> Prohibition through its effect upon the grape industry becomes an economic problem of the first magnitude in California, a problem that has been under- rather than overestimated by both sides. . . .
>
> Viewed from the economic standpoint, the suggestion of the prohibitionists that the grape growers turn their surplus product into grape juice, grape syrup, and grape preserves provokes a smile. Given the plants and the capital, the manufacturing would not be difficult. California could without trouble supply twenty or thirty million gallons of grape juice, but unfortunately the total grape-juice consumption of the United States, expensive advertising campaigns notwithstanding, barely reaches two million gallons a year. As for grape jam and grape syrup, how large a quantity of these commodities did you eat last year?[35]

In 1916, the California Grape Protective Association, made up of "only those who are dependent upon the vineyards and wineries for their livelihood," published a ten-cent booklet entitled *How Prohibition Would Affect California*. Its pages intended to "answer truthfully all the misleading arguments advanced by . . . opponents in an endeavor to discredit viticulture in California." Its topics concerned foremost the multiple ways prohibition legislation would threaten the livelihoods of the 150,000 Californians "employed in the Vineyards, Wineries, and Packing Houses," noting that vineyards contributed to the table grape and raisin industries as well, not just viticulture. They particularly highlighted the fact that the California grape industry represented an investment of $150,000,000.[36]

Beyond expressing the prevalent economic concerns, the booklet also appealed to Californians' pride in their state's history. This appeal included the unsubtle reminder that it was the Franciscan padres who had brought the grapevine to California—in the course of fulfilling God's work.[37] The wine interests also argued that effective, total prohibition would never work: many Americans were too fond of alcohol to give it up completely. Whereas wine, it so happens, was the ideal solution, a quintessential agent for temperance, as evidenced by European countries. Regions where people partook of wine only with meals were not troubled by alcoholism. In fact, the booklet implied, wine drinking was a sign of cultivation.[38]

This last view had long been strongly advocated by the California Grape Protective Association's founder, Italian Andrea

---

The California State Board of Health on Wine-Drinking Countries

Page thirty-seven of Andrea Sbarboro's *Temperance Versus Prohibition* includes a typewritten letter Sbarboro received from the president of the California State Board of Health:

November 22, 1905

My dear Mr. Sbarboro,
In your paper entitled "Wine or Tea, That is the Question?" you expressed sentiments which I have been advocating for years. If the people of this country were educated from babyhood up to drink wine, alcoholism would be a rare disease, as has been proven in wine-drinking countries. It is the forbidden fruit that tempts. In my experience, in families where the wine flows freely, drunkards are the exception, whereas many of the offspring of teetotalers and wine abhorrers, who have not tasted [alcohol] until they have almost grown to be men, become drunkards.

—MARTIN REGENSBURGER, President, California State Board of Health

Source: Sbarboro, *Temperance Versus Prohibition*, 37.

"The Food Value of Wine"

"The proper way and the proper time to drink wine" is "at the table with the daily meals." "Drinking between meals is a bad American habit, which is responsible for a great deal of indigestion and intemperance. On the other hand, the fruit acids in wine when taken with more solid food aid and promote digestion."

Alcohol in Wine a True Food

"Two American scientists, Professors Atwater and Benedict, determined . . . [with] rigorously exact methods . . . that the potential energy of alcohol transformed in the body into energy as completely as other food." They specify the benefit of diluted wine taken throughout the day: "in the proportion of one gramme per kilogramme of body weight, alcohol in the form of wine is a food just as sugar or starch is a food."

. . . "The fruit acids . . . not only promote the flow of saliva and the gastric juices, but also aid in converting into sugar the starchy matters of the food, while the salts in wine go to nourish the bones and tendons of the body."

Wine as a Temperance Agent

Wine plays an important part as a temperance agent. The wine-drinking people of Europe are the most sober and temperate people in the world. All over France and Italy, where practically every man, woman, and child drink more or less wine every day, the use of strong liquors, which are responsible for drunkenness, is very small. It is a good sign, therefore, to find Americans learning to use wine with their meals, and this habit will make for temperance in this country just as it does in Europe.

The true temperance advocate, as well as the physiologist, therefore favors the proper use of light wine at the table and in the family. The more our people drink wine the better it will be for their health and temperance. The advice of the Apostle Paul to Timothy is just as good today as it was nineteen hundred years ago: "Use a little wine for thy stomach's sake and thine other infirmities."

Source: Twight, "Food Value of Wine," 45–50.

Sbarboro. Sbarboro considered moderate wine-drinking to be the best course for temperance, a message he promoted in speeches and with publications such as his 1909 *Temperance Versus Prohibition*.[39]

While the association did enjoy some successes, its achievements were hampered by two problems. One was indecision on whether to align itself with all other liquor interests in opposing prohibition entirely, or to maintain its asserted moral high ground that prohibition was fine for other alcoholic beverages, just inappropriate for wine. The second problem was one that plagues many organized groups: frequent strife among its members.[40]

The American Wine Growers' Association too had a public-education program. Its favorite item of literature was Professor Edmund H. Twight's essay "Wine—A Food," which details the nutritional value of wine and counsels, "We should always use wine with food and in the same way as food, that is, temperately."[41]

But in the end, the efforts of the grape growers and winemakers were as unsuccessful as those of the hard-liquor and beer industries. In the blinding light of hindsight, it can seem that the California wine industry's best argument was that wine is unlike liquor—that wine, an emblem of cultivation, is in fact an agent of temperance, a tool the Drys could capitalize on. If wine had reached that pinnacle of public opinion in advance of these considerations, would the history of Prohibition have turned out differently? One wonders again what might have happened had there not been that assassination in Sarajevo, or had a German U-boat missed its target in 1915. Had the eminences of the European wine community tasted California's vintages—and deemed them superb—would their judgment have given the industry sufficient argument to finagle the exclusion of wine from Prohibition? Perhaps not—and yet, one cannot help but wonder.

THE EIGHTEENTH AMENDMENT

Even Herbert Asbury, the able chronicler of Prohibition, admitted that the chaos of war and the lobbying for and against wartime prohibition in the Food and Fuel Control Act made the course of the constitutional amendment in the Congress "somewhat confused."[42] What is not confused is what followed. On August 1, 1917, by a vote of 65–20, the Senate approved the resolution that the proposed Eighteenth Amendment—criminalizing the production, transport, and sale of alcohol (though not its consumption or private possession)—be submitted to the states for their ratification. Though this resolution was a big step forward for the Drys, Asbury notes that the Wets believed there was sufficient opposition to kill the amendment, since a majority of only thirteen states in either house of Congress would block it. "The Wets were confident that they could hold thirteen states till doomsday, . . . ignor[ing] completely . . . that the Anti-Saloon

League had been manipulating state legislatures for some ten years, and that the Drys had brought most of them into the fold before they went after Congress."

The Wets had grossly miscalculated. The terms of the resolution required that the amendment be ratified by at least thirty-six states within seven years; it was ratified in just thirteen months. (The first state to ratify was Mississippi; the thirty-sixth, Nebraska.) California, as it happens, was the twenty-second state to vote for ratification. In the end, only Rhode Island and Connecticut declined.[43]

As Daniel Okrent puts it: "The original Constitution and its first seventeen amendments limited the activities of government, not of citizens. Now there were two exceptions: you couldn't own slaves, and you couldn't buy alcohol."[44]

The Eighteenth Amendment reads, in its entirety:

SECTION 1. After one year from the ratification of the article the manufacture, sale, or transportation of intoxicating liquors within, the importation thereof into, or the exportation thereof from the United States and all territory subject to the jurisdiction thereof for beverage purposes is hereby prohibited.

SECTION 2. The Congress and the several States shall have concurrent power to enforce this article by appropriate legislation.

SECTION 3. This article shall be inoperative unless it shall have been ratified as an amendment to the Constitution by the Legislatures of the several States, as provided in the Constitution, within seven years from the date of the submission hereof to the States by the Congress.[45]

The Eighteenth Amendment thus consists of but three sentences. The second clause, giving the states and the Congress "concurrent" power to enforce Prohibition, led to tiresome legal quarrels over the rights and obligations of the Congress and the states under the Eighteenth Amendment. The first clause, though, contained the matter that mattered: it "prohibited" the "manufacture, sale, or transportation of intoxicating liquors . . . for beverage purposes." *Prohibited* is an English word with a clear meaning. But what are "intoxicating liquors"? Were beer and wine included? And what does the phrase "for beverage purposes" mean?

The Eighteenth Amendment required an act of Congress to flesh out its full intended meaning, as well as to set up the enforcement mechanism. That act was the National Prohibition

Act, better known as the Volstead Act. The legislation's full title conveys its portent: "An act to prohibit intoxicating beverages; and to regulate the manufacture, production, use, and sale of high-proof spirits for other than beverage purposes; and to ensure an ample supply of alcohol and promote its use in scientific research and in the development of fuel, dye, and other lawful industries [and practices, such as religious rituals]."

Federal enforcement of Prohibition was placed in the charge of the Bureau of Internal Revenue, part of the Treasury Department. The Volstead Act gave the bureau vast powers of search and seizure, provided for substantial fines and prison terms for violation of the act's provisions, and appropriated $2 million for enforcement for the year 1920. Those funds would be utilized by the 1,520 ready and able enforcement agents of the Prohibition Unit of the bureau.[46]

As 1919 wound down, all the constituent parts necessary for the prohibition of trade in alcohol were in place. At 12:01 AM on January 17, 1920, Prohibition went into effect. The Drys were exultant.

On January 15, 1920, Americans were greeted with the news that, two days hence, all privately owned liquor in warehouses and safety-deposit vaults would be subject to seizure. The announcement sent Wets into a panic, as Asbury details:

> The San Francisco Chronicle described the movement of liquor those last few days as "gigantic." The streets were jammed with trucks and wagons, and the sidewalks were crowded with men hauling boxes and crates. "Fair ladies sat in limousines behind alluring barricades of cases," reported the Chronicle. "Business men in runabouts had cases on their knees. . . . On every face was stamped that extraordinary and inexplicable expression of triumph mingled with apprehension which the possession of irreplaceable treasure in a predicament of extraordinary peril is wont to imbue."[47]

Many historians have spoken of the surprising assumption prohibitionists had maintained throughout their ascent: that the rule of law would solve all. While the demoralized Wets scrambled and bemoaned, even the meekest among them possessed individual agency—and many more were not so meek. As our able chronicler, Herbert Asbury, captures, the Drys "had expected to be greeted, when the great day came, by a covey of angels bearing gifts of peace, happiness, prosperity, and salvation, which they had been assured would be theirs when the rum demon had been scotched. Instead they were met by a horde of bootleggers, moonshiners, rum-runners, hijackers, gangsters, racketeers, triggermen, venal judges, corrupt police, crooked politicians, and speakeasy operators, all bearing the twin symbols of the eighteenth amendment—the Tommy gun and the poisoned cup."[48]

THE EFFECT OF PROHIBITION ON THE WINE INDUSTRY

Daniel Okrent tells us that, at the onset of Prohibition, the combined industries of wine, beer, and spirits made up the "fifth largest industry in the nation."[49] And though Prohibition had a devastating effect on the wine industry overall, there were some surprises as well. An early one stemmed from the provision in the Volstead Act that allowed for home manufacture of "[mostly] non-intoxicating fruit juice." The result was a bursting market for fresh grapes, with prices skyrocketing from $10 to $100 per ton. Needless to say, grape growers took full advantage: in 1919, California had roughly 300,000 acres of vineyards; in 1925, that acreage had almost doubled.[50] And while wine grapes enjoyed the largest market, table grapes and raisins saw increased sales as well.[51]

But aside from this planting spurt, those in the wine industry—who had theretofore made their living through perfectly legal activities—had to find alternative sources of income. And while the history of the Dry era is replete with the derring-do of the bootlegging trade, the same was not true for the wine industry—perhaps in part because of the domestic aura of homemade sherry and the solemnity of sacramental wine. In any case, historians haven't traced large-scale illegal trafficking in the fermented grape. As for the commercial wine industry, Prohibition's highest intent, to put the kibosh on liquor traffic in the United States, succeeded rather well. With the onset of Prohibition, many wineries simply went out of business, as is readily indicated in the annual production figures for the first few years of the regime. In 1919, the country's winemakers produced 55 million gallons; in 1920, that figure was 20 million; in 1922, 6 million; and in 1925, just more than 3.6 million gallons.[52] One significant casualty was the California Wine Association, which had begun dismantling and selling off as soon as it was clear that Prohibition was inevitable.[53]

Thanks to a few exemptions in the Volstead Act, there was some legal production of wine during Prohibition—just not for use as a beverage. Surprisingly, wine has a few industrial uses, as in the manufacturing process of paints, solvents, chemicals, textiles, rubber goods, film, and smokeless powder. Wine also found

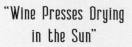

"Wine Presses Drying in the Sun"

The Volstead exemption allowing for home manufacture of very-low-alcohol wine naturally inspired a homemaking trend—particularly in Italian and French families, for whom a meal is not a meal without wine. The *New York Times* offered this description of the Italian neighborhood of North Beach in San Francisco: "A walk through the Italian quarter reveals wine presses drying in the sun in front of many homes. The air is heavy with the pungent odor of fermenting vats in garages and basements. Smiling policemen frequently help the owners of these wine presses to shoo away children who use them for improvised rocking horses."

Source: *New York Times*, April 28, 1929, section 3.

a legal outlet in food manufacture; Pinney tells us that the Colonial Grape Products Company, a "combination of wineries
around the state carpentered together in 1920 from parts of the
wreck of the California Wine Association," "had an extensive
trade with Campbell's Soup for sherry as seasoning, and with the
Bayuk Cigar Company for wine to cure tobacco leaves."[54]

Lesser-employed options included producing wines for
medicinal purposes and for the manufacture of vinegar.[55] (Paul
Masson proudly possessed the only permit in the country for
producing "medicinal champagne."[56]) An interesting twist is
that some established wineries were permitted to both produce wine for nonbeverage purposes and store whatever stock
they hadn't yet sold—which allowed them to bolster the dream
of repeal with actual product saved up for the magnificent day,
should it ever come.[57]

A more substantial exemption permitted the production of
sacramental wine, which was the reason wine had first been made
in California. Several California entities made use of this option,
starting with, as would be expected, religious organizations like
the Jesuit novitiate in Los Gatos and the Christian Brothers novitiate in Martinez. Family producers of sacramental wine included
the Concannons of Livermore, the Sebastiani family of Sonoma,
and the Bisceglias of the San Joaquin and Santa Clara Valleys. The
Livermore Wente family partnered with Napa's Beaulieu Vineyard in making wines for the Archdiocese of San Francisco. Operating in both Napa and San Joaquin Valleys, the Cella family,
under the name Roma Wine Company, found several ways to
prosper during Prohibition. In addition to shipping grapes, they
"made sacramental wines, a 12 percent alcohol wine sauce for can-
ners, a 6 percent wine sauce for cooks, and salted cooking sherry,
as well as grape juice and concentrate."[58]

But while the Cella family fared well during Prohibition, the
market they took advantage of was small. Over the subsequent fourteen years, the annual sale of sacramental wine, which peaked in
1924 at nearly 3 million gallons, averaged just 1.5 million gallons per
year—mostly because the government eventually cracked down on
the ersatz home-grown "churches" who'd received permits to produce putatively sacramental wine.[59] As for the market opportunities of other legally sanctioned grape products, recall what Walter
V. Woehlke was quoted earlier asking: "As for grape jam and grape
syrup, how large a quantity of these commodities did you eat last
year?" And so other measures were necessary—and readily taken.

Forbidden Fruit: Sun-Dried California Wine Grapes

Directions for Making Three Gallons

- Soak five pounds of California Dried Wine Grapes in cold water. After 12 hours run the liquid off and keep for later use.

- Crush the grapes in a small mill or meat-chopper. The pulp is the [*sic*] soaked in water and pressed.

- Put all the juices in a three-gallon crock, fill with water to the top, add two pounds of sugar, and let ferment at a temperature of 55° to 65° Fahrenheit for one week.

- Skim off and siphon into a cask or three-gallon demijohn.

- Cork with a vent hole bung (a bung with a hole bored through, allowing the excess gas to escape, at [the] same time preventing the entrance of air), and keep fifteen days fro [*sic*] after-fermentation.

- Add the beaten whites of two eggs for clarifying.

- Bottle, then immerse bottles with the mouth only projecting in a large vessel of water. Loosen the corks and heat the water to a uniform temperature of 180° Fahrenheit. Then remove the bottles, cork, and seal tightly and place in an inverted position in the cellar.

—Bebe Company, 233 Sansome Street, San Francisco

Source: Heintz, *California's Napa Valley*, 274.

How much wine was illegally made and sold in California during Prohibition is something we'll never know. Louis M. Martini told of being offered $175,000 in cash for 100,000 gallons of wine—and refusing. Other winemakers no doubt accepted similar offers, hiding the transactions behind claims of hijackings and thefts, "reports of broken hoses causing hundred-gallon spills, and fires that mysteriously destroyed wine-laded casts"—as Ruth Teiser and Catherine Harroun tell us. Another ploy was to present to federal agents for inspection casks of seemingly sacramental red wine (actually water) before supposedly being shipped to, say, a church in Cleveland—just to account for the grape usage of a separate, true wine sale.[60] For those winemakers who took their chances, the risk was apprehension by one of the Bureau of Internal Revenue's initial 1,520 agents. (Given that the U.S. population in 1920 was more than 100 million, that meant there was one agent for every 70,000 persons. As would be expected, the number of agents increased soon after, to more than 3,000.)[61]

The legality of home winemaking led to some rather imaginative Prohibition-era moneymaking schemes. As early as 1920 the California Wine Association offered "a harmless grape jelly" that could be made less harmless with the mere addition of water.[62] Some manufacturers of grape juice, especially concentrate, included on their products warning labels that dutifully informed the consumer precisely what they must *not* do with its contents—lest they unintentionally convert the juice to wine.[63] (Recall that the Volstead Act prohibited buying or selling formulas or recipes for homemade liquors.) Others sold wine labeled as grape juice.

Bolder manufacturers went further, as Daniel Okrent shares in *Last Call*. First came the Vino Sano Grape Brick, "a solid, dehydrated block of grape juice concentrate mixed with stems, skins, and pulp. The size of a pound of butter, it came in a printed wrapper instructing the purchaser to add water to make grape juice, but to be sure not to add yeast or sugar, or leave it in a dark place, or let it sit too long before drinking, because 'it might ferment and become wine.'"[64]

A later iteration expanded on the theme. Fruit Industries, Ltd., made up of a number of winemakers headed by Paul Garrett, offered with Vine-Glo both product and service, as the following advertisement conveys:

> Now is the time to order your supply of Vine-Glo. It can be made in your home in sixty days—a fine, true-to-type guaranteed beverage ready for the Holiday Season. Vine-Glo . . . comes to you in nine varieties: Port, Virginia Dare, Muscatel, Angelica, Tokay, Sauterne, Riesling, Claret, and Burgundy. It is entirely legal in your home—but it must not be transported. . . . You take absolutely no chance when you order your home supply of Vine-Glo, which Section 29 of the National Prohibition Act permits you.[65]

Daniel Okrent takes it from there: "A Fruit Industries agent would deliver a varietal grape juice . . . in five-, ten-, twenty-five- or fifty-gallon cans, add yeast and citric acid, and insert a tube to vent off gases. Every few weeks the agent would stop by to monitor progress; after sixty days he would arrive with bottles, foil capsules, corks, and labels, even tissue to wrap the bottles in."[66] Fantastically, as Thomas Pinney relates, "this complete domestic service was assisted by a large grant to the grape growers from the federal farm relief program."

Though Fruit Industries, Ltd., was sublimely confident in the legality of its product, and managed to evade prosecution for a time, by 1931 the threat of a Justice Department lawsuit ended its bold run.[67]

With or without guidance from Vino Sano Grape Bricks or Fruit Industries, the consumption—and, ergo, the production—of wine increased dramatically during Prohibition. In *Winemaking in California,* Teiser and Harroun note that "in the years just before Prohibition, [if] everybody in the United States had shared equally in the total amount of wine consumed, each man, woman, and child would have downed a little more than half a gallon a year. During Prohibition, however, the figure rose. It averaged more than three-quarters of a gallon." Note that these estimates are based on "grape tonnage and include illegal as well as legally produced wine."[68] Other sources back up that level of increase. *Fortune* magazine states that while in 1918 total wine consumption was 51 million gallons, by 1928 that figure had more than tripled, to about 160 million gallons—an increase of 109 million. (Interestingly, during those years consumption of liquor had only doubled.)[69] Thomas Pinney cites the Wickersham Commission as suggesting that, *conservatively,* 111 million gallons of homemade wine were produced during each putatively Dry year—roughly matching *Fortune*'s increased consumption figure. Pinney suggests that one reason wine enjoyed increased consumption was the fact that it was easier to make decent homemade wine than it was to make decent homemade beer.[70]

PROHIBITION IN SAN FRANCISCO

Assemblyman T. M. Wright of Santa Clara County authored California's "Baby Volstead" law, the Wright [Prohibition Enforcement] Act, which was ratified in 1921. He deemed San Francisco, New York, and Chicago to be the country's three wettest cities during Prohibition.[71] In her 1927 book *Does Prohibition Work?,* sociologist Martha Bensley Bruere states that New Orleans was the wettest. Others have suggested Baltimore. But the most recent serious writer on the subject, Daniel Okrent, gives the crown to Detroit—the "City on a Still," as historian Mickey Lyons aptly nicknamed the Motor City's reputation during those fourteen years of Prohibition.[72] Okrent writes: "In at least four major cities—Baltimore, San Francisco, New Orleans, and Detroit—not once was there a lull in the wet storm that blew in on the heels of the Eighteenth Amendment."[73]

San Francisco was particularly ill suited for enforced abstinence. Since its Gold Rush days, it had been a city of *immod-*

This advertisement for Vine-Glo appeared in the *Chicago Tribune,* December 4, 1930.

eration, in industry, commerce, things culinary, and all things forbidden—much of which was lubricated with alcohol. (San Francisco's embrace of vice was so notorious, and colorful, that Herbert Asbury devoted a whole book to the subject, his 1933 *The Barbary Coast.*) For example, tabulating the number of liquor licenses issued in 1890 (three thousand), added to the likely number of establishments operating without license (two thousand), suggests that in that year San Francisco had more watering holes per capita than any other city in the country—twice that of the famously wet cities of New York and Chicago.[74]

San Francisco's proud tradition of drinking prevailed into the Prohibition era, thoroughly imbuing its bibulous City Hall with a disinclination to enforce the land's drinking laws, even to the extent of reprimanding two veteran police captains in 1921 for enforcing those laws. The rebuke went further in 1926, when the Board of Supervisors adopted a resolution opposing police enforcement of Prohibition.[75]

Historian Kenneth Rose believes that San Francisco's pronounced anti-Dry stance resulted from its history being distilled with a particular mix of ethnicities and nationalities. The Prohibitionists, he noted, were largely rural, "native" (meaning, having been here for a generation or two), and Protestant. San Francisco by contrast was, first, the quintessence of nonrural, with a healthy majority of immigrant families, many of whom hailed from such drink-favoring countries as Germany, Italy, Ireland—even Russia. And though the Chinese aren't famous for tippling, San Francisco's Chinatown lost no time contributing to the fun. Rose writes: "Chinatown's famed 'opium dens,' . . . which had been popular with tourists since the 1870s, were often fakes maintained by the Chinatown Guides Association. By the twenties, speakeasies had joined opium dens on the itineraries of whites slumming in Chinatown." Even the sacramental wines of the city's Jewish community contributed to San Francisco's capacity of absorption.[76]

Fortunately, San Francisco's talent for rivaling other wet cities didn't come with their same level of violence. But this isn't to say crime wasn't rampant, or that it never turned bloody. In San Francisco in 1924, bootleggers were being arrested at the rate of approximately six hundred *per month*. Even Prohibition agents were indicted for battery, mayhem, and murder. All the same, in San Francisco vice was relatively orderly, organized, and protected by the authorities.[77] Although Al Capone owned at least one San Francisco speakeasy—hidden below the Warfield theater and connected to the Golden Gate Theater via an underground passage[78]—he mostly left it alone. In the end, San Francisco managed to, as Merritt Barnes puts it, "avoid the horrors of gangland violence so common in cities like Chicago and New York in the same years."[79]

Prohibition was altogether a mad time in San Francisco.

THE CHANGING TIDE REGARDING
THE "NOBLE EXPERIMENT"

The U.S. Constitution was designed to be a document of substance and solidity. To amend it—to add to or subtract from it in any way—requires the endorsement, the ratification, of three-fourths of the nation's states. By this means, the significance and heft of its laws couldn't be subject to mere whim or fleeting sentiment; each potential amendment is to be considered with the respect and seriousness it is due. Statistics bear out that founding intention: since 1789, when the Bill of Rights was first submitted to the states for consideration, nearly 11,700 amendments have been proposed; of those, only 27 have been ratified.[80] And only one has been repealed—within fourteen years of its passage. How on earth did that happen?

Senator Morris Sheppard of Texas, author of the Dry amendment, stated: "There is as much chance of repealing the Eighteenth Amendment as there is for a hummingbird to fly to the planet Mars with the Washington Monument on its tail."[81] And yet 1924, a mere four years after the Eighteenth Amendment went into effect, registered a shift in American sentiment regarding the "noble experiment." In that year nearly sixty bills were introduced in the House of Representatives to water down Prohibition, so to speak, by legalizing low-alcohol beer. Also in that year the United States needed to negotiate several international treaties regarding the patrol of waters outside U.S. jurisdiction, and more money was needed for the Coast Guard. And in an epically violent year a new form of Prohibition death was added: poisonings from bootlegged booze.[82]

Even before the Crash of 1929 and the onset of the Great Depression, Prohibition had become a national fixation, and not of a good sort. Written material on the subject was everywhere, from the lengthy book to the merest leaflet. Magazines and newspapers only fed the national fetish; indeed, one New York newspaper published on average six articles on Prohibition every day—for eight years. The Justice Department, the U.S. Attorneys offices, and the federal courts were overwhelmed with Volstead Act cases. Prohibition was a nagging headache for local officials as well. In 1926, Chicago mayor William E. Dever testified before Congress, saying, "It is an everyday—yes, an hourly—difficulty with us in Chicago. . . . It is almost impossible to give anything like good government along general lines. . . . I find myself immersed in it, to the very great damage of the city, from morning until night."[83]

Enforcement of the Volstead Act was a daunting dilemma. Neither the federal government nor the states gave to those charged with enforcing it sufficient resources with which to do so correctly—because there was no political will to enforce it correctly. For Prohibition's first fiscal year, $2 million had been appropriated for its enforcement; that amount had to be more than tripled for 1921. Overall the annual figure averaged $10 million. And yet, Prohibition Commissioner James M. Doran estimated that $300 million was what was truly needed. This was because effective enforcement called for "all of the forty-eight states cooperat[ing] without stint and regardless of expense; or, lacking that cooperation, . . . Congress [needed to] appropriate enough money to set up a new judicial system, to hire thousands of additional prosecutors, to build hundreds of new prisons, and to establish a huge national police force with virtually unlimited powers of search and seizure." The federal government could little afford a drastic increase in enforcement spending, but at the same time there was no reason to believe the states would step up. From the first, the states had simply passed whatever laws the Drys demanded—but then pointedly declined to enforce them.[84] By 1927, few states were willing to finance enforcement of their own Prohibition laws.[85]

As for the Drys themselves, their leadership declined dramatically following their gargantuan successes. Their brilliant leader and the general counsel of the Anti-Saloon League, Wayne B. Wheeler, died in 1927, leaving a vacuum that was never refilled. The Reverend Earl L. Douglass wrote in his 1931 *Prohibition and Common Sense* that the Anti-Saloon League was "limping, to say the least." At the same time, the Wet cause was gaining steam, with groups such as the American Legion and the nation's labor unions advocating repeal. The Voluntary Committee of Lawyers considered the Eighteenth Amendment "inconsistent with the spirit and purpose of the Constitution." The full New York State Bar Association added its own plea for repeal—including returning the issue to being just a matter for the states to determine for themselves. This example was quickly emulated by bar associations in several other cities. And as for the Wet leadership: gone were the bumbling brewers and distillers. In their stead rose the likes of the Association Against the Prohibition Amendment and the Moderation League, whose membership included prominent lawyers, bankers, and directors of major national corporations: General Motors, the Pennsylvania Railroad, Western Union, Metropolitan Life Insurance—even three Du Ponts.[86] The dice had not been given their final throw, but their numbers were coming up right.

Then came the Depression. The Wets howled—and whooped—that the Depression was the product of Prohibition. Economists backed them up with the inexorable, ineffable things that economists expostulate, and the argument took hold. In 1932, in nominating Franklin Roosevelt as candidate for president at its national convention, the Democratic Party also specified: "We favor repeal of the Eighteenth Amendment." Like Carry A. Nation swinging her hatchet in turn-of-the-century taverns, Roosevelt upon taking office took his axe to Prohibition, starting by slashing the Prohibition Bureau's funding. But the more significant breakthrough resulted from his request to Congress—readily supplied—to slip into the Volstead Act an allowance for low-alcohol beer. As of April 7, 1933, when the Cullen-Harrison (Beer Permit) Act went into effect, the influence of gangsters was largely erased from the American liquor scene; thereafter, speakeasies, which only days before had required Mob protection to operate, exuberantly hocked their wares in the light of day. The final blow: both the Senate and the House of Representatives passed a resolution that walked back the Eighteenth Amendment as if running a film reel in reverse: submitting a repeal amendment to the states for ratification. It took. As Detroit Prohibition historian Mickey Lyons relates: "At 5:32 and 30 seconds on December 5, 1932, Utah—after dragging its proverbial feet to make sure Pennsylvania and Ohio voted first—voted for Repeal. Being the thirty-sixth state to vote in favor, they officially rang in the repeal of Prohibition. The vote itself took a couple of minutes to be officially recorded, as it was interrupted by nearly two solid minutes of raucous cheering from an ecstatic Congress."[87] The Twenty-First Amendment to the U.S. Constitution was ratified in just over nine months. Prohibition had been voted out of existence; Repeal would take effect twelve months later.

History Unwinding Itself

Some of the ways in which Prohibition was undone mimic ways in which it was brought into being. As mentioned previously, the Dry movement had begun with temperance; it was only when that approach proved insufficient that the movement progressed toward the extreme stance that it took. Similarly, Herbert Asbury tells us that no one hoping to dial back the law's prohibitions imagined that it could be just wiped away; instead, proponents angled for a softening of the Volstead Act's proscriptions.

It's also been noted how effective—perhaps essential—the meeting of minds between women's groups and temperance groups had proven to be. Interestingly, the "first organization to abandon the double talk about modification... and [instead] demand outright destruction of the Eighteenth Amendment seems to have been the Women's Committee for Repeal of the Eighteenth Amendment, which in 1927, 'tired of taking a halfway position,' changed its name from the Women's Committee for the Modification of the Volstead Act."

Source: Asbury, *Great Illusion*, 316–17.

The pertinent part of the amendment reads simply, "The eighteenth article of amendment to the Constitution of the United States is hereby repealed." In the end it was the Great Depression that broke the back of Prohibition, the "dry camel," in Herbert Asbury's parlance.[88]

THE FUTURE OF THE WINE INDUSTRY?

Prohibition was the fourth major setback in scarcely more than forty years for the forever fledging California wine industry. As Thomas Pinney puts it:

> The measure intended to kill Demon Rum in this country managed to give it hardly more than a flesh wound. Liquor of all kinds continued to be made by one means or another, and people, perhaps in larger numbers than ever before, continued to drink liquor of all kinds. Yet the interruption to the normal growth and functioning of wine growing in this country had disruptive and destructive effects that are still being felt and will continue to be felt for as long as one can foresee.[89]

Considering that, it's remarkable that today there's any California wine to be found better than swill.

It was noted earlier that winegrowers experienced an expanded market for grapes in the early years of Prohibition. But as could be expected, the home market for grapes reached a saturation point—after which grape prices plummeted, and growers abandoned their vineyards or yanked out their vines.[90]

Many acres of newly planted vineyards did survive the price drop, but they were acres of pretty, insubstantial grapes. While professionals knew that a wine grape's appearance was its least salient attribute, the amateur home winemaker favored varieties like Alicante Bouschet, whose deeper color, larger clusters, and thicker skin helped it to still look luscious when it arrived in the mail. Other grape growers planted table grapes, like Flame Tokay and Emperor. We know from the industry's previous crises that acre upon acre of inadequate grape varieties can't be quickly remedied; decades would pass before California rebounded from this deficiency.[91]

Though many California wineries managed to ride out the Dry years, they were but a fraction of those in existence at its onset. Of those still standing, vineyards planted with inferior varieties were just one of many shortcomings. Wineries were in disrepair, their broken and obsolete fittings and equipment rusted.

Experienced winemakers had left their California wineries for countries where wine could be made legally. And of course many former wine drinkers had simply dropped the habit—or, faced with the scarcity of the Depression, needed to spend their few dimes on more essential commodities. All in all, California's grape growers and winemakers slouched from the gloom of Prohibition into the murk of the Depression.

Though the wine industry would rise again from the ignoble experiment of Prohibition—just as it had risen from the phylloxera epidemic, the earthquake and fire of 1906, and the empty seats at the 1915 Panama-Pacific International Exposition—this time the recovery would take much longer. The realization of that promise foreseen by the early California wine men did not begin until more than thirty years after the repeal of Prohibition. Before then, though, the dark years of the Depression, World War II, and the Korean and Cold Wars would have their separate and collective effects. The recovery from this fourth setback to the California wine industry did not hit its stride until the Vietnam War.

Notes

1. Husmann, "Resistant Vines," 46–47.

2. Note that, when lowercased, *prohibition* refers to efforts to prohibit the use of alcohol; when capitalized, *Prohibition* indicates specifically the period between January 17, 1920, when the Eighteenth Amendment went into effect, and December 5, 1933, when the Twenty-First Amendment went into effect.

3. Boorde, *Compendyous Regyment*, 252–53.

4. Ward, *Trip to New-England*.

5. Asbury, *Great Illusion*, 5–6.

6. Rorabaugh, *Alcohol Republic*, 20–21.

7. Pinney, *History of Wine in America*, 1:426–27; Okrent, *Last Call*, 9.

8. Boorde, *Compendyous Regyment*, 254.

9. Reverend Lyman Beecher, "The Nature and Occasions of Intemperance," *Six Sermons on Intemperance* (Boston: T. R. Marvin, 1828), 20, qtd. in Tyler, *Freedom's Ferment*, 323.

10. Pinney, *History of Wine in America*, 1:429, citing Asbury, *Great Illusion*, 12–13 (for 1810 figure); Tyler, *Freedom's Ferment*, 372 (for 1985 figure); and *Wines and Vines* 67 (July 1986): 22 (for 1985 figure).

11. Pinney, *History of Wine in America*, 1:426.

12. Davis, *Antebellum American Culture*, 393. In 1860, the average retail price of whiskey in the United States was thirty cents a gallon. Thomann, *Liquor Laws*, 196.

13. Pinney, *History of Wine in America*, 1:428.

14. Kobler, *Ardent Spirits*, 60.

15. Pinney, *History of Wine in America*, 1:425–26 and n2. Note that, in prohibitionist parlance, "Demon Rum" referred to any alcoholic drink.

16. Douglass, "Intemperance and Slavery." See also frederickdouglass .infoset.io/islandora/object/islandora%3A92#page/1/mode/1up.

17. Pinney, *History of Wine in America,* 1:427–30, citing in part Kobler, *Ardent Spirits,* 60, 62, 70–73.

18. Ibid., 1:430, citing in part Virginius Dabney, *Dry Messiah: The Life of Bishop Cannon* (New York: 1949), 6.

19. Ibid., 1:431, in part citing Kobler, *Ardent Spirits,* 56–57.

20. Ibid., 1:431; Asbury, *Great Illusion,* 60.

21. Kobler, *Ardent Spirits,* 90. Kobler's figures, from 4.8 gallons to 6.43, "computed from statistics of the U.S. Dept. of Commerce and the Bureau of Internal Revenue."

22. Okrent, *Last Call,* 12.

23. Teiser and Harroun, *Winemaking in California,* 170–71; Powell, "Dashaway Association," 467–71, citing in part Bushnell, *Characteristics and Prospects of California,* 23.

24. Pinney, *History of Wine in America,* 1:432, citing in part Ostrander, *Prohibition Movement,* 69, 72.

25. Sullivan, *Companion to California Wine,* 271.

26. Kerry C. Kelly, "The Volstead Act," U.S. National Archives and Records Administration, page last reviewed February 24, 2017, archives .gov/education/lessons/volstead-act.

27. Andersen, "Give the Ladies a Chance," 137.

28. Okrent, *Last Call,* 16.

29. Pinney, *History of Wine in America,* 1:432–33.

30. Asbury, *Great Illusion,* 98–100.

31. Pinney, *History of Wine in America,* 1:423.

32. Asbury, *Great Illusion,* 100–101. Though the Anti-Saloon League began its tenure eschewing political aspirations, shortly after the Eighteenth Amendment was ratified it changed its tune, proclaiming with glorious fanfare that it was "the strongest political organization in the world."

33. Ibid., 101–2.

34. Meers, "California Wine and Grape Industry," 21.

35. Woehlke, "Grape and Prohibition."

36. California Grape Protective Association, *How Prohibition Would Affect California,* 1, and back cover (unnumbered p. 66).

37. Ibid., 6–7; Meers, "California Wine and Grape Industry," 20.

38. Meers, "California Wine and Grape Industry," 19–22.

39. Sbarboro, *Temperance Versus Prohibition.*

40. Meers, "California Wine and Grape Industry," 21.

41. As qtd. in Teiser and Harroun, *Winemaking in California,* 171.

42. Asbury, *Great Illusion,* 129–30.

43. Ibid., 131–33.

44. Okrent, *Last Call,* 3.

45. "The Constitution: Amendments 11–27," U.S. National Archives and Records Administration, page last reviewed on October 6, 2016, archives .gov/founding-docs/amendments-11-27.

46. Asbury, *Great Illusion,* 134–36.

47. Ibid., 145–46.

48. Ibid., 137.

49. Okrent, *Last Call,* 3.

50. Pinney, *History of Wine in America,* 1:438, citing Teiser and Harroun,

"Volstead Act, Rebirth, and Boom," 57; Ostrander, *Prohibition Movement in California,* 181.

51. Ostrander, *Prohibition Movement in California,* 181.

52. Pinney, *History of Wine in America,* 1:436, citing Cherrington, *Standard Encyclopedia of the Alcohol Problem,* 6:2877.

53. Ibid., 2:8.

54. Ibid., 2:2, 9, 16; citing in part Horace O. Lanza, "California Grape Products and Other Wine Enterprises," interview by Ruth Teiser (Berkeley: Regional Oral History Office, Bancroft Library, University of California, 1971), 10.

55. Ibid., 1:436.

56. Lukacs, *American Vintage,* 219.

57. Pinney, *History of Wine in America,* 2:9.

58. Teiser and Harroun, *Winemaking in California,* 180.

59. Pinney, *History of Wine in America,* 2:9 and n36; U.S. Department of the Treasury, Bureau of Industrial Alcohol, "Table 9. Wine Shipped or Delivered for Sacramental Purposes During the Fiscal Years 1922–1933, Inclusive," *Statistics Concerning Intoxicating Liquors: December 1932* (Washington, D.C.: Government Printing Office, 1933), 20–21, babel.hathitrust.org/cgi/pt?id=umn.31951d00152032v;view=1up;seq=27.

60. Teiser and Harroun, *Winemaking in California,* 180–81.

61. U.S. Census Bureau, U.S. Census Report, 1921: "Statistical Abstract of the United States," 53, www2.census.gov/prod2/statcomp/documents/1921-02.pdf; Asbury, *Great Illusion,* 135.

62. Ostrander, *Prohibition Movement in California,* 179.

63. Sullivan, *Companion to California Wine,* 272.

64. Okrent, *Last Call,* 335.

65. Ostrander, *Prohibition Movement in California,* 179.

66. Okrent, *Last Call,* 335.

67. Pinney, *History of Wine in America,* 1:437.

68. Teiser and Harroun, *Winemaking in California,* 178.

69. "The Wines of the U.S.: Can Wine Become a National Habit?," *Fortune* (February 1934), repr. March 25, 2012, fortune.com/2012/03/25/can-wine-become-an-american-habit-fortune-1934.

70. Pinney, *History of Wine in America,* 2:20 and n79.

71. Rose, "Wettest in the West," 290, citing *San Francisco Examiner,* January 9, 1924.

72. Mickey Lyons, *Prohibition Detroit* (blog), prohibitiondetroit.com/web.

73. Okrent, *Last Call,* 257–59. The "four major cities" statement appears on page 257.

74. Rose, "Wettest in the West," 284, 285. For the figures of San Francisco's drinking establishments Rose cites Asbury, *Barbary Coast,* 123, 124. For the per capita detail, Rose cites Ostrander, *Prohibition Movement,* 81.

75. Rose, "Wettest in the West," 286, citing Ostrander, *Prohibition Movement,* 65.

76. Rose, "Wettest in the West," 286, 288, citing Asbury, *Barbary Coast,* 166, regarding the opium dens.

77. Rose, "Wettest in the West," 287, 290, 294.

78. Stephanie Foo, "Sights and Sounds of Central Market: The Warfield," *Crosscurrents,* KALW, November 22, 2011, http://kalw.org/post/sights-and-sounds-central-market-warfield#stream/0.

79. Merritt Barnes, "'Fountainhead of Corruption': Peter P. McDonough, Boss of San Francisco's Underworld," *California History* 58, no. 2 (Summer 1979): 144, as qtd. in Rose, "Wettest in the West," 287n23.

80. U.S. Senate, "Measures Proposed to Amend the Constitution," www .senate.gov/reference/measures_proposed_to_amend_constitution.htm.

81. Asbury, *Great Illusion,* 316.

82. Rose, "Wettest in the West," 286–87.

83. Asbury, *Great Illusion,* 317–18.

84. Ibid., 318–19.

85. Pinney, *History of Wine in America,* 2:5, citing J. C. Burnham, "New Perspectives on the Prohibition 'Experiment' of the 1920's," *Journal of Social History* 2 (1968).

86. Asbury, *Great Illusion,* 315–21.

87. Mickey Lyons, "24 Golden Rule Drunks: National Repeal Day Was a Dud in 1933," *Prohibition Detroit* (blog), prohibitiondetroit.com/web/ 24-golden-rule-drunks-national-repeal-day-was-a-dud-in-1933. Note that while only two states had refused to ratify the Eighteenth Amendment, ten states didn't ratify the Twenty-First.

88. Asbury, *Great Illusion,* 328.

89. Pinney, *History of Wine in America,* 1:425.

90. Ibid., 1:438.

91. Ibid.

PART THREE

◦⸻◦

After Prohibition

Doldrums, Mondavi, and a Tasting in Paris

Wine needs no apology. It is one of the good
things of life. While hard liquor is drunk for its
effect, wine is drunk patently for pleasure.

—HUGH JOHNSON,
"American Wine Comes of Age," *Time*, 1972

CHAPTER 9

Repeal, Replant, Replenish, Revive

1933–1940s

You cannot make good wine out of bad grapes, and . . .
you cannot make fine wine out of ordinary grapes.

—Leon D. Adams,
"Revitalizing the California Wine Industry," 1974

Most California wine, in short, is belly wash.

—*Fortune,* "The Wines of the U.S.," 1934

EVEN IN THE LAST few years of Prohibition, rumblings of an approaching repeal had begun. Upon the election of progressive president Franklin Roosevelt, after which the end of Prohibition felt inevitable, dormant wineries worked toward a renewed market for wine, and licenses to operate wineries were actively sought by old and new vintners alike. Among those shuttered wineries that revived upon Repeal were Simi of Healdsburg and Petri of Escalon and San Francisco.[1] Among those who had maintained legal trade throughout the Dry spell were the Christian Brothers novitiate and the Cella family's Roma Wine Company. In 1930, sniffing Prohibition's demise in the air, the Christian Brothers bought the Sequoia Estate, renamed it Mont La Salle, and positioned themselves to become a significant enterprise after Repeal. And since the Roma Wine Company was already well functioning throughout the Depression—thanks to their creative line of grape products: sacramental wine, wine sauce, cooking sherry, and the like—following Repeal it became the state's leading winemaker for a number of years.[2]

An early gouge into the Volstead Act was proposed on March 14, 1933, by Representative Thomas Henry Cullen of New York: the allowance to drink a "light" beer, containing just 3.2 percent alcohol. The wine industry lobbied vigorously for the bill to include an analogous light wine, of about 10 percent alcohol, but the best they could get was the same 3.2 percent allowed for beer. (Recall that beer averages about 5 percent alcohol, whereas table wine averages 12 percent; while it's not too much of a stretch to reduce beer to 3.2 percent, there were no 3.2 percent wines to be found.) All the same, the passage of the Cullen-Harrison (Beer Permit) Act—in effect just three weeks after being first proposed—began for the wine industry the legal trudge out of Prohibition. Many wineries no doubt saw little point in producing wine-water, the need for which they likely considered would be short-lived; in truth it was. But several wineries did opt to produce and market light wines during this period: Italian Swiss Colony made a burgundy and a sauterne, and Scatena Brothers of Healdsburg made a sparkling "Clarette."[3]

When Repeal took effect on December 5, 1933, the bungs were pulled from their casks and wine was sold for the first time in fourteen years. But given that the restored legality of wine did not restore the lost market, especially for premium wines, the opening of the gates hardly heralded the triumphal return the industry had hoped for. In the midst of the Great Depression, Americans stuck to their old, cheaper standbys: beer and spirits. Indeed, historian Thomas Pinney points out that the "effective agitation for repeal was largely an Eastern affair," and for the East Coast, beer and spirits were the objective, not wine. And so the industry needed to regain—or develop anew—the public's taste for its product. On the plus side, the increase in homemade wine had introduced many Americans to the fermented grape, as well as to the names of some of its varieties. But there was a downside to that introduction as well, since it's doubtful much of that homemade wine inspired loyal consumers—especially since amateur winemakers favored grapes less suited to making flavorful wine.

Reinvigoration of the California wine market centered on the grape. But though plentiful clusters hung from post-Prohibition vines, a large percentage of them were either table or raisin varieties. Those grapes grown particularly for wine production were predominantly undistinguished, high-yield varieties that had been grafted over the previous high-quality varietals. Indeed, many large fruit growers entered the wine business simply to have an outlet for their surplus grapes. These large growers—Di Giorgio Fruit Company, California Growers Winery, and California Grape Products, among others—glutted the market with grapes and created a chronic surplus that plagued the industry until long after World War II. Adding insult to injury, a large amount of the grapes crushed for wine production were not wine

Compulsory Distillation to Address Grape Surplus

Historian Thomas Pinney relates how, during the post-Prohibition era, "the surplus crop was the chief headache of the trade, and much ingenuity and experiment went into trying to find a remedy." This was the result of expanded vineyards (overplanted in the Prohibition era) producing bumper crops in a few particularly clement growing seasons. Given that these plentiful grapes encountered the contracted market of the Depression, the question was what to do with the excess. The 1938 California Agricultural Prorate Act proposed that the state "convert a large part of the perishable crop into long-lived brandy," the latter being a product that could be shelved until the market welcomed it. The measure, which would be compulsory, required a two-thirds majority to pass; the Wine Institute's active endorsement of the proposal soon produced that majority. As a result, "each grower, if he wished to sell his crop, had to deliver 45 percent of it to the Control Commission for distillation into beverage brandy or high-proof spirits.... The rest of the harvest could be sold to wineries at a guaranteed minimum price. [This was] the real object of the plan."

The problem was that these surpluses existed only for raisin grapes—and yet this compulsory distillation, as it was called, applied to wine grapes as well. Defending the makers of table wine, lawyer H. H. McPike stated: the "Prorate plan contemplates almost confiscation of forty-five percent of dry wine grapes to be converted into brandy on [the] false premise that there is a dry grape surplus. No such surplus exists." Though the approach was deemed successful from the perspective of the wine industry as a whole, continued opposition to the "prorate steamroller" brought on its demise after only one year.

Sources: Pinney, *History of Wine in America*, 2:110–11 and n79, citing H. H. McPike to President Roosevelt. "Surplus crop" statement on p. 110; and Pinney, 2:112 and n88, citing *Wine Review* 7 and Adams, *Wines of America*.

grapes—they were table and raisin grape rejects; being made into wine, or distilled into brandy, was their last resort.[4] Julia Flynn Siler notes: "The wines hurried on to the market in 1934, often by speculators with little winemaking experience, were probably the worst ever produced in the nation's history."[5] (Well, maybe the worst produced in the nation's *commercial* history.)

Vintners who wished to make good wines found themselves in the same conundrum the still-nascent industry had experienced decades earlier. In his 1889 "Plain Talk to the Winemen," Eugene Hilgard had specified that one couldn't develop a reliable market for good wine using inferior grapes or methods.

He had called for research and experience to be codified into a guide of best practices—and he had done just that.[6] And Charles Wetmore in his 1894 "Treatise on Wine Production" had noted: "As a rule, the wine maker is not rich. . . . He is not in a position to develop a wine market." Wetmore had also highlighted the unfortunate economics of the business, one where "quality and quantity are inversely related." At the time, many winegrowers had resorted to what had worked previously: "grafting back to more prolific varieties."[7]

But the trouble was, in the 1890s the industry had had the likes of Hilgard and Wetmore to study best practices and then proselytize them; in the 1930s, the circumstances were very different. As Pinney relates: "No research had been carried out. No instruction had been given to a younger generation. A tradition had been broken, and an orderly growth cut off."[8] James T. Lapsley captures the post-Prohibition climate in a nutshell: "The cold reality at Repeal was that winemaking in California was a poorly organized, highly competitive, and undercapitalized industry attempting to meet the unknown demand of a fragmented national market from an oversupply of low-quality grapes, all in the depths of the Depression."[9]

The wine industry needed financing if it was to survive this latest perilous setback. Bank of America was one of very few institutions willing to fill that need, which did save the industry—but the strict requirements of the bank's short-sighted vision hurt almost as much as it helped. Funders clumped the wine and grape industries together as one market, for which they saw no need for more than one type of grape. And yet, as we know, the fecund *Vitis vinifera* fueled three different markets: wine, table grapes, and raisins, each with its own best grape varieties. In these circumstances, many growers struggled to remain in business, especially those with small plots of wine-specific varietals. A typical complaint by growers voiced post-Prohibition echoed similar objections from industry members post-phylloxera. The concern: sufficient compensation for growing the better grape varieties, such as Riesling, Chardonnay, and Pinot Noir, as compared to the "ordinary" varieties of Carignane, Burger, and Zinfandel—especially since the yield for the premium grapes was but a fraction of the yield for the more standard varieties. (During Prohibition, bootleggers had appreciated that additional volume could be produced by multiple pressings of Alicante Bouschet grapes.[10]) John Daniel, owner of Inglenook—one of the few fine wineries in

California—bitterly resented that banks wouldn't approve larger loans for wine made from superior varieties. Indeed, as Leon D. Adams tells us, the banks, the U.S. Department of Agriculture, and the California Department of Agriculture "all thought of the grape industry as a single industry, and wine merely as the salvage outlet because its use of grapes came last on the calendar." And of the industry's personnel, they thought: "Oh, those wine men. They're just a bunch of ex-bootleggers!"[11] As Frank Schoonmaker and Tom Marvel put it at the time: "The main reason why fully nine-tenths of the wine from California for the next seven or eight years will necessarily be of second-rate quality is because it will necessarily come from vines that can produce only second-rate wine grapes."[12]

While these second-rate grapes did not hold promise for the production of premium wine, they were ideal for the reigning preference for sweet, fortified, anonymous bulk wine: primarily port, muscatel, and sherry, as well as Angelica and Tokay. The California wine industry was for the most part relegated to a market that sought only an uninspired, cheap commodity. Writing in 2017, Esther Mobley explains: "Unlike Port, which is fermented about halfway and then fortified with neutral brandy, angelica is fermented barely or not at all. You pick the grapes ultra-ripe, crush them into grape juice, then add brandy to heighten the alcohol level and prevent further fermentation. The result, often, is a dessert wine that tastes more like molasses than fruit."[13]

Prior to Prohibition, dry table wines had enjoyed a moderate popularity. But post-Repeal, Americans preferred wine that had been "fortified" with a distilled spirit, usually brandy, making it strong and sweet. Several explanations have been offered for this shift. For starters, sugary soft drinks had gained in popularity during Prohibition, and so the winemakers needed to meet that new American craving for sweet drinks. Second, "unlike dry table wines," Pinney tells us, "fortified wines would not spoil—or at least they would not spoil so quickly, or so perceptively, since the added alcohol and sweetness masked defects in wine quality."[14] A drink less likely to spoil is certainly a wiser purchase in a period of want such as the Depression. Another possibility: it may simply be that fortified, "dessert" wines resembled distilled spirits, but at a lower price. Indeed, the tax on fortified wines was minuscule compared to that levied on distilled spirits. For whatever reason, fortified wine was the alcohol of choice—and no more so than on skid row.[15] By 1937, California stores stocked five bottles of fortified wine for every one bottle of table wine. It would be thirty years before table wine would regain its previous prominence in the market.[16]

———— ❧ ————

AND SO THE MAJORITY of California wineries during the Depression produced fortified wine, which they sold in bulk to giant distributors, who bottled and shipped it. And though these wines did have a market, they hewed to a remarkably low standard. Burke Critchfield, Bank of America's principal representative to the California wine industry at the time, noted how "concoctions made of raisins, dried grapes, concentrate, extracts, water, and sugar were put out as 'wine' in elaborate packages, with intriguing vintage statements, sometimes 'guaranteed.'"[17] In *Vintage: California Wine Labels of the 1930s,* Frances Dinkelspiel writes: "These labels hark back to a dark time in the California wine industry at the height of the Great Depression. . . . Their bucolic scenes and titles invoking royalty were an invitation to set troubles aside and find cheer in a glass. Unfortunately, few could enjoy what they sipped. Most of the wine made in California in the 1930s was downright awful."[18] *Fortune* magazine concurred; in 1934 it observed: "Most California wine, in short, is belly wash."[19]

Commercial winemaking of the era functioned under the same ills Eugene Hilgard had railed against in 1889. Post-Repeal wine was made with inferior grapes, yes; but also, perhaps more so, the winemaking was plagued by sloppy methods, the result of both ignorance of even basic technology and an indifference to the quality of the wine produced. The art of winemaking that had been lost over the fourteen years of Prohibition resulted in the same lessons needing to be relearned, namely that wine must be produced in a scrupulously clean, cool, controlled environment. What took place instead would make the perfectionist winemaker weep. Wines were fermented at higher temperatures. Deplorably maintained, outdated equipment led to lactic acid bacteria and mold. Add to the list metal contamination, tartrates, protein instability in white wines, and refermentation in the bottle. In brief, myriad shortcomings resulted in wines of dubious drinkability on the shelf. Additionally, some wineries shipped out their product before it was ready—simply because the entities holding the mortgage demanded it, their concern about cash flow obliterating any concern about the inadequacy of their underaged product.[20]

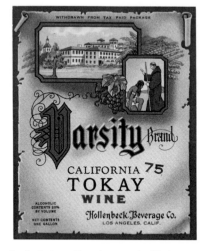

In depicting a Franciscan padre "doing God's work," this Varsity Brand California Tokay wine label harks back to the higher purpose that wine served *before* Prohibition. Hollenbeck Beverage Co., Varsity Brand California Tokay Wine. From the California Wine Label and Ephemera Collection, Kemble Special Collection 07-012. Courtesy of the California Historical Society.

But ignorance of best practices was not the only culprit; in many ways indifference to the quality of the wine being produced, as noted above, was more damning. After all, uninformed winemakers who take pride in their enterprise can ameliorate their shortcomings, but indifferent winemakers or financiers, lacking the desire to overcome their failings, can doom their product.

Unfortunately, problematic winemaking wasn't just to be found at the fortified bulk wineries. In 1937, Beaulieu Vineyards, one of the premier producers of the day, experienced a disastrous occurrence of tainted wine produced for a plum contract with a prominent East Coast importing firm—an unprecedented opportunity during this precarious time. As a result, nearly all of the large order of wine was returned. The (newly appointed) Beaulieu winemaker, André Tchelistcheff, later recalled: "There was refermentation in the bottle, there was a breakdown of mineral salts in the bottle, wines murky, muddy in the glass . . . it was a tragedy."[21]

Fortunately, Beaulieu had strong financial backing from its owner, Georges de Latour, which insulated it from both bankruptcy and the undue influence of bottom-line-blindered banks. And in Tchelistcheff Beaulieu had a winemaker who strove to create an excellent product. He identified the problem to be a reaction between the acid in the wine and the iron in their equipment, which produced significant iron oxide—rust. He remedied this concern by utilizing Pyrex glass instead, an expensive but effective solution. In this case, the well-funded Beaulieu could afford both the experimentation and retrofitting required to address the problem; unfortunately, the fact that the problem occurred at an upscale winery indicated just how low the industry's "best practices" overall had fallen. Other wineries could ill afford the means to solve their own particular shortcomings, and Beaulieu couldn't build trust in California wine all on its own.[22] The wine industry found itself in yet another pickle.

The Gallo Enterprise—Part One

While the 1930s produced forgettable wine, it did provide the foundation of a wine empire that would grow to become the largest in the world. The history of this particular empire begins a few decades earlier.

Louis Gomberg, the wine industry's first statistician, has noted that "traditionally in this country the table wine market has consisted primarily of immigrants who brought over their wine-enjoyment practices and way of life from Europe—mostly Italians, French, and Spanish, and a few other western Europeans."[23] This was precisely the market that Italian brothers Giuseppe (Joe) and Michelo (Mike) Gallo tapped into when they emigrated from the winemaking region of Piedmont, Italy, to turn-of-the-century San Francisco. Biographer Ellen Hawkes relates:

> The pensiones that catered to Italians usually had small saloons where locals gathered at night to drink the red wine so reminiscent of home—what many called 'dago red.' . . . On the side of each [wine] barrel was stenciled the name of the company supplying the wine. The customers . . . ordered their wine by name, choosing from among the several brands that in those days included Italian Swiss Colony and [Lachman and Jacobi]. The names, the brothers learned, did not always refer to a winery, but to the company that bought wine in bulk from winemakers, then barreled it and sold it to pensiones. It was a rudimentary form of distribution that met the needs of Italian communities where wine was considered an essential part of everyday life.

Starting with just a secondhand truck, barrels stamped with Gallo, and a small office in Oakland, the brothers started the Gallo Wine Company by the end of 1906—when San Francisco was only eight months into its post-disaster reconstruction. Not long after, Joe and Mike married two sisters who were daughters of Italian winemaker Battista Bianco.[24]

In 1910 Joe Gallo established a saloon in his name; in time he also ran a hotel, and started a business selling liquor. During Prohibition, Joe did what many winegrowers did: grow and ship grapes rather than wine, capitalizing on the home winemaking market. Mike also did as many did in the era: enter the bootlegging business. One young local later recalled: "To us, Mike Gallo was as notorious and powerful as Al Capone"—this assessment due in part to the fact that "everybody knew that he had done [time] in San Quentin."[25] Later, Joe assisted in his brother's shady enterprises in Livermore, which included producing brandy and wine for the "'soft-drink parlors' or cigar and tobacco shops" that had replaced pre-Prohibition saloons. In the early 1920s, Joe—now "Joe Sr.," after the birth of his third son, Joe Jr.—bought vineyard properties planted with Zinfandel grapes in the San Joaquin Valley. His older sons, Ernest and Julio, worked with him in his grape-growing and, likely, wine-producing business—this latter detail officially denied, of course. In another Prohibition trend,

Underground Winemaking During Prohibition

When the stock market crashed on October 24, 1929, wine grape prices plummeted—along with most other commodities. In response, Joe Gallo Sr. did what many other grape growers had done: he dug underground tanks for storing crushed grapes. As Ellen Hawkes notes: "Winemaking had gone underground, and while the technology of cement tanks would be perfected later, even in their rudimentary form they became a crucial part of the bulk-wine business well before Repeal. In fact, recognizing an innovation in wine production and storage methods, even those winemakers who were not bootlegging began to install underground tanks in order to stockpile a supply of wine in anticipation of its predicted legalization." Robert Mondavi would add: "If you had an underground tank, you were in the winery business for all intents and purposes."

Source: Hawkes, *Blood and Wine*, 82–83.

The Gallos and the Franzias and the Mondavis

The business and personal lives of the Gallo family have criss-crossed those of their cohorts. Ernest Gallo married Amelia Franzia, the daughter of Giuseppe Franzia, founder of one of the pioneer California wineries in Ripon. Mike Gallo, the uncle of Ernest and Julio (and brother of Joe Sr.), in 1928 took Sam Sebastiani as a partner in the Woodbridge Winery near Lodi. Joe Gallo Sr. and Cesare Mondavi, father of Peter and Robert Mondavi, both sold wine grapes during Prohibition to Paul Alleruzzo in Chicago. And when Joe Gallo Sr. sent Julio to New Jersey to oversee grape sales, young Julio was befriended by Jack Riorda, wine-maker-turned-grape-shipper at Prohibition-era Italian Swiss Colony.

Source: Hawkes, *Blood and Wine*, 62, 69–70, 74, 96.

Joe also produced grape juice—as well as, most likely, wine labeled as juice.[26]

In June 1933, by which time five states had ratified the Twenty-First Amendment, Joe Sr. took out two loans totaling $31,000 in cash. A few weeks later he and his wife, Susie, were found shot to death, an apparent murder-suicide. Their estate was inherited by their three sons: Ernest, twenty-four; Julio, twenty-three; and Joe Jr., thirteen—Joe Jr. under the guardianship of his older brothers.[27] Not two months after their parents' deaths, Ernest and Julio founded the E. & J. Gallo Winery in Modesto, Stanislaus County. (By this time the $31,000 cash loan from just a few weeks prior had disappeared.) Later Ernest and Julio would claim that what became the largest winery in the world had been started on only $5,900.23 of their savings—that it decidedly had not been begun by their father.[28]

Aided by their fathers' grower contacts and neighbors, the three sons heavily invested their labor toward the enterprise, though not always wholeheartedly or equally. The youngest, Joe Jr., claims that, though he was made to work at the winery—under Ernest's hectoring supervision—from the time of his parents' death he was excluded from his brothers' partnership and any ownership interest in the business. In future years he would assert that their father, not his two brothers, had founded the winery, and that he accordingly had an ownership interest in it. But Ernest and Julio steadfastly denied Joe Jr.'s claim, and successfully excluded him from the winery's profits. Decades later, Joe Jr. and his son, Mike, began the Joseph Gallo Cheese company. For their efforts they were sued—also successfully—by the older brothers for using their trademarked family name.[29]

From the beginning, the goal had been to build E. & J. Gallo Winery into an enterprise that would dwarf all other wine ventures. They achieved this dream through innovative and aggressive sales tactics, a constant drive to expand, and hard, hard work. Early efforts at expansion included building a vast new winery with a capacity of 1.5 million gallons in concrete tanks, the newest technology to hit the industry, with an assembly-line operation that could process one ton of grapes in one minute.[30]

Expansion, drive, and *innovation* would remain watchwords for the Gallo empire. Later efforts involved building a vertical integration system and seeking to control their own distributorships.[31] William Heintz notes, "In due course the Gallos had organized the first truly national wine distribution system."[32] In so doing they—or Ernest, to be more precise—sought to bypass the middlemen, the wine and beer distributorships that already in this post-Prohibition era were a powerful political and economic force in California, to the chagrin of many other individual growers and wineries. Thus, though the Gallo enterprise was an enormous competitor to the smaller entities in the trade, it also greatly aided them in challenging the status quo of the Depression years.

JOINING FORCES—
COOPERATIVES, GUILDS, AND INSTITUTES

In 1934, the University of California calculated that it cost a small, premium, three-ton-an-acre vineyard in Sonoma County $19 to produce one ton of grapes. But since those grapes sold for only $15 to $20 per ton, the profit margin of this era was dismal for small entities.[33] Following Repeal, the market dominance of increasingly enormous operations—of the likes of E. & J. Gallo Winery, Roma Wine Company, California Growers Winery, Mission Bell Winery, and Di Giorgio Fruit Company—forced smaller wineries and growers to the margins, or worse. Between 1934 and 1942, 554 wineries were forced out of business, their lack of premium wine grapes overwhelmed by a glut of common wine and raisin grapes.[34] And so many growers joined cooperative wineries, whereby small growers could operate much like bulk producers, pooling their grapes and securing large, more lucrative contracts with distributors.[35] Among the most successful early cooperatives was the Napa Valley Cooperative Winery. Within this cooperative, growers increased their revenue by as much as $7 to $10 per ton.[36]

But the consolidation didn't stop with just wineries joining production forces; some created large-scale marketing entities as well. In 1937, three large cooperative wineries in the Central Valley launched California Wine Sales, which marketed their products with a larger capacity than they could have managed on their own. Indeed, they were "convinced that such marketing associations [were] the salvation of the cooperative winery." In 1943, California Wine Sales was renamed the Wine Growers Guild; it was successful for decades thereafter.[37]

A similar consolidation had taken place not long before California Wine Sales was formed. After Repeal, only a few of the most profitable wineries could afford to actively market their wines. Most wineries produced anonymous bulk wine, which was subsequently labeled by the bottlers under numerous names. The only distinguishing marking on the label was often

CALIFORNIA. The industry needed advocates to distinguish its wine and reclaim its pre-Prohibition prestige. They had various other concerns as well, as Thomas Pinney relates: "New federal and state regulations, new taxes, and new requirements for compliance with all the inconsistent rules affecting interstate commerce; besides these burdens, there was an uninstructed public and an absence of clear standards for the production and labeling of wine."[38]

With these matters in mind, in 1933 the Grape Growers League—formed in 1932 by notable table wine figures like the Rossis of Italian Swiss Colony and Georges de Latour of Beaulieu Vineyards—became the Wine Producers Association. Their goal was to bring about full Repeal, or at least the legalization of the commercial wine trade within the Volstead Act. In the same year, a counterpart venture was formed by the California Sweet Wine Producers in the fortified wine trade. The following year, in order to advocate for their common goals of promoting California wine, the two joined forces as the Wine Institute. Their agenda: oppose adverse legislation, support simplification of regulations, sponsor research, keep members informed about activities, educate the public about wine, and promote wine as "a food product and temperance beverage."[39]

Thirty-two wineries initially signed on as members of the institute. Within its first seven months, it negotiated tax and license fee reductions in many states, secured new permissions for bulk sales, reduced federal regulatory red tape, worked toward educating the restaurant and hotel trade in wine sales, and recommended minimum prices for grapes that exceeded previous rates. In the Wine Institute's annual meeting of 1935, secretary-manager Harry Caddow emphasized the importance of the grape grower, "upon whom, as everyone knows, the welfare of the entire viticultural industry depends."[40]

One figure who served as the imagination and impetus behind the Wine Institute during its formative years was Leon D. Adams.[41] Adams was a San Francisco journalist who championed wine as an ideal means for "civilizing American drinking." Adams knew the industry's dirty little secret: many winery owners *themselves* believed that wine would never amount to more than the beverage of choice, its bottles wrapped in brown paper bags, for the denizens of skid row—"winos."[42] Adams's original goal for the Wine Institute was to have table wines declared a nonintoxicating beverage that would not be sold in bars but be reserved for home

Lionizing Leon D. Adams

In her 1974 interview with Leon D. Adams, Ruth Teiser characterized him as one who "saw the possibilities of the wine industry in California when very few people did, . . . that [he] more than anyone else went right about working on the development of that industry." One of Adams's initial concerns—doctrinal differences in the industry—he describes as follows: "You see, the principal people in the wine industry didn't understand wine. They never drank it: they drank whiskey."

But Adams was wine's staunch advocate. As Maynard A. Amerine writes in his introduction to the interview, Adams credited Andrea Sbarboro's pamphlets on temperance as the "source of his fascination with the wine industry. He himself says his career goal was 'to civilize American drinking, [to] teach Americans to use wine.'" In fact, he wrote his 1958 book *The Commonsense Book of Wine* in order to do just that. Historian Charles Sullivan asserts that the book "helped sweep away some of the meaningless rituals and taboos that had hindered the American public's acceptance of table wine as a part of everyday life." Historian Thomas Pinney states that the 1973 publication of Adams's *The Wines of America* only deepened his status, making him the "standard authority on the subject."

Again from Amerine: "[With his goal to civilize American drinking,] Mr. Adams thus becomes a missionary for wine"—though "historians may find that he was more than just a missionary, and that his impact on the American wine industry extended to much more than just civilizing American drinking."

Sources: Amerine, introduction to Adams, "Revitalizing the California Wine Industry," iii; Adams, "Revitalizing the California Wine Industry," 65; Sullivan, *Companion to California Wine*, 2; Pinney, *History of Wine in America*, 2:31.

and restaurant use.[43] Although this goal was unrealistic, Adams knew he needed to convince the winery owners of the value of wine as an integral part of a good meal before he could possibly hope to convince the public of that fact.

But first, the quality of the product California was marketing had to improve dramatically. The wine producers with the most political influence, however—Gallo, Sebastiani, Simi, and cooperative wineries that were members of Fruit Industries— refused to produce premium wines, or even to join the Wine Institute. These wineries, Adams recalled, saw no reason to contribute a substantial sum of money (dues were assessed based on the members' gallonage inventory) to a cause that would not directly represent them.[44] So the Wine Institute and its advertising

Gallo "Dinner Bell" Wine Label

This label for E. & J. Gallo Winery's Dinner Bell semi-sweet California Red Table Wine tells consumers how "Dinner Bell helps make a good meal better." From the California Wine Label and Ephemera Collection, Kemble Special Collection 07-059. Courtesy of the California Historical Society.

Though E. & J. Gallo didn't respond to Leon Adams's exhortation to join the Wine Institute, it did agree with his assertion that the public needed to be taught that wine is an integral part of a good meal. Accordingly, the label for Gallo Wine Company's Dinner Bell semisweet California Red Table Wine tells consumers all they need to know about the wonders to be found within the bottle, starting with: "Dinner Bell helps make a good meal better."

> This wine is made from grapes raised in Northern California produced solely from vines grown from imported cuttings . . . which grapes are selected for their high quality, color, sweetness, and soundness. Note its distinctive flavor. This wine has been especially produced for the American family and helps make a good meal better.
>
> This delicious wine can be served chilled or at room temperature.
>
> Try Dinner Bell white table wine with cream dishes, soups, salads, chicken, fish, or any mildly flavored food. Try Dinner Bell red table wine with game, roast beef, steaks, turkey, pot roast, chops, macaroni, and other full-flavored meals.

Thus spoke the label's "Jolly Old Gallo, Father of Wine."

Source: Miya and California Historical Society, *Vintage*, unnumbered page.

arm, the Wine Advisory Board, primarily promoted the premium wineries that produced but a tiny fraction of the wine distributed around the country.

The Wine Advisory Board became a major advocate for the select, small-scale wineries of Napa and Sonoma during the 1930s and 1940s. After selling Italian Swiss Colony to National Distillers in 1942, Edmund Rossi became manager of the board and actively pursued educating the wholesalers and retailers who sold California wine. One way he did this was through the literature they disseminated about wine. Instead of following the established practice of offering bulky booklets, intended more for the wine savvy, Rossi opted for less expensive, smaller leaflets written for those who knew next to nothing about wine. Since the leaflets cost less to produce, the board could afford to print more—thus reaching more readers. One angle they used capitalized on the view that wine should ideally be paired with food—that wine in fact enhanced the dining experience. They produced leaflets on cheese and wine, meat and wine, fish and wine. As Rossi shared in an interview with Ruth Teiser, the idea was to identify

The Wine Institute Seeks to Increase Consumption of California Wines

In *Bottled Poetry: Napa Winemaking from Prohibition to the Modern Era*, James T. Lapsley shares some of the ins and outs of post-Repeal marketing efforts. Essentially, the Wine Institute, which was a voluntary organization, had from its beginnings seen the need for substantial market development. Aided by passage of the

> California Marketing Act of 1937, which allowed the development of agricultural commodity marketing boards,...the Wine Institute...backed the creation of a new marketing order, the Wine Advisory Board, which would collect gallonage assessments from California producers, .75 of a cent per gallon for dry wine and 1.5 cents per gallon for sweet wines [about 5 percent of value] to be used for market development.
>
> Under the law, 65 percent of producers had to vote in favor of the proposed marketing order, and its proponents used the logic of "a rising tide lifts all ships" to urge the marketing order's passage. Harry Caddow of the Wine Institute argued that the potential U.S. wine market had "scarcely been scratched," and that wine had "the greatest marketing opportunity ever opened to an American farm product." Clearly, an over-supply of grapes existed, as evidenced by the 1938 prorate, which forced distillation of 45 percent of the grape crop. Did the industry want to control production or expand consumption? "All the pro rates, all the legal measures whereby quantities are regulated are, to our belief, not a fraction so important as intelligent means of stimulating consumption," the *St. Helena Star* editorialized. The industry was convinced and voted overwhelmingly in favor of the Wine Advisory Board, which officially came into existence on October 24, 1938.

Source: Lapsley, *Bottled Poetry,* 85 and references cited.

doors through which a new consumer of wine could be reached: "Some people who don't like wine, like cheese, and some people that don't like cheese, like wine. So we figured that there must be something in the combination that had its appeal. . . . The only question was of reaching that particular public. . . . The same thing with fish. Lot of people don't like fish, but maybe with wine they'd like it."[45] The salesmen employed by the Wine Advisory Board became a surrogate sales force for many small-scale wineries that couldn't afford their own marketing. Among the wineries showcased frequently were the elite four from Napa: Inglenook, Beaulieu, Beringer, and Larkmead.[46]

LEGACY WINERIES AND EMPASSIONED WINEMAKERS

Here is Sebastian Collins in Kevin Starr's novel *Land's End* describing the wineries of Napa Valley:

> Around eleven o'clock we entered the Napa Valley. Vineyards stretched away on all sides of us, reaching towards the foothills on the eastern and western edges of the valley. To our left, we could see the Inglenook Winery of Captain Gustav Niebaum, a stone fantasy resembling the castle of an Eastern European fairytale. Chateau Montelena and Chateau Beaulieu—next seen—evoked the South of France. We passed the great stone winery built by the Beringers, a Gothic-like affair, three stories tall, reminding me of the Rhineland. Greystone Cellars, done in the grand manner of Richardsonian Romanesque and set on a commanding knoll, dominates the central Napa Valley like a great cathedral devoted to the worship of the vine.[47]

It could easily be said that the wineries Inglenook, Beaulieu, Beringer, and Larkmead all worshipped the vine. These four were established Prohibition survivors of Napa Valley who were restored following Repeal by new generations of vineyardists and winemakers.

Some notable vintners—such as Finnish fur trader Gustave Niebaum, who founded Inglenook in 1879—arrived at viticulture from previous ventures; others, like German brothers Jacob and Frederick Beringer, knew from the start that winemaking was their calling. Jacob Beringer's first foray into the California industry began with Charles Krug in 1869. In 1875, the brothers founded their own winery near St. Helena, their vineyards dubbed Los Hermanos (The Brothers). They maintained operation during Prohibition producing sacramental wines, then returned to making award-winning table wines post-Repeal. In later years Beringer has been best known for its Cabernet Sauvignon; its private reserve is considered of "world-class stature." It remained a viable enterprise well into the twenty-first century.[48]

The Beringers' fellow vintners John and Felix Salmina—uncle and nephew—purchased S. P. Connor's Larkmead winery in 1895. Their acclaimed winemaking was readily restored after Prohibition; Sullivan notes that "only Beringer won more medals at the new State Fair competition in 1936." Furthering their reputation, in 1937 Larkmead earned first-place prizes for its Zinfandel and

Cabernet. Unfortunately, the enterprise could not maintain its prestige after the death of Felix Salmina, at which point it entered the corporate labyrinth fated to so many wineries before.[49]

Two of the named Napa four merit deeper description, starting with Beaulieu, the one winery of the group that actually flourished during Prohibition.

Beaulieu Vineyards

Beaulieu Vineyards began production in 1900 under the direction of Frenchman Georges de Latour. On account of his strong established relationship with the Catholic Church before Prohibition, Beaulieu became the primary producer of altar wine for Catholic dioceses across the country. Its success allowed it to continue to plant premium varietals at a time when other growers felt forced to downgrade their grapes. But though expanding while others contracted, Beaulieu also shared in the wealth, arranging with the Wentes in Livermore to make high-quality white wines for the Beaulieu label. De Latour furthered the reach of the Beaulieu name via his own marketing apparatus and distributing company. And with financial success also came recognition: Beaulieu wines entered into competitions were judged to be among the very best produced in the latter half of the 1930s—notwithstanding the 1938 debacle, when thousands of cases of "tragically" tainted wine were returned from a major sale. Beaulieu bounced back from that debacle the following year by winning three gold medals at the Golden Gate International Exhibition. One of those winners became the gold standard for Cabernets for the next four decades.[50]

Inglenook

Despite Beaulieu's dominance in the minds and palates of the wine judges in the latter 1930s, Beaulieu's own winemaker, Russian André Tchelistcheff, would later confess that he "always personally considered Inglenook [not Beaulieu] the first château," an attribution that very much derived from Inglenook's dedication to excellence. Inglenook's owner, John Daniel Jr.—grandnephew of Gustave Niebaum, the Finnish fur trader who founded Inglenook in 1879—and German winemaker George Deuer evaluated every vintage against Daniel's exacting, "exquisite standards." Wine that didn't make the grade they'd pronounce unworthy of the Inglenook label, after which it was instead consigned to bulk distributors. Tchelistcheff notes that it was John Daniel's wealth,

The Winemaking Sorcery of Inglenook

Though only vague details are known about Inglenook winemaker George Deuer's methods, James Laube posits some theories in his *Wine Spectator* article "The Glory That Was Inglenook." He notes that the flavorful grapes cultivated on the old Niebaum estate likely benefited from minimal human intervention—beyond occasional thinning to maintain a healthy fruit-to-vine ratio. Deuer also likely filtered his wine so as to remove tainting bacteria, an endemic concern at the time. Indeed, "only the cleanest, most meticulously made wines could escape the dangers to quality posed by . . . contamination." In addition, unlike some winemakers, Deuer maintained the common French practice of blending in touches of wines—notably Zinfandel or Petite Sirah—that would augment an Inglenook Cabernet's body, texture, and color. Altogether, Deuer's various exacting methods, whatever they were precisely, created wines whose legend persists to this day.

Source: Laube, "Glory That Was Inglenook," 65, 67.

inherited from Niebaum, that "permitted" them to maintain this stringent standard.[51] James Laube adds: "Back then, Napa's winemaking conditions were abysmal. This was in a time when the most expensive wines sold for $1 or $2 a bottle; vintners could ill afford the luxury of not selling every drop they made. But Daniel didn't [stand by] wines he didn't like."

The wines that did make the grade were legendary. Motivated by the motto "Pride, not profits," Daniel and Deuer set themselves to creating only the finest wines. Their exacting methods included using only estate-grown ripe grapes that were crushed and pressed in basket presses before being fermented in large casks. The juice was then aged for two to three years—not in small oak barrels, as other wineries used, but in massive tanks, which minimized oxidation. This approach no doubt contributed to the remarkably long life these wines have enjoyed.[52] Indeed, modern critics have declared many of its vintages of the 1940s and 1950s among the best ever produced in California.

Unfortunately, not all beautiful stories enjoy a beautiful end. The "luxury of not selling every drop they made" was not a luxury that could be maintained indefinitely. After years of financial strain, in 1964 John Daniel sold Inglenook to United Vintners—with the understanding that he would still "oversee winemaking" and that Inglenook would be maintained as "the Tiffany of the California wine industry." Sadly, Daniel's expectations would not be fulfilled. Infuriated at the sale, George Deuer burned his winemaking notes. And since the taciturn Deuer had been close-mouthed throughout his years of employment at Inglenook, he had never shared the secrets of his winemaking methods. Thus the magic of Inglenook can never be re-created—unless by accident—and critics and wine lovers can only speculate on just how Inglenook produced such enchanting wines.

The four quality producers of the Depression era provided a hope that someday, if the industry and public could shift their preferences from spirits and beer to wines, and fine wines at that, these wineries could flourish. Additional hope was sparked when, in 1937, Larkmead, Beringer, and Inglenook received a *diplôme d'honneur* at the Paris Exposition. In response, the *St. Helena Star* wrote that the honor confirmed "our area is second to none in the production of the world's best."[53] The honor was indeed great, but the wine industry would need much more than a *diplôme* in order to gain the reliable reputation it coveted—as well as the market security that would come in turn.

Louis M. Martini Winery

The California wine industry has had its share of figures known for their impassioned personalities. George Deuer was one, as evidenced by both his secretive dedication to precise methods and the indignant destruction of his precious notes. Louis M. Martini was another. Industry elder Leon Adams tells us: "The ego of Louis Michael Martini was expressed in two ways: one was in arguing, and the other was in producing a very fine product." Though he'd produced wine in California for decades, in 1940 Martini introduced an entire line of varietal wines under his own label that "ranked overnight...with the very finest premium wines of California."[54] Martini was thus among the first following Prohibition to make wine labeled with the name of the grape and the vintage, wines made from the Cabernet Sauvignon, Barbera, Johannisberg Riesling, and Sylvaner grapes he'd planted on his nearly six hundred acres in Sonoma.

The particulars of Martini's personality were evident in both his dedication to the industry and his dealings with his peers. In 1944 he helped to start the regional trade group Napa Valley Vintners. Six years earlier, Martini had also been among the original founders of the Wine Institute. Interviewed in 1973, he told Lois Stone and Ruth Teiser: "You see what happened, I realized at the time that you've got to have some kind of an association to get together, not to protect yourselves but to present a unified front, everybody together." But a unified front can waver within a realm that welcomes multiple opinions. In time he took a disliking to an advertising campaign the institute produced—since it, in his opinion, did little to promote fine wine—to the extent that he refused to pay his gallonage assessments.[55] But it would appear Martini's objection went deeper than that. He believed that advertising in general was futile, "only good for promoting something that is not up to the quality that people want.... People buy what they want, and make the market."

Martini's account of his displeasures with the institute conveys much about the vagaries of interpersonal relations:

> Five of us agreed to put the first money up [$500]...and hire a manager.... We agreed to put up $1,000 later. Then we got heavy taxes at the end at the year. Then they got a man I didn't particularly like....
>
> Then they wanted [Harry] Caddow for manager, Caddow and Leon Adams; and I wanted somebody else. I said, "Why don't we

wait? Why are we in a hurry?" Well, Rossi and Lee Jones wanted Caddow. They overruled me. Then [Burke] Critchfield took over and wanted to do everything himself. Well, I got disgusted and didn't join. The hell with it.[56]

Martini was confident that if he stuck to his quality winemaking principles the market would follow. It would appear that his stance was a viable one, at least for him, since the Louis M. Martini Winery still exists today.

Martin Ray Winery

The study of personality and passion continues with vintner Martin Ray. A former stockbroker who *prospered* during the Depression, Ray was a longtime, disciplined disciple of winemaker Paul Masson; indeed, he may have been even more fanatical than his mentor in his zeal to produce fine wines. Paul Lukacs writes that Ray "had an arrogance that some people attributed to genius and others to near insanity."[57] To his assiduous training he brought a palate educated on the best European wines he could acquire. From his Table Mountain vineyards, planted in the early 1940s with Cabernet, Chardonnay, and Pinot Noir—at a time when, as Thomas Pinney relates, "these wines were so rare in California as to be practically invisible"—he produced what some consider the region's only superb wines of the day. His exacting methods, developed during his tenure with Paul Masson, began with unirrigated vineyards, the grapes from which would be crushed within an hour of picking. After fermentation they were aged in oak until they were "ready"—usually ten years. Then they were bottled by hand and affixed with a high price tag. Ray thought the price and the quality of his wines would speak for themselves. He made his opinion clear: "Quite frankly I would like people to be shocked, shocked first at the type of wines that can be made in California, and second, by the prices which people are willing to pay for them when at their best."[58]

In sharp contrast to fellow impassioned winemaker George Deuer, Ray opposed blending; he firmly believed a bottle of wine labeled as varietal should contain grapes only from that varietal. Ray was headstrong and never joined the Wine Institute, attended fairs, or engaged in any sort of mass distribution. Yet he gained a fiercely loyal following of wine lovers who whispered his name among those of the greatest winemakers of the time. Ray also realized that his quest to produce fine wine was of great importance to the wine industry. In 1955 he proclaimed: "The market for fine wines is limited, yet the market for all other wines is supported by it."[59] And the market still supports it; as with Louis M. Martini, the Martin Ray Winery makes excellent wine to this day.

Taken together, Ray exhibited the fierceness of purpose that the wine world would not again see until Robert Mondavi made his entrance.

A Third World's Fair and World War II

In the mid-1930s, in a bid to jolt the region out of Depression doldrums, San Francisco took on hosting a third world's fair. This time the celebration recognized the completion of the city's two new bridges: the San Francisco–Oakland Bay Bridge, opened in 1936, and the Golden Gate Bridge, dedicated in 1937. The Golden Gate International Exposition, held on Treasure Island, ran from February 18, 1939, through October 29, 1939—and again from May 25, 1940, through September 29, 1940.

The theme of the fair was Pageant of the Pacific. The *Christian Science Monitor* thought "it ought to be in the West, and have a tang of the Orient about it . . . at the last frontier of civilization's forward march, yet looking out upon the most ancient lands and the most exotic peoples."[60] And indeed it did. The 1940 publication *San Francisco: The Bay and Its Cities* offers lavish descriptions of the exposition, starting with its island host: Treasure Island "appears like a 'stately pleasure dome' conjured up by the magic of modern science from Kublai Khan's Xanadu. By night this unearthly effect is enhanced by panchromatic floodlighting which transforms the exposition's towers and pavilions into a floating city of emerald and vermilion palaces."

The fair's theme was to be found in various iterations throughout the fantastic creation:

> Midway down the Avenue of Palms rise two massive Mayan-Incan pyramids . . . supporting huge stylized elephant figures—the exposition's main gateway to its great circular Court of Honor. Here the slim octagonal Tower of the Sun . . ., pierced by airy embrazures and surmounted by a spire, rises 400 feet. . . . From the facades of the pavilions which enclose [the immense oblong Court of the Seven Seas] protrude the rearing prows of galleys with carved figureheads, suggestive of travel and adventure. This *via triumphalis* set with standards and lanterns opens into the Court of Pacifica . . ., across whose fountain and sculptures gazes [the] amazonian statue

Pacifica, symbolic of peaceful co-operation between the Americas and their Pacific neighbors, stationed against a gleaming backdrop of tubes and metal stars designed to produce melodious sounds.[61]

Of course, members of the wine industry saw in the fair a stellar opportunity for promoting their viticultural cause. The Wine Institute erected a Wine Temple in the Food and Beverages Palace to create "publicity and promotion of California wine on a scale far beyond anything that could be attempted by a few producers exhibiting independently."[62] Four of those who signed on—Beringer, Inglenook, Larkmead, and Beaulieu—collectively promoted Napa's "four points of superiority . . . soil, climate, proper varieties of grapes, and proper aging."[63] But the institute couldn't inspire the broad participation and enthusiasm it sought; not even 9 percent of the state's 560 wineries exhibited, and the temple received scant attention. Even the wine competition underwhelmed—except in the view of the winners, who included Wente of Livermore and Paul Masson (by then owned by Martin Ray). California's second largest agricultural commodity could not solidify its identity. And yet, Thomas Pinney notes, perhaps the opportunity did benefit the industry internally; the prizes won by their wines certainly boosted morale and likely invigorated the motivation to reach greater heights. James Lapsley adds: "Participation by Napa producers . . . was also a statement that they were among the industry leaders, that in this instance they were on par with Roma, Petri, Shewan-Jones, or Italian Swiss Colony."[64] (Beaulieu took home the grand prize for its Cabernet, though it was entered as a burgundy.)[65]

So the exposition produced only a tepid return for the winemakers for the great effort and expense expended on it. Many in the wine industry had sought what San Francisco's previous world's fairs had offered: a strong gust to propel it out of its doldrums—in this case, the Depression, by then in its tenth year. But the shot in the arm it needed would come later—initiated, perversely enough, when German tanks and planes stormed into an unsuspecting Poland on September 1, 1939, setting off World War II. As the escalating war paralyzed that continent, East Coast importers of superior French and Italian wines found their supplies cut off—and turned to California to fill the void. Indeed, the *New York Times* reported in 1940: "Producers here believe that they have the best chance they have ever had to build up demand for American wine in this market."[66]

The next boon for California wine—and for the country's economy as a whole—came soon after the United States entered the war, on December 8, 1941, the day following Japan's attack on Pearl Harbor. Wineries supported the war effort as the sole provider of tartrates, used in the manufacture of explosives, from the deposits scraped from inside storage tanks.[67] Another benefit resulted from the requirement that many grapes, including Thompson Seedless, be dehydrated into raisins for food rations. This latter directive greatly decreased the supply of low-quality grapes available to wineries—producing a corresponding leap in price for wine-quality grapes. During the war the price for a ton of wine grapes would more than triple, from $15 a ton to $50 a ton.[68] In addition, the scarcity of low-quality grapes broke the Depression-era trend of crushing raisin grapes for wine; consequently, the vintages made in this time improved significantly. And though other alcoholic beverages were requisitioned for troops on the battlefield, wine was not—which greatly increased both its appeal and consumer demand.[69] Altogether, even with a price ceiling on wine and brandy, for the first time in decades growers and wineries alike enjoyed a profitable bottom line.

Profit in any arm of the alcohol industry does not go unnoticed for long. The entrance into the war inspired four large American distillers to try their hand in the wine business. First, Schenley, Seagram's, National Distillers, and Hiram Walker and Sons stepped in to produce brandy. Then, when the War Production Board announced that all production of whiskey would stop on November 1, 1942, distillers scrambled to add wineries to bolster their portfolios. Within a few years, the distillers held nearly two dozen properties and controlled one-quarter of California's wine production. And though the appearance of these large corporations worried many small winery owners and growers, their invasion during this time was nonetheless advantageous. Wine was in a seller's market, but a majority in the wine industry neither knew how to sell it nor had the means to capitalize on that market. The distillers, though, who aggressively marketed whiskey, applied the same principles to wine. When consumers responded, everyone in the industry benefited. Plus, fears of long-term disruption, even industry takeover, proved to be unfounded: when the war ended, the distillers, likely preferring their established trade, significantly retreated from the world of wine.[70]

The wartime economy required critical and timely advances in the distribution of wine. Recall that the industry at the time predominantly sold bulk wine that was shipped in tank railroad cars to bottlers. But during the war the rules of the game had changed. First, tank railroad cars were diverted to military use, throwing a wrench in the primary mode of shipping wine. So wineries once again needed to bottle their wine; fortunately, most developed bottling lines quickly and transitioned smoothly to the traditional distribution method, which again became the standard. Second, the price of grapes had soared. And third, the price ceilings set for bulk wine ($0.28 per gallon in 1943) were much lower than those for bottled wine ($1.55 per gallon). With these latter two changes, the bulk wine trade lost all profitability. By the end of the war, the bulk wine market had fallen from 80 percent of distribution to a meager 5 percent.[71]

By war's end in August of 1945, California wine had made significant strides. The quality of wine, and the means of production and distribution, had improved measurably. And though consumer demand still had a distance to cover, larger entities such as wine merchants, hotels, and restaurants had a new appreciation for wine labeled by its varietal. But to fully capitalize on the new distribution of quality wines, and to permanently trend upward the trajectory of California wine in particular, vast acreages of superior grape varieties would have to be planted. So advocated Frank Schoonmaker, an influential wine critic and promoter, echoing the arguments made at various times throughout the trade's history.[72] This degree of replanting, though, could only be accomplished outside the oppressive reach of Bank of America. Fortunately, there was a player in a position to challenge that bank: the E. & J. Gallo Winery.

THE GALLO ENTERPRISE—PART TWO

The Gallo brothers benefitted enormously from the war—and perhaps not entirely aboveboard. Ernest rapidly adapted to the new demand for bottling by acquiring several insolvent bottlers at the beginning of the war. To attract attention to Gallo products, he chose a "high-shouldered, tapered quart" bottle (which holds ~945 milliliters of wine) instead of the standard amber-colored "fifths" bottle (which holds 750 milliliters, or one-fifth of a gallon—what we think of as a standard wine bottle). Ernest Gallo later recalled: "This quart departed from the tradition. . . . Wine is a beautiful color, and why not take advantage of the appeal?" Another novelty was to include a recipe on the label, which added to the rising public consciousness of seeing wine as an integral part of a good meal.[73]

As for the actual war effort, Ernest established Tartar Incorporated to produce the cream of tartar used in explosives manufacturing.[74] But the winery's large-scale wartime venture was to distill molasses into industrial-strength alcohol—"torpedo juice, [they] called it"—for the government, which paid E. & J. Gallo Winery its cost plus 10 percent. According to one account, Ernest claimed exaggerated costs, making him a war profiteer. In any case, the war was lucrative: by 1945, E. & J. Gallo Winery had a huge accumulation of working capital.[75]

In anticipation of the end of the war, Ernest and Julio approached wine-grape growers with a well-received offer to agree to buy, a year in advance, their entire following year's harvest, at a substantially higher price per ton than the growers were then receiving. In return, of course, the growers could sell to no one else. Then the Allied victories in Europe and Japan ended both the war and wartime price controls on wine. But when wineries seeking to ramp up production sought their requisite grapes, they found a smaller supply than expected. Once again, just as had been the case after Prohibition, reinvigoration of the California wine market centered on the grape.[76]

E. & J. Gallo Winery sought to outcompete rivals in every aspect of winemaking—bottling, distributing, marketing, and selling. The winery constructed enormous production and storage facilities that rivaled those of Italian Swiss Colony, Cresta Blanca, and Guild (the new owner of the Roma Wine Company). In the decade following the war, Julio fine-tuned the E. & J. Gallo signature winemaking style, offering light and sweet red and white wines. Theirs was also among the first wineries to adopt aluminum screw-top caps to avoid leakage from unreliable corks.[77] But outcompeting their smaller rivals didn't necessarily mean that Gallo trampled those rivals. In the 1950s and 1960s, 60 to 75 percent of the wine produced in Mendocino, Napa, and Sonoma Counties entered the market inside an E. & J. Gallo bottle. But much of that wine had been produced by Gallo's smaller rivals. While of course many wineries would have preferred to bottle and sell wine under their own labels, the option to sell their product to Gallo certainly kept them afloat.[78]

Some of Gallo's innovations in sales and marketing reveal much about Ernest's astute approach to the business. To sell well, a wine had to be seen as recommended—but Gallo couldn't invest much in advertising. Even more pertinently, Ernest believed the wine seller had no reason to favor Gallo wines. "Why should a retailer carry it?" Ernest Gallo noted in an interview. "He had all the wine he wanted." So they took another approach: Gallo salesmen offered to stock retailers' shelves for them, which allowed them to position Gallo wines in the most prominent spots.[79] With tactics like these, Gallo soon became a well-known brand throughout the state.

As E. & J. Gallo Winery gained ever-greater purchasing power, it began to compete with the existing behemoths of the wine industry. And though its rapid expansion and emphasis on cheap bulk wine was definitely unnerving to small producers, it's nonetheless true that Gallo helped to restore an industry that was being misdirected and degraded under the lending control of Bank of America. In the 1930s and 1940s most banks focused their financial investments toward industry, so Bank of America had little competition in its financing of agricultural enterprises. Bank of America also had an especially constricting grip on small, struggling wineries: since its process was to combine the wine it purchased and then sell it in bulk, it mandated quality standards of all incoming wine. As the great winemaker André Tchelistcheff relates: "In the 1940s, when I had my own laboratory, Bank of America was my best client, because Bank of America had control of all small wineries, and there was a compulsory necessity every month to give a chemical analysis report to Bank of America." The bank was requiring these monthly chemical analyses as just one part of its overall dominion over its winery borrowers. It controlled all aspects of their operation, from the grape growing, harvesting, crushing, aging, and blending to marketing. As Tchelistcheff concludes: "Bank of America was choking the wine industry." And as noted earlier, they frequently tried to force premature wines on the market—just to favor their balance sheet.[80] Charges were even leveled against Bank of America for conspiring to fix sweet wine prices and terms of sale.[81]

The Gallo brothers had loathed and rebelled against Bank of America from the beginning of their adventures in wine. They had taken out their first loans from the much smaller Capital National Bank of Sacramento.[82] Following the war, as E. & J. Gallo Winery ascended to a position of power in the industry, the Gallos continued to defy Bank of America's near-monopoly on wine lending, in part by demonstrating to small wineries that there were financing alternatives. Gallo also helped to revive cooperatives.

Even Beaulieu Vineyard's André Tchelistcheff would late in life applaud E. & J. Gallo Winery's role in the financial rescue of the industry. As he shared with Ruth Teiser and Catherine Harroun in 1979: "I saw the crisis after Repeal: compulsory distillation. I saw the crisis when the fine quality grapes were sold for $25, $30 a ton, and the cost of production was about $38 to $40." But "Gallo removed the control of banks. Gallo, in expansion of purchasing power, restored the industry. Without Gallo, the industry would never have survived."[83]

And so, despite the Gallo brothers' aggressive and, at times, ruthless business tactics, their winery had nonetheless stabilized a reeling industry. Their innovative sales tactics and highly efficient bulk production also set the standard for years to come. And given the continued expansion of E. & J. Gallo Winery, as of the early 1990s, according to *Fortune* magazine, "one out of every four bottles of wine sold in the United States is made by Gallo." The family winery begun by Ernest and Julio had become, by far, the largest winery in the world.[84]

Doldrums Reckoning

Ernest and Julio Gallo were powerful agents in steadying the California wine industry following the Great Depression and World War II. Two other men, Louis M. Martini and Martin Ray, were catalysts in the forming of a consciousness and the forging of a zeal for the quality California wines could achieve. Although neither Martini nor Ray attained the acclaim enjoyed by their counterparts at Inglenook and Beaulieu, both were strong-willed, visionary men who burnished the image of California wine through their work—and served as a bridge to the next generation.

Martin Ray and Louis M. Martini saw the trajectory California wine could take. Along with John Daniel and André Tchelistcheff, they maintained the belief through the doldrums of the 1930s that California could become known for its fine wines, not its sweet, bulk wines. These men in turn would heavily influence a young ambitious man named Robert Mondavi, whose family would take the reins of the Charles Krug winery. Mondavi was the catalyst for a crucial shift of attitude toward California wine—both in the industry and in the consumer. But the foundation he built on would have been unstable without Ray, Martini, Daniel, Tchelistcheff, de Latour, Adams, and, yes, the Gallo brothers having solidified it first.

When America repealed Prohibition at the end of 1933, the nation was in the midst of the most severe economic crisis in its history, the Great Depression of 1929–41. And since the last four years of Prohibition were also the first four years of the Depression, the California wine industry wasn't exactly jump-started upon Repeal. In subsequent years it largely languished—and then, fast-forward a bit: World War II ended the Depression, a tremulous peace was purchased in 1945, and an anxious America went back to making wages and families instead of war. And some made wine.

To get a sense of what wine was in vogue after the war, we can look to the charming 1948 book *Dining Out in San Francisco and the Bay Area* by Raymond Ewell, wine critic and bon vivant. Ewell pairs his various restaurant reviews with a few words about wine—California wine in particular. So as to introduce the uninformed of the pleasures to be uncorked with California vintages, he offers his readers a handy list identifying the "Label Designations of Equivalent California Wines" in terms of the more standard "European Types."

Raymond Ewell's Table of California Equivalents to European Wine Types

EUROPEAN TYPES	LABEL DESIGNATIONS OF EQUIVALENT CALIFORNIA WINES
Rhine and Moselle wines	Riesling, Johanisberg [*sic*] Riesling, Traminer, Sylvaner, Moselle
White Burgundy, Chablis, White Rhône wines	Pinot Blanc, Pinot Chardonnay, Chablis
Red Burgundy, Red Rhône wines	Pinot Noir, Red Pinot, Burgundy, Gamay
Graves (Dry White Bordeaux)	Sweet Semillon, Sweet Sauterne, Haut Sauterne, "Châteaux" wines
Claret (Red Bordeaux)	Cabernet, Cabernet Sauvignon, Claret, Zinfandel, Mourestel Chianti, Barbera, Grignolino

Source: Ewell, *Dining Out in San Francisco*, 87.

He adds that the "best California wines are thought by many connoisseurs to be the equal of many of the well-known European wines." (Compare this assessment with the 1907 *Joe Tilden's Recipes for Epicures*—mentioned at the end of chapter 5—written by another bon vivant, one who failed to mention one California vintage in a chapter about wine.)

Ewell has another detail for diners that boded well for California wine in the day: "California wines are served in nearly all San Francisco restaurants. . . . Eastern United States wines are practically never found, and Chilean wines very rarely. In the post–war period European wines have been very variable and unreliable. There are, of course, many good ones on the market, but one can't be sure—until you have opened the bottle. In general, your chance of getting a wine of good to excellent quality in this year 1948 is better if you stick to the better California wines than if you buy European wines—and a lot cheaper, too."

He shares two additional points:

All the best California table wines come from vineyards within sixty-five miles of San Francisco—in Napa, Sonoma, Alameda, and Santa Clara counties. Other wine growing areas in the state are too hot and dry to produce good table wines. This generalization does not necessarily apply to dessert wines.

The best California wines are usually bottled at the winery, so beware of wines which are obviously bought in bulk and bottled elsewhere. It takes a very skillful wine blender to produce consistently good wines in this way, of which there are not very many in California. A notable exception is the Napa and Sonoma Wine Co., which buys wines in bulk, ages, blends, and bottles them, and produces some excellent wines. (Ewell, *Dining Out in San Francisco,* 86, 89)

It could be said that Raymond Ewell's pointers exemplify the global status of California wine at the time: well worth the recommendation, but not widely known. The state's vintners certainly had their work cut out for them.

Following the triple blows of Prohibition, the Depression, and the Second World War, the California wine industry crawled back into the light like wine barrels reemerging from underground cellars. Remarkably, many of the early California wine names survived, even revived. But nothing came easily for the California wine industry following the war. One Napa Valley winery produced what are arguably the finest California wines ever made, but few took notice just then. In time, though, the genius, generosity, and vigor of one man—who must rank with Jean Louis Vignes, Agoston Haraszthy, and Charles Kohler in the history of California wine—raised California wines to the peak of the elite wine world, two hundred years after California winemaking began.

Notes

1. Similar to the treatment of *prohibition/Prohibition* in chapter 8, the word *repeal,* when lowercased, refers to the general revoking of an amendment; whereas, when capitalized, *Repeal* refers to the specific passage of the Twenty-First Amendment revoking the Eighteenth Amendment.

2. Teiser and Harroun, *Winemaking in California,* 180.

3. Pinney, *History of Wine in America,* 2:8, 30–32.

4. Ibid., 2:31–33, 61, 64 and n50.

5. Siler, *House of Mondavi,* 17–18.

6. Hilgard, "Plain Talk to the Winemen."

7. Wetmore, "Treatise on Wine Production," 35.

8. Pinney, *History of Wine in America,* 2:33.

9. Lapsley, *Bottled Poetry,* 24.

10. Hawkes, *Blood and Wine,* 51.

11. Adams, "Revitilizing," 40, 63–64, 68–69. His "salvage outlet" statement appears on page 64; the "wine men" statement—said by one of Bank of America's Giannini brothers to Burke Critchfield—appears on page 40.

12. Schoonmaker and Marvel, *Complete Wine Book,* 37, qtd. in Lapsley, *Bottled Poetry,* 41.

13. Mobley, "Mission Revival," L14.

14. Pinney, *History of Wine in America,* 2:57–58, citing in part Amerine, "University of California," 16.

15. Gomberg, "Analytical Perspectives," 9.

16. Pinney, *History of Wine in America,* 2:57–58; see also 83–86.

17. Critchfield, "Status of California Wine," 326, qtd. in Pinney, *History of Wine in America,* 2:55.

18. Dinkelspiel, foreword to *Vintage,* unnumbered p. v.

19. "The Wines of the U.S.," *Fortune* 9 (February 1934), 118, qtd. in Pinney, *History of Wine in America,* 2:55.

20. Pinney, *History of Wine in America,* 2:56, and n16.

21. Lapsley, *Bottled Poetry,* 39, 62; Tchelistcheff, "Grapes, Wine, and Ecology," 62.

22. Lapsley, *Bottled Poetry,* 63.

23. Gomberg, "Analytical Perspectives," 9. See also "Louis Gomberg; First to Statistically Analyze Wine Industry," *Los Angeles Times,* December 5, 1993, articles.latimes.com/1993-12-05/news/mn-64108_1_wine-industry.

24. Hawkes, *Blood and Wine,* 23–25.

25. Ibid., 28–29, 38, 39, 43.

26. Ibid., 42–43, 50–53, 95.

27. Ibid., 105, 112, 118.

28. Ibid., 121, 124.

29. Ibid., 121–24, 138–39, 295, 395.

30. Ibid., 133–36.

31. Ibid., 146.

32. Heintz, *California's Napa Valley*, 314.

33. Pinney, *History of Wine in America*, 2:63 and n44, citing William C. Ockey, "The Cost of Producing Wine Grapes," *Wine Review* 3 (March 1935), 24, table 7.

34. Ibid., 2:62, citing "Resumé of the Number of Wineries That Have Given Up Their Bonds Since the Repeal of Prohibition," Wine Institute memo dated June 22, 1942, copy in the Wine Institute library. See also Lapsley, *Bottled Poetry*, chap. 2.

35. Ibid., 2:61–63, 66.

36. Lapsley, *Bottled Poetry*, 25, 27 and n10, citing "History of Napa Valley Co-operative Winery," *St. Helena Star*, April 30, 1937, 8.

37. Pinney, *History of Wine in America*, 2:2, 67, citing in part "Cooperative Marketing Agency Organized," *Wine Review* 5 (December 1937): 25.

38. Ibid., 2:95–98.

39. Ibid., 2:95–96, citing "Program Wine Producers Meeting," October 20, 1934, Wine Institute Library.

40. Ibid., 2:96–98, citing in part Harry Caddow, "Annual Meeting of the Wine Institute, *Wines & Vines* 16 (September 1935): 12.

41. Tchelistcheff, "Grapes, Wine, and Ecology," 88.

42. Adams, "Revitalizing," 63–65.

43. Edmund A. Rossi, "Italian Swiss Colony," 77–78.

44. Adams, "Revitilizing the California Wine Industry," 66, 68.

45. Rossi, "Italian Swiss Colony," 86–87.

46. Lapsley, *Bottled Poetry*, 86–87.

47. Starr, *Land's End*, 801–2.

48. Teiser and Harroun, *Winemaking in California*, 85; Sullivan, *Companion to California Wine*, 25.

49. Sullivan, *Companion to California Wine*, 186.

50. Lapsley, *Bottled Poetry*, 8–12, citing in part "Wine Juries Select California Blue Ribbon Wines for 1939," *Wines & Vines* 20, no. 10 (October 1939): 14–15.

51. Tchelistcheff, "Grapes, Wine, and Ecology," 68.

52. Laube, "Glory That Was Inglenook," 62, 65, 67.

53. Lapsley, *Bottled Poetry*, 17, citing "Diplôme D'Honneur Award Confirmed," *Wines and Vines* 19, no. 9 (September 1938): 21, and "Editorial," *St. Helena Star*, August 12, 1938, 2.

54. Adams, "Revitilizing," 72; Sullivan, *Companion to California Wine*, 203.

55. Martini and Martini, "Wine Making in the Napa Valley" 31–33, 41, 40, 43. The campaign frequently pictured an ideal housewife's table setting, complete with fine glassware, a bottle of wine on the table, and the tag line: "Mrs. Gotrock serves wine. Why don't you?" As it happens, wine industry statistician Louis Gomberg concurred about the campaign, saying "it sold no one." Gomberg, "Analytical Perspectives," 22.

56. Martini and Martini, "Wine Making in the Napa Valley," 41, 43.

57. Lukacs, *American Vintage*, 220–21.

58. Pinney, *History of Wine in America*, 2:150–52 and nn73, 74.

59. Lukacs, *American Vintage*, 221; see also 218–23.

60. Lewis Rex Miller, *Christian Science Monitor*, qtd. in Federal Writers' Project, *San Francisco*, 368.

61. Federal Writers' Project, *San Francisco*, 368–69.

62. Lapsley, *Bottled Poetry,* 83–84, citing "California Wine Display at the 1939 Golden Gate International Exposition," *Wines & Vines* (February 1938): 16.

63. "Ready for Fair Opening," *St. Helena Star* (February 17, 1939), 1, qtd. in Lapsley, *Bottled Poetry,* 84n70.

64. Lapsley, *Bottled Poetry,* 83–84; Pinney, *History of Wine in America,* 2:117, citing in part "The California Wine Temple," *Wine Review* 7 (March 1939), 84.

65. Lapsley, *Bottled Poetry,* 40.

66. Ibid., 96; Pinney, *History of Wine in America,* 2:119, in part citing Plan Liquor Promotion, *New York Times,* June 23, 1940, III: 7.

67. Pinney, *History of Wine in America,* 2:132; see also note 66 on page 423, where Pinney cites the wartime uses of tartrates to be found in H. A. Caddow, "War and the Wine Industry," *Wines & Vines* 23 (May 1942): 15–16.

68. Gallo, "E. & J. Gallo Winery," 27. In 1942 the Office of Price Administration set price ceilings on both wine and brandy; it set none on grapes. Gomberg, "Analytical Perspectives," 14.

69. Lapsley, *Bottled Poetry,* 100.

70. Pinney, *History of Wine in America,* 2:126–29.

71. Gomberg, "Analytical Perspectives," 14–15, 17; Lapsley, *Bottled Poetry,* 100–101, citing in part "New Wine Ceiling Regulation," *Wines & Vines* (October 1943), 10–11, re: price ceilings for bulk and bottled wine.

72. Pinney, *History of Wine in America,* 2:137–38.

73. Gallo, "E. & J. Gallo Winery," 24–26.

74. Pinney, *History of Wine in America,* 2:423n66. Georges de Latour founded Beaulieu Vineyards with income from producing cream of tartar before Prohibition.

75. Hawkes, *Blood and Wine,* 156–57.

76. Ibid., 165–66.

77. Ibid., 167.

78. Heintz, *California's Napa Valley,* 310.

79. Gallo, "E. & J. Gallo Winery," 26.

80. Tchelistcheff, "Grapes, Wine, and Ecology," 71.

81. Critchfield, "California Wine Industry," xvi.

82. Pinney, *History of Wine in America,* 2:65, citing Ernest and Julio Gallo, with Bruce B. Henderson, *Ernest and Julio: Our Story* (New York: Times Books, 1994), 69.

83. Tchelistcheff, "Grapes, Wine, and Ecology," 71.

84. Hawkes, *Blood and Wine,* 17–18.

CHAPTER 10

Robert Mondavi's Contagious Passion for Wine

1950s–1970s

The use of table wines [will] surpass
considerably that of dessert wines.

—Edmund A. Rossi, "The Coming Expansion of
the Table Wine Market," 1944

Wine to me is passion. It's family and friends. It's warmth
of heart and generosity of spirit. Wine is art. It's culture.
It's the essence of civilization and the Art of Living.

—Robert Mondavi, *Harvests of Joy*

In times of severe hardship, human concerns reduce to those of sheer survival; when mere subsistence is paramount, the concept "quality of life" is a luxury. Such could be said of the long period of want for the wine industry. During Prohibition, wine struggled for its very existence. During the Depression, wine struggled for market share—a game in which only fortified wines readily succeeded. But the stabilizing factors of World War II and its aftermath once again offered actors in the wine industry the chance of considering—and determining—just what California wine could be.

A few foundational elements and attributes had helped to develop the wine industry. These were facility in creating demand, technologic innovation, and passion for craft—as well as, less nobly, pursuit of personal gain. As for the latter, it's undeniable that the Gallo brothers' lust for market share inspired innovative production and marketing practices that were then adopted by other winemakers. The same can be said of the big distillers' stint in winemaking; their aggressive marketing modeled much for smaller entities to emulate. More substantially, the E. & J. Gallo Winery broke the stranglehold that the Bank of America had had on the industry. Their wildly successful product also heightened consumer demand for wine.

These four elemental attributes remained very much in play as the wine industry headed into its next era.

THE STATE OF THE WINE INDUSTRY—
LATE 1940S–1950S

"In the early 1940s, the fledgling Napa Valley wine industry faced a number of problems, including price controls and a daunting shortage of labor, bottles, and rail cars for eastern shipment of wine." So reads the website of the still-extant Napa Valley Vintners. Convinced of the mutual benefit of shared information and innovation, in 1944 seven vintners—John Daniel Jr. of Inglenook, Fernande de Latour of Beaulieu Vineyard, Charles Forni of the Napa Valley Cooperative Winery, Louis M. Martini, Robert Mondavi of CK Mondavi & Sons, Felix Salmina of Larkmead, and Louis Stralla—created an "association, a vintners forum, . . . [wherein they could] exchange ideas and work as a group to overcome some of [the] obstacles they faced. . . . The vintners believed they could solve industry-related problems better collectively than as individuals."[1] The group met every month in St. Helena, each time drinking wine provided by a different member winery. Decades on, "the vintners are all good friends," a *San Francisco Examiner* reporter writes, "despite the competition of the marketplace, and they often help each other out with production problems."[2] Louis M. Martini offers a more succinct description of the association: "Its main function is eat, drink, and be merry. We meet monthly for business."[3] Tchelistcheff concurs, saying it's "epicurean, not administrative."[4]

In the first few years of their joining convivial forces, the Napa vintners experienced the postwar changes to the industry. At war's end, European vintners resumed production, and their wines were still the preference of the East Coast merchants. As an industry newsletter later reported: "Americans, as a rule, are suckers for any article of foreign origin."[5] In addition, now that other alcoholic beverages were no longer requisitioned for the troops, those who'd previously sought wine merely as a substitute drink happily returned to their favorite ale or spirit, which the brewers and big distillers were all too willing to provide. As a result, in 1947 the return to the standard supply-and-demand economy brought on a nationwide crash in wine prices that upended the market. Established wineries such as Inglenook and Beaulieu emerged relatively unscathed from

In 1947, after a lapse of six years, wine judgings were resumed at the California State Fair, the accepted competing grounds for California's finest wines. Gold, silver, and bronze medals were awarded to Larkmead wines. Shown here is Larkmead Sauterne, winner of the Gold Medal, highest award in its class.

PRODUCED AND BOTTLED BY
LARKMEAD VINEYARDS
ST. HELENA, NAPA COUNTY, CALIFORNIA

This advertisement, which appeared in the October 1947 issue of *Wines & Vines*, boasts of the gold medal Larkmead Vineyards won at the 1947 California State Fair. The promotion turned out to be a swan song. By the end of the year Larkmead had become a crushing station for Italian Swiss Colony.

In 1950 the Napa Valley Vintners Association erected this sign welcoming tourists to the "world famous wine growing region" of Napa Valley. Photograph courtesy of the Napa Valley Vintners Association.

this latest setback, in many ways on account of the wine-drinking public's deep acquaintance with their brand. But other wineries weren't so fortunate. One of these was Larkmead, which by war's end was owned by a midwestern partnership. Though it had won several medals at the 1947 California State Fair, as boasted in an October 1947 advertisement, that prestige didn't foretell brighter days ahead. By the end of that year, Larkmead had become a crushing station for Italian Swiss Colony; a few years after that, Larkmead shuttered altogether.[6]

In witnessing the demise of Larkmead, the Napa Valley Vintners saw the need for promoting Napa Valley wines as belonging to a premium class—distinct from, as Paul Lukacs puts it, "skid-row fortifieds or undistinguished table blends."[7] They particularly felt that the statewide promotional efforts of the Wine Advisory Board did premium wine a disservice, that consumers of lesser California wines "erroneously assumed that all California wines are inferior."[8] The trick was to convey to the public that excellent wine was to be found from all the Napa Valley wineries, not just those with the established prestige of Inglenook and Beaulieu. In one effort to this end, the vintners erected a large road sign identifying Napa Valley as a WORLD FAMOUS WINE GROWING REGION; that the vintner members were listed on the sign pitched them as being the premium winemakers of that region. The vintners also joined with San Francisco in launching a particularly clever promotion: a "sponsored" cable car, which every day gave to a "lucky passenger" one bottle of Napa Valley wine.[9]

Of course, the Napa Valley Vintners also continued the pursuit of making better and better wine.

THE SCIENCE OF FINE WINE— VITICULTURAL INNOVATION

Many benefits that derived from the war didn't dissolve at the onset of peace. Just as the loss of transportation via rail car had motivated wineries to develop their own bottling facilities, many postwar California wineries and vineyards took pride in their technological innovation. And though some of this technology was imported from Europe, much originated at their doorstep, in the Department of Viticulture at the University of California at Davis.

In 1936, in his first task at the fledgling department, young researcher Maynard Amerine set out to determine which grape varietals grew best in which parts of the state. (This was precisely the study that Agoston Haraszthy had advocated be done with his thousands of imported vines back in 1861.) Over the course of five years, tracking "the growing conditions at each vineyard site—when the vines bloomed and the grapes ripened, how hot the weather got, [and] the average number of hours of sunlight," Amerine studied 140 different varieties of grape. Each was made into small batches of wine, the chemical compounds of which he also analyzed. As for the primary findings of all this study: climate, especially heat, largely determines how successfully varietals grow, and certain grapes fare better than others in certain regions. As Paul Lukacs conveys in *American Vintage: The Rise of American Wine,* "Temperature was the single most important factor in grape growing, and thus the single most important factor in determining wine quality." In cooler regions, grapes took longer to ripen, their skins were darker, and their fermented juice more acidic. In hot regions, many varieties of grapes simply couldn't make good wine. These lessons, considered in general, had been discovered through the experience of the industry's forebears, recent and past, but the researchers offered more than just generalities. From their data, Amerine and department chair Alfred Winkler constructed a master map of California that visually portrayed the state's five different climatic viticultural growing regions—which could then be matched to grape varieties identified as ideal for that region. They published their cutting-edge findings in 1944, in the *Composition and Quality of Musts and Wines of California.*[10]

While in time this comprehensive guide became essential for growers and winemakers alike, some converted more quickly than others. Notably, the study didn't identify profitability: it identified which grapes would create the highest-quality wine in any particular region—and those varieties happened to be ones favored by those passionate about their craft. For example, in the early 1950s Robert Mondavi and André Tchelistcheff advocated planting finer varietals like Cabernet Sauvignon and Sauvignon Blanc, both of which the guide recommended for Napa Valley. But these, as well as most other superior grapes, tended to have much lower yields. And so, initially, many growers were reluctant to replant with the varieties for which their vineyards were best suited, as those varieties produced merely a third of the yield of the established vines, but did not fetch three times the price. Most growers knew too well the vagaries of the winegrowing business, and could ill afford to adopt an artisan mindset without a market anxious to receive it. It didn't help that in 1953 the journal *Wines & Vines* reported that grapes earned less per acre than almost any other fruit—in some cases three to five times less. But in time, as demand shifted, and the fine-wine movement gained purchase, growers increasingly converted to superior varietals.[11]

In the meantime, the impetus of the mass producers and bulk growers would still benefit those concerned with craft. The big industry players always wanted to know how to wrest more profit from the grape, especially through increasing yields, and had the means to support the necessary research. For example, in 1947 the Roma Wine Company funded a viticultural science program at Fresno State College.[12] Some smaller players initiated research as well; in the late 1940s, Mondavi and Tchelistcheff established the Napa Enological Center Library to study various aspects of wine-making.[13] Decades later, Mondavi would establish the Robert Mondavi Institute for Wine and Food Science within the College of Agricultural and Environmental Sciences at UC Davis.[14]

Other vineyard concerns were long-standing—pests and pestilence. In *Bottled Poetry,* James T. Lapsley relates how most existing vineyards in Napa Valley "were forty to fifty years old and coming to the end of their economic lives. Virus diseases were endemic . . . [but] no practical means to control viruses existed." Fortunately, the apparatus existed with which to develop that control. In 1951, UC Davis launched a program to "select and import healthy, high-yielding clones of important wine grape varieties, to heat-treat these selections to eliminate viruses, and to propagate and provide certified cuttings to commercial nurseries." Additional trials sought rootstock capable of resisting the longtime nemesis of the grapevine, phylloxera, as well as its fellow parasite, the nematode.[15]

One invaluable figure in this realm was the wealthy financier James D. Zellerbach, who in 1952 founded Hanzell Vineyards. He was inspired by the Château du Clos du Vougeot in the Burgundy region of France, whose wines he loved and sought to replicate, namely Pinot Noir and Chardonnay. He'd been introduced to both in Burgundy, when he headed the Marshall Plan rebuilding of Europe after World War II. To achieve his goal he consulted with experts of the day, including André Tchelistcheff and To-Kalon vineyardist Ivan Schoch, as well as numerous researchers from UC Davis. Zellerbach enlisted this cadre of specialists so as to help him adapt French winemaking techniques to his Sonoma vineyard's soil and climate. One such technique involved fermenting white wines in cold stainless-steel fermenting tanks so as to replicate the temperature of France's Burgundy region, which produced unparalleled crisp, fruity Chardonnays. He also aged his Pinot Noir in small French oak barrels, another nod to Burgundy. Charles Sullivan considers use of both techniques revolutionary at that time in California.

Sullivan also credits the Hanzell "cellar master" R. Bradford Webb for his use of malolactic fermentation, yet another effort in replicating a Burgundy-region advantage. There, barrel-aged

Pinot Noir naturally underwent a second, "malolactic" fermentation wherein more strident malic acid converted to a smoother lactic acid and carbon dioxide—resulting in mellower wines. But in California this second phase didn't reliably occur. Furthering research pioneered at UC Davis, Webb induced this process by adding malolactic bacteria to the wine. George Taber identifies the 1959 Hanzell Pinot Noir as being the first wine in history for which malolactic fermentation was actively induced.[16] Unfortunately, Zellerbach's funding of cutting-edge methods ceased upon his death in 1963. But not all was lost: developments like these inspired other winemakers to continue in the same vein.

Altogether, studied application of the technology of this period greatly advanced the quality of California wines. Author Paul Lukacs credits the standardization of wine, "in terms of both quality and style," as having helped to "make it a mainstream consumer product." He continues: "Americans were not the first to bring machines into the vineyard . . . Louis Pasteur and his followers did that. Yet because American producers accepted tradition only as a means of information, and existing facts only as a lesson in doing better, they more than their French, German, or Italian counterparts took Pasteur's work to a new level of accomplishment. In effect, they created modern, commercial wine as we know it today."[17]

These forward strides in winemaking innovation were essential to wine finally achieving the heights its advocates sought. Equally essential, though, was the hard work and dedication of those passionate about winemaking as a craft. Enter the Mondavi family.

Charles Krug and C. Mondavi & Sons

The early story of the Mondavi family parallels in several respects that of the Gallo family—less the Gallo tragedy. Just as Giuseppe and Michelo Gallo had begun producing wine for Italian pensiones, fellow Italian immigrant Cesare Mondavi did the same, for his own saloon in his own pensione boardinghouse. When Prohibition shut down all trade in wine, he traveled to California on behalf of the local Italian-American Club on a mission to secure grapes for home winemaking. Quickly enamored of the state, Cesare Mondavi bought a vineyard in Lodi in 1922, where he cultivated wine grapes for the home market.

Lodi, just north of Stockton, was thus the site of the original Mondavi business in California—just as Modesto, south of

Starting in the Prohibition era, C. Mondavi & Sons shipped wine grapes—such as the Zinfandel "Valley Beauty" grapes shown on this box-end label—from their headquarters in Lodi, California.

Stockton, was the site of the Gallos' first business. And just as sons Ernest and Julio helped their father in the vineyards, Cesare Mondavi's two sons, Peter and Robert, helped their father in tending his vines and shipping their grapes. But Cesare Mondavi impressed upon his sons more than just how to run a grape-growing business; he also modeled for them the importance of a reputation for integrity.[18] As Robert recounted years later:

> My father told my brother and me over and over that this was the basis for success. All the people he bought from and sold to in the grape business regarded him as a trusted friend. And in fact those friendships would become the foundation for his later wine business. He relied on them after Repeal when he transformed his grape-shipping business into a winery, and many of the dealers who had bought and distributed his grapes then bought and distributed his wine. Their faith in his grapes was transferred to his wine.[19]

Cesare's faith in grapes transferred to his sons as well—as did his belief that there was a great future for table wine, despite the midcentury trend. After graduating from Stanford University in 1936, Robert studied viticulture for a summer at the University of California at Berkeley. Robert then moved to Napa, where he worked as a "low-paid 'cellar rat'" assisting Jack Riorda at the Sunny St. Helena Winery (now Merryvale). Before long Robert conducted experiments in his own "primitive" lab, where he studied the batches of wine they produced. Peter Mondavi followed a similar path, just a year later: first Stanford, then graduate work in enology at UC Berkeley, where he first experimented with cold fermentation.

In 1940, Robert took over management at Sunny St. Helena, having during his time there helped expand its production from 500,000 gallons to over 1,000,000. In 1943, Robert urged his father to buy the renowned Charles Krug Winery in St. Helena. Cesare consented, with one condition: that the brothers build the business together. They were in full agreement—except that Peter couldn't share in the earliest phase, on account of serving in World War II. (Robert was exempt because the grapes he grew aided the war effort.) So Robert set to modernizing Charles Krug's aging winery without Peter—and making dry table wines, not fortified wine. Robert and Cesare sold wine under two labels: they bottled the bulk wine produced at Sunny St. Helena at a lower price under the CK label; their better wine carried the Charles Krug label.

While the wine Robert produced during the war fared very well, the firm known as C. Mondavi & Sons made an even bigger name for itself upon Peter's return, when he was able to resume the innovations in cold fermentation that he had pursued at UC Berkeley. Within a short time, Peter's wines won awards at the California State Fair, their first gold in 1949.[20] The Mondavi star was ascending.

Of course, the fruits of Peter's technological innovation and passion for craft weren't enough to build their business; C. Mondavi & Sons also needed to nurture a market for its wines. To that end they signed with national distributor McKesson & Robbins in 1947—the same year the wine market crashed, for which reason the contract was canceled. As James Lapsley relates:

> Believing that "new wines needed to be marketed in new ways...the Mondavis decided to build their own sales force. . . . None of the San Francisco wholesalers approached by Robert Mondavi were interested in the wines or in helping to build an unknown brand. If the Mondavis could not 'push' the wine through the system, as McKesson & Robbins might have done with its marketing clout and established relationships, then they had to 'pull' the wine through by creating a demand for it at the consumer and restaurant level, so that distributors would receive requests for it and want to carry the brand."[21]

This latter task Robert fulfilled with a flair and a warmth that few could resist. He believed that to create a demand for their wine they needed to first create an appealing atmosphere for drinking wine. And so in 1949 C. Mondavi & Sons opened a visitor center, which welcomed to its tasting rooms all those interested in sampling fine wine, be they weekending couples or a full-slated convention. They also held large tasting events, hosting hundreds of guests at a time. Through these tastings they seduced the palates of the restaurant owners and retailers in attendance,

Bottles and Bins logo courtesy of the Charles Krug Winery.

who then pressured wholesalers to carry their wines—the same wholesalers who'd previously declined them.[22]

In that same year C. Mondavi & Sons also launched one of the first winery newsletters, edited by Francis "Paco" Gould. Called *Bottles and Bins,* the newsletter promoted fine Napa and California wines, not just those from Charles Krug. By 1952, more than seven thousand subscribers had delved into the world of California wine through its pages.[23]

These promotional efforts, including the Visitors' Room, on-site educational programs, and *Bottles and Bins* newsletter, made large strides toward creating that customer "pull" their wines needed. And as people became acquainted with Charles Krug's quality, its allure increased.[24]

THE DEMAND FOR FINE WINE—TEMPTING PALATES

The Mondavis' hundreds of guests and thousands of subscribers notwithstanding, in the early 1950s, the average consumer had little interest in table wines. Martinis or Manhattans were the drink of preference, and those who indulged in the grape drank only French wine. In a move to improve table wine's image and reputation, in 1951 several vintners formed the Association of Chateau Wine Growers, including André Tchelistcheff of Beaulieu, Robert and Peter Mondavi of Charles Krug, the Taylors of Mayacamas Vineyards, J. Leland ("Lee") Stewart of Souverain Cellars, and Fred and Eleanor McCrea of Stony Hill Winery. They believed that to burnish the image of Napa Valley wine, they needed to improve the quality of all Napa Valley wine. To do this, they determined among themselves that all their wine must meet agreed-upon standards, which they ensured by conducting regular tastings of each winery's vintage. Only those wines that met their approval received a label guaranteeing its quality. In this step they opted to improve on the requirement set by the Bureau of Alcohol, Tobacco, and Firearms that any wine labeled as being a particular varietal needed to contain at least 51 percent of that variety. In form with their dedication to high standards, the Chateau Wine Growers decided varietal classification should require that a wine contain 85 percent of that grape variety.[25]

Unfortunately, the Chateau Wine Growers lacked the funding they needed to pursue their mission, and so the organization disbanded by 1952. But in its wake member Robert Mondavi recognized the need for more official accreditation and marketing. In 1955 he and others formed the Premium Wine Producers of

California (PWPC), a statewide group of premium wineries, which could then seek funds from the state-run Wine Advisory Board. The PWPC also became an advisory committee to both the Wine Advisory Board and the Wine Institute of California. In determining who qualified as a premium wine producer, they decreed the first official definition of *premium wine,* determined by purchase price: those who produced a wine that retailed at more than $1 per "fifth" (again, 750 milliliters, or one-fifth of a gallon, a "standard" wine bottle) were eligible to join the organization.

The PWPC then launched an extensive public-relations program—involving television, radio, and magazines across the country—that portrayed wine as an essential element of the "good life." They also took advantage of a trend that surged in popularity in the mid-1950s: the blind taste test. At these "comparative tastings," a community's "opinion molders, such as restaurant owners, newspaper and magazine editors, radio and television personalities, and members of wine and food societies," were invited to blindly sample California wines pitted against European wines of the same varietal; happily, the stateside wines reliably held their own against the imports.[26] In another boon for the wine camp, in October 1955 the journal *Wines & Vines* reported that a "private survey of wine drinking habits" produced "two startling conclusions: women were more likely to buy wine for home consumption than men, and people would buy more wine if it were readily available."[27]

With efforts like these, premium wine from California began to make a name for itself. But the premium winemakers still produced just 5 percent of California's table wine.[28] In terms of market share, the likes of Beaulieu, Charles Krug, and Inglenook were crushed beneath the boot heels of their Italian American compatriots—the likes of E. & J. Gallo and the Petri Wine Company. And yet, despite their enviable hold on the market, those competitors were troubled by use of the word "premium" in the PWPC's name, considering it dismissive of their bulk wine. They were also displeased that marketing funds issued by the state—to which they contributed the lion's share—would in effect belittle their product. In the face of their objections, in 1958 "premium" was stricken from the name Premium Wine Producers of California. Though lobbying continued on both sides, and compromise measures attempted, in 1964 the Wine Advisory Board voted to dissolve the fine-wine public-relations program altogether, hiring instead an industry-wide public relations employee.[29]

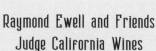

Raymond Ewell and Friends Judge California Wines

In 1948, food and wine critic and San Francisco bon vivant Raymond Ewell described in his *Dining Out in San Francisco and the Bay Area* how he had conducted blind wine tastings with friends assessing various California wines. His conclusions:

- Individual tastes and preferences in wines vary a great deal.

- There was some but not a very definite relationship between prices and the ratings by the group, since low-priced wines were frequently rated higher than more expensive ones.

- *Wines from the following wineries received consistently high ratings:* Wente Bros., Beringer Bros., Fountain Grove, Beaulieu Vineyard, Louis M. Martini, and Napa & Sonoma Wine Co.

- *Wines from the following wineries also received some high ratings, but not enough wines were tested to reach any conclusion regarding their consistency:* Charles Krug, Souverain Cellars, Los Amigos Vineyard, Grape Gold, Inglenook, and Concannon Vineyards.

- *Wines from 12 other wineries whose wines were tested received only low ratings.*

So the big players once again prevailed; unfortunately, so seemingly did the old reputation: in 1959, Stanford Wolf of premium winery Cresta Blanca noted that, in the East, the term *California* was "synonymous with cheapness."[30] And yet, the jury was not yet out, and the 1960s saw some surprising boosts to the industry. For one, wine was favored by the American counterculture; "hippies" drank wine, not the martinis of their parents' generation.[31] In 1961 Julia Child and her coauthors published the masterpiece *Mastering the Art of French Cooking.* In it she championed wine as a regular partner in a French meal, which didn't necessarily have to be "fancy cooking."[32] Paul Lukacs notes that in the mid-1960s a "number of factors—increased foreign travel, the Francophile tone of the Kennedy years, greater middle-class affluence, and more—led millions of Americans to sample table wine. [Then,] in 1967, sales of table wines passed those of fortified wines for the first time since Prohibition."[33] Wine was booming: in one decade, American consumption had doubled.[34] The demand for wine that Cesare Mondavi had predicted had arrived; not surprisingly, the large corporate interests took notice. Recall that John Daniel Jr. sold Inglenook to United Vintners in 1964. In 1966, Korbel Champagne was distributed by the owners of Jack Daniels. In 1967, Almaden sold to National Distillers. In 1969, Beaulieu was sold to Heublein. Seagrams already owned Paul Masson.[35] Knowledgeable winemakers knew they needed to seize the market before a wholesale corporate takeover once again diluted the quality, and reputation, of California wine.[36]

Furthering the Mondavi Dream

Though Cesare Mondavi didn't live to see the sale of American table wines surpass sweet wines—he died in 1959—he did get to enjoy the sea change that led to that momentous milestone. He also experienced the expansion of the Charles Krug Winery; by the 1960s, its six-hundred-acre vineyards could annually produce two million gallons of wine: varietal and generic table wine, as well as dessert wine. They were also widely acclaimed: "between 1949 and 1956, the [Mondavi] brothers won thirty-nine gold medals at the State Fair for their table wines."[37]

In 1962, a year after Julia Child first celebrated French cooking, Robert Mondavi visited nearly fifty wineries of Europe. There he experienced for himself the beauty of pairing a fine meal with fine wines, and marveled at the subtlety and complexity of the wines he tasted. He noted the methods the French wineries employed, particularly the concept of small: producing wine in small batches—a far cry from bulk manufacture—and aging in small oak barrels.[38] (These inspirations paralleled those of James D. Zellerbach with his Hanzell wines.) He was also struck by the sense of artistry he perceived in the winemakers. As Paul Lukacs relates, Mondavi observed that "the best American wines . . . still were widely viewed as forms of liquor. They competed with spirits and fortifieds for public attention, and the people who made and sold them treated them as such. For in America, . . . wine, like whiskey, was [still] tainted with a suspicion born of the country's hard-drinking past." Mondavi himself explained: "The contrast was stark: we were treating wine as a business; the great European châteaux were treating wine as high art." Robert returned to California with a transformed concept of the heights to which California wine could aspire.[39]

It was perhaps at this juncture that a long-standing discontent between Robert and Peter Mondavi progressed toward the irreparable.

The Mondavi brothers had competed since childhood. While that competitive spirit can likely be credited for their great success, it also stoked resentment, especially of Peter toward Robert. Though only a year younger than Robert, Peter was the youngest of the four Mondavi children, and had always been seen as the baby brother. And though financially the brothers were equals in the firm—Cesare, Rosa (Cesare's wife), Robert, and Peter held equal shares—Robert was still general manager, and Peter's boss. Indeed, when the aging Cesare retired from his duties, he consigned them to just Robert, not to both brothers.

The brothers had long had incompatible views of how to build the winery business. In 1946, Robert had convinced Peter to buy a large quantity of bulk grapes. When prices plunged the next year, the loss—$371,000—nearly did them in. Peter later claimed this untimely gamble set them back ten to fifteen years.[40]

Peter also recounts: "As things got better, [Robert] got more active, more expansive in what he wanted to do. . . . He's a salesman. He was on the promoter side . . . [while] the rest of the family was on the more conservative side."[41] Put succinctly, Robert always strove for better and bigger; Peter was content with very good and big enough. It was Robert who had urged that they acquire To-Kalon vineyards in 1962, a $1.35 million expansion that produced another quarter million gallons of fine varietal wine, nearly doubling their output.[42] It was Robert who insisted that they always reinvest their profits toward further improvement, bringing significant growth every year.[43] It was Robert who pushed for adopting some of the winemaking techniques he'd witnessed in France. And it was Robert who berated Peter, in 1958, for a drop in the quality of their wine. Sales staff had repeated customers' complaints of their wines being "flat-tasting and oxidized." Robert blamed Peter's shoddy oversight of the operation; Peter blamed the impossibility of keeping up with premature expansion—indeed, the impossibility of keeping up with Robert's excessive expectations.[44]

Separate from that 1958 blip in quality, which was more than made up for, Peter was proud of the success of Charles Krug. And though he earnestly sought to maintain that success, and worked long hours to achieve it, he also wanted to enjoy their considerable accomplishment—not to be endlessly criticized for what they had not yet produced. Peter and the rest of the family often argued for rewarding themselves with their profits, not continually pushing for more. But Robert was not satisfied; he believed Charles Krug could ascend to a higher level, and that the rest of the family needed to emulate his drive to achieve that.

Perhaps inevitably, simmering irreconcilable differences erupted into a violent disbanding of the brothers. In 1965—when they were both in their fifties—a heated argument led to a physical fight that ended with Robert and Peter grappling in the sandy loam, Robert's livid hands throttling Peter's purple throat.

The aftermath was as ugly as the fight. The rest of the Mondavi family—mother Rosa, and sisters Mary and Helen—sided with Peter. Robert was removed as general manager of Charles Krug, and told to take a six-month leave of absence. Later, he learned that his son Michael would not be allowed to join Charles Krug. Later still, he was expelled altogether: fired from the family business, left with nearly nothing.[45]

Though Cesare Mondavi would have been heartbroken at this turn of events—after all, he'd envisioned C. Mondavi & Sons as a family enterprise, and required that the brothers build it together—in some ways this breakup, though painful on both sides, may have been the only feasible solution to the family's incompatible views. With Robert's dismissal—and a great deal of friction removed—the winery would be able to continue in the manner that the majority of the Mondavi family preferred. In any case, the blowup sowed the seeds for a transformation of California wine.

Though critical with his own family, Robert had always been supportive of his peers. He had been part of the founding spirit of the Napa Valley Vintners, who formed in large part to help one another with the obstacles they encountered in their business. Given his longtime generosity in sharing ideas, and numerous efforts fostering the improvement of all Napa Valley, Robert found he had many friends after his ejection from Charles Krug. Just as Cesare had learned that his Prohibition customers' faith in his grapes transferred to his post-Repeal wine, one by one, fellow vintners like Louis M. Martini pitched in with money to help Robert start up a new winery. Buoyed by his aspirations and others' belief in his prospects, he started over, with a small 11.6-acre parcel of the To-Kalon vineyard, next to Highway 29, the route leading to the established wineries that attracted visitors all year.

Mondavi wanted to make his new winery an architectural proclamation. He hired Los Angeles architect Clifford May to design it in the style of the old hacienda ranch home, with an imposing tower and expansive outdoor spaces. Robert "want[ed] the building to declare, 'Here is a heart and soul. . . . This is not a factory, this is a home.'" That "home," though, nonetheless included both traditional and cutting-edge technology capable of making exquisite wine, from some of the valley's best grapes.[46]

It also represented the very movement Robert had so long worked to foster. As historian Paul Lukacs notes, "the construction of the Robert Mondavi Winery marks the effective beginning of American wine's rise in both quality and prestige. What happened there helped ignite the revolution in American tastes.

Architect Clifford May designed the Robert Mondavi Winery in the style of the old hacienda ranch home so as to declare, in Robert's words: "This is not a factory, this is a home." Courtesy of Constellation Brands.

It also helped change broad public attitudes toward wine in general, and American wine in particular."[47]

Robert Mondavi was able to crush and produce wine in his first year, 1966. For the first harvest he hired Warren Winiarski, who had previously worked at Souverain Cellars under Lee Stewart. Author Julia Flynn Siler offers a take on Mondavi's first crush:

> [For grape growers,] crush is a moment of death as well as birth. The life that they have nurtured from bud break through harvest is coming to an end; another is about to begin. . . . Warren Winiarski reflects, "I never saw a grower sad, but solemn. They're glad that it's happening but it's a mixed feeling. They've worked all that season to make these grapes what they are and now they are being crushed, being destroyed in order to be reborn into a different substance. They're glad but also a little bit mindful of destruction."

Winiarski possessed an attention to detail and a passion for wine-making that of course appealed to Mondavi. In turn, Winiarski appreciated Mondavi's high-achieving, technology-infused operation. But in that first winter, much of the wine was produced outside, as the winery was still under construction.[48]

Ultimately, Winiarski felt the need to strike out on his own. To replace him, in 1968 Mondavi lured Croatian Mike Grgich, offering him the space to come into his own after working under André Tchelistcheff at Beaulieu. In exchange, Grgich introduced the technology of malolactic fermentation that he had learned from Tchelistcheff. As mentioned earlier, this secondary fermentation converts malic acid to lactic acid and carbon dioxide—making red wines smoother and mellower.[49]

Grgich found himself in a frenetic atmosphere with few rules and an incessant demand to produce, which was in part why Winiarski had moved on. Mondavi's approach was, as Cyril Ray puts it, a "frustrated satisfaction in *not* being satisfied, an excitement in trying every year to beat himself at his own game."[50] But Grgich was up to the task in this breakneck operation, and produced fine wines from the start. In a 1969 blind taste test of the best California Cabernets, Mondavi's—Grgich's—came out on top, vaulting him into elite company. For Grgich, however, this sudden success came at a cost; he felt overworked and underacknowledged. When he realized that Robert intended his son Michael to be his successor in the winery, Grgich felt what Winiarski had felt before him: "Everyone who is devoted to making something wants to have complete control of the material—finally

As Lukacs notes, quoting Winiarski: since "'their tastes and aspirations were formed elsewhere,' they brought to a sleepy industry new energy and vision—the desire to 'pursue excellence.'"[59]

California's wine boom had begun.

Notes

1. "History of the Napa Valley Vintners."

2. Heintz, *California's Napa Valley,* 336, citing in part Tom Eurch, "Lunch with the Brotherhood," *San Francisco Examiner,* October 13, 1974, magazine section.

3. Martini and Martini, "Wine Making in the Napa Valley," 42.

4. Tchelistcheff, qtd. in Sullivan, *Napa Wine,* 240.

5. "French Wine Blues," *Bottles and Bins* (July 1950): 2, qtd. in Lapsley, *Bottled Poetry,* 152.

6. Lapsley, *Bottled Poetry,* sixth unnumbered page after page 110.

7. Lukacs, *American Vintage,* 185.

8. Lapsley, *Bottled Poetry,* 146, citing in part Walter S. Richert, "Regional Promotion of Wines," *Wines & Vines* (August 1949): 14.

9. Ibid., 146 and n2.

10. Lukacs, *American Vintage,* 179–82.

11. Ibid., 186–87; Heintz, *California's Napa Valley,* 317 (see also p. 320).

12. Lukacs, *American Vintage,* 182–83.

13. Heintz, *California's Napa Valley,* 316–17.

14. "About Us," Robert Mondavi Institute for Wine and Food Science, robertmondaviinstitute.ucdavis.edu/about.

15. Lapsley adds: By 1959, "virus-free certified stocks...provided the basis for the vineyard expansion that took place in the 1960s." *Bottled Poetry,* 177–78.

16. Taber, *Judgment of Paris,* 68–70; Sullivan, *Companion to California Wine,* 146. On his page 70 Taber notes that in France Émile Peynaud was also experimenting with induced malolactic fermentation, but no one on the West Coast was aware of this at the time.

17. Lukacs, *American Vintage,* 177–78.

18. Hawkes, *Blood and Wine,* 25, 62–63.

19. Robert Mondavi, qtd. in Hawkes, *Blood and Wine,* 63.

20. Siler, *House of Mondavi,* 18–24. George Taber adds that Peter did "trailblazing work" on the pressing of grapes and filtering of wines. Taber, *Judgment of Paris,* 71.

21. Lapsley, *Bottled Poetry,* 191–92, citing in part Robert Mondavi, "Creativity in the California Wine Industry," interview by Ruth Teiser, 1984 (Berkeley: Regional Oral History Office, Bancroft Library, University of California, 1985), 27.

22. Siler, *House of Mondavi,* 25; Heintz, *California's Napa Valley,* 333; Lapsley, *Bottled Poetry,* 192.

23. Siler, *House of Mondavi,* 29.

24. Ibid., 33.

25. Heintz, *California's Napa Valley,* 315–16.

26. Lapsley, *Bottled Poetry,* 150–53.

27. Heintz, *California's Napa Valley,* 315, citing "What the U.S. Public Thinks About Wine," *Wines & Vines* 36 (October 1955).

28. Lapsley, *Bottled Poetry,* 141 and n12.

29. Ibid., 156–57.

30. Ibid., citing Stanford Wolf, as quoted in minutes of the standing committee, Academy of Master Wine Growers, April 15, 1959, 5.

31. Taber, *Judgment of Paris,* 81.

32. Child, introduction to *Mastering the Art of French Cooking,* 1:xiv.

33. Lukacs, *American Vintage,* 187.

34. Heintz, *California's Napa Valley,* 321, citing statistical issues of *Wines & Vines.*

35. Lapsley, *Bottled Poetry,* 187.

36. Lukacs, *American Vintage,* 153.

37. Sullivan, *Companion to California Wine,* 175–76, 219.

38. Siler, *House of Mondavi,* 36–37.

39. Lukacs, *American Vintage,* 150–51.

40. Siler, *House of Mondavi,* 33, 36.

41. Peter Mondavi, qtd. in Siler, *House of Mondavi,* 33.

42. Siler, *House of Mondavi,* 63.

43. Lapsley, *Bottled Poetry,* 173, 188.

44. Siler, *House of Mondavi,* 33, 34.

45. Ibid., 38–39, 49, 51–54.

46. Ibid., 62–63, 65.

47. Lukacs, *American Vintage,* 133.

48. Siler, *House of Mondavi,* 67, 75–78 . The quoted portion appears on page 78.

49. Taber, *Judgment of Paris,* 70, 124–25.

50. Ray, *Robert Mondavi,* 59.

51. Siler, *House of Mondavi,* 81, 82–83.

52. "American Wine Comes of Age," *Time,* November 27, 1972, 84.

53. Johnson, *Hugh Johnson's Modern Encyclopedia of Wine,* 439.

54. Lukacs, *American Vintage,* 154.

55. Taber, *Judgment of Paris,* 118–19, 128–29.

56. Ibid., 107–8, 111–12.

57. Lukacs, *American Vintage,* 210–12, 216, 217.

58. Ray, *Robert Mondavi,* 59–60.

59. Lukacs, *American Vintage,* 211.

CHAPTER 11

Stellar Cellars and the Judgment of Paris

1960s–1976

> We are in competition with each other. We are
> not in competition against each other.
>
> —ROBERT MONDAVI, quoted by Joseph E. Heitz,
> "Creating a Winery in the Napa Valley," 1985

> Great wine is not an accident of climate and geography.
> It is a creative act of men. California's greatest asset
> is a set of wine makers who want to make the finest
> wine in the world. They may succeed, and if they do
> they will inevitably bring a new meaning to "finest."
>
> —ROY BRADY, 1975

T O T H E A N C I E N T G R E E K S, Eris was the goddess of strife, and she did not take kindly to offense. When she learned she was the sole deity not invited to the wedding party of Peleus and Thetis, she sowed the seeds of discord, tossing into the festivities a golden apple with the inscription FOR THE FAIREST. Three goddesses, Hera, Athena, and Aphrodite, claimed the apple was intended for her. To resolve the argument, Zeus, king of the gods and husband of Hera, sent the goddesses to consult Paris, son of King Priam of Troy. Their journey took them to Mount Ida, where Paris tended sheep in pastoral exile—a preventative against his fulfilling a prophecy that said he'd be the ruin of Troy. Since Paris was the handsomest of all mortal men, to him fell the lot of judging to which goddess the apple was entitled. Hoping to sway his vote, Hera offered worldly greatness; Athena offered glory on the battlefield. But Aphrodite's offer was irresistible— she promised Paris could have the most beautiful woman in the world as his wife. That woman was Helen, wife of Menelaus, King of Sparta. After Paris awarded Aphrodite the golden apple, with her divine assistance Paris abducted Helen and carried her off

Frederick John Kluth, *The Three Goddesses at the Judgment of Paris*. Acrylic on canvas, Kent, Ohio, May 26, 2009, 30" x 40". Image courtesy of the artist.

to Troy.[1] And so, Helen's was the face "that launched a thousand ships," as Christopher Marlowe coined. What became known as the Judgment of Paris brought on the rape of Helen, a ten-year war, and the annihilation of the great civilization of Troy.

In 1976—the year of America's bicentennial—an English wine merchant named Steven Spurrier sowed a great strife in the wine world: he staged a high-stakes competition, for which he chose Paris as judge. But this time Paris was the capital of France, not the pretty prince of Troy, and the competition judged not the fairest goddess, but the finest wines—those from France versus those from California.

The journey of California wine to its own Mount Ida was the consequence of healthy but supportive competition among a series of winemakers who held deep respect for one another. We've seen how the cooperative spirit inspired by Robert Mondavi invigorated his wine-craft compatriots, and how he essentially incubated both Mike Grgich and Warren Winiarski, both of whom had worked under Beaulieu's André Tchelistcheff. Tchelistcheff in turn had prophesized the coming dominion of small winemakers like Grgich and Winiarski, proclaiming grandly, "The apostolic mission of the future belongs to the small wine grower."[2] Indeed, after retiring from Beaulieu in 1973, Tchelistcheff began his "third career" as a winemaking consultant so as to nurture the new talent. As he relates, the choice "answered all my philosophical goals. I thought my . . . experience . . . and my general know-how . . . should guide me towards the process of building a new generation of winemakers. . . . Youth is tomorrow, far more important than today. . . . [And] in every region there are several . . . factors that eventually will guide us to a new success in the California wine industry."[3]

Distinct from previous generations of California winemakers, the new generation of boutique winemakers sought not simply to earn a living but to master and perhaps enhance an ancient craft. This lofty motivation melded with an evolution in their approach to that craft. The newcomers didn't maintain an "apostolic" adherence to the state's more clinical scientific methods—the scriptures of the University of California at Davis, for example. They were also deeply inspired by the French "holistic" approach to making wine. While Mondavi and Tchelistcheff also aspired to create excellent wine, they relied on precise, slicing-edge technology to do so. But the newer vintners viewed themselves more as enologists or viticulturists. As Richard Graff of Chalone Vineyard puts it, "Most Americans, most scientifically trained enologists, look at wine in a very linear, very objective manner. But the other way of looking at it is holistically. Wine is perceived as coming from a vineyard, and the function of the winemaker is to permit the grapes to achieve their maximum potential." The fact that Graff himself was a scientifically trained enologist, having studied at UC Davis, demonstrates this fusion of method. Graff was inspired to apply a traditional French winemaking mentality to the beneficial technological advancements of the day.[4]

That the wines crafted in this "boutique" era received such exquisite attention made them truly superb; that they were produced in such limited volumes made them highly desired.[5]

Crafting a Masterpiece

Let us now spend some time with a few of these new vintners, seeing a bit of how they nurtured their grapes before harvesting, crushing, fermenting, and aging them in the hope of crafting something approaching a masterpiece in a glass.

Joseph Heitz Cellars

Starting a boutique winery required a large commitment, especially if one did not arrive from an established career with a reliable stream of investment capital. Joseph Heitz was among those who struggled to reach the top.

Following World War II, Heitz worked at his first wine job: doing "pickup" work at the Italian Swiss Colony plant outside

Clovis in central California. Inspired to pursue the craft, he earned a degree in winemaking from UC Davis in 1948, after which he secured a job overseeing quality control for Gallo. In 1951 he moved to Beaulieu Vineyards, where he worked closely with Tchelistcheff as a lab assistant; eventually he was promoted to manager.[6]

In 1958 Heitz moved to Fresno to establish the enology curriculum at Fresno State College, where he taught for four years. But he then moved on, lured by the siren song of the vine. With a $5,000 loan, Heitz and his wife, Alice, purchased a winery south of St. Helena that came with eight acres planted solely with Grignolino vines. In the first year, a damaging frost followed by withering heat dramatically reduced the yield, producing only 312 gallons of wine. In the second year, Heitz and his young son were in a car accident, which left Joe bedbound just when he needed to produce the next vintage. Defeated, Heitz decided to give up his dream/scheme—but the Napa Valley spirit of cooperation wouldn't allow it. Friends and business rivals alike assisted Alice in keeping Heitz Cellar afloat. Even the government inspector (a fellow student from Davis) completed forms for them on the QT.[7]

With the help of their friends the Heitzes carried on, each year a bit better, and bigger, than the last. At first the winery stocked only nine barrels, a portable crusher, a hand corker, and a hand labeler. They could fill but one bottle at a time. Joe harvested grapes with his children and a neighbor. As he told Ruth Teiser in a 1985 interview, "If you don't have equipment you make it up in labor. We still do that somewhat, because you have to have a certain volume to justify fancy equipment."

In contrast to previous Napa generations, Heitz chose not to grow the majority of his own grapes, preferring to buy in bulk from other growers. He claimed later that, although he knew winemaking, he knew but little about growing fine wine grapes.[8] As the years went on, Heitz continued to grow only Grignolino, though he produced more than a dozen wines ranging from sherry to Cabernet Sauvignon.[9]

In 1963—through happenstance involving a bottle of Heitz Cellars wine given as a housewarming gift—the Heitzes met Tom and Martha May, who'd just purchased a twelve-acre Napa Valley property planted with two-year-old Cabernet Sauvignon vines. Rechristened Martha's Vineyard, the property was soon producing among the most select Cabernet grapes in all of

Napa—indeed, in all of California. An intriguing hint of mint in the rich flavors of the grape added to their allure. The entire first significant harvest, of 1965, was claimed by Joe Heitz.[10]

Heitz blended that first Martha's Vineyard harvest with other local grapes, as he had always done with Cabernet. But the next year, 1966, Heitz bottled a vintage of just the Mays' grapes, labeled HEITZ CELLAR MARTHA'S VINEYARD CABERNET SAUVIGNON. And though he had sold his first Cabernet for $1.63 a bottle, he'd learned that wine connoisseurs—in his words, "real wine people who knew wine and knew values"—were more likely to buy higher-priced wines. So he priced that first Martha's Vineyard Cabernet at $7 a bottle. Given that only the best French wines sold at that price, he chose to represent what he saw as high quality via his high price, just as Martin Ray had done before him. As Heitz recalled for Ruth Teiser, "Most of the world thinks, anything that's imported, they're willing to pay more for. Well, I helped change that around. California wines are great and they should demand the price they deserve."[11]

Heitz's reputation soared following the release of his Martha's Vineyard Cabernet Sauvignon. Before, Heitz had just scraped by with little money to advertise his wines; now, publicity came knocking. His Cabernet Sauvignon was featured in *Town & Country* magazine, along with a full-page photograph of Martha's Vineyard. Famed English wine critic Harry Waugh sang the praises of subsequent Martha's Vineyard releases even before he'd

Heitz Cellar Martha's Vineyard Cabernet Sauvignon wine label. Courtesy of Heitz Wine Cellars.

tasted them.[12] By 1972, business booming, Heitz was able to expand, and built a large stone winery and offices near St. Helena.

In just ten years, despite his early bad luck, Heitz had become a respected winemaker in the Napa Valley, as well as a mentor to the rising young "boutique" generation. Mike Robbins, the owner and winemaker of Spring Mountain, absorbed much of his winemaking knowledge from what George Taber dubs the "local wine brotherhood: Robert Mondavi, Joseph Heitz, and André Tchelistcheff." Bob Travers, the winemaker of Mayacamas, worked for Heitz for a year before buying his own winery in 1968. Heitz wholeheartedly gave back to the community that had helped him grow Heitz Cellar from a seeming curse into a budding boon.[13]

Warren Winiarski and Stag's Leap Wine Cellars

"Winiarski was like a scientist in his lab, only the lab was the entire Napa Valley." So wrote George Taber, describing the practiced, measured approach Warren Winiarski took when considering exactly where in Napa he'd like to start a winery, assessing soils and judging where frost was most problematic.[14] Though he wasn't a scientist per se, he did approach winemaking with an academic, even scholarly mindset, having pursued a PhD in political theory from the University of Chicago. He'd first experienced the "good life" that comes with wine while studying Niccolo Machiavelli in Italy; back in Chicago, he read up on winemaking and became inspired by the process of striving to produce excellence. (In theory, this fascination was inevitable: *Winiarski* means "vintner's son" in Polish.)[15]

Winiarski became particularly intrigued by what he read about Martin Ray in John Storm's 1955 *An Invitation to Wine*, as he related to Ruth Teiser when she interviewed him in the early 1990s: "[Ray] had the ability to infuse qualities of uncommon interest, almost of magic. He had the ability to instill such a high degree of enthusiasm for what he was doing. . . . [H]e was a very compelling figure, a very compelling spirit . . . [W]hat had probably [had] the greatest impact and attractiveness [to me] were the grand style wines [made] by this man who seemed such a powerful presence to all who met him, to be larger than life itself up on this isolated mountain."

Winiarski was in essence a Martin Ray fan before he'd even tasted Ray's wines; but once he did, they were a "revelation," he told Teiser. "The wines were extraordinary, stunning, a degree of artistic excellence that I had not experienced in California wines before. . . . They were excellent not for their regional qualities, not for their here-and-now qualities, but they could be at any time, in any place, and anyone would recognize them for quality." It was precisely that excellence that inspired Winiarski. "It was unquenchable, then, this desire to put this thing together and make it work. I thought to myself that it is people and their endeavors that really make this turn around—such stunning examples of excellence, such exquisite pleasure to accompany food and dining."[16]

To get a sense of the wine-artisan's life, Winiarski spent a week working with Martin Ray up on Ray's "isolated" Table Mountain vineyards, during which time the two mutually tested out the possibility of Winiarski apprenticing with Ray. As Winiarski later recalled:

> I helped them bottle. It was a fantastic experience. They bottled with a siphon hose from a barrel. Everything had its special magic. . . . Martin had accumulated a number of bells from schoolhouses. . . . On occasions, when visitors came, they rang those bells. It was like a cathedral with all its bells ringing. It was ceremonial; it was formal; it was very special. It called for your taking strong notice, that this was not without its "breath of divinity," for it invited comparison with its churchlike original. The quality of the life there—there was nothing ordinary; not a thing was left to its ordinary disposition. [Everything] tried to be heightened, enhanced, increased in meaning.

Though ultimately Ray deemed Winiarski "too independent" to apprentice at his winery, Winiarski was hooked, and decided to make a go of the winemaking life—for which he moved to California in 1964, where he found a promising fit with Lee Stewart at Souverain.[17] From there, as we know, Winiarski headed to Robert Mondavi, before striking out on his own.

While working at Souverain Cellars, Winiarski had been struck by the degree to which Lee Stewart's wines expressed their fruit. In contrast, he felt many grapes produced in California did not realize their "full potential for excellence." He vowed to change that in his approach to winemaking.[18]

Deciding when exactly to harvest grapes was the first step in achieving the harmony Winiarski sought for his wine. Taber relates the care with which this "vintner's son" approached his harvest for the fall of 1973:

> He kept a close eye on the weather, always concerned about the possibility of heavy rains, which could cause mold and damage

the crop. Another danger was excessive heat, which can dehydrate the grapes, and in extreme cases turn them into shriveled raisins on the vine. If the damaged grapes are not removed, the resulting wine will have a burnt-fruit taste. . . . Winiarski used a hand-held refractometer to measure the percent of sugar in a drop of juice, giving its reading in Brix. . . . Winiarski knew he was near harvest when the Brix went over 23 degrees.

No instrument, though, is better than a winemaker's sense of taste, and as the grapes continued to mature, Winiarski sampled more individual berries and sometimes clusters of grapes. Fields do not mature uniformly, and berries at the top of a cluster taste different from those at the bottom. . . .

By the end of September, . . . the flavors were good, promising the wine would have layers of tastes; the skins had a wonderful grainy texture from the tannin, foretelling structure and a long life for the wine; and finally the weather was warm, so waiting any longer would produce more sugar and thus more alcohol later, which would make the wine too powerful.

Winiarski sought "directed understatement," so he dared not leave the crop too long. "The ripeness and richness of the Cabernet had to be combined with restraint."

Indeed, Winiarski sought harmony and balance in all his wines: soft fruit offset hard tannins, strong Cabernet Sauvignon blended with gentle Merlot. (In French, *cabernet sauvignon* means savage or wild Cabernet.)[19] The wine was fermented for six days in modern, temperature-controlled stainless steel tanks that he personally monitored. After undergoing a secondary malolactic fermentation, the wine was exposed to oxygen in a splash tank to kick-start the aging process, and then transferred into Nevers oak barrels imported from France that Winiarski had pretreated by hand. Later the Cabernet Sauvignon was blended with Merlot at a ratio of 9:1. The Winiarski family hand-bottled all eighteen hundred cases of his 1973 vintage themselves. Harry Waugh commented that Winiarski's wine "represented a swing from California's 'huge Cabernet Sauvignons' to a wine of 'more finesse and elegance, in effect more along the lines of the Medocs from Bordeaux.'"[20]

Mike Grgich and Chateau Montelena

From day one, Croatian Miljenko (Mike) Grgich was given full rein over winemaking operations at Chateau Montelena. And step one was designing and retrofitting the winery with first-rate equipment and technology, since Jim Barrett believed "you don't make world-class wine with second-rate equipment."[21] Step two was planting the hundred-acre vineyard with phylloxera-resistant St. George rootstock, onto which they grafted Cabernet Sauvignon vines. While Grgich waited for those vines to mature, the winery bought grapes, principally from the Sonoma Valley, with which Grgich made white wines.

Fortunately, "full rein" meant Grgich was allowed to monitor and influence how the grapes were grown. This was a significant coup since, as Taber relates, grape growers and winemakers approach their objective from opposite directions: the grower, who is paid by weight, wants to produce luscious, heavy clusters; whereas the winemaker wants to cultivate smaller, more flavorful berries. And yet Grgich had the finesse to ensure all parties were satisfied. This approach was part of Grgich's genius—and a bit surprising at that, given that he was known for his reticence and serious disposition. It could be said that Grgich approached the entire winemaking process with a gentle, reasoned determination: he knew exactly what he wanted, and he knew why.[22]

For example, like Martin Ray had done before him, Grgich ignored the conventional vineyard-care guidelines encouraged by the University of California experts: the preventative application of sulfur so as to discourage mold and mildew, and watering once a week. Instead, Grgich went without the sulfur if he detected no telltale spores; he is quoted as saying, "Don't monkey with God in making wine. God is the best winemaker. Leave nature alone." He also deprived the vines of water, bringing them to the brink of dehydration before reviving the grapes with a brief splash of irrigation in the middle of summer. This treatment prevented the grapes from growing too large, which produced a more concentrated, intense flavor.[23]

Grgich's approach to the Chardonnay grapes differed somewhat from Winiarski's with his Cabernet and Merlot. Winiarski did all his testing for sugar in the vineyard, whereas Grgich took randomly picked grapes back to the lab for study. And Grgich's white grapes offered indications of ripeness that Winiarski's dark berries did not. As the sugar heightened, the white berries, previously green, turned more golden, with a translucence that revealed their seeds when held to the sun. Grgich also waited for the vines to sag under the weight of the ripened clusters. He even listened to the grapes: with a higher sugar content, a grape squeezed between his fingers created a squeak much like the sound of rubbing grains of sugar together. There were a few additional signs that peak harvest time was near: a rush of starlings drawn to the ripest berries, preparing for their winter migration, and the occasional shriveled "raisin" on the vine.

Harry Waugh called Grgich a "true perfectionist." Grgich exhorted his cellar hands to treat every step in the winemaking process with care. When it came time to crush the picked grapes, he'd explain: "It's like hugging a friend. You don't want to squeeze so hard that you break your friend's ribs." Though Chateau Montelena used a crusher they'd bought from Inglenook, the actual press was of a new "bladder-squeezing technology"; instead of utilizing a screw press that essentially ground the juice out of the grapes, an inflated rubber tube slowly squeezed the grapes against a screen. By gently squeezing the grapes without fully crushing them, they avoided splitting the seeds, thus preventing the seeds' bitter tannins from leaking into the juice.[24]

Grgich also fermented his Chardonnay longer than Winiarski did his Cabernet: forty-five days rather than just six or so; and at half the temperature: roughly forty-five degrees rather than as much as ninety degrees. The lower temperature preserved the aroma and fruitiness he sought. Various other Grgich methods included striving to prevent the juice being exposed to oxygen, which darkens its freshness. (Note this is a concern with white wine in particular; Winiarski had intentionally exposed his Cabernet to oxygen.) Another was "divining" just when the juice in its stainless-steel tanks, its pulp settling to the bottom, was ready to be pumped out; leaving the sediment behind preserved the grape's fruitiness. And though others espoused the secondary malolactic fermentation for red wines, that was not a procedure Grgich performed on white wines, as he wanted the wine to be "crisp" rather than "flabby." And even though Winiarski and Grgich both aged their wine in French oak barrels, they chose different oak: Nevers oak for the red, Limousin for the white. The aging process "pulled in the hints of oak," and deepened the Chardonnay's hue and aroma. Both vintners also blended their wines. Then, after the Chardonnay was bottled—by machine rather than by hand—came the final phase. Taber writes: "Bottle aging is the anaerobic process when the aromas of the grapes and the aromas and extractives of the oak are married into the bouquet. Grgich called this process, which takes one to two years, 'the wine honeymoon.'"

As for Grgich's first wines: the previously mentioned Johannesburg Riesling sold well, but it was the Chardonnay that the winery prized—and that Grgich took most pride in.[25] As he recalled in an interview with Ruth Teiser in 1992: "I started with them on a small scale. The first wine is still considered the best Chardonnay ever produced in California—vintage '72. . . . I put all my body and soul into it—my own wine."[26]

THE STATE OF THE WINE INDUSTRY—1970S

In the fall of 1970, *Wines & Vines* printed an article titled "Bank of America Lays It on the Line; It's a Rosy 10 Years Ahead for Wine."[27] Bank of America had forecast that annual consumption of wine would rise from 250 million to 400 million by 1980—an assessment they reached by considering the rising disposable income that would be available to the "forty million young adults" who would hit drinking age within the decade.[28] After that first announcement, others prophesized even higher pinnacles would be attained.

Inevitably, a deluge of investment poured into the California wine industry following the predictions. Corporations such as Heublein, Nestlé/Pillsbury, Coca-Cola, and Seagrams showed renewed interest in the market, and heavily promoted brands old and new. Individual investors and aspiring winemakers alike dove headlong into the scrum.[29] Select Cabernet Sauvignon and Chardonnay grapes, which once fetched less than nearly every other agricultural crop in the state, sold for as much as a thousand dollars a ton.[30]

National publicity added to the fervor. On November 27, 1972, *Time* magazine's cover announced, "American Wine: There's Gold in Them Thar Grapes," alongside a wine jug adorned by Ernest and Julio Gallo, by then in their sixties. The accompanying article noted that American consumer attitudes were evolving: "the wine boom is evidence of a growing ease and worldliness in American lifestyles."[31] The rising consumer demand for the sophisticated and appreciated drink that wine had become began to transform winemaking into a (more reliably) profitable enterprise. James Lapsley notes: "The technological transformation of *vin ordinaire* into a beverage readily enjoyable to Americans was a key in helping wine maintain a place at the U.S. table."[32] Indeed, Cyril Ray considered even "California's best jug-wines [to be] the best-made, best-balanced, cleanest, and most consistent *vins ordinaires* in the world."[33]

Wineries became tourist attractions. Fortunately, many of the Napa Valley wineries had been inspired by Robert Mondavi's welcome-mat promotional concepts begun in the early 1950s, and already boasted tasting rooms, winery tours, and lawn events. Adding to the allure, in 1973 Brit Peter L. Newton founded Sterling winery atop the crest of a knoll, where the grand, modern winery, reached only by an aerial tramway, stood out against its conventional old, weathered stone brethren. Tourists swarmed to Sterling to take in the view of Napa on the ride up. Meanwhile, residents and fellow winemakers were appalled that a quiet, oak-covered hillside had become but a tourist tower.[34]

But the 1973 surge in capital investment soon encountered disappointment. Both the Arab oil embargo and a national economic recession caused bulk wine sales to plummet.[35] Two years after the release of the Bank of America report, wine consumption leveled off at 7 percent growth a year, while production continued to grow at 10 percent a year. The wine industry abounded in surplus.[36]

Steven Spurrier and the Second Judgment of Paris

In his youth at Holbrook Hall in Derbyshire, England, Steven Spurrier had enjoyed rearranging the bottles in his family's cellars. After he'd wandered into adulthood, he worked a bit in the London wine trade, even though as landed gentry he didn't need to work at all. He also spent a lavish seven months studying and tasting wine while touring France, Germany, Portugal, and Spain. But by the autumn of 1970, when nearly thirty and living in Paris, Spurrier still had not found his calling—until he happened upon a small wine shop called Les Caves de la Madeleine. On the spot, he inquired if he could buy it.

Though the shop was indeed for sale, its owner, widow Madame Fougeres, felt uneasy about selling to an *Englishman*, however posh a gentleman he might be. And so, to prove himself worthy, for six months with no wages Spurrier toiled in the shop and delivered cases of wine throughout Paris. At the end of his servitude, when he was finally allowed the purchase, Spurrier changed the shop's selection of wines from *vin ordinaire* to the highest-quality French vintages.

In time Spurrier also proved himself to France's wine elite, and gained enough respect to judge tastings throughout France. Later, Spurrier and a friend founded a small school, L'Académie du Vin, which offered wine-appreciation classes in English. The school was an even bigger success than the shop, and eventually attracted even French students and aspiring sommeliers. American journalist Patricia Gallagher ran the school, while Spurrier ran the shop. Every few months they would host an event to promote both enterprises. In the spring of 1975, that event took the form of a wine tasting comparing the 1970 vintages of "Bordeaux's elite First Growth" red wines. As George Taber tells us, "No one in France had ever staged such a face-off of the great wines."[37]

The advancements in the wineries of the New World were making themselves known in the Old World too, and Spurrier soon received his own lessons in California wine. In the early 1970s, Parisians' concept of wine from the Golden State was the only one readily available: screw-top bottles of Paul Masson—by then owned by Seagrams and not to Martin Ray's exacting standards—and these in truth were only intended for Americans thinking fondly of home. It was European wine that Spurrier dealt in; he thought "California wines were 'rather cooked'": both high in alcohol and rather burnt tasting. But at a dinner party the American wine writer Alex Bespaloff strove to convince him otherwise. Later, two additional figures became "evangelists for the new California wine pioneers": Robert Finigan, the author-publisher of *Robert Finigan's Private Guide to Wines* newsletter, and the *New York Times* wine reporter Frank J. Prial. All three separately assured Spurrier and Gallagher that the contemporary vintners considered French wine their "model of excellence." These evangelists considered good California wines to be "surprisingly good—not up to French standards, but nonetheless interesting." And Gallagher's fiancé described wine he'd tasted in Napa Valley as "pleasantly surprising."

In time, perhaps encouraged by Bespaloff and Finigan and Prial, California winemakers began calling at the shop to leave bottles of their best vintages and to describe the evolution taking place in California wine. Both Spurrier and Gallagher were impressed with the depth and clarity of the wines they sampled. Somewhere in the mix Gallagher got the idea to put the best California vintages on display in Paris to show how far American wines had come. They decided that America's bicentennial year of 1976 would be an ideal premise for showcasing California wines in a blind tasting with French wines, an event to reinforce the partnership and affinity between America and France throughout their history. Thus was their tasting conceived, and Spurrier and Gallagher began preparing for an informal afternoon event.[38]

They decided that the French wines included would be reds from Bordeaux and whites from Burgundy. As for the latter, recall that, though to many the term "burgundy" indicates red wine, and likely common wine at that, it originally indicated that a wine, white or red, hailed from the Bourgogne region of France.[39] Taber tells us that the region's white wines have "long been considered without equal." Indeed, Alexandre Dumas believed that a particular Chardonnay, Montrachet, should be "sipped only while kneeling and with the head bowed." This last view in many ways epitomized what the French thought about their best wines—as worthy of nothing less than reverence.[40]

Patricia Gallagher consulted Robert Finigan regarding which California wines to compare with the French vintages. For the red category, Finigan chose Warren Winiarski's Cabernet Sauvignon, which he considered an "exceptional effort" in a "Bordeaux style." The white category was a bit trickier, since the California vintages tended to be more "full mouthed" than the French. Ultimately, he selected Chateau Montelena and Chalone as contrasting examples of premium California Chardonnays. He judged Chalone as having some "stunning, minerally wines suggestive of the better Meursaults and Pulignys," while Chateau Montelena's first few Chardonnays had "impressed [him] with Burgundian accuracy accented by an extra touch of Californian ripeness."[41]

Finigan produced for Gallagher a list of wines that, perhaps surprisingly, did not include established, prominent California names like Beaulieu, Inglenook, or Robert Mondavi—only the latter of which was still independently owned. Instead, Finigan chose to showcase the new generation of boutique winemakers, "where newer and more exciting things were taking place." In March of 1976, Spurrier traveled to California to make the final selection of wines for the tasting. He opted to match six California Cabernet Sauvignons with four French Bordeaux reds, and six California Chardonnays with four Burgundy whites.[42]

As for the French candidates for the tasting, Spurrier purposely selected vintages from his shop that he believed would easily defeat the California wines. His intention was to showcase that not *all* California wine came from a screw-top jug, that there were some interesting developments going on in the Golden State. It went without saying that all the French vintages would be preferred. The California winemakers concurred; none imagined besting the French selections.[43]

California Wines Selected for the 1976 Paris Tasting

Cabernet Sauvignon
- 1972 Clos du Val Winery
- 1969 Freemark Abbey
- 1970 Heitz Cellars Martha's Vineyard
- 1971 Mayacamas Vineyards
- 1971 Ridge Vineyards Monte Bello
- 1973 Stag's Leap Wine Cellars

Chardonnay
- 1974 Chalone
- 1973 Chateau Montelena
- 1976 David Bruce
- 1972 Freemark Abbey
- 1973 Spring Mountain
- 1972 Veedercrest Vineyards

Spurrier next assembled a panel of nine distinguished judges, nearly all of whom were well known and respected in French wine circles. These included the inspector general in control of the production of premium French wines—and the author of several books on the subject; the editor of two French wine review publications; a Bordeaux-born chef and restaurateur; a head sommelier from another top restaurant; and the owner of a vineyard that had long produced some of the most highly acclaimed French wines ever bottled. Also on the panel: the French-language teacher at L'Académie du Vin, who made up a title of "president of the Institute Oenologique de France" so as to not shrink too much alongside his prestigious fellow judges. Curiously, in his invitation Spurrier had described the event as a tasting to celebrate the up-and-coming California wines. He neglected to mention that French wines would be included as well.

Spurrier and Gallagher then invited the press, particularly the wine critics for the *Le Monde* and *Le Figaro* newspapers and the esteemed *Gault&Millau* restaurant guide. But to their chagrin, a mere week before the tasting Spurrier and Gallagher learned that no one from the press planned to attend. As author George Taber puts it: "A tasting of California wines? No one in the French press saw a story there." Indeed, Taber himself—at the time a Paris-based reporter for *Time* magazine who'd taken the Académie's wine course—had tossed aside the press release he'd received for the event. It took Gallagher's earnest persuading to convince him to be their sole journalist in attendance.[44]

Despite all the effort and expense they'd put into the tasting, Spurrier and Gallagher approached the event with no particular objective other than an afternoon of fun—and a chance to promote both Les Caves de la Madeleine and L'Académie du Vin. They were nothing more than curious about how the California wines would be judged in comparison with their French counterparts.

———

ON MAY 24, 1976, on a sunny Monday afternoon in Paris, the retinue of distinguished French judges assembled at the Inter-Continental Hotel. Spurrier introduced the event as part of America's bicentennial celebration, one intended to showcase the intriguing wines emerging from California. His announcement that several similar French wines had been added to the lineup produced no demur. Since the tasting was "blind," all of the wines

Defining a Wine's Attributes:
Eye, Nose, Mouth, and Harmony

"Master sommelier" Tim Gaiser, author of *Taste Wine Like a Pro,* offers a few words on how to assess a wine's numerous attributes.

❧ **EYE:** *Color* and *Clarity.*

Color/hue might be considered: STRAW ▪ YELLOW ▪ GOLD ▪ BROWN (white wines) or PURPLE ▪ RUBY ▪ GARNET ▪ BROWN (red wines).

Clarity includes "brightness"—how much it reflects light—as well as the presence of any sediment. Clarity might be considered: CLOUDY ▪ HAZY ▪ DULL ▪ BRIGHT ▪ BRILLIANT.

❧ **NOSE:** *Bouquet,* the full aromatic experience, often including "fruit, earth, and wood."

Some define *aroma* as indicating what fruity scents are present (perhaps citrus or tropical—more specific examples follow) that derive from the grape itself; and *bouquet* as indicating scents that derive from the techniques or materials used to make the wine, especially how it was aged (as in oak or redwood barrels).

❧ **MOUTH:** *Body* and *Taste,* but also *Palate.*

Body speaks to a wine's weight or "mouthfeel": CRISP ▪ LIGHT ▪ MEDIUM ▪ FULL ▪ SYRUPY ▪ FLABBY.

Taste would first be identified as DRY or SWEET, but the category also includes flavors, as in fruity (APPLE ▪ APRICOT ▪ CHERRY ▪ FIG ▪ MANGO ▪ PLUM), earthy (CHALK ▪ DAMP EARTH ▪ MUSHROOMS ▪ SLATE ▪ WET LEAVES), or woody (CARAMEL ▪ SAWDUST ▪ SMOKE ▪ SPICE).

Another consideration is that of *palate,* wherein one "confirms the nose" and "assesses structure." Confirming the nose especially concerns how the taste compares to the aroma—if the expectations of the nose are fulfilled on the tongue. In assessing structure one considers the wine's tannins, acidity, alcohol, and finish/aftertaste. As Tim Gaiser says, "The general rule in wine tasting: the longer the finish, the better the wine—no matter who made it, where it's from, or how much it costs."

❧ **HARMONY:** Balance; synthesis of all of the above.

An additional consideration is *complexity*, the extent of a wine's flavors and bouquet combined with how much it changes on the palate. A simple wine offers just a few aromas in the glass and will change very little as you taste it. A complex wine offers many different aromas in the glass and will "change dramatically—and pleasantly—as it travels across your palate. . . . It will continue to change and develop in the glass, revealing even more nuances over time." A simple wine is a nursery rhyme; a complex wine is a chamber quartet.

Source: Gaiser, "Catch and Release: Using the Deductive Tasting Technique," TimGaiser.com.

had been poured into neutral bottles, as there are subtle but noticeable differences between the shapes of the two countries' wine bottles. The wines were to be tasted in random order to further obscure their origin. Scoring for the tasting was conducted on a standard twenty-point scale with four equally weighted criteria for eye, nose, mouth, and harmony.[45]

The tasting began with the white wines. George Taber—the entire press contingent—noted such comments as "This soars out of the ordinary" and "This is nervous and agreeable." But a confusion came over the judges as they started to realize that distinguishing the upstart California contestants from the exalted French ones wasn't the child's play they'd expected. They began to talk among themselves, quibbling about the wines' origins.[46] One judge proclaimed, "Ah, back to France!" while tasting a California entrant. Another, sampling the French Batard-Montrachet, announced, "This is definitely California. It has no nose."[47]

The child's play turned out to be a shake-up. Every judge had ranked a California Chardonnay as being the best of the whites. According to six of the nine judges, that top ranking was earned by Chateau Montelena; the remaining three judges had preferred Chalone. California Chardonnays also claimed three of the top four spots in the tasting. The judges were stunned. They could not comprehend how they could have so overwhelmingly chosen California wines—or, how the California wines had so thoroughly duped them.

One of the judges, Claude Dubois-Millot, later admitted: "We thought we were recognizing French wines, when they were

In 2013, Stag's Leap Wine Cellars produced a Cabernet Sauvignon celebrating the fortieth anniversary of their winning entry at the 1976 Paris tasting. Stag's Leap Wine Cellars 2013 S.L.V. Cabernet Sauvignon 40th Anniversary Vintage label, courtesy of Ste. Michelle Wine Estates.

California and vice versa. At times we'd say that a wine would be thin and therefore California, when it wasn't. Our confusion showed how good California wines have become."[48]

The tasting continued with the reds. This time, Taber notes, the judges were "more intense and more circumspect." They were also better at distinguishing whether a sample was Californian or French. Spurrier had expected this; while they might have felt cocky when judging the whites, their consternation (and perhaps a bit of shame) from those results required that they be much more deliberate with the reds. Plus, the French reds had another advantage: the judges would have been deeply familiar with the French entries, whereas they were tasting the challengers for the first time.

Consternation and deliberation played a larger role in the judging of the reds, but they did not rule the day. This time French wines earned three of the top four slots, and scored better overall. But it was Warren Winiarski's Stag's Leap that received the top rating, besting the French Château Mouton Rothschild. The victor once again hailed from California.[49]

Following the announcement, some of the judges praised a few of the California wines they'd tasted. Some offered comments like: "We clearly saw that the California whites can stand up to the French whites. They are certainly the best—after France. They have come a long way, but they have a long way to go." Other statements were more snide or haughty. One judge was downright irate; Odette Kahn, editor of the *Revue du Vin de France,* demanded and redemanded that Spurrier return her scorecards. He would not. The results were final; California had upset the best of France.[50] As for those scores, the Wikipedia page for the "Judgment of Paris" provides all the judges' scores for each wine.[51]

———

No one involved—Spurrier, Gallagher, or any of the Californian vintners and owners—foresaw what came next. On June 7, 1976, buried in the Modern Living section of *Time* magazine, was a story titled "The Judgment of Paris" that read: "Last week in Paris, at a formal wine tasting organized by [Steven] Spurrier, the unthinkable happened: California defeated all Gaul." That day, wine stores across the country sold out of the winning wines from the competition.

The story resounded with the American public. Though some had already known that California was producing world-class wines, most didn't—until the Judgment of Paris both affirmed and publicized that fact. The implications of the tasting were described and celebrated in newspapers and magazines from coast to coast. Some of the facts of the tasting were magnified, taken out of context, or fabricated altogether. The significance of the event, though, remained: some California wines were of an exceptionally high quality, and should be considered on par with the finest French wines.[52]

The French largely ignored the results of the tasting, initially choosing not to report on the event; several pooh-poohed the results once they did. Despite efforts to dismiss the affair's significance, many of the judges were blamed for setting back the reputation of French wine. When George Taber set out to write his 2005 book *Judgment of Paris: California vs. France and the Historic 1976 Paris*, several of the judges declined to speak with him, even twenty-five years after the fact. Steven Spurrier for years faced vigorous accusations that he had sought to undermine the reputation of French wine; in his own words, he was *"persona non grata* in Bordeaux and Burgundy."[53]

Some of the complaints made in the Francophone defense were that the tasting was inexpertly handled, that a twenty-point score was insufficient, that nine judges were insufficient, that it was unfair to pit six California wines against only four French, and that the French wines would inevitably improve with age and thus had competed prematurely. As it happens, several subsequent tastings were held in the ensuing years, including a Wine Olympics in Paris 1979, in which over sixty judges assessed over three hundred wines from over thirty countries. In another event there were ninety-nine experts on the tasting panel. Spurrier also held tenth- and thirteenth-anniversary rematches, which allowed the French reds significant time to show their age. In all these contests, as would be expected, the rankings shuffled around a fair amount. But one point remained constant: while the French wines were undeniably excellent, the California wines held their own.[54]

In 1991, Warren Winiarski offered his thoughts on the Judgment of Paris: "Sam Aaron [distinguished wine merchant and connoisseur of New York City] once told me, after the Paris tasting, that in the Paris tasting we were struck by lightning. That's certainly true. This was a tremendously energizing event, circumstance, and happening. However, we did climb to the top of the tree, or the top of the hill, in order to be exposed to the possibility of being struck by lightning. One could also say that."[55]

Thoughts on the Significance of the 1976 Paris Tasting

Is such a tasting a valid judgment on the quality of the wines involved? Probably not. . . . The variables involved in this kind of tasting are incalculable. Only the most naïve reader would conclude anything other than that on a certain day a certain group of French wine specialists agreed that California turns out some fine wines.

—FRANK J. PRIAL, "Wine Talk," *New York Times*, June 16, 1976

The Paris tasting destroyed the myth of French supremacy and marked the democratization of the wine world. It was a watershed in the history of wine.

—ROBERT PARKER, wine critic, 2001, quoted in Taber, *Judgment of Paris*

With the immediate and widespread publication of the Paris results, several of the tasters disdained their very own conclusions, with excuses ranging from not understanding the scoring system to not comprehending the importance given a tasting they thought of no particular consequence. But *le chat* was quite clearly out of *le sac*, like it or not: the best California wines were recognized as playing prominently in the big leagues as they had never been seen before. Even in the twenty-first century, Paris 1976 stands as the event that brought California's best to the world's attention.

—ROBERT FINIGAN, *Corks and Forks: Thirty Years of Wine and Food*, 2006

If we hadn't had a reporter from *Time*, there would have been no fuss at all.

—STEVEN SPURRIER, quoted in Taber, *Judgment of Paris*, 1996

Before the Paris tasting, Winiarski's Cabernet Sauvignon and Grgich's Chardonnay had been selling for only $6 to $7 a bottle, whereas premium French wines could fetch three to four times that price. After the tasting, once the wine sellers realized what had happened, the winning California wines could command much higher prices—at least while inventory lasted. (The prices rise still. On January 22, 2017, a bottle of the winning red, 1973 Stag's Leap Wine Cellars Cabernet Sauvignon, sold at auction for $1,300 on WineBid.com.[56] Seven years earlier, Decanter.com reported that "one of the few remaining bottles of ex-cellar 1973 Chateau Montelena Chardonnay has been sold by Spectrum Wine Auctions for $11,325."[57])

Fortunately for California, the Judgment of Paris coincided with the wine industry's recovery from the demand slump of 1974 and 1975; as a result, all California wineries began to bump up their prices, gradually matching those of their French counterparts.[58] The number of wineries in the state bumped up too. In 1977, Mike Grgich founded Grgich Hills Estate. Many others followed suit, most seeking to contribute to the evolution of California wine.[59]

In the 1960s and 1970s, the likes of Mondavi, Tchelistcheff, Martini, and others had significantly improved the quality of California wine; they'd also attracted the interest, talent, and investment of a new generation of winemakers, winery owners, and growers. But despite all the innovation, increasing quality, and reverberating buzz, in the years leading up to the 1976 tasting the wine lists of upmarket restaurants on both coasts still often lacked a single California offering.[60] But with the Paris tasting, California wines had proven they could grace the table of any fine restaurant.

Notes

1. *Bulfinch's Mythology*, 211–12.
2. Lukacs, *American Vintage*, 217.
3. Tchelistcheff, "Grapes, Wine, and Ecology," 155, 157.
4. Lukacs, *American Vintage*, 232.
5. Ibid., 233.
6. Taber, *Judgment of Paris*, 177.
7. Heitz, "Creating a Winery," 29–32; Taber, *Judgment of Paris*, 177.
8. Heitz, "Creating a Winery," 32–37, 48. Heitz's comment about equipment and labor appears on page 33.
9. Taber, *Judgment of Paris*, 177.
10. Tom May, interview by author, April 9, 2003.

11. Heitz, "Creating a Winery," 39, 49.

12. Tom May, qtd. in Heitz, "Creating a Winery," 323, citing William Heintz, "Martha's Vineyard of Napa Valley: A Historical Overview," April 1989, private research study for the Mays, 69.

13. Taber, *Judgment of Paris*, 172, 179–80.

14. Ibid., 108.

15. Carol Emert, "The Winiarski Way," *SF Gate*, Thursday, April 1, 2004, sfgate.com/wine/article/THE-WINIARSKI-WAY-In-1976-Warren -Winiarski-s-2800232.php.

16. Winiarski, "Creating Classic Wines," 12–13, 15–16.

17. Ibid., 14–20. The extracted quotation appears on page 17.

18. Ibid., 21, 13.

19. Taber, *Judgment of Paris*, 134–35, 140.

20. Ibid., 137–41, quoting in part from one of Harry Waugh's diaries. See also pages 135–41 for Taber's fascinating step-by-step tour through the process of Winiarski's second vintage.

21. Ibid., 120.

22. Ibid., 143–45.

23. Ibid., 143–44, 148. The "monkey with God" statement appears on page 148.

24. Ibid., 146–47.

25. Ibid., 143, 147–50.

26. Grgich, "Croatian-American Winemaker," 24.

27. John A. Knechel, "Bank of America Lays It On the Line; It's a Rosy 10 Years Ahead for Wine," *Wines & Vines* 51 (September 1970): 3, cited in Pinney, *History of Wine in America*, 2:459n72.

28. Pinney, *History of Wine in America*, 2:240–41 and references cited.

29. Lapsley, *Bottled Poetry*, 200–201.

30. Heintz, *California's Napa Valley*, 345.

31. Ibid., 363–64.

32. Lapsley, *Bottled Poetry*, 200.

33. Cyril Ray, *Robert Mondavi*, 60.

34. Heintz, *California's Napa Valley*, 345.

35. Mondavi, *Harvests of Joy*, 180.

36. Heintz, *California's Napa Valley*, 347.

37. Taber, *Judgment of Paris*, 7–9, 11–12, 14–15.

38. Ibid., 15–16.

39. Sullivan, *Companion to California Wine*, 40.

40. Taber, *Judgment of Paris*, 24.

41. Finigan, *Corks & Forks*, 120–22.

42. Taber, *Judgment of Paris*, 155–58.

43. Ibid., 185.

44. Ibid., 159–63.

45. Ibid., 198–200.

46. Ibid., 200–201.

47. Lapsley, *Bottled Poetry*, 203; Taber, *Judgment of Paris*, 3.

48. Taber, *Judgment of Paris*, 201, 202.

49. Ibid., 202–4.

50. Ibid., 204–5.

51. "Judgment of Paris (wine)," *Wikipedia*, en.wikipedia.org/wiki/ Judgment_of_Paris_(wine).

52. Taber, *Judgment of Paris*, 213–16.

53. Ibid., 217–19.

54. Ibid., 220–24.

55. Winiarski, "Creating Classic Wines," 62.

56. "1973 Stag's Leap Wine Cellars Cabernet Sauvignon," WineBid, January 22, 2017, winebid.com/BuyWine/Item/6037216/1973-Stags-Leap-Wine-Cellars-Cabernet-Sauvignon.

57. Maggie Rosen, "'Judgment of Paris' Montelena Fetches US$11,325," *Decanter,* July 23, 2010, decanter.com/wine-news/judgment-of-paris-montelena-fetches-us11325-53483/#KuptCCvsJsstJyxe.99.

58. Mondavi, *Harvests of Joy,* 185–86; Taber, *Judgment of Paris,* 216.

59. Mondavi, *Harvests of Joy,* 191.

60. Robert Finigan, interview by author, November 2, 2009.

CHAPTER 12

Now That They've Seen Paris—
The California Wine Industry
Meets the Twenty-First Century

1976–Present

> The difference between good wine and fine wine is a
> fleeting moment on the palate; it takes a lot of study and
> tasting to understand it. . . . You don't need four hundred
> words of vocabulary to describe *alcoholic grape juice*.
>
> —Bob Trinchero,
> Sutter Home Vineyards

WHEN ROBERT MONDAVI learned the results of the 1976 Paris tasting, he was "tickled to death, . . . happy and proud," for his "alumni" winemakers Warren Winiarski and Mike Grgich, and for California wine as a whole.[1] But the event occurred at a turbulent time in his personal history. In 1972, Robert had filed a lawsuit against his brother and mother over being fired from Charles Krug in 1966. April 1976, the month prior to the tasting, had seen the beginning of a trial that would last for several months, its testimony a story of family discord worthy of a latter-day Aeschylus. The pathos and spectacle of that story, a family feud filled with accusation and recrimination, was keenly reported by the Napa Valley press. In the background of that personal saga lay the continuing story of California wine itself. Though the state's wineries and vintages had reached great heights, would they be able to build on that success? Or would internal struggles and jarring economic forces once again endanger the progress that had been made? To begin answering those questions we return to Robert Mondavi, starting with his share of the success, failure, and controversy that have marked California's wine industry since 1965.

In September 1972, Robert Mondavi was informed that his family intended to dissolve the C. Mondavi & Sons partnership and form a new one, C. Mondavi and Company, of which his share would be limited. When he balked, they proceeded in forming a partnership that excluded him completely. In a lawsuit filed on November 21, 1972, Robert asked the court to order the dissolution of the new partnership Peter and Rosa had created. He also demanded both a full accounting of their assets and asked to be awarded damages for their actions taken against him. Robert engaged as his principal lawyer the brilliant and multitalented John Martel, who was as gritty and confident as his client.[2] Peter and Rosa were defended by Joseph Alioto, one of the country's great trial lawyers who was also the thirty-sixth mayor of San Francisco. Alioto had filed a counterclaim, arguing that Robert—who (amazingly) still sat on the Charles Krug board—should be barred from that position since Robert Mondavi Winery was a direct competitor of Charles Krug. In turn, Martel asked the court to dissolve Charles Krug as a corporate entity on the basis of mismanagement. This stance was one Robert Mondavi had been reluctant to take; his decision to proceed with such a serious accusation would have long, forking ramifications.[3]

The trial of *Robert Mondavi v. C. Mondavi & Sons* began in Napa on April 22, 1976. From the first day, the rhetoric seethed violet. An observing lawyer later recalled that the opening statements by Martel and Alioto "made the Scopes trial look like a cotillion intermission." Unfortunately, no transcripts exist of the trial, and the two lawyers in their written briefs wrote in appropriately measured tones. The case, assigned to Judge Robert D. Carter of Modesto, was tried without a jury.

The trial was not attended by Rosa Mondavi, who was suffering from pancreatic cancer. When her health declined even further toward the end of the trial, Robert visited her every morning before that day's session began.[4] Then, on the bicentennial day of July 4, 1976, Rosa suffered a stroke and died. Robert writes: "Even during the worst of the trial, we remained close. We had meals together and there was no animosity between us. In the end, after raising her family and accomplishing so much here in America, my mother simply couldn't bear to see her sons battle it out in court. I think it simply broke her big maternal heart."[5]

Following the brief respite for Rosa's death and funeral, the trial trudged on. Robert Mondavi held his ground throughout

Joe Alioto's withering and days-long cross-examination, which in the end landed no punches; Robert's steady and sturdy answers to Alioto's hostile questions only fortified the credibility of his account of things. Then, during his cross-examination of Peter Mondavi, John Martel provoked Peter into revealing his lifelong resentment of Robert, while also elucidating that no evidence justified Robert's expulsion from Charles Krug.

On August 12, 1976, Judge Robert D. Carter handed down his "Intended Decision," a searing denunciation finding that the Mondavi family had engaged in "deliberate and calculated execution of a scheme to defraud Robert." Charles Krug was ordered to be sold, the proceeds to be divided equally among all shareholders, including Robert. In addition to his share, Robert was also awarded $539,885 plus a nearly equal amount in attorneys' fees.[6] In his thoughtful and extraordinarily long decision—159 pages—Judge Robert D. Carter wrote: "A man's reputation must be earned, and...'once withered is hard to revive.'"[7]

Vindicated by the validation he'd received with the judge's decision, and perhaps also calmed by it, Robert ultimately let Peter buy back Charles Krug, agreeing to not pursue further legal action against him. Peter in turn dropped his appeal, and turned over cash and property amounting to some $11 million. The property was hundreds of acres of prime vineyards, including the To-Kalon holdings that Krug had purchased before ousting Robert. With the proceeds, Robert bought out the last outside stake in the Robert Mondavi Winery—without once forgetting the dear price all involved had had to pay throughout the feud.[8]

State of the Wine Industry—Corporate Interests, Vineyard Management, and Technological Advancement

Robert Mondavi regained individual ownership at a time when individual control was becoming increasingly scarce among Napa Valley winemakers. This was in part because, though the Judgment of Paris certainly signaled a strong ascent in the state's wine industry, it did not lead to immediate solvency for many wine growers. As Mondavi said about the effect of the 1976 tasting: "Not all the old barriers to California wine crumbled overnight, but we had made a nice dent or two."[9] Wineries mired in debt took advantage of newfound corporate interests, who swooped in to get a piece of the pie. Just as had been done before, many of these corporations sacrificed the quality of established premium brands in favor of significantly increased production of anonymous bulk wines.

Even the soft-drink industry saw opportunities in Napa. Sterling, the white gleaming winery on the hill, sold to Coca-Cola in 1977, which promptly eliminated three of its varietal wines. (Coca-Cola later sold to Seagrams in 1984.)[10] Corporations entering the market soon discovered, though, that managing a winery posed challenges distinct from managing a liquor or food company. Costs were high, ironically pushed up by the recent success in Paris. Profits appeared on financial statements only in the long term. Additionally, corporations found themselves in competition with a growing population of independently wealthy winery owners with a dogged motivation to succeed. Many corporations' winery experiments lasted only a few years. In 1976 alone Pillsbury sold Souverain, John Hancock Life Insurance sold Monterey Vineyards, and Newcastle Breweries sold Simi Winery.[11]

Then foreign interest in the California wine industry arose. Within a week of buying Almaden from National Distillers in 1987, Heublein turned its entire wine business over to Grand Metropolitan Holding Company of Great Britain. Grand Metropolitan, which also held an interest in Beaulieu, Inglenook, and Christian Brothers, would become one of the largest corporations in the California wine industry, second only to E. & J. Gallo.[12]

Between 1977 and 1981 the number of wineries in Napa Valley more than doubled, from 51 to 110. Many of the new wineries were founded by well-financed individuals who weren't fazed by price inflation, the Arab oil embargo, or the general downturn in the industry. These figures approached the operation of a winery quite differently from a corporation. Their goal was not so much to make a profit from the investment (though profit was ever preferable to loss) but to live more back-to-the-earth while producing high-quality wines they could take pride in. Squeezed between the corporations and these new wealthy entrepreneurs were the older farming families who had owned and tended the vines of Napa Valley for decades. The director of the Napa Valley Grape Growers Association is quoted as saying, "This is no longer just a farming area. It's a label, like Calvin Klein." Another in the association surmised that only 100 to 150 "real farmers" remained.[13] Many of these older families had no choice but to sell out. Those who held on to their land endured unfair contracts enforced by the large, usually corporate-owned, grape-buying wineries.

But not all corporate involvement depleted the region's cachet. One interesting development concerned liquor giant Heublein. In the late sixties, employee Andrew Beckstoffer was instrumental in Heublein purchasing United Vintners and Beaulieu Vineyards, making it the largest vineyard owner in Napa County. But Heublein soon discovered what a high-risk business vineyard ownership can be. As we've seen, the quality and yield of the crop can fluctuate wildly from year to year, and poor harvests can lead to significant losses. In 1973, seeking to escape the risk of vineyard management, Heublein reconfigured its relationship with Beckstoffer, whereby the latter assumed management of what came to be known as Vinifera Development Corporation. In essence, Beckstoffer oversaw the grape-growing end of the business, while Heublein retained the right of first refusal on all of Vinifera's grapes, as well as received all proceeds.[14]

Unfortunately, the Vinifera Development Corporation quickly hit rough waters. High interest rates combined with a sharp drop in the price of grapes in 1975 and 1976 resulted in massive losses. Disenchanted, Heublein opted to release all vineyard management associations. So in 1977 Beckstoffer negotiated with Heublein to acquire 100 percent of Vinifera. Though the acreage he controlled was cut in half, and his debt totaled $2.6 million, he gained outright ownership of a business foundation from which he could steadily grow his vineyard-management enterprise. And though Beckstoffer had begun in the corporate world, by then he had fallen in love with Northern California and premium winegrowing—and he believed in the long game. Indeed, from the beginning of Vinifera Development his mission statement was to be a "large-volume, high-quality grower of Northern California coastal premium wine grapes through the development and application of modern business and viticultural technology *our way* to realize above-average return from farming services and grape sales while building an estate in vineyard real estate."[15] As for building an estate, over the years Beckstoffer gradually acquired additional vineyards in Napa, Mendocino, and Lake Counties. In time, he became the largest independent grower on the north coast, owner of more than 2,100 acres of vineyards.[16]

Part of doing things "his way" involved improving the rights of the grape growers, for which reason in 1975 Beckstoffer helped to found the previously mentioned Napa Valley Grape Growers Association (NVGGA). One early NVGGA success was facilitating passage, headed by Senator Claire Berryhill, of the California Crush Report, which required wineries to report what they paid for grapes—details growers had never been privy to before. An additional implementation was for the growers to tabulate their

"THERE'S BLOOD ON THOSE GRAPES"

BOYCOTT non-UFW GRAPES LETTUCE and GALLO WINE

UNITED FARM WORKERS OF AMERICA—AFL-CIO

Stating "There's Blood on Those Grapes," this poster exhorts that everyone "boycott non-UFW grapes, lettuce, and Gallo wine." Image from the 1975 UFW Gallo boycott campaign, used with permission of the United Farm Workers of America. The poster reads, in part: "If you want to help 2 million farm workers, join our boycott of table grapes and Gallo wine. Don't buy table grapes unless they have the U.F.W. eagle on the label. Don't buy Gallo Wine or any other wine made in Modesto, CA. (If it says MODESTO, it's made by Gallo.) And don't buy any of the Gallo names, like Thunderbird, Ripple, Andre Cold Duck, Boone's Farm, Madria Madria Sangria, Tyrolia, Carlo Rossi, Red Mountain, or Josef Steuben. Do buy Paul Masson, Christian Brothers, Almaden, Italian Swiss Colony, Perelli-Minetti, Viedel, or Novitiate of Los Gatos. If enough of us join the boycott, the growers will get the message. And America's farm workers will get the union they deserve."

The Rights of California Farmworkers

Andrew Beckstoffer has identified the class structure of wine-growing as follows: "Like in all of agriculture, the processor is the first-class citizen, like the processor winery; the producer farmer is a second-class citizen; the farmworker is a third-class citizen." While Beckstoffer strove to improve the working conditions for the grape growers, others joined in support of the grape farmworkers. An early effort occurred in 1963, when the mostly Filipino Agricultural Workers Organizing Committee (AWOC) in Delano, California, initiated a strike of table grapes when they were denied minimum wage for their labor. In a show of solidarity, this strike was soon bolstered by the National Farm Workers Association (NFWA), co-founded in 1962 by Mexican American civil rights activists César Chávez and Dolores Huerta. Soon after the two groups fused to become the United Farm Workers of America (UFW) labor union. Their persistent, nonviolent efforts, which included consumer boycotts, marches, and community organizing, effected a collective bargaining agreement in 1970, when the first grape contracts were signed.

The authors of *The Fight in the Fields: Cesar Chavez and the Farmworkers Movement* paint a grim picture of the interpersonal politics of these concerns. They share that "union lawyer Jerry Cohen respected some of the agribusinessmen for their pride and their hard work. But by 1970, he had become convinced that some ranchers thought it beneath them to deal face-to-face with Mexican farmhands. Not only did they refuse to look Chávez in the eye, they considered Huerta and César inscrutable, and tried to funnel bargaining positions through white attorneys. 'Some of them didn't like the notion of dealing equally with people of a different race,' Cohen says bluntly. And even if they realized it was becoming socially unacceptable to say such things publicly, Cohen believes many ranchers were dogged by one single question: 'Are we going to have Mexicans telling us how to run our damn operations?'"

As part of a second boycott on grapes—as well as on lettuce and Gallo wines—on February 22, 1975, several hundred protestors embarked on a UFW-led 110-mile march from San Francisco to the E. & J. Gallo Winery in Modesto. When they reached Modesto on March 1, their numbers had swelled to fifteen thousand. This time their persistence led to the June 4, 1975, passage of the California Agricultural Labor Relations Act (ALRA), which was written to "ensure peace in the agricultural fields by guaranteeing justice for all agricultural workers and stability in labor relations."

Sources: Beckstoffer, "Premium California Vineyardist," 67; Rainey, "Farm Workers Union"; Ferriss and Sandoval, *Fight in the Fields*, 163; Griswold del Castillo and Garcia, *Cesar Chavez*, 127; Agricultural Labor Relations Act of 1975, Cal. Stats. 1975, Third Extraordinary Session, c. 1 sec. 1 at 4013.

vineyard production costs. Thus armed with the two new sets of data, in 1976 growers demonstrated that their proceeds didn't cover their production costs. The following year, the NVGGA developed the "bottle price" formula to determine fair prices for grapes, whereby growers received one hundred times the retail price of a bottle of wine for every ton of grapes they sold. That this system rapidly gained footing augmented the status of growers in the early 1980s.[17]

In reviewing historical vineyard management in the Napa Valley, Beckstoffer recognized a significant pattern: the most successful growers had always solved their financial difficulties with a higher-quality crop. In the nineteenth century this had meant planting better varieties; in the twentieth, it meant utilizing technological advances. Regardless, the primary goal was crop quality, not increasing yields—precisely the opposite of the corporate approach. The lucky timing of innovations in vineyard technology inspired Beckstoffer to take on a significant challenge: to increase both the quantity and quality of grapes. Rising to the challenge, Beckstoffer became an ardent and master student of the vine.[18]

Many of the viticultural practices adopted by Beckstoffer originated from groundbreaking work begun by New Zealand researcher Dr. Richard Smart in the early 1980s. Utilizing the teachings of "canopy management" pioneer Dr. Nelson Shaulis, Smart was an advocate of adjusting the amount of sunlight allowed to hit the fruit and leaves, which led to the development of different trellis systems to suit different vineyards' soil, climate, and varietal.[19]

Dr. Smart also advocated constant regulation of soil moisture. One particularly clever approach concerned reducing the amount of water that reached rootstock by planting ground-cover grasses that "suck the moisture out of the soil, thus denying it to the roots at certain times of the year." Implementing these viticultural practices removed some of the risk from climatic swings—of grave concern to the grape grower. With an adjustable trellis system, it was possible to cool the vine when it was exceedingly hot or warm the vine during a freeze. Implementation of drip irrigation, which developed in Israel, proved to be the most efficient method of maintaining adequate soil moisture. Beckstoffer notes: "We would not have the Chardonnays and the Pinot Noirs or the Merlots that we have now without drip irrigation." Spacing between rows was reduced—for both viticultural and economic reasons. Various means of airing the vines—including planting the

Advances in Viticulture: Dr. Richard Smart

In an interview with Carole Hicke in 1999, Andrew Beckstoffer described the changing theories regarding best vineyard practices:

In the past it had just been photosynthesis and lower yields—that's the way you got quality. . . . Well, Dr. Smart . . . said that the quality comes when you balance the vine between vegetation and fruit, and you let sun into the grapevines and onto the fruit. So we began to change all of our trellis systems in the 1980s. We would lift and separate so as to efficiently get sunlight into the vines. . . . What that did is it changed our quality, it changed yields, it changed the costs, it changed all of our viticultural practices. Where in the past we would go in and we would prune the vines and we would cultivate the ground clean, and then we would pick the grapes at high sugar, now we don't do that anymore. We go in and manipulate the vines. We'll prune them, and then we'll shoot-thin [thin the shoots], and then we'll pull leaves, and then we'll cluster-thin [thin the clusters], then we'll pick twice—that type of thing. So all of those things changed. . . . But also we would adjust vine row direction so that the wind would give us natural sanitation, so we didn't have to put so many toxins on to eliminate the molds and the fungus. . . . The idea of the trellis system helping us be environmentally sensitive as well as producing better fruit is the thing that started in the mid-1980s.

Source: Beckstoffer, "Premium California Vineyardist," 118.

vine rows in line with wind flow, which blew off fungus spores—reduced the need to fumigate the crop.[20]

Beckstoffer shares: "The soils and the climates were given to us by nature and by ancestors. . . . What we must add to the heritage is our viticultural techniques, and that's where this generation is making its addition, and if we are environmentally sensitive, we won't screw up the soils, but we will improve the balance, we will improve our contribution through our viticultural techniques."[21]

When a new phase of phylloxera hit in the 1980s, growers needed to plant new rootstocks. Taking advantage of that necessity, they opted to plant genetically superior "clones" of the preferred varietals, clones selected not just for disease resistance and higher yields, but also for wine quality, a trend begun in France. And if the land was in Napa Valley, with its characteristic well-drained, volcanic soils and alluvial fans, Beckstoffer preferred one varietal in particular: Cabernet Sauvignon.

Cabernet Sauvignon

Andrew Beckstoffer firmly believed in the value of knowing his trade, which in his case meant knowing exactly what works best where and why—down to the level of microclimate. For his holdings in the Carneros region of Napa, for example, the dominant grape is Merlot, "because it needs a cooler climate and ripens earlier," whereas Chardonnay prevails in Mendocino, which has a maritime climate. He knew that high-quality Cabernet grapes could do well only in certain locations—in particular, the cooler St. Helena, Rutherford, and Oakville areas of Napa Valley. In addition, since Cabernet grapes are manipulated less in the winemaking stage than are other varietals, he foresaw the wisdom of producing top-quality Cabernet Sauvignon grapes. Beckstoffer began to plant multiple clones of the Cabernet varietal as well as Petit Verdot and Cabernet Franc, which can be blended in to improve Cabernet. As he expressed to Carole Hicke in 1999, he'd long wanted to "do vineyard-designated wines to express the characteristics of a single vineyard site," but winemakers had been concerned that the resulting wine would be "one-dimensional," not "multifaceted and interesting." So, following the example of climate-similar Bordeaux, Beckstoffer planted multiple clones of Cabernet, as well as some Cabernet Franc, Petit Verdot, and Merlot, all so as to create "diversity, complexity, personality. . . . The winemaker can then blend all of those and show off the site."[22]

To follow are a few winemakers who did just that.

Justin Meyer and Silver Oak Cellars

Like Andrew Beckstoffer, Justin Meyer glimpsed the potential
for Cabernet Sauvignon long before anyone else did. After fifteen years at Christian Brothers, where, as a monk, he was assistant to the legendary winemaker Brother Timothy, in 1972 Meyer
renounced the celibate lifestyle and started a specialized, Caber-
net-only winery, one of the first devoted to a single varietal. He
and his partner named it Silver Oak Cellars, because it is "halfway between Silverado Trail and Oakville." Given the white-wine
craze at the time, fellow winemakers thought Meyer was crazy to
focus on a red wine, and a single one at that. But he was unde-
terred; knowing how well Cabernet was suited to the climates
in the Napa and Sonoma Valleys, he decided to take his chances.
As he told Carole Hicke in 1999: "I guess I picked one wine for
two reasons: that it was kind of a reaction to my days at Christian Brothers, where we made so many wines it was hard to do
them all right, and it was kind of in keeping with [my thinking]
that Cabernets were what Napa and Sonoma did best, so why
not devote our attention to that. This is a pretty common concept in France."[23]

Silver Oak Cellars Napa Valley Cabernet wine label. Courtesy of Silver Oak
Cellars.

Silver Oak produces a "silky smooth" Alexander Valley Cabernet, which is 100 percent Cabernet, as well as a "more austere,
tannic" Napa Valley Cabernet, into which is blended Petit Verdot, Merlot, and Cabernet Franc. And though Meyer, who died in
2002, lavished more credit on the grapes than on the winemaking,
that isn't to say he wasn't particular about his methods. All their
wines are aged in American oak; Meyer preferred its more "vanilla
aroma," as well as the fact that the wine extracts less wood tannin
from American oak. He also barrel-aged for thirty months—about
half again as long as the competition's standard of eighteen to twenty-four months. The extended aging process continues in the bottle as well, between twelve to eighteen months for the Alexander
and nearly twenty-four months for the Napa. Meyer noted: "That
was one of our goals: to distance ourselves from the competition by
giving the wine special aging." And though it was "painful" at first—
bottling wine for years before selling any—once they hit the market the wines more than made up for the wait. "The marketing concept of only one varietal has been magic," he said.[24] And since Silver
Oak's production is limited, most restaurants are allotted only a
certain number of cases per year. For some of those restaurants,

The Genetic Ancestry
of Cabernet Sauvignon

In 1997 Dr. Carole Meredith and
Dr. John Bowers of the University
of California at Davis examined the
genetic background of the noble
Cabernet Sauvignon grape, the
staple red-wine grape of the Bordeaux region of France and a mainstay of the California red-wine fleet.
They determined from the grape's
DNA that the first Cabernet Sauvignon vine was a hybrid between
Cabernet Franc and Sauvignon
Blanc. We know from Silver Oak's
Napa Valley Cabernet that Cabernet Franc is a fellow red grape,
but it was a surprise to many to
learn that the other ancestor is a
white grape. As the *Economist* reported at the time: "Philologists
may scoff that such a parentage
was obvious from Cabernet Sauvignon's name, but it was not. *Sauvignon* simply means 'wild,' and the
name is assumed to indicate that
the first example was found growing that way, and that the grape
was so called to distinguish it from
the Cabernet Franc. Though it has
long been suspected that Cabernet Sauvignon and Cabernet Franc
are related, the relationship to Sauvignon Blanc has come as a bit of a
shock to those with a nose for such
things."

Source: "Secrets of the Cabernet," *Economist,*
May 3, 1997, 72.

Meyer told Hicke, their allotment is so small they don't dare to include the Silver Oak vintages on their wine lists—or they'd sell out
in just a few months. Instead, they hand-sell to their customers in
the know. There is a quantity restriction in their tasting rooms as
well: one bottle per customer. And though all the customers wish
Silver Oak produced more wine, Meyer was content as things were.
"We're closed on Sundays. It's just a kind of religious belief of mine
that, 'The Good Lord has taken care of me, and I am going to recognize Sunday as a day of rest.'"[25] So Silver Oak makes exactly the wine
they want to make—and when they are done they rest.

Robert Mondavi, Baron Philippe de Rothschild, and Opus One

Another foray into the single-varietal, small production realm
was made by a partnership that took the wine world by surprise:
Robert Mondavi and Baron Philippe de Rothschild—the former the son of an Italian immigrant, the latter the scion of a European family with rich ties to both winemaking and banking.
Their joint-effort Cabernet-based wine, made in the Bordeaux
manner in Napa Valley with Mondavi/To-Kalon grapes, was
initially called Napamédoc—Médoc being the region of France
that was home to the baron's Château Mouton Rothschild. Later
the collaborators settled on the name Opus One, to convey the
idea that the wine would be the first "opus" or "work" of a master composer.[26]

The unexpected partnership formed because Baron Philippe
had long wanted to, in his words, "ally" with a California winery—
something he chose to pursue during a period when the business climate in France was feeling a bit shaky. A close advisor had
informed him that Robert Mondavi was "the one person who
shares your vision and passion."[27] Mondavi later described their
shared vision: "Our aim was to create a wine like no other, a great
wine with its own style, character, and breeding."[28] Even the wine
label had its own style and character, designed to stand out in
a crowd. Indeed, the baron was among the first in the world to
treat the wine label as a work of art, beginning with the Cubist-
inspired design for his 1924 Château Mouton Rothschild. An
elaborate, hand-crafted label would before long become a point
of pride, and in many ways a marketing necessity, for all of California's premium wines.[29]

Another intriguing detail: the 1970 Château Mouton Rothschild had placed second in the 1976 Paris tasting, after Stag's Leap
Wine Cellars. Given how the French press had scoffed at the idea

that California wine could match the tradition-rich prestige of French wine, some might have thought that a grand scion of that prestige would never deign to collaborate with an upstart Californian. And yet, the unlikely duo bottled their first vintage in 1979, just three years after the Judgment of Paris.

Opus One was very much a product of collaboration. Though Mondavi and the baron later bought land and built a magnificent winery in Napa, their earliest vintages were produced at Mondavi's winery using grapes from his To-Kalon vineyards. To this Californian foundation were added two particularly French winemaking methods. In order to separate out sediment in the aging process, they "racked" or transferred the wine to another barrel every three months, as is done in Mouton; the barrels themselves were made from French Nevers oak.[30] And though Robert's son, Timothy Mondavi, in theory collaborated as an equal winemaker, there was no doubting that Rothschild's premier winemaker, Lucien Sionneau, was the far more experienced of the two. Theirs was an interesting process, finding the perfect meld of French winemaking techniques and American technology. Sionneau's successor at Mouton, Patrick Léon, recounts: "We started out with two different wine cultures and two different perspectives. . . . In essence, it was science versus nose. The Americans were very strong with testing and analysis, but they were less strong in the art of the *assemblage,* the blending of fine wine." Léon in particular felt that a great winemaker needed to have a strong nose—but the "true artist" also needed *un petit grain de folie:* "a touch of whimsy or folly."

As for the blending of their wine, it was predominantly Cabernet Sauvignon, of course, with Cabernet Franc and Merlot added; this Bordeaux trio would prevail for all Opus One vintages.[31] And as for wine's reception on the market: at the inaugural Napa Valley Auction on June 21, 1981, the first twelve-bottle case of Opus One fetched $24,000, more than double the expected price. At a cost of $2,000 per bottle, it was the most expensive case of California wine ever sold at auction. And this for a wine that at the time still aged in its Nevers oak barrels, a few years away from its 1984 release.[32] Mondavi and Rothschild released both their 1979 and 1980 Opus One vintages in 1984, priced at $50 a bottle. They sold out immediately.

In his autobiography Robert Mondavi writes: "Our 1979 vintage turned out well, but not as well as we had hoped. Lucien Sionneau's French palate, of course, favored elegance and finesse;

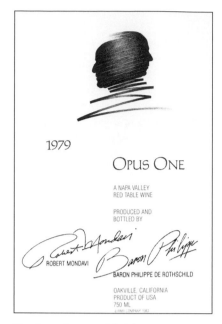

The Opus One wine label, featuring profiles of both winemakers—Robert Mondavi (*left*) and Baron Philippe de Rothschild (*right*)—was designed by Susan Roach Pate. Courtesy of Opus One Winery.

Tim was more accustomed to . . . the bold, intense richness of our Cabernets. It took them a little time to establish the right balance and harmony."[33] It also took the wine a little time to reach its own balance and harmony. Brisk initial sales notwithstanding, critical reception of the first vintages seems to have been underwhelming. And yet, in more recent years the following has been said of the first Opus One vintage: "Just like a really fine Bordeaux, it needed over twenty-five years to develop and mature to the sublime wine that it is today."[34] Both Wine-Searcher and *Decanter* give it a score of 90/100 (or above), and estimate it will reach its maturity between 2016 and 2020. As for its tasting notes, *Decanter* offers this description: "The inaugural vintage of Opus One, made from the same raw materials as the 1979 Mondavi Reserve, is still going strong, bursting with cedary black fruit, wood smoke, asphalt, and forest floor. On the palate the wine is mellow, layered, and harmonious."[35]

After sales of later vintages hit a lull, the duo launched a unique promotion called Vintage Debut, whereby Opus One was available by the glass at restaurants for about $10. This greater exposure expanded their fan base, which in turn nudged the bottle price up to $70, and then $80—the most expensive wine to be had in Napa Valley. Opus One became known as the country's first "ultra-premium" wine.[36]

ZINFANDEL

Our varietal study continues with another grape: Zinfandel. To begin with some backstory, we turn to Paul Lukacs and his *American Vintage: The Rise of American Wine:*

> Most inexpensive varietals were (and are) fashioned in the stylistic image of elite premium wines—those made by boutique American producers and by prestigious European, particularly French, estates. The one exception was Zinfandel, a *vinifera* variety of uncertain origin with no European model to either imitate or rebel against. Back in the 1880s, Zinfandel had been one of California's most widely planted grapes. During Prohibition, it enjoyed popularity with home winemakers, and after Repeal it served primarily as a blending grape for inexpensive generic red wines. In the 1950s and 1960s, some producers did make varietal Zinfandels. Because the grape often ferments to a high degree of alcohol, these wines proved popular among drinkers who liked their wines heady and strong. Connoisseurs liked to call them America's own.[37]

In *Zin: The History and Mystery of Zinfandel,* David Darlington notes how Zinfandel is "a grape that has never been considered the equal of the *vignobles* of Europe—which had, in fact, been the primary ingredient in the generic red jug products of California's past, and a wine that, to the extent that it had any reputation at all, was traditionally known as a 'cheap claret' suitable for picnics and everyday drinking but certainly not for elegant dinner parties or occasions of any importance." Zinfandel was a "varietal that had always been known as a poor man's grape because of its high productiveness and low price."[38]

In his book *Zinfandel: A History of a Grape and Its Wine,* Charles L. Sullivan particularly credits the "enthusiastic entrepreneurs of the 1960s [for making] a juggernaut out of the fine Zinfandel phenomenon."[39] One of those entrepreneurs was Ridge Vineyards. Although their website states they've produced single-vineyard wine since 1962, they've been making wine since the late nineteenth-century. Their first vintage, labeled Monte Bello Winery, was bottled in 1892. In 1900, their Cabernet Sauvignon won a gold medal at the Paris Exposition; their 1971 Ridge Vineyards Monte Bello Cabernet ranked fifth in the 1976 Paris tasting.[40] In the early 1960s, the winemakers at Ridge Vineyards discovered that Zinfandel grapes grown from thirty-year-old vines produced wines with an alluring, complex character. Their first vintage from these vines dates from 1964; in 1973, critic Roy Brady wrote of "that big spicy style of Zinfandel, which had become virtually extinct before Ridge Vineyards took the lead in its resurrection."[41]

Another acclaimed winemaker, David Bruce, bottled his own Zinfandel in 1965. But it was Robert Mondavi's 1966 Zinfandel that garnered the most early attention, thanks in part to the recommendations of restaurateurs. At his seventh-annual "vintage festival" dinner in 1970, Hank Rubin at his inspired Pot Luck Restaurant in Berkeley included Mondavi's 1966 Zinfandel on the menu, offering the following description: "[Zinfandel] is made in two styles; one a light, fruity wine to be drunk young, the other, like the one tonight from Robert Mondavi's Napa Valley winery, more like a Cabernet, full, heavy-bodied, improving with age." (Indeed, Sullivan also refers to the "growing number of Zinfandel-made-like-great-Cabernet lovers.") His praise of the early Zin makers continues: "It was the 1968 Joseph Swan Zinfandel that lit the fuses not already sizzling on the powder keg. In retrospect, it and his subsequent 1969 Zin seemed to be the final blasts in the modern Zinfandel revolution."[42]

The year 1968 also plays a role in our next wander with this intriguing grape.

Bob Trinchero and Sutter Home Winery

Just as Justin Meyer and then Andrew Beckstoffer had seen the market mystique in Cabernet Sauvignon, Louis (Bob) Trinchero had been drawn to Zinfandel. But whereas the lure for Cabernet Sauvignon had been Napa's particular climate, Trinchero was drawn more to the grape's appeal to the consumer.

The Trinchero story begins as have many shared within these pages: with Italian immigrants making wine in the New World. In this case, brothers John and Mario Trinchero helped their father, Luigi, make wine in Prohibition-era New York. In 1948, John and Mario set to awakening from its Dry slumber the Sutter Home Winery in Napa's St. Helena. (Note that Sutter Home had no vineyards of its own.) Fast-forward two decades, by which time the role of family winemaker had been taken up by Mario's son Bob.[43] Around this time Sutter Home made a range of different wines. But Bob shared Justin Meyer's view, that producing a range of wines spreads you thin, whereas the "château concept" of focusing on just one wine provides the opportunity of making an excellent wine. In 1968, Trinchero expressed to a friend, Darrell Corti, his frustration at the soaring prices of Napa Valley grapes, by then $200 per ton; Corti suggested he consider the much more affordable Zinfandel grape grown in Amador County, east of Sacramento.[44] Trinchero's first taste of 1965 Amador County Zinfandel won him over. Sutter Home biographers Kate Heyhoe and Stanley Hock note how "it was virtually black in color, with a huge bouquet of ripe, spicy, blackberry fruit, a thick, chewy texture, and incredibly intense, robust flavors."[45] The 1968 Sutter Home Amador County Zinfandel, released in 1971, was equally well received—so well received that Trinchero began focusing his efforts more on Zinfandel and less on his other wines.[46]

Since Sutter Home wasn't the only winery making Zinfandel, Trinchero sought to make a bolder statement, to "out-zin the competition." Along his journey with the grape he experimented with extracting some of the juice just after crushing, which led to the red skins having in effect a more concentrated impact on the juice that remained. This experiment indeed produced a more robust wine for the 1972 vintage, as well as hundreds of gallons of the extracted, pale juice. Furthering his experimentation, he aged this juice into a dry wine that he bottled under the name Oeil de Perdrix (eye of the partridge), which in France indicates a white wine made from red grapes. But to appease the decree of the Bureau of Alcohol, Tobacco, and Firearms that wine labels must include an English-language description, the Sutter label included the words "a White Zinfandel wine." But as the wine wasn't particularly prized by its maker—"a winemaking byproduct, it was very much a commercial afterthought"—it was sold only in their tasting rooms.[47] But then one year a happy accident occurred when a vintage experienced a "stuck fermentation," meaning the fermentation process inexplicably ceased before all the sugar had been converted to alcohol, producing a sweeter, pink-tinged wine. That 1975 Sutter Home White Zinfandel took the wine world by storm.[48]

When Carole Hicke interviewed Bob Trinchero in 1991, he offered his thoughts on the wine's popularity. "The average American is raised on Kool-Aid and Coca-Cola. How can they jump directly into Cabernet Sauvignon? They just can't. You need an entrance vehicle, and that doesn't mean that just because they like the entrance vehicle they're going to go to Cabernet; they may stay with the entrance vehicle. The idea is to get Americans to drink wine, not to intimidate them."[49] White Zinfandel was an unpretentious, unintimidating wine that stood in stark contrast to the elitist attitude of many in the wine industry, an attitude Trinchero despised. "Nobody has built a wall of intimidation for the wine consumer like the wine writers. It's their elitism that really bugs me—they make people think they need a PhD to appreciate wine. The difference between good wine and fine wine is a fleeting moment on the palate; it takes a lot of study and tasting to understand it.... You don't need four hundred words of vocabulary to describe *alcoholic grape juice*."[50]

In 1979, Sutter Home sold twenty thousand cases of White Zinfandel.[51] Despite this success, competing wineries scoffed at Trinchero's operation, certain he was prospecting on a "flash in the pan" that would prove to be fool's gold when demand for his liquid confection collapsed. By 1985, however, Sutter Home had become the largest winery in Napa Valley, capable of producing twenty-four thousand cases of wine a day. In time all the principal wineries in Napa, including Mondavi, scrambled to add White Zinfandel to their production lines. By 1987, California wineries collectively produced 5 million cases of White Zinfandel per year—2.5 million by Sutter Home alone.[52]

The Joy of Zinfandel, the Intellect of Cabernet

From day one, Zinfandel has so much forward fruit that it's sensual to drink right away. Its appeal is immediate, whereas Cabernet needs time to develop. You *can* have a very sensual experience with old Cabernet, but you can have a comparable experience with young Zinfandel—which is why, in a restaurant, I'd be more likely to order a Zinfandel than a Cabernet. The roundness and depth of flavor in Zinfandel—it's sheer joy, whereas the pleasure of Cabernet is more intellectual. You might say Zinfandel is romantic and Cabernet is baroque. Zinfandel is perhaps a full orchestra, where Cabernet is a chamber quartet.

Source: Paul Draper, qtd. in Darlington, *Zin*, 24.

This label graced the first Sutter Home Oeil de Perdrix White Zinfandel. It reads: "This wine is made from 100% [Deaver Vineyard] Zinfandel grapes. At harvest time the grapes are crushed and the juice is separated from the skins immediately, hence a White Zinfandel, with just a blush of the grape. It has a hint of sweetness and can be served chilled at any time." Courtesy of Trinchero Family Estates.

Back when more posh wineries had scoffed at Sutter Home's White Zinfandel, Trinchero had scoffed at the impenetrable traditions surrounding fine wine:

> The wine industry . . . has spent so much time perpetuating a wall of intimidation to the consumer. . . . We [even] force our consumer to go out and spend five dollars for a tool to open our package . . . and pulling a cork is not that easy. Instead of saying, "Why don't we put it in flip-top cans or whatever," no, my God, that's not traditional. . . . Well, I can tell you right now that we have run tests. . . . We find that a screw cap is superior to a cork. At best, the wines were the same. At worst, we found variations in the wines that were corked. . . . Corks do a lousy job in sealing wine. . . . [But] I'm not ready to come out with screw caps because I don't think the consumers are ready for it.[53]

With his White Zinfandel, Trinchero toppled the pillars of intimidation that had confronted the American consumer, producing a wine from Napa that catered to American tastes, not French tastes. Sutter Home's biographers Heyhoe and Hock concur, telling us: "White Zinfandel taught the Trincheros two important lessons . . . : it pays to break with tradition, and it's best to satisfy consumer tastes, not your own. In doing so, [the Trincheros have] actively shaped the character of the wine industry."[54]

The Mystery, and Ascent, of Zinfandel

The history of the Zinfandel grape includes a few protracted mysteries. First: what are its ancestral origins—from where does it hail? It was long thought that there was no European grape of that name.[55] Second: whatever it is, how did it find itself in California? In 1941, Frank Schoonmaker wrote in *American Wines:* "If an absence of apparent ancestors is proof of divine origin, certainly the Zinfandel grape is entitled to a whole collection of legends."[56]

Historians are nothing if not sleuths. Fortunately for this volume, Charles Sullivan pursued the Zinfandel mystery to its end, as declared by the title of his 1978 article "A Viticultural Mystery Solved: The Historical Origins of Zinfandel in California." Sullivan begins his argument asserting that Arpad Haraszthy was the source of the claim that Colonel Haraszthy was the first to bring Zinfandel to California—as part of the large collection of cuttings he brought back from Europe. As historians have found no evidence to support that claim, and not for lack of searching, Sullivan concludes that Arpad in effect falsely promoted the story, whether or not he was intending to deceive.[57] Sullivan told David Darlington: "Haraszthy did plant Zinfandel in different vineyards in the 1860s; he may even have [inadvertently] imported it in one of the standard New England collections during the 1850s. But there is not one instance where Agoston Haraszthy ever used the word *Zinfandel* in print."[58]

As for the comment "he may even have imported it in one of the standard New England collections," in his article Sullivan posits that there were "four possible ways" Zinfandel might have made its way to California, all of which derive from the fact that Zinfandel had been a table grape in New England since the 1830s.[59] This is a claim first put forth by Robert A. Thompson in 1885, one supported with significant evidence.[60] More than one theory suggests the confusion derives from Zinfandel being known under another name: Black St. Peters. One thought was that this grape arrived at a nursery on Long Island in the 1820s, "probably from the Imperial collection at the Schönbrunn in Vienna," as Darlington tells us. The vines could have been collected for the Imperial collection from any number of locations, some perhaps as far away as Greece.[61]

As it happens, there is substantial evidence to support the claim made by Antoine Delmas: that he imported Zinfandel from France, though called Black St. Peters, of which in 1854 he provided cuttings to none other than General Vallejo.[62]

Sullivan pursued the subject well after the 1978 publication of his article. (Indeed, in 2003 he published an entire book on the varietal: *Zinfandel: A History of a Grape and Its Wine*.) But even before then he'd traced the variety's initial importation to George Gibbs of Long Island circa 1829; Gibbs in turn received it from Vienna, Austria. But even those details are incomplete. Sullivan notes that "there is no record of the name under which those vines traveled, for there has been no vine named Zinfandel in Europe." In any case, it became popular as a table grape on the East Coast. When, come the Gold Rush, some Easterners opted to swap the Atlantic for the Pacific, they imported Zinfandel grapes to the West Coast as well. In 1862, members of the Sonoma Horticultural Society made wine from Zinfandel grapes; General Mariano Vallejo's French winemaker, Victor Fauré, likened it to "a good French claret."[63]

So concludes the means of arrival. But what of the grape's origins? In 1985 Rich Kunde, president of the Sonoma County

Grape Growers, lodged a complaint with the U.S. Bureau of Alcohol, Tobacco, and Firearms about an Italian wine being marketed in California, labeled ZINFANDEL. The back label explained that the wine was made from Italian Primitivo grapes, and that "it can now be affirmed with resonable [*sic*] certainty . . . that the Primitivo grape cultivated in Puglia, Italy, and Zinfandel are the same vine." Never mind the irony that California winemakers had long labeled inferior, blended table wines as "Burgundy," "Chablis," and "Chianti," expropriating those names from noble European regions. Was the Italian claim correct? Nine years later, in 1994, Dr. Carole Meredith of the University of California established using DNA fingerprinting that Primitivo and Zinfandel are indeed the same variety of grape.[64]

<hr/>

AS IT HAPPENS, the mystery and ascent of Zinfandel go hand in hand: as Zinfandel surged in popularity, so too did the mystery of its origin as a subject of debate. Similarly, the White Zinfandel craze also provoked interest in its original red incarnation. And since the large producers of White Zinfandel had no need for the premium Zinfandel grapes, the grapes were readily available to those wishing to make more artisan red Zinfandel—wineries like Ridge Monte Bello, Ravenswood, and Rosenblum Cellars. In the late 1980s, red Zinfandel gained acceptance as one of the premier varietals in California. Following a tasting of Ravenswood's Zinfandel vintages from 1986, critic Robert Parker proclaimed the winery was "making some of the greatest wines in California." When questioned whether he would ever bestow a perfect 100-point score on a Zinfandel, Parker responded, "Yeah, I just haven't had the guts."[65] Deep, rich, and appealing, red Zinfandel had once again stepped into the California spotlight.

After hitching itself to White Zinfandel's success in the 1980s, red Zinfandel enjoyed its own success in the 1990s: between 1995 and 1999, its production doubled, from 1.5 million to 3 million cases. By the end of the decade, Zinfandel Advocates and Producers (ZAP) held the Guinness record for the world's largest one-varietal tasting, and lobbied to achieve a congressional designation for Zinfandel as "America's Heritage Wine."[66] Zinfandel had been accepted as a legitimate, fine varietal to be sipped with the likes of Cabernet Sauvignon and Chardonnay.

In another book by Charles Sullivan, *Napa Wine: A History from Mission Days to Present,* the region is described as one might describe an exalted wine: "The Napa Valley is a unique commodity that demands a premium, like buying a unique painting. It's a unique socioeconomic environment that takes a certain clientele." This was quoted from a Bank of America economist, no less. As the birthplace of elite wines that fetched astonishing prices, by the 1980s Napa had become an exclusive area to live, a place where opulent wineries and gaudy mansions flecked the landscape—and where vineyard land could in turn fetch up to $25,000 per acre.[67] The year 1981 saw the inaugural Napa Wine Auction, which was sponsored by the Napa Valley Vintners to publicize the region's excellent wines while raising funds for local hospitals. That first auction, which included pre-sale of Opus One's first vintage, raised $324,142 in total; in 1989, that figure reached $850,000, and included $55,000 for nine bottles of Stag's Leap 18-liter Cabernet Sauvignon.[68] All told, there was status in having a Napa Valley address. And the benefit was self-reinforcing; in 1988, the *New York Times* noted that inclusion of Napa Valley on a wine label justified an addition of two dollars or more to the wine's price tag.[69]

This wasn't what the area's first generations of settlers had intended. Far-sighted county planners had long before implemented land-use laws to protect Napa's valuable agricultural land. In 1966, as Sullivan puts it, "conservationist leader William Bronson called for the creation of a national vineyard to save the Napa Valley from the bulldozer." Spurred by popular support, in 1968 Napa Valley became one of the United States' first agricultural preserves. Within this "Ag Preserve" initiative was adopted an aggressive zoning policy intended to both discourage residential development and prevent commercial interests uninvolved with agriculture or winemaking from gaining a toehold. Except within the limits of the small towns scattered along Highway 29, development of any new residence required a parcel of land of at least twenty acres. In 1979, that amount was increased to forty acres.[70] As the result of this protection, by the early 1990s Napa Valley was among the most expensive and coveted agricultural land in the world. Prime undeveloped land sold for more than $100,000 an acre.[71]

Despite strict land-use regulations, development began to invade the Napa Valley from within a Trojan horse of "winery operations." Wineries began marketing activities unrelated to the production and sale of wine, including concerts, cooking classes, and art exhibits—all intended to extract maximum profit from an exploding tourist industry. Those tourists, 2.5 million of them as of 1988, reportedly added about $160 million annually to the local economy, but they also created significant traffic congestion along Highway 29.[72] As wineries began to seem more like gift shops than wineries, the grape-grower leadership in the valley, led by Andrew Beckstoffer of the Napa Valley Grape Growers Association, sought to refine the definition of a winery. The growers believed wineries should be crushing grapes; they should be making and selling wine, not T-shirts. In opposition stood the Napa Valley Vintners, who in 1983 had become the Napa Valley Vintners Association (NVVA), a formal trade organization. The NVVA supported a definition that comprised a wide variety of wine-related activities, stating that "efforts to curtail some of the marketing techniques would put the entire industry at a competitive disadvantage." In a related dispute, the growers objected to wineries that received and processed a majority of their grapes from outside the Napa Valley and nonetheless labeled the wine NAPA VALLEY. The growers felt that the designation should require that no less than 75 percent of the grapes processed in a winery be grapes harvested in Napa County. To the NVVA's adamant resistance Beckstoffer proclaimed, "We don't see how you can preserve Napa County's agriculture by setting up processing plants for other than Napa County grapes."

Responding to an assessment that "a number of wineries in the valley were nothing but retail stores," in August 1988 the Napa County Board of Supervisors imposed a seventeen-month moratorium on new winery applications.[73] During the moratorium, Beckstoffer continued to argue for a winery definition ordinance that would tie the definition of a winery to the protection of the agricultural preserve. Finally on January 17, 1990, a compromise was agreed on and Ordinance No. 947 passed: the 75 percent rule was included, but it applied only to new wineries and expansions of established wineries. And though established wineries retained the right to offer open-house tours and tastings, new wineries could not: all such visits required an appointment. Overall, it was a victory for the growers, serving to slow what might otherwise have been unrestricted development. And yet it lacked permanence, agreed to by elected officials whose preferences might not be shared by their successors. As Sullivan notes, "the future of Napa wine seemed to hang on a tenuous thread of public policy."[74]

Indeed, the passage of the Winery Definition Ordinance hardly deterred wealthy people from testing the elasticity of the agricultural-preserve status of the valley. Growth slowed in Napa County during the 1980s, but as the 1990s dawned, and as wineries became more profitable, pressure grew to permit more development.

Environmentalists and proponents of the agricultural pre-serve knew the preserve sat on a fragile legal foundation, for the law creating the preserve could be modified or repealed al-together with the vote of but three of the five county supervi-sors. And several supervisors were beginning to listen to pro-development arguments. When James Hickey, longtime stew-ard of the agricultural preserve and head of the County Planning Department, was forced to resign in 1989, environmental activists realized they needed to work quickly to remove the agricultural preserve and the watershed management from the supervisors' hands. They lobbied to include a proposition on the November 1990 ballot requiring that all modifications to the status of the agri-cultural preserve and watershed management be decided by voters until 2020. The 20/20 Vision proposition passed overwhelmingly, demonstrating popular support for the slow-growth movement and mindset, and a fervent wish to preserve Napa for agriculture.[75]

But, despite the efforts of growers and longtime residents, commercialization and tourism steadily increased in the valley. As James Conaway puts it: "By the beginning of the 1990s, the perspective of value had reversed, at least for vineyards—the hills were up, the valley down—and the renaissance was approaching its zenith." As property values rose to new heights—the price for homes for sale started at $1 million, and many McMansions re-placed once-quaint cottages—locals began to feel out of place, as well as pushed out. The annual number of tourists visiting in-creased by the millions, putting the valley second only to Disneyl-and as a California tourist destination. That reversed perspec-tive of value applied to landowner intentions as well as property value: incomers weren't drawn by the desire to craft premium wines; they sought, as Conaway posits, an association with an "expression of husbandry and cultural accomplishment" as "tes-tament to their material and spiritual worth."[76]

One particularly flashy example was filmmaker Francis Ford Coppola's purchase in 1996 of the historic Inglenook, which, as an established winery, was not subject to the terms of the Winery Definition Ordinance. What had once been a venerable estate now housed, indoors and out, extensive memorabilia from Coppola movies: the gunboat from *Apocalypse Now,* the desk used by Marlon Brando's Don Corleone in *The Godfather.* Since corporate giant Heublein still controlled ownership of the name "Inglenook," Coppola christened the winery Niebaum-Coppola. Its gift shop sold, among other non-wine items, binoculars, bocce balls, candlesticks, cards, chessboards, chocolates, cigars, flashlights, handbags, mechanical birds, spaghetti sauce, and yo-yos. Coppola claimed he was carrying out Niebaum's vision for the winery, and yet Niebaum, a seafarer and fur trader, hadn't exactly envisioned his winery as a tourist way station that peddled trinkets like those sold on San Francisco's Fisherman's Wharf. On the contrary: as Conaway notes, "Niebaum had allowed no tourism and no deviation from the narrow path of a great wine estate."[77]

The Cultural Perception of Wine

In his 1978 book *Wines in America,* Leon D. Adams hypothesized that, enhanced by the success at the Judgment of Paris, the annual per capita consumption of wine would increase to five gallons within a decade. (In 1978, the per capita figure was 1.96 gallons.[78]) Given that he saw table wine as being on its way to becoming America's "national mealtime beverage," he declared: "The wine revolution . . . has only begun." In a talk given in 1986, "What's Going On Here Anyhow?" he repeated the claim.[79] This stance was a reasonable assumption. After all, American wine had come of age; though still relatively young, it had proven itself worthy of standing alongside world-class vintages. It had survived crippling disease, pests, and natural disasters. It had prevailed through governmental restriction as well as through fickle consumers once that restriction was lifted. It had repeatedly ridden the waves of corporate intrusion. And it had overcome internal obstacles, from shoddy practices to disappointing crops to unscrupulous dealers. Fluctuations in the market were to be expected, but by the latter half of the twentieth century, the wine industry had come too far to ever be defeated. Hadn't it? Just as the phylloxera again reared its microscopic head, threatening viticulture in the 1980s, so returned another antagonist set on the industry's destruction: neo-prohibitionists.

Modern–Day Public Opinion and Policy Regarding Alcoholic Beverages

In 1970 the U.S. Congress, responding to rising public concern over the deleterious effects of addictive substances, created the National Institute on Alcohol Abuse and Alcoholism (NIAAA). In 1972, the Center for Science in the Public Interest (CSPI), founded just the year before, petitioned that labels of all alcoholic beverages include a list of their ingredients, a demand they made of both the Food and Drug Administration (FDA) and the Bureau of Alcohol, Tobacco, and Firearms (BATF). This latter effort floundered for a while, but in 1977 the NIAAA and the CSPI found common cause when the NIAAA strongly advised pregnant women against drinking alcohol; the FDA also sought to require that alcoholic beverage labels warn consumers about "fetal alcohol syndrome." Again, progress was made, but nothing solid resulted. Then in 1985 the process repeated, this time concerning the FDA's announcement of the health hazards caused by sulfites; this time it stuck, literally: in 1987, wine bottles were required to include warnings about the sulfites lurking within. By 1989, that warning was required to include the risks of birth defects, impaired driving, and general "health problems."

In addition:

- Efforts made by Mothers Against Drunk Driving (MADD) brought about passage of the National Minimal Drinking Age Act of 1984.

- In 1985, the group Project SMART (Stop Marketing Alcohol on Radio and Television), a coalition of education, religious, and public health activists, took aim at liquor advertising on TV and radio. Nothing came of it.

- In 1986 California passed Proposition 65; as a result, all sellers of alcohol were required to prominently display the following: WARNING: DRINKING DISTILLED SPIRITS, BEER, COOLERS, WINE, AND OTHER ALCOHOLIC BEVERAGES MAY INCREASE CANCER RISK, AND, DURING PREGNANCY, CAN CAUSE BIRTH DEFECTS.

In 1988, CSPI sought a sixty-six-fold increase of the tax on wine, from 17 cents per gallon to $11.37. In 1991, the federal excise tax on table wine was raised to $1.07 per gallon for larger producers.

Source: Pinney, *History of Wine in America*, 2:351–53 and references cited (nn29–34).

Starting in the 1970s, anti-alcohol groups railed shrill against the wine industry with the same vigor they used against whiskey. But as of the mid-1980s, the wine industry appeared unscathed. In 1980, per capita consumption cracked the two-gallon mark, and rose steadily thereafter, reaching 2.43 gallons in 1986. But then came the descent, a fall as steady as the previous rise.[80]

The California wine industry soon realized that the neo-prohibitionists' gospel on the negative effects of alcohol on American life was having a significant deleterious effect on national consumption. A countercase needed to be made—much as the wine industry had sought during Prohibition—to represent wine as a beverage distinct from other alcoholic drinks, one to be enjoyed in moderate amounts with meals. Robert Mondavi, the de facto ambassador of California wine, took up the responsibility of presenting the argument.[81] Otherwise, he writes, "any warning label would destroy everything we had built."[82]

To counter the rising neo-prohibitionist voices, in 1988 he launched the Robert Mondavi Mission Program, which was "designed to educate Americans about wine and its role in American culture and society, . . . illustrat[ing] the benefits of moderate consumption as well as the detriments of abuse."[83] Mondavi began by printing his position on his own wine labels: "Wine has been with us since the beginning of civilization. It is the temperate, civilized, romantic mealtime beverage recommended by the Bible. Wine has been praised for centuries by statesmen, philosophers, poets, and scholars. Wine in moderation is an integral part of our culture, heritage, and gracious way of life."[84]

Mondavi's articulate preaching on the beneficial aspects of fine wine began to draw attention from many quarters. On November 17, 1991, the CBS program *60 Minutes* aired a segment on the "French paradox": the curious fact that, though the French have a diet rich in butterfat, and hence cholesterol, they have a much lower risk of heart disease than do Americans. The paradox was explained by the fact the French drink red wine with meals, which has the effect of neutralizing the harmful effects on the human cardiovascular system of the cholesterol-rich French food. Of course, this only complemented Mondavi's promotion of wine as an "integral part of our culture, heritage, and gracious way of life," and served to quiet much of the neo-prohibitionist rant against wine.[85]

THE SPECTRUM OF THE MODERN-DAY WINE MARKET

This resurrection of Prohibition-era rhetoric, decades after Repeal, provides a segue to a modern-day phenomenon that emerged from actual Prohibition.

From the time of Repeal onward, wholesalers had gained a remarkable degree of control over the wine industry. In the old saloon days before Prohibition, a two-tier system existed in which producers of alcohol were dominant over retailers. Upon Repeal, the so-called three-tier system was established, wherein most states required producers to sell their wares to only licensed wholesalers or distributors, not to the retailers themselves. Though the intention had been to thwart the chance of producers monopolizing the market, monopolies had emerged anyway; only this time it was among the distributors rather than the producers. In the 1960s, ten thousand wholesalers had competed for distribution contracts, but by the year 2000 only three hundred remained, and the five largest wholesalers controlled one-third of the market. To this day, though small wineries can always distribute locally, many are impeded from selling to states that require the wholesaler intermediary—a continuing concern to be sure.[86]

In addition to financial and regulatory concerns, the late twentieth-century wine industry found itself in new waters in terms of the market for its product. While the watchwords of *passion for craft* and *personal gain* remained very much in play, the spectrum of this range expanded considerably. We begin at the high end.

Harlan Estate and Cult Wines

While individuals like Robert Mondavi strove to maintain the public image of wine, others focused on taking its quality to a new level. An admirable example of the latter is wine artist Bill Harlan, who credits the inspiration to create a first-growth California winery to a trip he took with Mondavi, visiting the vineyards and estates of Bordeaux and Burgundy.[87]

In 1984, Harlan acquired premium Napa Valley land on the Rutherford-Oakville Bench, near Martha's Vineyard. There he planted Bordeaux varietals and established a winery following the principles of France's first-growth estates: based on the land, family-owned, and carrying minimal debt. He also took to heart the meticulous care in winemaking that we've seen from Warren Winiarski and Mike Grgich. In other words, Harlan tolerated no

Harlan Estate wine label, Oakville, Napa Valley. Courtesy of Harlan Estate.

vineyard practices that could in the least diminish the quality of his grapes. His methods included "green harvesting," which entailed removing many of the berries in the middle of the growing season, before they turned from green to red. Though this practice reduced yield, it intensified the flavor of the grapes that were later harvested. And the grapes were picked by hand—not by machines—and selected strictly for their taste. Come harvest time, additional practices included efforts to reduce bruising of the picked fruit, as well as picking through the night to ensure the berries' flavor would not be changed by exposure to the sun.[88]

From its first commercial vintage, released in 1990, Harlan Estate has produced two excellent wines: Harlan Estate and the Maiden. Each vintage—no more than two thousand cases—sells for hundreds of dollars per bottle. Some in the industry, like *The Wine Cellar Insider,* attest that "Harlan Estate produces a unique expression of California Cabernet Sauvignon: . . . rich, deep, concentrated, and intense, . . . [with] a sense of elegance and purity of fruit that meshes perfectly with all the power."[89] Various tasters through the years have agreed, giving Harlan wine very high scores.

Altogether, Bill Harlan is considered a master steward of the land. His focus on perfection created a new flight of wines in California: cult wines.

The publication *Wine Spectator* coined the expression "cult wines"—then made them a California phenomenon. With a readership of nearly four hundred thousand, *Wine Spectator* can raise a wine from obscurity and send it to heights of acclaim—or destroy a reputation like a withering Dorothy Parker review. And just as Harlan's wines inspired the term, his fastidious and studied practices inspired other vintners to make their goal the creating of exquisite wine, regardless of cost. Indeed, some have spent fortunes in that quest.

It was in the spring of 2000 when *Wine Spectator* first wrote of "California's Cult Wines," explaining "Who They Are and Why They're Red Hot."[90] (Author James Conaway considers the article a "canonization of the cult of the macerated grape.") Most of the wines included could not be purchased for less than $200 a bottle, and were such strong and tannic Cabernet Sauvignons that they were scarcely drinkable until middle age. Of this trend, an anonymous longtime Napa Valley winemaker remarked in derision, "Some of these winemakers are making extract, not wine. They've lost sight of wine as something that goes with meals."

A Nose for Bordeaux

The spectacular prices of modern-day wines inevitably led to some spectacular schemes to defraud gullible collectors. One particularly impressive scheme was effected by Rudy Kurniawan, a well-off wine connoisseur with tricksterism in his blood. And he was very well off indeed; as Bianca Bosker relates in the *New Yorker,* "in 2006, the auction house Acker Merrall & Condit broke records selling off thirty-five million dollars' worth" of "treasures from his cellar." (It was suggested that Kurniawan needed the sale in order to fund his lavish tastes, which included spending one million dollars on wine *per month*.) A later sale of post-WWII vintages of Domaine Ponsot Clos Saint-Denis (1945 and 1949, plus 1966) went sour when someone pointed out that 1982 was the first year Domaine Ponsot produced that particular wine. This observation triggered an investigation into what is now considered history's most egregious case of wine fraud, leading to a ten-year prison sentence for its brazen actor.

How could a ruse of this magnitude be contemplated, let alone carried out? The manufacture of ersatz wine labels and cellar-aged bottles is comprehensible. But what of the elixir within those bottles? What of the well-aged connoisseur's practiced nose for body, palate, and harmony? Writer Bosker points out that since the vintages Kurniawan concocted are not readily available, and were never particularly consistent, tasters of the fraudulent wines had little to go on. Tasting notes of one of these wines echo—in both a sad and humorous manner—the confused yet haughty comments at the 1976 Judgment of Paris, with assessments like "fantastic," "very real," and "as good as it gets." Whereas an expert wine-store taster considered the same vintage to be "garbage," tasting of "skunk juice."

It turns out that Kurniawan had a nose for blending, and had created the wines following "recipes for faking aged Bordeaux." But though a wine-store buyer detected Kurniawan's putatively vintage "skunk juice," would the fraud have been detected if not for inexpert research on just which vintages to fake? One can only wonder.

Source: Bosker, "True-Crime Documentary." This article is a review of the 2016 film *Sour Grapes.* As for Kurniawan's tricksterism: evidence suggests that two of his uncles carried out their own nefarious schemes "defrauding Indonesian banks of hundreds of millions of dollars."

"Wine has become a talent show. . . . It isn't who can capture the terroir anymore, but who can capture the wine writer."[91] Indeed, many cult producers seemed to be more inspired by the prestige of producing the next champion wine than by the pure satisfaction of—as Bill Harlan put it—"capturing the season in a bottle."[92]

In any case, the grand showcase of cult wines is the previously mentioned Napa Valley Wine Auction. Established by Robert Mondavi and Pat Montadon in 1981, since 1983 it's been held at Harlan's Meadowood Napa Valley luxury resort.[93] At one auction more than two hundred local vintners contributed wine, and two thousand visitors each paid $1,000 just to attend—with all proceeds donated to charity. Recall that at the first auction, a case of the still-unbottled first vintage of Opus One fetched $24,000, its cost of $2,000 per bottle making it the most expensive case of California wine ever sold at auction. Compare that to the auction in 2000, when a single Imperial bottle of the cult wine Screaming Eagle went for $500,000. That year's total was $10,000,000, double that of the previous year.[94]

As an aside: In 2005, Robert and Peter Mondavi collaborated on a conciliatory vintage, the first since their feud. Using grapes from both family vineyards, they produced one barrel of Cabernet blend called Ancora Una Volta ("once again"). It brought in $400,000 at that year's Napa Valley auction.[95]

Fred Franzia and Two-Buck Chuck

While cult producers focused on producing a few thousand cases of ultra-premium wine, Fred Franzia, head of the Bronco Wine Company, was doing just the opposite: selling as much wine as possible for the lowest price. (Given that he is the nephew of Ernest and Julio Gallo, this isn't too surprising.) In 2002, Franzia introduced (and coined the term) "super-value wines," and began marketing the Charles Shaw brand solely at Trader Joe's stores for $1.99 a bottle. What became known as "Two-Buck Chuck" revolutionized California's bulk-wine industry; within a year, Charles Shaw was the fastest-growing wine brand by volume in the United States.

Franzia was able to keep his prices at basement levels by several means. One was by exploiting a glut in both midgrade wine grapes and good-quality bulk wine (some of it from Franzia's friend Michael Mondavi).[96] Another was by managing his own distribution in California, effectively eliminating the middleman. This was a considerable coup, given that the three-tier system otherwise required there be a buffer between the producer and the retailer.

In discussing Two-Buck Chuck we get a sort of reprise of our Paris-tasting tale—a low-brow one, that is. In what some have called the Judgment of California, the Charles Shaw 2005

California Chardonnay won two gold medals at the 2007 California State Fair Commercial Wine Competition: Best of California and Best of Class.[97] Respected *Wine Spectator* senior editor James Laube describes that vintage as "clean and intense, with ripe, vivid citrus and pear flavors that end with a refreshing lemony edge." Note, though, that many other Charles Shaw wines earn comments that would make any other winemaker wince. Laube describes the 2004 Charles Shaw Merlot as being "on the medicinal side of herbal, with thin weedy flavors that give the fruit notes a sourness." Wine writer Karen MacNeil said of a Charles Shaw Cabernet, "I don't understand how people put this in their mouths."[98] In another amusing take, *Thrilllist* ran an article called "We Made a Sommelier Taste All the Trader Joe's Two Buck Chuck." The Chardonnay earned one of its more nuanced assessments: "Soapy lavender. It reminds me of my dad's bathtub." The White Zinfandel was deemed "pure liquefied, alcoholic Jolly Rancher."[99]

All humorous commentary aside, Franzia laughed all the way to the bank. By 2009 he owned 40,000 acres of vineyards and annually crushed 350,000 tons of grapes; that he also in that year sold 20 million cases of wine made him the fourth-largest winery in the United States. His cavernous volume of production allows him to buy huge wine lots on the bulk wine market for bargain prices, resulting in huge profits: as of 2009 annual revenues had reached $500 million.[100]

But the Franzia story is not lacking in controversy, especially given two significant examples of not playing fair in the industry. In 1993, eight years before the launch of Two-Buck Chuck, Franzia and Bronco Wine Company were indicted on federal charges of conspiracy to defraud. The crime? Selling one million gallons of wine masquerading as Zinfandel and Cabernet Sauvignon when they were in fact lesser varietals—a practice almost as old as the California wine industry itself. Pleading no contest, Bronco paid a $2.5 million fine.[101]

A decade later, rival winemakers objected to the fact that Franzia released three wines labeled as being made from Napa Valley grapes when in fact the majority of the vinted grapes had been grown in Lodi, California, south of Sacramento. This practice went against the state law, tightened in 2000, that required that any county listed on a wine label be the origin of at least three-quarters of that vintages's grapes. The Napa Valley Vintners initiated lawsuits that entangled Franzia for years, nearly making their way to the U.S. Supreme Court. Finally, in April 2006, Franzia conceded defeat; he renamed the Napa Ridge line Harlow Ridge and agreed to use Napa grapes in the Rutherford Vintners and Napa Creek wines.[102] Needless to say, fellow vintners weren't particularly pleased with Franzia and company. As Dana Goodyear notes in the *New Yorker,* "there are some in the Napa Valley who refuse to call Charles Shaw by its cute nickname. To them, it's Two Buck Upchuck."[103]

All chicanery and raillery and lawsuits aside, Franzia's Two-Buck Chuck revolution nonetheless provided a counterweight to the cult-wine frenzy, much as White Zinfandel had become a foil against the elitism of premium wines a generation earlier.

Jess Jackson and Kendall-Jackson Wine Estates

Between the extremes of cult-wine and super-value wine exists a happy-medium price niche. That market was claimed by Jess Jackson, a longshoreman turned policeman turned lumberjack turned trial lawyer turned vintner, who produced his first Sonoma Valley Chardonnay in 1983. In the early 1990s, his $14 Kendall-Jackson Vintners Reserve Chardonnay, priced in the "ultra-premium" price bracket, was applauded as one of the best bargains for a high-quality wine on the market. By 1994, Jackson was selling 1.7 million cases of Kendall-Jackson a year. That same year he lured winemaker Charles Thomas, who had been with Mondavi since 1978, for his Artisans and Estates brand. By 2004, Jess Jackson had a net worth of $1.8 billion, making him one of the few billionaires in the wine industry.[104]

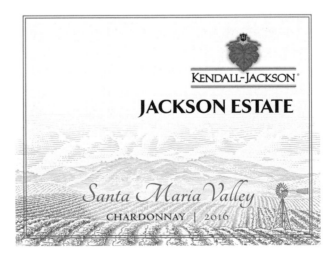

Kendall-Jackson Jackson Estate Santa Maria Valley 2016 Chardonnay wine label. Courtesy of Kendall-Jackson.

That Jess Jackson had successfully wooed a beloved Robert Mondavi winemaker said much about the state of that company at the time. By then it was Robert's sons, Michael and Timothy, who equally headed the firm, which as of June 1993 had become a publicly traded corporation. But fraternal squabbling—by now a seeming occupational hazard for Mondavi companies—had led to Timothy being demoted from co-CEO to managing director and winegrower. What this change truly augured was Michael's favoring of multiple lines along the entire price scale over Timothy's dedication to crafting excellent wine, Timothy having taken to heart his experience working with the Château Lafite winemaker for Opus One. But expanding into multiple brackets stretched the company thin over many costly, experimental ventures, including a disastrous attempt to introduce Mondavi wine to Disneyland.[105] All the while Jess Jackson remained firmly committed to the ultra-premium bracket, where he more than prospered.

Although in the ensuing years the Robert Mondavi winery attempted to appear small and personal to its hundreds of thousands of annual visitors, it had in reality been transformed into more of a volume producer than a quality producer. By 2000 most of Mondavi's wines priced at under ten dollars a bottle. Julia Flynn Siler handily sums up the reality the firm faced as it entered the twenty-first century: "Upscale consumers had become enamored of highly concentrated 'cult' wines from tiny, artisan producers—a group of customers that Timothy and Robert identified more closely with. Everyday wine drinkers, in contrast, were moving toward inexpensive foreign imports from Australia and elsewhere, pushed by low-cost retailers such as Costco. For a company that sold wines at both ends of the range and whose capitalization was by then around $600 million, the market's radical polarization touched off a corporate identity crisis."

The expansion of the Mondavi empire came at the cost of its founding principles. One was collegiality within the valley. Another was quality. As for the former, Andy Beckstoffer was dismayed when both Mondavi brothers brought legal action regarding his wanting to use the name To-Kalon on a wine he was releasing—especially given the fact that the wine was produced from grapes grown in part from the historic To-Kalon vineyards. As for quality, various cost-cutting measures that Robert would have abhorred were readily employed throughout the winemaking process once Michael was at the helm. In their vineyards they also managed to undo the best practices painstakingly realized over California's entire winegrowing history. Again from Siler: "The Napa vineyards had become an unmanageable jungle of eight different trellising systems, a mishmash of rootstocks, and wrong varieties planted in the wrong soil.... Almost inevitably, the production and wine growing problems seeped into the bottle."[106]

In December of 2000, Robert Parker in his bimonthly *The Wine Advocate* excoriated the Robert Mondavi Winery for producing mediocre, "collectively superficial" wines—this assessment the result of his reviewing thirty-five of their most recent vintages. He prefaced his rebuke by sharing: "No one in the United States has done more to promote the image of fine wine than Robert Mondavi and his family. They have had a profound positive impact on American culture and we all have benefitted from it." But he did not pull any punches as to the wines themselves. With the exception of the 1997 Cabernet Sauvignon To-Kalon Reserve, he judged the Mondavi lineup to be "indifferent, innocuous wines that err on the side of intellectual vapidness over the pursuit of wines of heart, soul, and pleasure." Upon publication of the widely read newsletter, the price of Mondavi stock dropped 14 points.[107]

On November 4, 2004, the Robert Mondavi Corporation announced its sale to Constellation Brands Inc., a New York company renowned for wine of little quality; thereafter cheaper "lifestyle" wines would be released under the Robert Mondavi name.[108] In so doing the Mondavi Corporation buried the passion for perfection that Robert Mondavi had founded the winery on almost four decades earlier. Robert Mondavi himself would be buried almost four years later, in 2008. The Constellation purchase epitomized more than any other takeover the newest wave of conquered citadels of the California wine industry.[109]

AND WHAT OF THE OTHER vintners in this spectrum discussion? Harlan Estates continues to receive stellar praise for its wines. Kendall-Jackson Wine Estate & Gardens remains a vibrant enterprise. And at the bottom rung of the quality ladder, Fred Franzia gives no indication of ceding his dominion over the bulk-wine market; by January 2016, sales of Two-Buck Chuck had surpassed the one-billion-bottle mark.[110]

This chapter began with two questions: *Though the state's wineries and vintages had reached great heights, would they be able to build on that success? Or would internal struggles and jarring economic forces once again endanger the progress that had been made?* Some of the answers are mixed. Though both internal struggles and economic forces led to the corporate buyout of the Robert Mondavi Winery, the man himself clearly left a lasting, bountifully positive mark on the industry—including a $25 million endowment establishing the Robert Mondavi Institute for Wine and Food Science at UC Davis.[11] On the other hand, though Napa Valley remains a prime tourist destination, ever attracting outside dollars by the millions, few independent vintners, or growers for that matter, remain from the 1960s and 1970s, which many consider an irreparable loss.

Yet other answers have no downsides. Corporate interests again tried a hand at the wine game, but their efforts did nothing to discourage or dampen the prospects of tiny operations like Silver Oak and Justin Meyer—who, like Joseph Heitz before him, has found a way to make a bootstrap enterprise viable, even profitable. And though the winds of prohibition again stirred the waters, that threat was neatly and readily quelled. As another plus, the advances to viticulture produced by the likes of Dr. Richard Smart—and promoted by the likes of Andy Beckstoffer—benefit all, nearly indiscriminately. Altogether it seems safe to say that, though present and future progress can always be endangered, California viticulture has come too far to be easily overthrown, let alone vanquished.

NOTES

1. Mondavi, *Harvests of Joy,* 185.

2. Siler, *House of Mondavi,* 97–98, 100–101.

3. Ibid., 100.

4. Ibid., 115.

5. Mondavi, *Harvests of Joy,* 189–90.

6. Siler, *House of Mondavi,* 120–21, 123–24.

7. Intended Decision, *Robert Mondavi v. C. Mondavi & Sons,* Napa County Superior Court Nos. 29917 and 30122, August 12, 1976, 113, citing in part Justice Cardozo.

8. Mondavi, *Harvests of Joy,* 190–91.

9. Ibid., 186.

10. Sullivan, *Napa Wine,* 317–18.

11. Pinney, *History of Wine in America,* 2:346–47.

12. Gomberg, "Analytical Perspectives," 38, 71–72.

13. Sullivan, *Napa Wine,* 322.

14. Sullivan, *Companion to California Wine,* 23; Beckstoffer, "Premium California Vineyardist," 26–27, 53–55.

15. Beckstoffer, "Premium California Vineyardist," 57, 59–61. The "large-volume" statement appears on page 57.

16. Sullivan, *Companion to California Wine,* 23.

17. Beckstoffer, "Premium California Vineyardist," 106–7, 132–37.

18. Beckstoffer, "Premium California Vineyardist," 122–23. In his professional CV, Dr. Smart names Nelson Shaulis as being considered the "father of canopy management": smartvit.com.au/wp-content/uploads/2016/01/informal-CV-photo-Dec-2015-shortened.pdf.

19. Beckstoffer, "Premium California Vineyardist," 120–21.

20. Ibid., 121–22, 124–26, 146. UC Davis scientists had previously recommended that the space between rows be large enough to allow tractors to drive through; to address this concern, Beckstoffer found narrower "equipment" (p. 84).

21. Ibid., 123.

22. Ibid., 91–93.

23. Meyer, "Justin Meyer and Silver Oak Cellars," 37, 54–55. The statement appears on p. 54.

24. Ibid., 54–56, 61.

25. Ibid., 63, 65, 67.

26. Siler, *House of Mondavi,* 168, 170–71; Teiser and Harroun, *Winemaking in California,* 237.

27. Siler, *House of Mondavi,* 166.

28. Mondavi, *Harvests of Joy,* 215.

29. Pinney, *History of Wine in America,* 2:342.

30. Siler, *House of Mondavi,* 170.

31. Mondavi, *Harvests of Joy,* 218.

32. Siler, *House of Mondavi,* 175–76.

33. Mondavi, *Harvests of Joy,* 221.

34. Ed McCarthy, "Opus One: American Royalty," *WineReviewOnline,* November 14, 2006, winereviewonline.com/mccarthy_opusone.cfm.

35. *Decanter* staff, "Opus One, Oakville 1979," *Decanter,* February 3, 2016, Taster William Kelley, decanter.com/reviews/napa-valley/opus-one-oakville-1979/#rAb3lFIQoVtx1Qiw.99. See also wine-searcher.com/wine-38290-1979-opus-one-napa-valley-usa. Decanter.com rates it as 93/100; Wine-Searcher.com offers 90/100.

36. Mondavi, *Harvests of Joy,* 221–22.

37. Lukacs, *American Vintage,* 200.

38. Darlington, *Zin,* 3.

39. Sullivan, *Zinfandel,* 108.

40. Ridge Vineyards, "History," ridgewine.com.

41. Brady, "Super Zin," 18.

42. Sullivan, *Zinfandel,* 108, 110–11.

43. Heyhoe and Hock, *Harvesting the Dream,* xiv–xv.

44. Trinchero, "California Zinfandels," 45, 49.

45. Heyhoe and Hock, *Harvesting the Dream,* 71.

46. Trinchero, "California Zinfandels," 49–50.

47. Lukacs, *American Vintage,* 201–2.

48. Heyhoe and Hock, *Harvesting the Dream,* xv–xvi. Note that another acclaimed winemaker, David Bruce, produced White Zinfandel in the

1960s; Sullivan deems his the first White Zin "sold as such in California in the twentieth century." Sullivan, *Zinfandel,* 108, citing in part Charles L. Sullivan, *Wines and Winemakers of the Santa Cruz Mountains: An Oral History* (Cupertino: CA: D. R. Bennion Trust, 1994), 341–69.

49. Trinchero, "California Zinfandels," 67.

50. Darlington, *Zin,* 206.

51. Lukacs, *American Vintage,* 202; see also Heyhoe and Hock, *Harvesting the Dream,* xvi.

52. Darlington, *Zin,* 190.

53. Trinchero, "California Zinfandels," 66–67.

54. Heyhoe and Hock, *Harvesting the Dream,* xvii.

55. The origin question of the variety's name goes down to the level of spelling. Different American writers have spelled it "Zinfindal," "Zinfardel"—as in, the "Black Zinfardel of Hungary"—plus "Zeinfindall" and both "Zinfenthal" and "Zenfenthal." Sullivan, "Viticultural Mystery Solved," 117, 120, 124, 127.

56. Darlington, *Zin,* 3–4.

57. Sullivan, "Viticultural Mystery Solved," 115–16.

58. Charles Sullivan, quoted in Darlington, *Zin,* 80.

59. Sullivan, "Viticultural Mystery Solved," 115, 120. See also, generally, 120–24.

60. *San Francisco Evening Bulletin,* May 1, 1885; *Santa Rosa Press Democrat,* August 5, 1903, cited in Sullivan, "Viticultural Mystery Solved," 117.

61. Sullivan, "Viticultural Mystery Solved," 118; Darlington, *Zin,* 78–80, 89.

62. Sullivan, "Viticultural Mystery Solved," 117–18, 123, and n43.

63. Sullivan, *Companion to California Wine,* 407–9.

64. Darlington, *Zin,* 1–4, 281–82; Sullivan, *Companion to California Wine,* 411. Some, like Jancis Robinson and coauthors Julia Harding and José Vouillamoz, now think it is the Tribidrag variety of Croatia; to this Sullivan adds that Dr. Meredith's DNA tests to that effect are to date inconclusive, while Darlington states she's determined they're closely related but not the same variety. Robinson, Harding, and Vouillamoz, *Wine Grapes,* xix; see also xx–xxi. Generally, see also Sullivan, *Companion to California Wine,* 407–11.

65. Darlington, *Zin,* 191, 213, 281. The "roundabout" statement appears on page 191.

66. Ibid., 281.

67. Sullivan, *Napa Wine,* 322.

68. Ibid., 325.

69. Gross, "Shall Tourists or Grapes Rule"

70. Sullivan, *Napa Wine,* 298–99.

71. Conaway, *Far Side of Eden,* 13.

72. Gross, "Shall Tourists or Grapes Rule"

73. Sullivan, *Napa Wine,* 240–41, 350–51.

74. Ibid., 352.

75. Ibid., 338, 355–56. See also 255n24.

76. Conaway, *Far Side of Eden,* 7–8, 13, 37. See also Comiskey, *American Rhone,* 234.

77. Conaway, *Far Side of Eden,* 36–38, 268–69.

78. Wine Institute, "Wine Consumption in the U.S."

79. Lukacs, *American Vintage*; 316; Pinney, *History of Wine in America,*

2:368, citing in part Adams, *Wines of America,* x. Adams repeated his claim in his 1986 talk, "What's Going On Here Anyhow?" A talk by Leon D. Adams to the Twelfth Wine Industry Technical Symposium at Santa Rosa, California, January 18, 1986. In Adams, "California Wine Industry Affairs," 49.

80. Wine Institute, "Wine Consumption in the U.S." Consumption decreased until 1993, when it hit 1.74 gallons. It has risen steadily ever since. As of 2015, the figure is 2.83, the current all-time high.

81. Sullivan, *Napa Wine,* 367–68.

82. Mondavi, *Harvests of Joy,* 258.

83. Hon. Mike Thompson of California in the House of Representatives, "Recognizing Robert Mondavi, Recipient of Winevision's First Annual 'Visionary Award,'" Thursday, June 29, 2000, 106th Cong., 2nd Sess., vol. 146, no. 86—Daily Edition, https://www.congress.gov/congressional -record/2000/06/30/extensions-of-remarks-section/article/E1160-3.

84. Mondavi, *Harvests of Joy,* 260–61.

85. Ibid., 262–63.

86. Pinney, *History of Wine in America,* 2:347.

87. "Harlan Estate Napa Valley California Cabernet Sauvignon Wine," *The Wine Cellar Insider,* thewinecellarinsider.com/california-wine/harlan -estate-california-wine-cabernet-sauvignon.

88. Bill Harlan, interview by author, April 9, 2003. Note that Harlan Estate was the first winery in the Napa Valley to practice green harvesting.

89. "Harlan Estate," *The Wine Cellar Insider.*

90. Laube, "California's Cult Wines."

91. Conaway, *Far Side of Eden,* 90–93. The "extract, not wine" statement is from page 93; the "talent show" statement appears on pages 92–93.

92. Harlan, interview.

93. Ibid.

94. Conaway, *Far Side of Eden,* 302, 305–6.

95. Sullivan, "Robert Mondavi 94," B5.

96. Siler, *House of Mondavi,* 308–10.

97. "The Judgment of California: Charles Shaw Chardonnay Is State's Best," *Napa Valley Register,* June 29, 2007, napavalleyregister.com/wine/ the-judgment-of-california-charles-shaw-chardonnay-is-state-s/article_ 09f74fcf-6cb8-5ac3-9400-9c99ff37bcd6.html.

98. Goodyear, "Drink Up," 58.

99. Ben Robinson, "We Made a Sommelier Taste All the Trader Joe's Two Buck Chuck," *Thrillist,* June 8, 2015, thrillist.com/drink/nation/ the-best-two-buck-chuck-at-trader-joe-s-cheap-wine-thrillist-nation.

100. Goodyear, "Drink Up."

101. "Bronco Winery Head Steps Down to Settle Wine Fraud Case," December 9, 1993, United Press International, upi.com/Archives/1993/ 12/09/Bronco-Winery-head-steps-down-to-settle-wine-fraud-case/ 1564755413200.

102. Jerry Hirsch, "Vintner Agrees to Drop 'Napa' from Wine Label," *Los Angeles Times,* April 29, 2006, articles.latimes.com/2006/apr/29/business/ fi-settle29.

103. Goodyear, "Drink Up," 58.

104. Siler, *House of Mondavi,* 4, 243–44, 249, 251.

105. Ibid., 230, 247, 250, 292–93.

106. Ibid. 302–3.

107. Ibid., 304.

108. Ibid., 331, 353.

109. Ibid., 326–28, 339–40, 356. In this newest wave we've learned that even cult wineries have succumbed to the siren song of lucre. In 2006, Jean Phillips, the independent owner of the cult Cabernet Screaming Eagle, sold out to Stanley Kroenke, an owner of Colorado sports franchises. Pierce Carson, "Jean Phillips Sells Screaming Eagle," *Napa Valley Register,* March 23, 2006.

110. Paul Franson, "Two Billion-Buck Chuck," *Wines & Vines,* January 26, 2016, winesandvines.com/buyersguide/?pLev=product&pId=122& articleId=163823. Despite the title of this piece, it specifically shares that Bronco Wine Co. "has delivered more than 1 billion bottles of Charles Shaw wine," as announced by Fred Franzia at the Unified Wine & Grape Symposium keynote luncheon on January 26, 2016.

111. "About Us," Robert Mondavi Institute for Wine and Food Science, http://robertmondaviinstitute.ucdavis.edu/about.

Conclusion

The main distinction between sparkling wines and
still wines is that the former are particularly apropos
for special or festive occasions, and in general
should be reserved for such occasions. Of course, if
life is one big gala event for you, dear reader, then
by all means drink champagne with all meals.

—RAYMOND EWELL,
Dining Out in San Francisco and the Bay Area, 1948

THIS STORY OF WINE in California has traveled a great distance within a relatively brief period of time. Franciscan friars from Spain planted the first wine grapevines in California. Scholars disagree on just when, so let's imagine the year was 1776. Just two centuries later, California wines were recognized as among the finest in the world in a blind tasting by French judges in Paris.

Few of the pioneering wine names continue to flourish today. Among them are Buena Vista, founded by Agoston Haraszthy in 1857, and Gundlach-Bundschu, established just months later in 1858, both in Sonoma. Concannon and Wente in the Livermore Valley date from the early 1880s, as does Chateau Montelena in Napa. But the intrepid few are vastly exceeded by the number of wineries that have fallen along the way, victims of terrain, or climate—actual or political—or human folly.

What ground we've covered on this journey. We've traveled with the explorers and the mission friars, both eventually heading northward. We've tramped with the likes of William Wolfskill and George Yount, from Kentucky through the Southwest to Los Angeles. Some in Southern California—like George Yount or Kohler and Frohling in LA, or the venerable General Vallejo in Monterey, or Agoston Haraszthy in San Diego—would also eventually head northward: for reasons of Pierce's disease, or seats in government, or the changing winds of the market, or just curiosity. And while most of the vineyards of Southern California lost their rootstock long ago, Northern California has proven to be more hospitable to the vine.

We've also covered extensive figurative ground. For example, we've seen there is both strength and discord in numbers. Indeed, there is wisdom in joining forces or pooling resources, whether to stay afloat, get ahead, or just to remain abreast. But we've also seen how combining entities can prove problematic if strong opinions disrupt the harmony, whether the debate be over phylloxera or prohibition. We've seen the folly of focusing on cost with little thought to craft, as well as the folly of abiding by craft with little thought to cost, as the brokenhearted heir of Inglenook learned too late. And we've seen people abusing as well as protecting the rights of others, from Don Benito Wilson's putative kindly treatment of the California natives, to attempts to tax immigrant gold miners, to Agoston Haraszthy's underpaying of his Chinese laborers, to the modern-day advocates for grape growers (Andy Beckstoffer) and grape pickers (César Chávez and Dolores Huerta). Fortunately, human rights practices improved over time; even the Chinese Exclusion Acts first passed in 1882 were eventually repealed—though not for six decades.

In chapter 5 it was noted that for California viticulture the transition from the nineteenth century to the twentieth was like the transition from childhood to adolescence, during which it was caught in two intertwining phases of self-assessment and inquiry concerning survival and identity. And what of the transition from the twentieth century to the twenty-first? California viticulture is by no means still adolescent, but for all its growth and advancement it is still plagued by concerns of survival and identity. These are both the more hard-edged concerns of finance, operations, and—that fickle fiend—the market at work throughout its history, as well as the more wobbly concern at play throughout all of history: the vagaries of human nature. These concerns have recurred in our narrative in different combinations, interweaving and loosening and reweaving into new formations. But one particular interplay repeats: the tussle over quality versus quantity.

Fortunately, sometimes what benefits the one benefits the other. For example, both camps require healthy vines planted in appropriate terrain. And though those seeking quality strive to make their wines enticing—via exacting methods of vineyard monitoring, harvesting, crushing, fermenting, more monitoring, aging, blending, and more aging—the reputable players in both camps agree that wine should at least be palatable, for which the fundamentals of appropriate temperature, sound grapes, and hygienic equipment are key. Also, when the bigger enterprises

The Ever-Trodden Path of Viticultural Science

The University of California at Davis has brought us phylloxera-resistant rootstock, has decodified the DNA of Zinfandel, and has even developed a complete lexicon for describing the aromas and flavors of wine. In 1869 a Napa Valley winemaker stammered to describe Zinfandel, finally settling on saying the wine has a "delightful flavor resembling the raspberry." The folks at Davis have given us more than a hundred nouns with which to describe wine, including, yes, *raspberry,* but also *black currant, raisin, prune, tobacco, vanilla, burnt toast, moldy cork, kerosene, leesy,* and *horsey.* The flavor lexicon has a rigorous taxonomy. *Cut grass* is a species of the genus *Fresh,* which is of the phyllum *Herbaceous. Wet dog* is of the kingdom of *Plonk.* The Davis denizens have even devised a colorful plastic wheel, called the Wine Aroma Wheel, on which the aromas are displayed taxonomically.

At the end of the twentieth century, the icon-clasting Davis scientists scandalized the French wine world with the revelation that some of the most patrician grapes of that patrician grape land are the bastard offspring of "an obscure white plonk." So wrote Roger Highfield, science editor of the London *Daily Telegraph.* The DNA studies showed that sixteen venerable varietals, among them Chardonnay, Aligote, and Gamay Noir, aren't just direct descendants of the Pinot variety (no particular surprise there)—they also descend from the Gouais Blanc. As far back as the Middle Ages Gouais Blanc was considered so middling a grape that attempts were made, unsuccessfully, to ban it. Even its name, derived from the derisive old French adjective *gou,* indicates its low station. So, as Highfield writes, "In the distant viticultural past, royalty mingled with a commoner."

Sources: Sullivan, "Viticultural Mystery Solved," 127; Highfield, "DNA Links," 3. Wine Aroma Wheel, copyright 1990, 2002 by A. C. Noble. For more, see winearomawheel.com.

funded research to ever improve their bottom line, the smaller entities benefitted from the resulting studies. And we've seen how the Gallo brothers' zeal for market share inspired innovative production and marketing practices that were then adopted by other winemakers. The same could be said of the big distillers' stint in wine: their aggressive marketing modeled much for smaller entities to emulate. And when the E. & J. Gallo Winery broke the stranglehold that the Bank of America had had on the industry, everyone benefitted.

Another shared concern is the bigger bugaboo of market, even though the two camps view it differently. While many lament the product of the likes of E. & J. Gallo, the fact remains that the

Gallo brothers didn't attain success by offering undesirable product: their initial consumers responded, and they responded in turn. In later years, wineries like the family-run Sutter Home also let consumer tastes steer their journey in winemaking—to yet another profitable turn.

We've seen how the history of wine in California is rife with repeating phases of antagonism. On one side are those who saw what wine could achieve and strove toward those heights. On the other side stand those who saw in the liquid grape no allure other than cash flow. It's been mentioned that before efforts were made to, shall we say, put a cork in the practice, early California wine was often adulterated in the barrel by unscrupulous merchants, who in blending it with swill essentially diluted it as one would water milk. The adulteration in turn sullied the name of California wine.

That particular practice was readily solved when the commandeering of rail cars during World War II forced the development of industry-wide bottling processes. But by the 1960s, the likes of Almaden, Paul Masson, Inglenook, and Italian Swiss Colony found their wine sullied not by wholesalers or merchants but by the corporate buyers of their vineyards and wineries—buyers who cared not a whit for the art and wit of winemaking; indeed, the buyers cared only for the dollar value of the names they had purchased. The corporate buyers made great money from those names, but as they degraded the wine, they degraded the names.

And yet, whereas previously the existence of low-quality, low-priced wine had soured the public's concept of all American wine, the most recent revolution in California wine has fully established that it produces many excellent alternatives, however widespread a lower-realm competitor might be; modern-day Two-Buck Chuck has done nothing to sully the reputation of its quality-focused compatriots. Who today sees all California wine as good for nothing more than cooking, or who views all Golden State wines as "cooked"? Consider the years it took to reach this point.

The quality and reputation of California wines remain high; they consistently rank among the best in the world. And though in previous years consumer dedication didn't necessarily follow suit, today wine sales continue a long trend upward. As mentioned earlier, annual per capita consumption of wine in the United States had in 1980 surpassed the two-gallon mark; it peaked in 1986 at 2.43 gallons, after which it began a steady

Appeasing a Connoisseur

San Francisco—notwithstanding its considerable youth relative to Boston, Philadelphia, and New York—possesses three of the five oldest restaurants in the United States. Tadich Grill is San Francisco's oldest, established in 1849. It serves traditional San Francisco fare without pretension.

One Friday afternoon in the late 1970s, a man and woman arrived at Tadich and took seats at the bar. The man, eager to flaunt before the lady his knowledge of wine, asked for the best rosé the place had to pour. Then as now, Tadich Grill had no rosé to offer by the glass. And so co-owner Bob Buich accommodated the request by concocting a mixture of red and white wines that could, to the eye, pass for a rosé. Two glasses of this meritage were presented to the couple, and the man did the manly thing: swirling the glass, inhaling the bouquet, then portentously savoring a sip. He then exclaimed it was the finest rosé he had tasted in his many travels, and asked what vintage it was.

The reply: "April."

decline. In 1993, it bottomed out at 1.74 gallons, after which it began a steady upward trend. It again hit the 2.43-gallon mark in 2007, two decades after first reaching that milestone. As of 2015, the figure is 2.83, an all-time high.[1]

And yet, consumption of wine in the United States still does not match the rates in many other countries.[2] As wine historian Paul Lukacs has remarked, "Quality has reached unprecedented heights, and American wines have become international style setters, but table wine still has little to do with daily home life in much of the country. In this regard, the wine revolution still has only just begun."[3] This opinion suggests that California viticulture still has significant ground to cover. But is its success truly determined by sheets of statistics?

In any case, California wine has certainly had its share of revolutionary figures—and long before the term "cult wines" was coined. Yet it's been the industry leaders, rather than the revolutionaries, that have truly furthered the success of California's viticulture. Some of this leadership has occurred by chance: Paul Masson didn't seek to inspire the young Martin Ray, just as Ray didn't know his written words would later inspire Warren Winiarski. Other efforts were very intentional. Both Eugene Hilgard and Charles Wetmore were determined to effect better practices in the industry, especially in planting resistant rootstock. Agoston Haraszthy advocated planting superior varietals; his son Arpad later advocated planting in superior terrain. And both Andrea Sbarboro, blowing into the winds of Prohibition, and Leon D. Adams, looking to disrupt the post-Repeal doldrums, sought to change public opinion about wine—each determined to save the industry.

But resilience stands as one of the greatest attributes of the figures in this history. Agoston Haraszthy dusted himself off from setback after setback to begin again. Robert Mondavi, ousted from his family's firm, rose to win again. And while his resilience derived greatly from his passion for wine, it can't be denied that the support of his fellow vintners—offering both encouragement and financial assistance—helped him to rise again. He'd earned that support from having always believed they all fared better when they helped each other. Other icons in this history had done the same, from Father José Sanchez teaching Wolfskill and Yount at Mission San Gabriel, to General Vallejo and Agoston Haraszthy sharing their vines, to Charles Krug and André Tchelistcheff consulting to fellow winemakers.

This history has shown that it is the genius of individuals that accounts for the inexorable innovation and continuing success of California wine. These individuals—like Jean Louis Vignes, Agoston Haraszthy, and the beloved Charles Kohler, as well as, more recently, Robert Mondavi and Jim Barrett and Bill Harlan, joined by Warren Winiarski and Mike Grgich and Bob Trinchero—were abetted by the equal genius to be found in University of California laboratories, but they weren't led by it. John N. Hutchison puts it best: "A long procession of enthusiastic, conscientious growers and vintners had poured their energies and their ambitions into a remarkable endeavor—to make California, within their lifetimes, a wine region that would challenge the products of a thousand years of European experience and glamour. Among them were rascals, slipshod greenhorns, and untalented managers, but on balance the California wine community was typified, as it is today, by its devoted application to making each vintage better than the last best one."[4]

Notes

1. Wine Institute, "Wine Consumption in the U.S."

2. "Table 7.1: Per Capita Wine Consumption by Country," Wine Institute, 2010, www.wineinstitute.org/files/2010_Per_Capita_Wine_Consumption_by_Country.pdf.

3. Pinney, *History of Wine in America,* 2:368.

4. Hutchison, "Northern California," 47.

Acknowledgments

Kevin Starr devoted decades to writing and telling how Californians dreamed, and dream. This book is the story of Californians dreaming of making one fine thing from the stuff of California—not gold gleaned from dirt and rock blasted from the Sierra Nevada, not waterworks to rival Roman aqueducts, not self-driving cars, but wine—wine made from grapes grown in the rocky dirt of California. Wine—making it, drinking it, reading of it—can bring joy, and this book is meant to bring that. It is also the product of many generous people, beginning with Kevin.

In 2002, Phil Wood, founder of Ten Speed Press in Berkeley, published my restaurant history of San Francisco, and urged me to write what is, at last, this book. So did Kimberley Cameron, my agent then and now. Doris and Charles Muscatine urged me too; over meals at Chez Panisse and Sam's Grill and Oliveto they made rich suggestions for topics to be treated, and often as not I found sources in Doris's own many books. (Charles proposed several allusions to Chaucer, none of which escaped the editor's culling blue pencil.) Kimberley and I have become ever closer friends; Phil and Charles and Doris have all, alas, passed, as has Kevin Starr, who died January 14, 2017.

Nicholas Littman, Jonathan Ritter, and Maria Brandt helped immensely with research. Nicholas helped with drafting too, and Maria also with securing the many needed permissions. Editor Kirsten Janene-Nelson worked tirelessly, meticulously, to sculpt the text and to select the art. Tom Christensen, author, translator, nonfiction editor of *Catamaran Literary Reader,* and former editor-in-chief of Mercury House, read a draft of the book, and suggested, and encouraged, and published in *Catamaran* a portion of an early draft of chapter 11.

Many in the wine industry have given me interviews and in other ways been of help, among them Bill Harlan of Napa's Harlan Estate; Tom May, who, with his wife, Martha, owned Martha's Vineyard in the Napa Valley (Tom, alas, passed away in 2017); Andy Beckstoffer; and the late Gil Nickel of Far Niente Winery.

Jerry Braun, name partner in the San Francisco law firm Farella Braun & Martel, which represented Robert Mondavi in the epic 1976 trial against Mondavi's mother and brother, sought to track down obscure facts from his law firm's archives. Richard Mendelsohn of the venerable wine-law firm Dickenson, Peatman & Fogarty in Napa similarly rummaged through records and files to find an odd fact here and there.

To my wife, Carol Sayers, an especially heartfelt thanks for encouraging me to continue with this book, especially when several years ago I was undergoing months of debilitating daily medical treatments, and for painstakingly (probably painfully) reading the manuscript for sense, typos, eye-rolling inanities, and nonsense.

Warren Hinckle finished editing *Who Killed Hunter S. Thompson?* only shortly before his death on August 25, 2016. To the end Hinckle hectored me to finish this book (sometimes over martinis and sand dabs at gatherings of the Warren Hinckle Round Table at Sam's Grill in San Francisco). His daughter Pia Hinckle, also a writer, also a great friend, helped me with a particularly tricky structural problem in the opening chapter of the book.

A number of scholars have given me succor and aid, among them Charles Faulhaber, director emeritus of The Bancroft Library at the University of California, Berkeley; and Peter Hanff, the library's deputy director. Each was especially helpful when I had difficulty locating documents at the Bancroft, such as the original "Haraszthy Family" manuscript. Professor Thomas Pinney is another such scholar. To Professor Pinney, whom I've yet to meet in person, I want to express a particular thanks for his thoughtful critique of an earlier draft of this book. In so many respects this book is the better for his comments. But I must tender to him a humble apologia for my not having fully accepted two suggestions he made. Those were to include much more historical information than I had and, second, to make the book less, in my words, "Northern California–centric." As to his second suggestion, Professor Pinney's magisterial history of wine in Los Angeles will fill a gap that, even after including more here about Southern California wine, I must still cop to. As to his first suggestion, there can be no one history of a time, such as the Middle Ages or World War II, nor of a place, such as California. I confess to a slashing selectivity, one that traces the historical trajectory of California wine as I happen to see it.

Another stellar scholar who helped and encouraged me is Professor Christopher O'Sullivan of the University of San Francisco.

Several years ago Professor O'Sullivan asked to read the then still-gurgling, not-yet-congealing manuscript, liked it, and asked to use it for his course in California history, and his lecture series on California wine. I replied, *But of course,* and during the several following years he continually urged me to put aside my day jobs and finish the book. All along he offered many helpful suggestions.

Justin Race, the dynamic new director of the University of Nevada Press, whom I'd not met until he accepted this book for publication, has been of great support in the short time of our association.

———— ∞ ————

TO BEGIN AGAIN, Kevin Starr was the preeminent historian of California. He was the preeminent historian of California *ever,* in the considered view of many, including Dana Gioia, his colleague and the poet laureate of California. To Kevin, a cherished friend who I never dreamed would not live to read these words of thanks, I offer special gratitude. Kevin too asked to read the manuscript, and made suggestions as others had. In late 2015 he also wrote a wholly gratuitous, glowing endorsement of the work. That endorsement, I have to think, helped the manuscript reach the last round of the California Historical Society Book Award competition for 2016. (One of the other three finalists was a book by Thomas Pinney. When he won, it was my decided pleasure to send him two magnums of California wine in congratulation—Northern California wine.) Kevin had for several years been caroling hosannas for the University of Nevada Press (as had Chris O'Sullivan), and when he learned that *Crush* had been named a finalist of the CHS Book Award, he wrote Justin Race urging him to publish it.

A generation separated the younger Chris O'Sullivan from Kevin Starr, but Chris shares rare qualities with Kevin—a deep and wandering intellect, a passion for our past that capaciously embraces the history of California, and the brimming grace of generosity.

My heartfelt thanks to all.

Chronology

1568 The first wine grapes planted in the Americas are planted in South Carolina.

1626 The first wine grapes planted on the West Coast are planted in New Mexico, at Mission Socorro along the Rio Grande.

1697 The Roman Catholic Society of Jesus, the Jesuits, begins establishing missions in Baja California.

1699 Mission San Francisco Xavier is founded. There, Jesuit Juan de Ugarte plants what is possibly the first vineyard in Baja California.

1767 Spain banishes the Jesuits from the New World. Their expulsion ushers in the era of Franciscan missions.

1769 July 16: Franciscan padres dedicate Mission San Diego de Alcalá, the first of a string of California missions that will in time incubate the California wine industry.

1778 First wine cuttings to be planted in Alta California are planted in 1778 or 1779 at Mission San Juan Capistrano.

1781 A small group of hardy settlers lays the foundation of the pueblo of Los Angeles.

1783 Pedro Fages plants a small vineyard in Monterey, making him the first outside the mission system to grow grapes in Northern California.

1798 By 1798, five missions produce wine: Santa Barbara, San Buenaventura, San Gabriel, San Juan Capistrano, and San Diego.

1820 By 1820, Los Angeles—the "City of Vineyards"—boasts of having fifty-three thousand vines in an area of fifty-three acres.

1821 September 27: Mexico establishes its independence from Spain.

1824 The first vineyards to be planted in Northern California are planted at the Franciscan mission in Sonoma County after 1823. 🦅 Joseph Chapman plants 4,000 vines in Los Angeles. In time he becomes the first U.S.–born winegrower in California.

1830 William Wolfskill and George C. Yount visit Mission San Gabriel, where Father José Sanchez likely shares his viticultural knowledge.

1830s Frenchman Jean Louis Vignes, a distiller and cooper by trade, arrives in Los Angeles, where he immediately recognizes the similarities of climate between Southern California and his native Bordeaux. In time he becomes California's first full-time professional winemaker.

1831 More than 100,000 wine-grape vines flourish in Los Angeles, producing half the total wine grapes in California.

1833 Mexico begins the process of secularizing the mission system.

1834 General Mariano de Guadalupe Vallejo takes over the vineyards at the Mission San Francisco Solano and plants his own, named Lachryma Montis Vineyard, from which he makes wine and brandy—all from the Mission grape. He also shares his cuttings with others, spreading the viticulture in the region.

1838 William Wolfskill buys a vineyard in Los Angeles and develops one of the most significant winemaking operations in the city. His grapes and wines sell throughout California. ✺ George C. Yount plants the first vines in Napa Valley with cuttings from General Vallejo's Lachryma Montis Vineyard in Sonoma.

1840s William Wolfskill experiments with which fruits grow best in the soil and climate of Southern California. He also plants in regular rows, in contrast to the more haphazard rows at the missions. ✺ Dr. John Marsh makes wine in Contra Costa County from the Mission, Isabella, and Catawba grapes of his small vineyard at the foot of Mount Diablo.

1841 Edward Bale plants a vineyard as part of a vast ranch in the St. Helena area of the Napa Valley.

1846 July: California becomes a territory of the U.S. by virtue of the Mexican War.

1849 From the start of the Gold Rush, San Francisco becomes the de facto center of the wine market.

1850s The intrepid phylloxera makes its first foray into Europe. ✺ Matthew "Don Mateo" Keller experiments with grape varieties other than the Mission.

1852 Agoston Haraszthy establishes the vineyard, nursery, and horticultural garden he names "Las Flores" in San Francisco.

1853 Benjamin (Don Benito) Wilson establishes his Lake Vineyard in Los Angeles and experiments with grape varieties other than the Mission. He produces a prized port and, in 1855, likely the first sparkling wine in California. He also experiments with the winemaking process, including aging his wines for longer periods.

1856 In Alameda County Clement Colombet buys the Agua Caliente Rancho, which soon thereafter boasts 60,000 vines and a winery. ✺ Agoston Haraszthy begins transplanting 13,000 vines from his other holdings to his Buena Vista Ranch in Sonoma.

1857 The Sainsevain brothers—nephews of Jean Louis Vignes who took over his El Aliso— are the second vintners to produce sparkling wine in California. ✺ George Yount's wines win prizes at the 1857 Napa County Fair.

1857–1860s Charles Krug plants vineyards in Sonoma and makes wine for fellow pioneers John Patchett, Edward Bale, and George Yount, becoming the first consulting winemaker in Northern California.

1858 The California State Agricultural Society reports on the viticultural advances at John Sutter's Hock Farm, including vine spacing and staking of vines. His 12,000 bearing vines produce 400 gallons of wine. ✺ Charles Lefranc replaces the Mission grapes at New Almaden Vineyards with various superior French varieties, resulting in the state's first commercial Bordeaux. ✺ Agoston Haraszthy submits his "Report on Grapes and Wine of California" to the California State Agricultural Society— perhaps the first written treatment on the subject. ✺ Charles Kuchel and Emil Dresel plant Rhine Farm in Vineburg; in time their enterprise is renamed Gundlach-Bundschu. Still run by a member of the Bundschu family, it claims to be the second oldest winery in California.

1860 The U.S. Census lists Santa Clara County as having 26 grape growers and winemakers, just one shy of Sonoma County's 27. Sonoma County produces 1,200 gallons of wine; Alameda County produces over 8,000 gallons; Napa produces nearly 9,000 gallons.

1860s California wine is exported to Australia, British Columbia, China, Hawaii, Mexico, Peru. Los Angeles Mission grape "port" is exported to Canada, Denmark, England, and Germany.

1861 Agoston Haraszthy imports from Europe "about 100,000 vines of 300 tagged varieties." He regularly proselytizes planting superior varieties. ❧ Charles Krug establishes his eponymous winery in Napa Valley—on a parcel of Edward Bale's Rancho Carne Humana—on which he plants 23 acres of superior varieties.

1862 Agoston Haraszthy publishes *Grape Culture, Wines, and Wine-Making.*

1863 Phylloxera is discovered in England and France. ❧ With nine silent backers Agoston Haraszthy founds the Buena Vista Vinicultural Society. The society produces 100,000 gallons of wine. In years following it also implements use of the dug-out hillside cellar, the redwood tank, and unirrigated vineyards.

1866 Arpad Haraszthy and Isador Landsberger produce the state's first commercially successful sparkling wine, which they name Eclipse.

1868 UC Berkeley establishes a College of Agriculture; it becomes the first state-run agricultural experiment station.

1869 The National Prohibition Party is established.

1870s Isaac De Turk becomes the leading grape grower and winemaker in Sonoma County. By 1888 his winery has a capacity of 1 million gallons. He ships his wines in bottles, not casks, and urges other winemakers to do likewise—to thwart unscrupulous merchants' attempts to profit through adulteration.

1872 Arpad Haraszthy promotes Northern California terrain in four articles, "Wine-Making in California," that appear in Bret Harte's *Overland Monthly.* As a result, lands previously considered worthless for agriculture are planted with grapes.

1873 Phylloxera is first discovered in California near Sonoma.

1875 German brothers Jacob and Frederick Beringer establish Los Hermanos winery in Napa County.

1876 Grapes cost more to pick than they receive on the market; one gallon of wine sells for just ten cents.

1877 onward Several vintners of the "Southern Vineyard" take advantage of phylloxera's advances in Europe by expanding their own enterprises.

1880 600 acres of vines have been destroyed by phylloxera in Sonoma County alone. ❧ In part to address the phylloxera scourge, the State of California establishes the Board of State Viticultural Commissioners; it is headed by Charles Wetmore. ❧ UC Berkeley establishes the Department of Viticulture and Enology as a center of research to bolster the developing California wine industry. It is headed by Eugene W. Hilgard, who conducts extensive viticultural studies—complete with a vineyard and wine cellar—on campus.

1880 onward German vintner and horticulture professor George C. Husmann arrives in CA. He is instrumental in guiding Europe out of its phylloxera era by sending them resistant rootstock from his home state of Missouri.

1880s Pierce's disease attacks vineyards in Anaheim. ❧ Eugene Hilgard (UC Berkeley) and Charles Wetmore (Board of State Viticultural Commissioners) advocate that CA vineyards be planted with phylloxera-resistant rootstock, then grafted with superior grape varieties. Their pleas are mostly ignored.

1881 The Korbel brothers harvest their first crop of grapes in Sonoma County. By 1899, the Korbel name is nearly synonymous with fine champagne. ❧ Genovese Andrea Sbarboro forms the Italian Swiss Colony winemaking collective. By 1900, it is the largest source of table wine in California.

1889 Frona Eunice Wait's *Wines and Vines of California* is released. She writes most glowingly of Gustave Niebaum's Inglenook. ❧ July 23: The *San Francisco Examiner* runs a series of articles proclaiming "Wine Is Too Cheap." ❧ August 8: In a follow-up to the "Wine Is Too Cheap" articles, Eugene W. Hilgard, dean of UC Berkeley's College of Agriculture, asserts that the industry's slump is the result of the sloppy practices of careless winemakers.

1890s In 1890, Napa has 18,000 acres of bearing vines; by 1900, only 2,000 remain. ❧ The approach of grafting superior wine-grape varieties onto resistant rootstock slowly becomes the accepted solution to phylloxera.

1892 Between 1889 and 1892, 10,000 acres of vineyards are destroyed by phylloxera in Napa County alone.

1894 Seven of the state's most prominent wine dealers join to form the California Wine Association (CWA). By consolidating resources, they soon dominate the market, selling their mutually produced and bottled wines under the CALWA brand. ❧ In an effort to counter the CWA, several wine producers form the California Wine Makers Corporation (CWMC).

1895 The Anti-Saloon League is founded.

1896 Paul Masson founds his winery in Santa Clara County, where he produces wines considered the "Pride of California."

1900 At the Paris Exposition, two California wines take gold medals for Cabernet Sauvignon: Howell Mountain and Monte Bello. ❧ Frenchman Georges de Latour founds Beaulieu Vineyards in Napa Valley. Its excellent wines are both financially successful and highly acclaimed.

1906 The great earthquake and fire destroy wineries and 15–30 million gallons of wine. (Others put the figure at 50 million, two-thirds of CA's entire stock.)

1907 The CWA opens its new facilities, Winehaven, in Contra Costa County. In 1908, it produces 675,000 gallons of wine. At that time it is the largest and most up-to-date winery plant in existence.

1909 Andrea Sbarboro of the Italian Swiss Colony Wine Company publishes *Temperance Versus Prohibition*.

1913 The State Board of Viticultural Commissioners is established as the result of legislation initiated by the Grape Protective Association.

1915 July 12–13: The prestigious Permanent International Viticultural Commission conference is held at the 1915 Panama-Pacific International Exposition in San Francisco. Several CA wines win prizes at the Wine Day tasting. ❧ George C. Husmann reports on the molasses pace of progress regarding phylloxera to the International Congress of Viticulture, while also claiming, "America...[has] saved the viticultural industry of the world."

1916 The California Grape Protective Association publishes *How Prohibition Would Affect California.*

1920 January 17: Prohibition goes into effect. The National Prohibition Act, better known as the Volstead Act, permits home manufacture of "[mostly] non-intoxicating fruit juice." Prices for fresh grapes skyrocket from $10 to $100 per ton. 🍇 August 18: Women attain the right to vote with the passage of the Nineteenth Amendment. Its success is due in large part to the prohibition movement. 🍇 Assemblyman T. M. Wright of Santa Clara County authors California's "Baby Volstead" law, the Wright [Prohibition Enforcement] Act, ratified in 1921.

1920–33 Prohibition is skirted via various means. Legal ones included grape juice, industrial uses, food manufacture, vinegar, medicinal purposes, and sundried grapes (with instructions on how to not "accidentally" create wine). Between 1920 and 1933, 43 million gallons of wine are sold legally, while perhaps as much as 135 million gallons are produced.

1928 Estimates suggest total annual wine consumption in the U.S. reaches 160 million gallons—more than triple the amount from 1918.

1932 The Grape Growers League is established; it strives to expand, if not completely restore, the legalization of commercial wine. 🍇 December 5: Prohibition is repealed with the passage of the Twenty-First Amendment.

1933 April: Passage of the Cullen-Harrison (Beer Permit) Act allows for the free consumption of 3.2 percent alcohol beer or wine. 🍇 The California Sweet Wine Producers is established in the Central Valley. With the Wine Producers Association it writes the National Recovery Administration code for the wine industry in the New Deal era, establishing fair practices and setting prices. 🍇 December 5: Official beginning of Repeal. 🍇 Ernest and Julio found the E. & J. Gallo Winery in Modesto, Stanislaus County. In time they build it into an enterprise strong enough to break the stranglehold the banks, especially the Bank of America, have on the industry.

1934 *Fortune* magazine declares that "most California wine...is belly wash." 🍇 The Wine Producers Association and the California Sweet Wine Producers join forces as the Wine Institute. Its agenda is to oppose adverse legislation, support simplification of regulations, sponsor research, keep members informed about activities, educate the public about wine, and advocate wine as "a food product and temperance beverage." 🍇 The Napa Valley Cooperative Winery is established.

1934–42 554 wineries are forced out of business, especially on account of the low profit margins.

1936 At the fledgling UC Davis Department of Viticulture and Enology, Maynard Amerine sets out to determine which grape varietals grow best in which parts of the state. 🍇 Martin Ray buys the La Cresta estate from his mentor Paul Masson and continues the Paul Masson brand.

1937 The California Marketing Act allows for the development of agricultural commodity marketing boards. The resulting Wine Advisory Board collects gallonage assessments from California producers to be used for market development. 🍇 Larkmead, Beringer, and Inglenook receive a *diplôme d'honneur* at the Paris Exposition.

1938 To address a surplus of grapes, the California Agricultural Prorate Act mandates that the state "convert a large part of the perishable crop into long-lived brandy." The act lasts only one year.

1939 John Daniel Jr., grandnephew of founder Gustave Niebaum, takes over operations at Inglenook. He and German winemaker George Deuer produce wine that modern-day critics consider among the best ever produced in California.

1940 Louis M. Martini wows the industry with the introduction of an entire line of varietal wines; he is among the first following Prohibition to make wine labeled with the name of its grape.

1942–45 WWII benefits to the wine industry include: being the sole provider of tartrates, used in the manufacture of explosives; increased prices for wine grapes; improved quality of wines; and increased demand for wine, since all other alcohol is requisitioned for troops.

1943 Martin Ray sells Paul Masson to Joseph Seagram & Sons, after which he founds his own winery on Table Mountain. 🍇 Cesare Mondavi buys the Charles Krug Winery in Napa Valley.

1944 Maynard Amerine and Alfred Winkler publish *Composition and Quality of Musts and Wines of California,* based on Amerine's work studying 140 different varieties of grape. 🍇 The trade group Napa Valley Vintners is formed so as to promote Napa Valley wines as belonging to a premium class.

1945 Frank Schoonmaker advocates vast replanting of vineyards with superior grape varieties.

1946 Innovations in the packaging and marketing of E. & J. Gallo wines include adopting aluminum screw-top caps to avoid leakage from unreliable corks and having salesmen shelve Gallo wines (in prominent spots) as a "favor" to wine stores. 🍇 State officials name Agoston Haraszthy the Father of California Viticulture.

1947 The return to the standard supply-and-demand economy after the war brings on a nationwide crash in wine prices that upends the market and drives some wineries, like the award-winning Larkmead, out of business. 🍇 In the late 1940s, Robert Mondavi and André Tchelistcheff establish the Napa Enological Center Library to advance the study of various aspects of winemaking.

1948 In *Dining Out in San Francisco and the Bay Area,* Raymond Ewell declares that "all the best California table wines come from vineyards within sixty-five miles of San Francisco—in Napa, Sonoma, Alameda, and Santa Clara counties."

1949 New owner Frank Bartholomew and winemaker André Tchelistcheff produce the first vintage of the revived Buena Vista Winery, with great success. 🍇 C. Mondavi & Sons opens a visitor center. It also launches one of the first winery newsletters, *Bottles and Bins.*

1950s–1960s 60 to 75 percent of the wine produced in Mendocino, Napa, and Sonoma Counties enters the market inside an E. & J. Gallo bottle—a practice that keeps many smaller entities afloat.

1951 UC Davis launches a program to "select and import healthy, high-yielding clones of important wine grape varieties, to heat-treat these selections to eliminate viruses, and to propagate and provide certified cuttings to commercial nurseries." 🍇 Several vintners form the Association of Chateau Wine Growers with the aim of improving the quality of all Napa Valley wine. Their agreed-on standard is that to receive a varietal classification a wine must contain 85 percent of that grape variety.

1952 Financier James D. Zellerbach founds Hanzell Vineyards. Hanzell begins fermenting white wines in cold stainless-steel fermenting tanks and aging Pinot Noir in small French oak barrels. Cellar master R. Bradford Webb also induces "malolactic" fermentation.

1955 The Premium Wine Producers of California (PWPC) is formed. It decrees the first official definition of "premium wine," determined by purchase price. It also holds blind taste tests, which surge in popularity in the mid-1950s.

1958 Leon D. Adams publishes *The Commonsense Book of Wine* in order to "civilize American drinking, [to] teach Americans to use wine."

1960s The six-hundred-acre vineyards of the C. Mondavi & Sons' Charles Krug Winery annually produce 2 million gallons of varietal and generic table wine and dessert wine.

1961 Julia Child and her coauthors publish the masterpiece *Mastering the Art of French Cooking*. It champions wine as a regular partner in a French meal.

1963 When they are denied minimum wage for their labor, the mostly Filipino Agricultural Workers Organizing Committee (AWOC) in Delano, CA, initiates a strike of table grapes. The strike is soon bolstered by the National Farm Workers Association (NFWA). Soon after, the two groups fuse to become the United Farm Workers of America (UFW) labor union. Their persistent nonviolent efforts, which include consumer boycotts, marches, and community organizing, effect a collective bargaining agreement in 1970, when the first grape contracts are signed.

1964 Ridge Vineyards resurrects the "big spicy style of Zinfandel" beginning with their first vintage in 1964.

1965 Long-simmering tensions between brothers Peter and Robert Mondavi culminate in Robert being expelled from the family business.

1966 Buoyed by the support of friends and fellow vintners, the Robert Mondavi Winery is established. 🐎 Joseph Heitz bottles a vintage of grapes grown by Tom and Martha May; labeled HEITZ CELLAR MARTHA'S VINEYARD CABERNET SAUVIGNON, it is priced at $7 per bottle, the price then of only the best French wines.

1967 Sales of table wines surpass those of fortified wines for the first time since Prohibition. 🐎 Almaden is sold to National Distillers.

1968 Napa Valley becomes one of the first agricultural preserves in the U.S. An aggressive zoning policy discourages residential development and restricts commercial interests uninvolved with agriculture or winemaking.

1969 Beaulieu Vineyards is sold to Heublein.

1970 The U.S. Congress, responding to rising public concern, creates the National Institute on Alcohol Abuse and Alcoholism (NIAAA). 🐎 The Bank of America forecasts that annual consumption of wine will rise from 250 million to 400 million gallons by 1980. The announcement triggers a deluge of corporate investment. 🐎 After consulting to winemakers in Napa Valley, Warren Winiarski founds Stag's Leap in Napa Valley. His methods include measuring the sugar levels in the grapes to decide when to harvest them and exposing the wine to oxygen in a splash tank to kick-start the aging process. 🐎 Jim Barrett revives Chateau Montelena with state-of-the-art infrastructure. Winemaker Mike Grgich joins him in 1972. Grgich makes white wine from purchased grapes. His first wine, from 1972, is considered by many to be the best Chardonnay ever produced in California.

2000 Only three hundred wholesalers remain; the five largest control one-third of the market. Many small wineries are impeded from selling to states that require the wholesaler intermediary. ❧ April 4: *Wine Spectator* magazine coins the term "cult wines"—and then makes them a California phenomenon. ❧ December: In his bimonthly *The Wine Advocate,* Robert Parker excoriates the Robert Mondavi Winery for producing mediocre, "collectively superficial" wines.

2002 Fred Franzia coins the term "super-value wines" and markets the Charles Shaw brand solely at Trader Joe's stores for $1.99 a bottle. What becomes known as "Two-Buck Chuck" revolutionizes California's bulk-wine industry. ❧ The Robert Mondavi Corporation is sold to Constellation Brands Inc. for $1.3 billion.

2005 Robert and Peter Mondavi collaborate on a conciliatory vintage. The one barrel of Cabernet blend called Ancora Una Volta ("once again") brings in $400,000 at that year's Napa Valley Auction.

2006 After protracted litigation initiated by the Napa Valley Vintners Association, Fred Franzia agrees to rename his Napa Ridge line "Harlow Ridge" and agrees to use Napa grapes in his Rutherford Vintners and Napa Creek wines.

2007 Annual per capita consumption of wine in the U.S. again hits the 2.43-gallon mark two decades after first reaching that milestone.

2008 The Robert Mondavi Institute for Wine and Food Science opens at UC Davis.

2014 Rudy Kurniawan becomes the first person to be tried and convicted in a U.S. federal court for counterfeiting wine; he is sentenced to serve 10 years in a federal prison.

2015 Annual per capita consumption of wine in the U.S. reaches 2.83 gallons, the all-time high.

2016 By January 2016, sales of Two-Buck Chuck have surpassed the one-billion-bottle mark.

Bibliography

Ackley, Laura A. *San Francisco's Jewel City: The Panama-Pacific International Exposition of 1915.* Berkeley: Heyday Books, 2015.

Adams, Burton Warren. "Wente Bros." In *The Vine in Early California,* edited by Joseph Henry Jackson. San Francisco: Book Club of California, 1955.

Adams, Leon. "California Wine Industry Affairs: Recollections and Opinions." An oral history conducted in 1986 by Ruth Teiser. Regional Oral History Office, Bancroft Library, University of California, Berkeley, 1990. digitalassets. lib.berkeley.edu/roho/ucb/text/adams_leon_ ca_wine2.pdf.

———. "Revitalizing the California Wine Industry." An oral history conducted in 1974 by Ruth Teiser. Regional Oral History Office, Bancroft Library, University of California, Berkeley, 1974. digitalassets.lib.berkeley.edu/roho/ucb/ text/adams_leon_ca_wine.pdf.

———. *Wines of America.* Boston: Houghton Mifflin, 1973.

Ambrose, Stephen, *Nothing Like It in the World.* New York: Simon & Schuster, 2000.

Amerine, Maynard. "The University of California and the State's Wine Industry." An oral history conducted in 1971 by Ruth Teiser. Regional Oral History Office, Bancroft Library, University of California, Berkeley, 1972. digitalassets. lib.berkeley.edu/roho/ucb/text/amerine_maynard_1972.pdf

Amerine, Maynard A., and Axel E. Borg. *A Bibliography on Grapes, Wines, Other Alcoholic Beverages, and Temperance: Works Published in the United States Before 1901.* Berkeley: University of California Press, 1996.

Amerine, Maynard A., and A. J. Winkler. *California Wine Grapes: Composition and Quality of Their Musts and Wines.* Berkeley: University of California, Division of Agricultural Sciences, Agricultural Experiment Station, 1963. archive. org/details/californiawinegr0794amer.

Andersen, Lisa. "Give the Ladies a Chance: Gender and Partisanship in the Prohibition Party, 1869–1912." *Journal of Women's History* 23, no. 2: 137–61.

Asbury, Herbert. *The Barbary Coast: An Informal History of the San Francisco Underworld.* New York: Knopf, 1933.

———. *The Great Illusion: An Informal History of Prohibition.* New York: Doubleday & Co., 1950.

Auerbach, Jeffrey A. *The Great Exhibition of 1851: A Nation on Display.* New Haven, CT: Yale University Press, 1999.

Baegert, Johann Jakob, S.J. *Nachrichten Von Der Amerikanischen Halbinsel Californien* [Account of the American peninsula of California]. Mannheim, Germany: Churfürstliche Hof- und Academie Buchdr., 1773.

———. *Observations in Lower California.* Translated by M. M. Brandenburg and Carl L. Baumann. Berkeley: University of California Press, 1979. ark.cdlib.org/ark:/13030/ft5r29n9xv.

Bancroft, Hubert Howe. *California Pastorat 1769– 1848.* San Francisco: History Company, 1888.

———. *History of California.* 7 vols. San Francisco: A. L. Bancroft & Company, 1884–86; History Company, 1888–90.

Banks, Charles Eugene, and Opie Read. *The History of the San Francisco Disaster and Mount Vesuvius Horror.* Chicago: Thompson & Thomas, 1906.

Beckstoffer, William Andrew. "Premium California Vineyardist, Entrepreneur, 1960s to 2000s." An oral history conducted in 1999 by Carole Hicke. Regional Oral History Office, Bancroft

Library, University of California, Berkeley, 2000. texts.cdlib.org/view?docId=kt3xon99t8&doc.view=entire_text.

Behr, Edward. *Prohibition: Thirteen Years That Changed America.* Boston: Little, Brown, 1996.

Belcher, Captain Sir Edward. *Narrative of a Voyage Round the World.* Vol. 1. London: Henry Colburn, 1843.

Bell, Major Horace. *Reminiscences of a Ranger: Early Times in Southern California.* Los Angeles: Yarnell, Caystile & Mathes, 1881.

Boorde, Andrew. *A Compendyous Regyment; or, A Dyetary of Helth Made in Mountpyllier Compiled by Andrew Borde, of Physycke Doctor . . .* London: Robert Wyer, 1542. Reprinted in *Andrew Boorde's Introduction and Dyetary with Barnes in Defence of the Berde,* edited by F. J. Furnivall. Millwood, NY: Kraus Reprint, 1981. archive.org/details/fyrstbokeofintroooboorrich.

Bosker, Bianca. "A True-Crime Documentary About the Con That Shook the World of Wine." *New Yorker,* October 14, 2016.

Brady, Roy. "Alta California's First Vintage." In *The University of California/Sotheby Book of California Wine,* edited by Doris Muscatine, Maynard A. Amerine, and Bob Thompson, 10–15. Berkeley: University of California Press, 1984.

———. Preface to a manuscript on California wine dated October 18, 1975. Roy Brady Papers, University of California, Davis, Shields Library.

———. "Super Zin: A Swan Song in Reverse." *Wine World* 2, no. 6 (August–September 1973): 18–20.

Brechin, Gray. *Imperial San Francisco: Urban Power, Earthly Ruin.* Berkeley: University of California Press, 1999.

Brewer, William H. *Up and Down California in 1860–1864: The Journal of William H. Brewer.* 1930. Reprint, Berkeley: University of California Press, 1974.

Briscoe, John, *Tadich Grill: History of San Francisco's Oldest Restaurant.* Berkeley: Ten Speed Press, 2002.

Brooks, Noah, "Restaurant Life in San Francisco." *Overland Monthly* 1, no. 5. (November 1868).

Bryant, Edwin. *What I Saw in California: Being the Journal of a Tour by the Emigrant Route and South Pass of the Rocky Mountains, Across the Continent of North America, the Great Desert Basin, and Through California in the Years 1846–1847.* New York: D. Appleton & Co., 1849.

Buena Vista Vinicultural Society. *Reports of the Board of Trustees and Officers for the Year Ending June 23, 1866.* San Francisco: Towne and Bacon, 1866.

Bulfinch, Thomas. *Bulfinch's Mythology.* 1834. Reprint, New York: Crowell, 1970.

Bushnell, Horace. *California, Its Characteristics and Prospects.* San Francisco: Whitton, Towne and Co., 1858.

Byles, Stuart Douglass. *Los Angeles Wine: A History from the Mission Era to the Present.* Charleston, SC: Arcadia, 2014.

California Grape Protective Association. *How Prohibition Would Affect California.* San Francisco: 1916. hdl.handle.net/2027/uc1.31175035119216.

California Midwinter International Exposition, San Francisco, Cal., January 1st to June 30th, 1894. Portland, ME: Leighton & Frey Souvenir View Co., 1894.

California State Agricultural Society. *Transactions of the California State Agricultural Society During the Year 1872.* Sacramento, CA: State Printer, 1873.

Carosso, Vincent P. *The California Wine Industry: A Study of the Formative Years, 1830–1895.* Berkeley: University of California Press, 1951.

Caughey, John. *California.* Upper Saddle River, NJ: Prentice Hall, 1940.

Chandler, Arthur, and Marvin Nathan. *The Fantastic Fair: The Story of the California Midwinter International Exposition, Golden Gate Park, San Francisco, 1894.* St. Paul, MN: Pogo Press, 1993.

Cherrington, Ernest H., ed. *Standard Encyclopedia of the Alcohol Problem.* Vol. 6. Westerville, OH: American Issue, 1930.

Child, Julia. Introduction to fortieth anniversary edition of *Mastering the Art of French Cooking,* vol. 1, by Simone Beck, Louisette Bertholle, and Julia Child. New York: Knopf, 2001.

"Chinese Immigration and the Chinese Exclusion Acts." Office of the Historian, Bureau of Public Affairs, U.S. Department of State. history.state.gov/milestones/1866-1898/chinese-immigration.

Clavigero, Don Francisco Javier, S.J. *The History of (Lower) California.* Translated and edited by Sara E. Lake and A. A. Gray. Stanford, CA: Stanford University Press, 1937.

Comiskey, Patrick J. *American Rhone: How Maverick Winemakers Changed the Way Americans Drink.* Berkeley: University of California Press, 2016.

Conaway, James. *The Far Side of Eden: New Money, Old Land, and the Battle for Napa Valley.* Boston: Houghton Mifflin, 2002.

Critchfield, Burke. "The California Wine Industry During the Depression." An oral history conducted in 1970 by Ruth Teiser. Regional Oral History Office, Bancroft Library, University of California, Berkeley, 1972. archive.org/details/caliwineindustooteisrich.

———. "The Status of California Wine in Eastern States." *Fruit Products Journal* 14 (July 1935).

Dana, R. H., Jr. *Two Years Before the Mast: A Personal Narrative of Life at Sea.* 4th ed. London: Edward Moxon, 1845.

Darlington, David. *Zin: The History and Mystery of Zinfandel.* New York: Da Capo Press, 1991.

Davies, Norman. *Europe: A History.* New York: Oxford University Press, 1996.

Davis, David Brion. *Antebellum American Culture: An Interpretive Anthology.* University Park: Pennsylvania State University Press, 1997.

Davis, William Heath. *Seventy-Five Years in California.* San Francisco: John Howell, 1929.

———. *Sixty Years in California: A History of Events and Life in California; Personal, Political and Military, Under the Mexican Regime; During the Quasi-Military Government of the Territory by the United States, and After the Admission of the State into the Union, Being a Compilation by a Witness of the Events Described.* San Francisco: A. J. Leary, 1889.

Dinkelspiel, Frances. Foreword to *Vintage: California Wine Labels of the 1930s,* by Christopher Miya and California Historical Society. Berkeley: Heyday Books, 2016.

———. *Tangled Vines: Greed, Murder, Obsession, and an Arsonist in the Vineyards of California.* New York: St. Martin's Press, 2015.

Douglass, Frederick. "Intemperance and Slavery: An Address Delivered in Cork, Ireland, October 20, 1845." In *The Frederick Douglass Papers—Series One: Speeches, Debates, and Interviews.* Vol. 1, *1841–1846,* edited by John

W. Blassingame and John R. McKivigan. New Haven, CT: Yale University Press, 1979.

Dumas, Alexandre. *Alexandre Dumas' Dictionary of Cuisine.* Edited and translated by Louis Colman. New York: Simon & Schuster, 1990.

Edwords, Clarence E. *Bohemian San Francisco: Its Restaurants and Their Most Famous Recipes—The Elegant Art of Dining.* San Francisco: P. Elder and Company, 1914.

Ewell, Raymond. *Dining Out in San Francisco and the Bay Area.* 2nd ed. Berkeley: Epicurean Press, 1948.

Federal Writers' Project of the Works Progress Administration. *Los Angeles in the 1930s: The WPA Guide to the City of Angels.* Berkeley: University of California Press, 2011.

Federal Writers' Project of the Works Progress Administration of Northern California. *California: A Guide to the Golden State.* New York: Hastings House, 1939.

———. *San Francisco: The Bay and Its Cities.* New York: Hastings House, 1940.

Ferriss, Susan, and Ricardo Sandoval. *The Fight in the Fields: Cesar Chavez and the Farmworkers Movement.* San Diego: Harcourt Brace & Company, 1997.

Finefield, Kristi. "San Francisco: Before and After the 1906 Earthquake and Fire." *Picture This* (blog). Library of Congress, April 18, 2012. blogs.loc.gov/picturethis/2012/04/san-francisco-before-and-after-the-1906-earthquake-and-fire/.

Finigan, Robert. *Corks and Forks: Thirty Years of Wine and Food.* Emeryville, CA: Shoemaker and Hoard, 2006.

Forbes, Alexander. *California: A History of Upper and Lower California . . .* London: Smith, Elder, 1839.

Fradkin, Philip L. *The Great Earthquake and Firestorms of 1906: How San Francisco Nearly Destroyed Itself.* Berkeley: University of California Press, 2005.

Fredericksen, Paul. "Haraszthy's Busy Last Years." *Wines & Vines* 28 (October 1947).

Gajanan, Mahita. "Who Invented Air Conditioning?" *Time,* July 26, 2016.

Gallo, Ernest. "The E. & J. Gallo Winery." An oral history conducted in 1969 by Ruth Teiser. Regional Oral History Office, Bancroft Library,

University of California, Berkeley, 1995. digitalassets.lib.berkeley.edu/roho/ucb/text/gallo_ernest.pdf.

Gardner, M. W., and William B. Hewitt. *Pierce's Disease of the Grapevine: The Anaheim Disease and the California Vine Disease.* Berkeley: University of California Press, 1974.

Gomberg, Louis B. "Analytical Perspectives on the California Wine Industry, 1935–1990." An oral history conducted in 1990 by Ruth Teiser. Regional Oral History Office, Bancroft Library, University of California, Berkeley, 1990. archive.org/details/analyticalperspoogombrich.

Goodlett, Joan. "Korbel." In *The Vine in Early California,* edited by Joseph Henry Jackson. San Francisco: Book Club of California, 1955.

Goodyear, Dana. "Drink Up." *New Yorker,* May 18, 2009, 59–65. newyorker.com/magazine/2009/05/18/drink-up.

Gregory, Tom. *History of Sonoma County, with Biographical Sketches of the Leading Men and Women of the County, Who Have Been Identified with Its Growth and Development from the Early Days to the Present Time.* Los Angeles: Historic Record Company, 1911.

Grgich, Miljenko. "A Croatian-American Winemaker in the Napa Valley." An oral history conducted in 1992 by Ruth Teiser. Regional Oral History Office, Bancroft Library, University of California, Berkeley, 1992. archive.org/details/croatianamericanoogrgirich.

Griswold del Castillo, Richard, and Richard A. Garcia. *Cesar Chavez: A Triumph of Spirit.* Norman: University of Oklahoma Press, 1997.

Gross, Jane. "Shall Tourists or Grapes Rule in the Napa Valley?" *New York Times,* May 30, 1988. nytimes.com/1988/05/30/us/shall-tourists-or-grapes-rule-in-the-napa-valley.html.

Guinn, J. M. "How California Escaped State Division. *Annual Publication of the Historical Society of Southern California* 6, no. 3 (1905): 223–32.

Hanna, Warren L. *Lost Harbor: The Controversy over Drake's California Anchorage.* Berkeley: University of California Press, 1979.

Hannickel, Erica. *Empire of Vines: Wine Culture in America.* Philadelphia: University of Pennsylvania Press, 2013.

Hansen, Gladys, and Emmet Condon. *Denial of Disaster: The Untold Story and Photographs of the San Francisco Earthquake and Fire of 1906.* San Francisco: Cameron and Company, 1989.

Haraszthy, Agoston. *Grape Culture, Wines, and Wine-Making.* New York: Harper & Brothers, 1862.

———. "Grape-Growing and Wine-Making in California." Reprinted in *The California Culturist: A Journal of Agriculture, Horticulture, Mechanism and Mining,* vol. 2, *June 1859 to May 1860,* edited by W. Wadsworth. San Francisco: Towne & Bacon, Printers, 1860.

———. "Report of Commissioners on the Culture of the Grape-Vine in California." In *Grape Culture, Wines, and Wine-Making.* New York: Harper & Brothers, 1862.

———. "Report on Grapes and Wine of California." In *Transactions of the California State Agricultural Society During the Year 1858.* Sacramento: John O'Meara, State-Printer for California, 1859.

Haraszthy, [Arpad?]. "The Haraszthy Family" manuscript. Bancroft Library, University of California, Berkeley.

Haraszthy, Arpad. "Instructions for the Jury of Awards, Midwinter Fair." *Annual Report of the Board of State Viticultural Commissioners for 1989–90.* Sacramento: State Printing, 1890.

———. *Wine Making in California.* San Francisco: Book Club of California, 1978. Originally "Wine-Making in California," *Overland Monthly,* May 1872.

Hawkes, Ellen. *Blood and Wine: The Unauthorized Story of the Gallo Wine Empire.* New York: Simon & Schuster, 1993.

Hayes, Benjamin. *Pioneer Notes from the Diaries of Judge Benjamin Hayes, 1849–1875.* Edited by Marjorie Tisdale Wolcott. Los Angeles: McBride Printing Company, 1929.

Hayne, A. P. "Phylloxera." In *Report of the Viticultural Work During the Seasons 1887–93, with Data Regarding the Vintages of 1894–95.* University of California College of Agriculture, Agricultural Experiment Station. Sacramento: State Printing, 1896.

Heintz, William. *California's Napa Valley: One Hundred and Sixty Years of Wine Making.* San Francisco: Scottwall Associates, 1999.

Heitz, Joseph E. "Creating a Winery in the Napa Valley." An oral history conducted in

1985 by Ruth Teiser. Regional Oral History Office, Bancroft Library, University of California, Berkeley, 1986. archive.org/details/winerynapavalleyooheitrich.

Heyhoe, Kate, and Stanley Hock. *Harvesting the Dream: The Rags-to-Riches Tale of the Sutter Home Winery.* Hoboken, NJ: John Wiley & Sons, 2004.

Highfield, Roger. "DNA Links Noble French Wines to Common Plonk." *London Daily Telegraph,* September 3, 1999.

Hilgard, Eugene W. "Letter of Transmittal." In *Report of the Viticultural Work During the Seasons 1887–93, with Data Regarding the Vintages of 1894–95.* University of California College of Agriculture, Agricultural Experiment Station. Sacramento: State Printer, 1896.

———. "Plain Talk to the Winemen." *San Francisco Examiner,* August 8, 1889.

"History of the Napa Valley Vintners." *Napa Valley Vintners,* 2017. napavintners.com/about/history.asp.

Hittell, John S. *The Resources of California.* 3rd. ed. San Francisco: A. Roman, 1867.

Hittell, Theodore H. *History of California.* Vol. 1. San Francisco: N. J. Stone & Co., 1898.

Holliday, J. S. *The World Rushed In.* New York: Simon & Schuster, 1981.

Husmann, George C. "Resistant Vines." In *Official Report of the Session of the International Congress of Viticulture Held in Recital Hall at Festival Hall, Panama-Pacific International Exposition, July 12–13, 1915,* by International Congress of Viticulture, Permanent International Viticultural Commission. San Francisco: Dettner Printing, 1915. archive.org/details/cu31924003740283.

Hutchison, John N. "Northern California from Haraszthy to the Beginnings of Prohibition." In *The University of California/Sotheby Book of California Wine,* edited by Doris Muscatine, Maynard A. Amerine, and Bob Thompson, 30–48. Berkeley: University of California Press/Sotheby Publications, 1984.

Hyatt, Thomas Hart. *Hyatt's Handbook of Grape Culture: Or, Why, Where, When and How to Plant and Cultivate a Vineyard, Manufacture Wines, etc, Especially Adapted to the State of California as, also, to the United States Generally.* 2nd

ed. San Francisco: A L. Bancroft & Company, 1867, 1876.

Jackson, Joseph Henry, ed. *The Vine in Early California.* San Francisco: Book Club of California, 1955.

James, Juliet. *Palaces and Courts of the Exposition: A Handbook of the Architecture, Sculpture and Mural Paintings with Special Reference to the Symbolism.* San Francisco: California Book Company, 1915.

Johnson, Hugh. "American Wine Comes of Age." *Time,* November 27, 1972, 76.

———. *Hugh Johnson's Modern Encyclopedia of Wine.* 2nd ed. New York: Simon & Schuster, 1987.

Keller, Matthew. "California Wines," Los Angeles, July 2, 1866. In *The California Scrap-Book: A Repository of Useful Information and Select Reading...,* edited by Oscar T. Shuck. San Francisco: H. H. Bancroft, 1869.

———. "The Grapes and Wine of Los Angeles." *Report of the Commissioner of Patents for the Year 1858—Agriculture.* 35th Cong., 2d Sess., Ex. Doc. no. 47. Washington, D.C.: William A. Harris, Printer, 1859.

King, John. "The Great Quake: 1906–2006: Grand S.F. Plans That Never Came to Be." *San Francisco Chronicle,* April 12, 2006. sfgate.com/bayarea/place/article/The-Great-Quake-1906-2006-Grand-S-F-plans-2537355.php.

Kobler, John. *Ardent Spirits: The Rise and Fall of Prohibition.* New York: G. P. Putnam's Sons, 1973.

Kohler, Charles. "Wine Production in California: An Account of the Wine Business in California, from Materials Furnished by Charles Kohler." Unpublished manuscript, 1878. Handwritten original and microfilm. Bancroft Library, University of California, Berkeley.

Lapsley, James T. *Bottled Poetry: Napa Winemaking from Prohibition to the Modern Era.* Berkeley: University of California Press, 1996.

Laube, James. "California's Cult Wines: Who They Are and Why They're Red Hot." *Wine Spectator,* April 4, 2000. winespectator.com/webfeature/show/id/Californias-Cult-Wines-_287.

———. "The Glory That Was Inglenook." *Wine Spectator* 26, no. 11 (October 31, 2001).

winespectator.com/webfeature/show/id/The-Glory-That-Was-Inglenook_1057

Leggett, Herbert B. *Early History of Wine Production in California*. San Francisco: Wine Institute, 1941.

Lewis, Oscar. *San Francisco: Mission to Metropolis*. Berkeley: Howell-North Books, 1966.

Lewis Publishing Company. *An Illustrated History of Sonoma County, California. Containing a History of the County of Sonoma from the Earliest Period of Its Occupancy to the Present Time*. Chicago: Lewis Publishing Company, 1889.

London, Jack. "The Story of an Eyewitness by Jack London." *Collier's*, May 5, 1906. See also the Virtual Museum of the City of San Francisco, www.sfmuseum.net/hist5/jlondon.html.

Lukacs, Paul. *American Vintage: The Rise of American Wine*. Boston: Houghton Mifflin, 2000.

Lyman, George D. *John Marsh, Pioneer: The Life Story of a Trail-blazer on Six Frontiers*. New York: Charles Scribner's Sons, 1940.

Lyons, Mickey. *Prohibition Detroit* (blog). prohibitiondetroit.com/web.

MacNeil, Karen. *The Wine Bible*. New York: Workman Publishing, 2001.

Marks, Ben. "Forgotten Kingpins Who Conspired to Save California Wine." *Collectors Weekly*, December 11, 2015. collectorsweekly.com/articles/california-wine.

Marryat, Frederick. *Second Series of a Diary in America, with Remarks on its Institutions*. Philadelphia: T. K. & P. G. Collins, 1840.

Martini, Louis M., and Louis P. Martini. "Wine Making in the Napa Valley." An oral history conducted in 1973 by Lois Stone and Ruth Teiser. Regional Oral History Office, Bancroft Library, University of California, Berkeley, 1973. digitalassets.lib.berkeley.edu/roho/ucb/text/martini_louis_m_and_louis_p___w.pdf.

Marx, Karl, and Friedrich Engels. "Review: January–February 1950." *Neue Rheinische Zeitung Revue* (January–February 1850). Reprinted in *The Penguin Marx Library*, vol. 1, *Political Writings*, edited by David Fernback. Harmondsworth, England: Penguin Books, 1973.

Maybeck, Bernard R. *Palace of Fine Arts and Lagoon*. San Francisco: Paul Elder and Company, 1915.

McGinty, Brian. *Strong Wine: The Life and Legend of Agoston Haraszthy*. Stanford, CA: Stanford University Press, 1998.

McGloin, John B., S. J. *San Francisco: The Story of a City*. San Rafael: Presidio Press, 1978.

McKee, Irving. "The Beginnings of California Winegrowing." *Historical Society of Southern California Quarterly* 29 (1947): 59–71.

———. "Jean Paul Vignes, California's First Professional Winegrower." *Agricultural History* 22, no. 3 (July 1948): 176–80.

———. "Three Wine-Growing Senators." *California* 37 (September 1947): 15, 28–29.

Meers, John R. "The California Wine and Grape Industry and Prohibition." *California Historical Society Quarterly* 46, no. 1 (March 1967): 19–22.

Meyer, Justin. "Justin Meyer and Silver Oak Cellars: Focus on Cabernet." An oral history conducted in 1999 by Carole Hicke. Regional Oral History Office, Bancroft Library, University of California, Berkeley, 2000. archive.org/details/justinmeyeroomeyerich.

Miller, Donald L. *City of the Century: The Epic of Chicago and the Making of America*. New York: Simon & Schuster, 1997.

Miya, Christopher, and California Historical Society. *Vintage: California Wine Labels of the 1930s*. Berkeley: Heyday Books, 2016.

Mobley, Esther. "Mission Revival: State's First Wine Grape, Circa 1760, Rides Again." *San Francisco Chronicle*, March 26, 2017, L7. sfchronicle.com/wine/article/Mission-revival-State-s-first-wine-grape-11023418.php.

Mondavi, Robert. *Harvests of Joy: My Passion for Excellence*. New York: Harcourt Brace, 1998.

Morison, Samuel Eliot. *Christopher Columbus, Mariner*. 1942. New York: Mentor Books, 1956.

Muscatine, Doris. *Old San Francisco: The Biography of a City from Early Days to the Earthquake*. New York: G. P. Putnam's Sons, 1975.

Muscatine, Doris, Maynard A. Amerine, and Bob Thompson, eds. *The University of California/Sotheby Book of California Wine*. Berkeley: University of California Press, 1984.

National Temperance Society. *The National Advocate* 44, no. 5 (May 1909).

Neuhaus, Eugene. *The Art of the Exposition: Personal Impressions of the Architecture, Sculpture,*

Mural Decorations, Color Scheme and Other Aesthetic Aspects of the Panama-Pacific International Exposition. San Francisco: Paul Elder and Company, 1915.

Newhall, Ruth. San Francisco's Enchanted Palace. San Francisco: Nowell-North Books, 1967.

Newmark, Harris. Sixty Years in Southern California: 1853–1913. New York: Knickerbocker Press, 1916.

Nolte, Carl. "Panama-Pacific Fair Changed San Francisco Forever." San Francisco Chronicle, February 14, 2015. sfchronicle.com/news/article/Panama-Pacific-fair-changed-San-Francisco-forever-6080573.php.

Northern California Historical Records Survey Project, Work Projects Administration. "Calendar of the Major Jacob Rine Snyder Collection of The Society of California Pioneers." San Francisco: Northern California Historical Records Survey Project, June 1940.

"Notes of Visiting Committees." Transactions of the California State Agricultural Society During the Year 1860. Sacramento: C. T. Botts, State Printer, 1861.

O'Connor, Charles J., et al. San Francisco Relief Survey: The Organization and Methods of Relief Used after the Earthquake and Fire of April 18, 1906. 1913. Reprint, New York: Russell Sage Foundation, 1974.

Official Guide to the California Midwinter Exposition in Golden Gate Park, San Francisco. San Francisco: G. Spaulding & Co., 1894.

Official History of the California Midwinter International Exposition. San Francisco, H. S. Crocker Company, 1895.

Official Report of the Session of the International Congress of Viticulture Held in Recital Hall at Festival Hall, Panama-Pacific International Exposition. San Francisco: Dettner Printing, 1915.

Okrent, Daniel. Last Call: The Rise and Fall of Prohibition. New York: Scribner, 2010.

Older, Cora Miranda. San Francisco: Magic City. New York: Longmans Green, 1961.

Ordish, George. The Great Wine Blight. New York: Charles Scribner's Sons, 1972.

Oshinsky, David. "Temperance to Excess." New York Times Book Review, May 23, 2010, 20.

Ostrander, Gilman Marston. The Prohibition Movement in California, 1848–1933. Berkeley: University of California Press.

Peninou, Ernest P., and Sidney S. Greenleaf. A Directory of California Wine Growers and Wine Makers in 1860: With Biographical and Historical Notes and Index. Berkeley: Tamalpais Press, 1967.

———. Winemaking in California. Vols. 1 and 2. San Francisco: Peregrine Press, 1954.

———. Winemaking in California. Vol. 3, The California Wine Association. Porpoise Bookshop, 1954.

Peninou, Ernest P., and Gail G. Unzelman. The California Wine Association and Its Member Wineries 1894–1920. Santa Rosa, CA: Nomis Press, 2000.

Pinney, Thomas. A History of Wine in America. Vol. 1, From the Beginnings to Prohibition. Berkeley: University of California Press, 1989.

———. A History of Wine in America. Vol. 2, From Prohibition to the Present. Berkeley: University of California Press, 2005.

———. "The Strange Case of Frona Eunice Wait and Major Ben C. Truman." Wayward Tendrils Quarterly 23, no. 1 (January 2013): 17–19. www.waywardtendrils.com/pdfs/vol.23_2013.pdf.

Powell, K. C. "The Dashaway Association: California's Mid-19th-Century AA." Drug and Alcohol Review 7, no. 4 (1988): 467–71.

Rainey, James. "Farm Workers Union Ends 16-Year Boycott of Grapes." Los Angeles Times, November 22, 2000. articles.latimes.com/2000/nov/22/news/mn-55663.

Rawls, Jim. Dr. History's Whizz-Bang: Favorite Stories of California's Past. Palo Alto: Tioga Publishing Company, 1991.

Ray, Cyril. Robert Mondavi of the Napa Valley. Novato, CA: Presidio Press, 1984.

Robertson, George. Statistical Report of the California State Board of Agriculture. In Report of the California State Board of Agriculture for the Year 1911. California State Board of Agriculture. Sacramento: Supt. of State Printing, 1912–1913.

Robinson, Alfred. Life in California: During a Residence of Several Years in That Territory, Comprising a Description of the Country and the Missionary Establishments, with Incidents,

Observations, etc., etc., by an American to Which Is Annexed a Historical Account of the Origins, Customs, and Traditions of the Indians of Alta-California. Translated from the original Spanish manuscript. New York: Wiley & Putnam, 1846.

Robinson, Jancis, Julia Harding, and José Vouillamoz. *Wine Grapes: A Complete Guide to 1,368 Vine Varieties, Including Their Origins and Flavours.* London: Penguin, 2012.

Robinson, W. W. *Land in California: The Story of Mission Land, Ranches, Squatters, Mining Claims, Railroad Grants, Land Scrip, Homesteads.* Berkeley: University of California Press, 1948.

Rohrbough, Malcolm J. *Rush to Gold: The French and the California Gold Rush, 1848–1854.* New Haven, CT: Yale University Press, 2013.

Rorabaugh, W. J. *The Alcohol Republic: An American Tradition.* Oxford: Oxford University Press, 1979.

Rose, Kenneth D. "Wettest in the West: San Francisco & Prohibition in 1924." *California History* 65, no. 4 (December 1986): 284–295.

Rossi, Edmund A. "The Coming Expansion of the Table Wine Market." *Wines & Vines* 25 (December 1944): 29, 47.

———. "Italian Swiss Colony and the Wine Industry." An oral history conducted 1971 by Ruth Teiser. Regional Oral History Office, Bancroft Library, University of California, 1971. digitalassets.lib.berkeley.edu/roho/ucb/text/rossi_edmund__w.pdf.

San Francisco Municipal Reports for the Fiscal Year 1905–6, Ending June 30, 1906, and Fiscal Year 1906–7, Ending June 30, 1907. San Francisco: Neal Publishing, 1908.

Sbarboro, Andrea. *Temperance Versus Prohibition: Important Letters and Data from Our American Consuls, the Clergy and Other Eminent Men.* 2nd ed. 1914. Reprint, Wentworth Press, 2016.

Schoonmaker, Frank, and Alexis Bespaloff. *The New Frank Schoonmaker Encyclopedia of Wine.* New York: Morrow, 1988.

Schoonmaker, Frank, and Tom Marvel. *The Complete Wine Book.* New York: Duell, Sloan & Pearce, 1934.

Scott, Mel. *The San Francisco Bay Area: A Metropolis in Perspective.* 1959. Reprint, Berkeley: University of California Press, 1985.

Shuck, Oscar T. *The California Scrap-Book: A Repository of Useful Information and Select Reading. Comprising Choice Selections of Prose and Poetry, Tales and Anecdotes, Historical, Descriptive, Humorous, and Sentimental Pieces, Mainly Culled from the Various Newspapers and Periodicals of the Pacific Coast.* San Francisco: H. H. Bancroft, 1869.

Serra, Junípero. *Writings of Junípero Serra.* Vol. 1. Edited by Antoníne Tibeser. Washington, D.C.: Academy of American Franciscan History, 1955–1966.

Siler, Julia Flynn. *The House of Mondavi: The Rise and Fall of an American Wine Dynasty.* New York: Gotham Books, 2007.

Simon, André L. *The History of the Wine Trade in England.* Vol. 1, *The Rise and Progress of the Wine Trade in England from the Earliest Times Until the Close of the Fourteenth Century.* London: Wyman & Sons, 1906.

———. *The Noble Grapes and the Great Wines of France.* New York: McGraw-Hill, 1957.

Singleton, Jill. "Lost Wineries and Vineyards of Fremont, California." museumoflocalhistory.org/wordpress2/wp-content/uploads/2014/10/Lost-Wineries-and-Vineyards-of-Fremont.pdf.

Soulé, Frank, John H. Gihon, and James Nisbet. *The Annals of San Francisco.* New York: D. Appleton & Company, 1855.

Starr, Kevin. *California: A History.* New York: Random House, 2005.

———. *Land's End.* San Francisco: McGraw-Hill, 1979.

Stegner, Wallace. "The Gift of Wilderness." In *One Way to Spell Man.* Garden City, NY: Doubleday & Company, 1982.

Stephens, H. Morse, and Herbert E. Bolton, eds. *The Pacific Ocean in History: Papers and Addresses Presented at the Panama-Pacific Historical Congress, Held at San Francisco, Berkeley and Palo Alto, California, July 19–23, 1915.* New York: MacMillan, 1917.

Stevenson, Robert Lewis. *The Silverado Squatters.* 1883. San Francisco: Mercury House, 1996.

Street, Richard Steven. *Beasts of the Field: A Narrative History of California Farmworkers, 1769–1913.* Stanford, CA: Stanford University Press, 2004.

Sullivan, Charles L. *A Companion to California Wine: An Encyclopedia of Wine and Winemaking from the Mission Period to the Present.* Berkeley: University of California Press, 1998.

———. *Napa Wine: A History from Mission Days to Present.* San Francisco: Wine Appreciation Guild, 1994.

———. *Sonoma Wine and the Story of Buena Vista.* San Francisco: Wine Appreciation Guild, 2013.

———. "A Viticultural Mystery Solved: The Historical Origins of Zinfandel in California." *California History* 57, no. 2 (Summer 1978): 114–29.

———. *Zinfandel: A History of a Grape and Its Wine.* Berkeley: University of California Press, 2003.

Sullivan, Patricia. "Robert Mondavi 94; Noted Vintner Who Raised Quality of American Wine." *Washington Post,* May 17, 2008, B5. washingtonpost.com/wp-dyn/content/article/2008/05/16/AR2008051603900.html.

Taber, George. *Judgment of Paris: California vs. France and the Historic 1976 Paris Tasting That Revolutionized Wine.* New York: Scribner, 2005.

Tchelistcheff, André. "Grapes, Wine, and Ecology." An oral history conducted in 1979 by Ruth Teiser and Catherine Harroun. Regional Oral History Office, Bancroft Library, University of California, 1983. digitalassets.lib.berkeley.edu/roho/ucb/text/tchelistcheff_andre__w.pdf.

Teiser, Ruth, and Catherine Harroun. "The Volstead Act, Rebirth, and Boom." In *The University of California/Sotheby Book of California Wine,* edited by Doris Muscatine, Maynard A. Amerine, and Bob Thompson. Berkeley: University of California Press, 1984.

———. *Winemaking in California.* New York: McGraw-Hill, 1983.

Thomas, Daniel J. "On Agricultural Statistics of the State." In *Transactions of California State Agricultural Society,* 1859, 323–48. Sacramento: C. T. Botts, State Printer, 1860.

Thompson, Bob, and Hugh Johnson. *The California Wine Book.* New York: Morrow, 1976.

Tilden, Joe. *Joe Tilden's Recipes for Epicures.* San Francisco: A. M. Robertson, 1907.

Tobriner, Stephen. *Bracing for Disaster: Earthquake-Resistant Architecture and Engineering in San Francisco, 1838–1933.* Berkeley: Heyday Books, 2006.

Todd, Frank Morton. Introduction to *Palace of Fine Arts and Lagoon,* by Bernard R. Maybeck, vii. San Francisco: Paul Elder and Company, 1915.

———. *The Story of the Exposition, Being the Official History of the International Celebration Held at San Francisco in 1915 to Commemorate the Discovery of the Pacific Ocean and the Construction of the Panama Canal.* New York: G. P. Putnam's Sons, 1921.

Transactions of the California State Agricultural Society. Sacramento: State Printer, 1859–1905.

Trinchero, Louis (Bob). "California Zinfandels, a Success Story." An oral history conducted in 1991 by Carole Hicke. Regional Oral History Office, Bancroft Library, University of California, Berkeley, 1992. digitalassets.lib.berkeley.edu/roho/ucb/text/trinchero_louis_bob__w.pdf.

Twight, E. H. "The Food Value of Wine." *American Practitioner and News* 43, no. 1 (January 1909): 45–50. archive.org/stream/americannews43loui#page/44/mode/2up.

Tyler, Alice Felt. *Freedom's Ferment: Phases of American Social History to 1860.* Minneapolis: University of Minnesota Press, 1944.

Vancouver, George. *A Voyage of Discovery to the North Pacific Ocean and Round the World . . .* [1790–95]. Vol. 2. London: Printed for G. G. and J. Robinson [etc.], 1798.

Wait, Frona Eunice. *Wines and Vines of California; or, A Treatise on the Ethics of Wine-Drinking.* Berkeley: Howell-North Books, 1973. Facsimile edition of the 1889 publication by the Bancroft Co., San Francisco.

Ward, Edward. *A Trip to New-England with a Character of the Country and People, both English and Indians.* London, 1699.

Webb, Edith Buckland. *Indian Life at the Old Missions.* Los Angeles, W. F. Lewis, 1952.

Wetmore, Charles A. "Treatise on Wine Production." Appendix B to the *Report of State Viticultural Commissioners, 1893–94.* Sacramento: State Printers, 1894.

Wilford, John Noble. "Wine Cellar, Well Aged, Is Revealed in Israel." *New York Times,* November 22, 2013.

Williams, Nigel. "How the Great Exhibition of 1851 Still Influences Science Today." *Guardian,* August 28, 2015. theguardian.com/science/blog/2015/aug/28/how-the-great-exhibition-of-1851-still-influences-science-today.

Wilson, Benjamin Davis. *The Indians of Southern California in 1852: The B. D. Wilson Report and a Selection of Contemporary Comment.* Edited by John Walton Caughey. 1952. Reprint, Lincoln: University of Nebraska Press, 1995.

Winchester, Simon. *A Crack in the Edge of the World.* New York: HarperCollins, 2006.

Wine & Spirit Education Trust. *Wine and Spirits: Understanding Wine Quality.* 2nd rev. ed. London: Wine & Spirit Education Trust, 2012.

Wine Institute. "Wine Consumption in the U.S." Crediting Wine Institute, DOC, BW166/ Gomberg, Fredrikson & Associates estimates. *Wine Institute,* revised on July 8, 2016. wineinstitute.org/ resources/statistics/article86.

"The Wines of the U.S." *Fortune* 9 (February 1934).

Winiarski, Warren. "Creating Classic Wines in the Napa Valley." An oral history conducted in 1991, 1993 by Ruth Teiser. Regional Oral History Office, Bancroft Library, University of California, Berkeley, 1994. archive.org/details/ creatingclassicwines00winirich.

Woehlke, Walter V. "The Grape and Prohibition." *Sunset* 37 (July–December 1916): 9–11, 92–94.

Index